BARRON'S

AP*

MUSIC THEORY

3rd Edition

Nancy Fuller Scoggin, B.M.E.
Joshua High School
Joshua, Texas

BARRON'S

For all my teachers and students—past, present, and future

About the Author: *Nancy Fuller Scoggin* taught instrumental music in Joshua, Texas, for thirty-two years, retiring as a full-time band director in 2013. She continues to teach AP Music Theory at Joshua High School. Her degree in music education is from the University of Southern Mississippi in Hattiesburg. She became a consultant for the College Board in 2001 and has been a presenter and consultant in the Southwest region and at the national level since 2003. She was a reader for the AP Music Theory exam for nine years and a member of the leadership team for five years. Ms. Scoggin enjoys teaching other high school music teachers about AP Music Theory through AP Summer Institutes in states across the country, including Arkansas, California, New Jersey, Oklahoma, and Texas.

Music illustrations and piano tracks by Mary Elizabeth/Voice of the Phoenix (http://voiceofthephoenix.com) using Sibelius 6 TruePianos, and Matthew Hindson's Scale Degrees font.

All inquiries should be addressed to:
Barron's Educational Series, Inc.
250 Wireless Boulevard
Hauppauge, New York 11788
www.barronseduc.com

ISBN-13: 978-1-4380-7677-5
ISSN: 2575-632X

PRINTED IN THE UNITED STATES OF AMERICA

9 8 7 6 5 4 3 2 1

10%
POST-CONSUMER WASTE
Paper contains a minimum of 10% post-consumer waste (PCW). Paper used in this book was derived from certified, sustainable forestlands.

Contents

As you review the content of this book to work toward earning a **5** on your APMT exam, here are five things that you **MUST** know above everything else:

Barron's Essential

1 **Vocabulary.** Most of the multiple-choice questions require you to know the basic terms of our musical language. Study the terms located on the first page of every chapter and study the chapter summary.

2 **Fundamentals.** Fundamentals are universally important in any field, and music theory is no exception. The two areas of significant importance are *key signatures and relationships* and *intervals*. Even these two areas are codependent. Build your knowledge on a solid foundation of these two areas and everything that follows will be easier.

3 **Part writing.** Part writing involves knowledge of many concepts rolled into one: chord spelling, inversions, Roman numerals, harmonic progression (T-S-D-T), resolutions, cadences, non-chord tones. The single largest component of part writing is correct chord spelling.

4 **Connect the dots.**
· See music: identify and understand; perform what you see
· Hear music: identify and understand; notate what you hear

The bigger picture is recognizing that when you part-write, you are creating a progression that is comparable to what you will hear in harmonic dictation. What you sing in the sight-singing portion of the exam is comparable to what you will hear and have to notate in melodic dictation. The information overlaps.

5 **Practice the exam.** Set time limits and time yourself when you are practicing. Practice using the same equipment for singing that you will use on the exam. Practice with the bubble sheets and—did I mention—time yourself.

Acknowledgments

There are many people I would like to thank for their contributions, well wishes, and enthusiastic support, most important my editor, Linda Turner. I would also like to thank the anonymous readers who so graciously offered their constructive comments and critical evaluations, and shared their wisdom and experience. Their input greatly influenced and shaped this project. I would also like to express my gratitude to Mary Elizabeth—the educator, author, and Sibelius wizard—for illustrating the music examples and generating the audio samples.

I would like to express my appreciation to a number of people who contributed their time and effort to this project by providing feedback and suggestions, reviewing questions, and sharing their expertise and love of music. A *big* thank you to Marcy Wells, Greenbrier, Arkansas; Vern Fosket, Sequim, Washington; and Casey Buck, Conway, Arkansas.

A personal thank you is extended to the administration of Joshua ISD, to my colleagues and friends in the music department: Steve Smoot, Lonnie Foster, Shannon Dow, Trent Fox, and Daniel Richardson. Thanks to Bob Small, my former high school principal, who had the vision, believed in me, and started me on this journey in AP Music Theory. I would also like to thank the many high school and college teachers I have met across the country at AP Readings and at summer institutes, who have encouraged and supported me in this effort. You have broadened my horizons and made me look deeper, think harder, and rejoice greatly in the knowledge that we have a shared passion. To my friends and family who listened to me talk endlessly about music theory and this project—I am eternally grateful and privileged to have you in my life. And to my students—the biggest thanks of all for many years of memories. This is for you and because of you.

For all of us who become teachers there is someone who is instrumental in shaping and molding the course of our careers. That person is our mentor, our teacher, our adviser, our friend. My mentor is Dr. Blaise Ferrandino, Professor of Music at Texas Christian University, Fort Worth, Texas. From the first summer institute I attended with Dr. Ferrandino in 1996 I knew my life had been impacted in the most positive and remarkable way. What I have learned at the feet of the master I have had the privilege of sharing with you in this book. Many of the processes and methods of teaching music theory I learned from him and developed through time with the wonderful students at Joshua High School.

Nancy Fuller Scoggin

Introduction

OVERVIEW OF THE AP MUSIC THEORY EXAM

The Advanced Placement (AP) Music Theory exam has two parts: the **Multiple-Choice** section and the **Free-Response** section.

Section I: Multiple-Choice is in two parts:

- **Part A** is multiple-choice questions based on recorded music. Part A questions are at varying levels of difficulty and range from identifying scale patterns and chord quality to listening to musical excerpts of various styles that test your listening skills in such areas as form, texture, harmonic progression, or error detection.
- **Part B** is non-aural multiple-choice. Part B is about fundamentals of music focusing on terminology, and visual score study and analysis.

Section I, Multiple-Choice, is 75 questions (42 of them based on recorded music) in approximately 80 minutes and is **45 percent of the total score**.

Section II: Free-Response is also in two parts:

- **Part A** consists of answering 7 questions in approximately 70 minutes. It is worth an additional **45 percent of the total score**. The first 4 free-response questions are also based on recorded music.

  - Free-response 1 and 2 (FR 1, 2) are melodic dictations that require you to listen to a short melody and notate pitch and rhythm accurately on the staff.
  - Free-response 3 and 4 (FR 3, 4) are harmonic dictations that require you to listen to a short four-part chorale and notate the soprano and bass. You must also write the Roman numeral chord symbols including appropriate inversions of the progression.
  - FR 5 is realizing figured bass, where you will be required to write a melody as well as the alto and tenor above a given bass line with figures and give the Roman numeral chord symbols.
  - FR 6 is part-writing from Roman numerals, where you will be required to write all four voices from the given Roman numeral chord progression.
  - FR 7 is composition by harmonizing a melody, writing an appropriate bass line, and indicating harmonic structure and cadences using Roman numeral chord symbols.

- **Part B** is an individually administered **sight-singing** portion that consists of 2 melodies to be performed and recorded and constitutes **10 percent of the total score**. You will have 75 seconds to practice each melody, followed by 30 seconds to record your performance of the melody.

How the Test Is Graded

Both the multiple-choice and free-response sections are designed to measure a wide range of music skills. The five-point scoring system is standard among all the AP exams:

Among Colleges and Universities that Accept AP Credit
A grade of **5** = **Extremely Well Qualified**. Almost all colleges and universities accept this score.
A grade of **4** = **Well Qualified**. Accepted by most colleges and universities.
A grade of **3** = **Qualified**. Accepted by many colleges and universities.
A grade of **2** = **Possibly Qualified**. Rarely accepted.
A grade of **1** = **No Recommendation**. Not accepted.

Your score from 1(low) to 5 (high) on this exam will take into account your performance on **both sections** of the exam. A passing grade of 3 (qualified) will be a **composite score**, which is accepted by many colleges and universities. However, some universities consider the **section subscores** individually and not just the composite, and look for a minimum score of 3 on *both* parts. *Therefore, if you earn a 2 on the aural section and a 4 on the non-aural (for a composite score of 3), it is possible to not receive college credit.*

Professionals from all over the United States, both high school teachers and college professors, gather for seven days of test grading known as the AP Reading. The seven free-response questions and two sight-singing examples have to be individually scored over the course of this one week of intensive grading. Each free-response question is graded by a different reader, so each question is an opportunity for a fresh start. More than 130 graders use the standards set by the leadership team as guidelines for scoring. All graders are supervised and are diligently checked and cross-checked for consistency of grading. Even the supervisors are monitored to ensure the quality of grading across the spectrum. All of this checking and rechecking has made the AP Music Theory exam one of the most reliable Advanced Placement exams for consistency of scoring.

Answering the Multiple-Choice Questions

The AP Music Theory exam is a timed exam consisting of 75 multiple-choice questions in Parts A and B. Each question has four possible responses, and you are asked to choose the correct answer. As with all multiple-choice questions, be careful to look at the terms within the questions very carefully. These include:

- All of the following except
- Includes
- Most likely
- Best fits
- Ends with or begins with
- Lengthened by
- Outside voices
- Only (as in "listen for the rhythm only")

These terms are clues. Use them to your advantage. Here are some other helpful hints.

- Read the questions twice.
- Underline or circle important words, such as those just mentioned, especially *except* and *only*, to help narrow down your choices and keep you focused on the requested task.
- This is a timed exam. Work as quickly as you can, and use your time wisely. Do not spend excessive time on one question. Keep working, filling in the answer sheet as you go. If you have time, return to questions you may have skipped.
- You are not expected to know all the answers.
- There is no penalty for wrong answers on the multiple-choice section, so you should answer *all* multiple-choice questions. Since there is no deduction for an incorrect answer, even if you have no clue, take a chance and guess!

Access audio at
http://barronsbooks.com/ap/mtheory/

Answering the Free-Response Questions

The seven free-response questions are also timed. Free-Response Question 1 (FR 1) is melodic dictation. The example will be played three times. There will be a 30 second pause after the first playing and 60 seconds following the subsequent playings. FR 2 is also melodic dictation. There will be four playings for this exercise. As in FR 1, there will be a 30 second pause after the first playing and 60 seconds following the subsequent playings. FR 3 and FR 4 are harmonic dictation, and each example will be played four times with a 30-second pause after the first playing and 60 seconds following the subsequent playings. You will then be allowed 45 minutes to complete the next three non-aural questions: figured bass realization (FR 5), part writing to the Roman numeral (FR 6), and melodic harmonization (FR 7). The suggested time is 15 minutes for FR 5, 10 minutes for FR 6, and 20 minutes for FR 7. In the test booklet the final three questions are printed on the left side with a page of staff paper on the right side for use as scratch paper. Make sure your final answer is on the left side answer page and not on the staff paper. Use a pencil!

Completing the Sight-Singing

There will be two sight-singing examples. One will be in major and one will be in minor. One will be in treble clef and one will be in bass clef. One will be simple meter and the other will be compound. The first pitch will be sounded, after which you will have 75 seconds to look over the music, *practice* singing the example, then record your performance of the example. Do not stop and start over. Sing confidently and clearly. You may use any form of syllables or numbers, or simply sing "la-la" for your performance. You may bring a pencil and mark on the music if you desire. The biggest mistake is *not* singing out loud during the allotted practice time.

How to Use This Book

BECOMING A THINKING MUSICIAN

TWELVE COGNATE AREAS (ELEMENTS)

Melody and Line	Tonality
Harmony/Counterpoint	Texture
Rhythm (Duration)	Form
Meter	Articulation
Notation and Terminology	Dynamics
Scales	Timbre

FIVE PROCESSES (ACTIVITIES WE DO WITH MUSIC) CORRESPONDING TO LANGUAGE

MUSIC: Listening → Performing → Analyzing → Notating → Composing

LANGUAGE: Hear   → Speak   → Read   → Write   → Create

SKILLS REQUIRED FOR THE AP MUSIC THEORY EXAM

Melodic dictation
Harmonic dictation
Sight-singing
Score analysis visual
Score analysis aural
Part writing
Realizing a figured bass
Harmonizing a melody

Cognate Areas (Elements) + Processes (Activities) = SKILLS

This is an **overlapping** or spiraling process.

Although the study of music is a fine arts subject, the teaching and learning of music concepts are very clearly associated with how language is learned. Think about how children are taught language—any language. We listen (aural) and then we learn to speak (oral). We hear others speaking; we try to model that sound. Parents recite words that children say back to them—single words identifying items. From there, children learn to speak multiple words, combining words into sentences and complete thoughts. Then the process becomes visual when the child learns to read and write the words, eventually formulating her own thoughts, creating her own ideas, and writing them down using correct grammar, capitalization, and punctuation. This is how music is learned.

We listen to music; we learn to speak it by singing or playing a musical instrument. We learn to read music, usually on one staff in a single linear fashion. If we continue our learning of the musical language, we are taught how to correctly notate and, eventually, to put our own musical thoughts and ideas on paper in the form of compositions using melodic shape and contour, chords, and cadences.

Our goal is to become "thinking musicians." This means that we are able to "hear with our eyes and see with our ears." In music, as in language, the eyes and ears are connected to the brain. We see music and our ear knows what it will sound like. We hear a melody and we can visualize what it looks like on the staff. A thinking musician understands and makes the connection by overlapping the activities of seeing, hearing, and notating. Overlapping is the process of singing a melody and then notating that same melody. It means that many of the fundamental skills are *both* visual and aural. We must be able to identify concepts visually, perform them, notate them, and then create something of our own that is similar. Many of the skills used in part writing are also used in harmonizing a melody or analyzing a score. When you prepare to sing a melody, you are identifying elements such as rhythm and meter, melodic patterns, and interval relationships that are also prevalent skills when notating melodic and harmonic dictation. This guide will help you use all the tools at your disposal, connect the information in an **IF–THEN** format, and present and highlight concepts that are overlapping.

CURRICULUM CONTENT

Chapters 1–7 focus on the **cognate** areas, the fundamental *elements* of music such as melody and rhythm, and each will begin with terminology important to that chapter and found in the exam. Understanding the terminology is essential to succeed on the AP Music Theory exam.

Chapters 8–16 focus on the **processes**, the *activities* that are associated with music—listening, performing, notating, analyzing, and creating.

Chapters 1–16 have multiple-choice **chapter review questions** based on written music. The questions focus on terminology, score study, and visual analysis. In these content chapters, review questions may not always mirror exam questions in wording, format, or substance; instead, they are used to review the subject matter in preparation for the test-taking strategy chapters.

The chapter review questions, and all multiple-choice practice questions, conclude with **answers explained** pages and *justification* for the correct answers to those questions. It is important to know not only the correct answer but why the answer is correct and the process used to determine the answer.

Aural units follow Chapters 3, 7, and 13. These include multiple-choice practice questions **with aural prompts** (found online: *http://barronsbooks.com/ap/mtheory/*) that ask questions based on what you *hear*.

TEST-TAKING STRATEGIES

Chapters 17–22 are devoted to test-taking strategies for all portions of the AP Music Theory exam. The review questions at the end of these chapters are designed to mirror exam wording, content, and difficulty level. Chapter 17 contains exam-level questions with tips and strategies for answering Part B (non-aural) questions. Chapter 18 contains similar information for Part A (aural) questions. Chapters 19–22 also include strategies for every free-response question and for sight-singing.

Practice tests are included. This guide contains **two complete practice exams**, including multiple-choice questions based on aural stimulus (Part A) and non-aural information (Part B), exercises for all seven free-response questions, and sight-singing.

You can access all the audio for the review chapters as well as for the practice tests online at *http://barronsbooks.com/ap/mtheory/*. These files are MP3 and downloadable to most devices.

Aural skills are one of the most difficult components of this exam; therefore, there are three separate aural skills content chapters *plus* three strategy chapters relating to:

Singing

- Chapter 4, "Aural Skills Part I: Fundamentals and Singing," works on the skill of singing. It contains **25 practice melodies**.
- There are an **additional 24 melodies** in "Strategies for Sight-Singing," Chapter 22.

Melodic Dictation

- Chapter 11, "Aural Skills Part II: Melodic Dictation," contains a **total of 23 exercises** for developing melodic dictation skills.
- An **additional 20 melodic dictation exercises** are found in "Strategies for Melodic Dictation: FR 1 and FR 2," Chapter 19.

Harmonic Dictation

- Chapter 15, "Aural Skills Part III: Harmonic Dictation," contains **47 progressive exercises plus 5 complete** harmonic dictations *and*
- Chapter 20, "Strategies for Harmonic Dictation: FR 3 and FR 4," contains **12 additional complete** harmonic dictations.

Appendix A contains additional information, charts, and study aids. Look for the arrow ➡ to lead you to additional information located in Appendix A.

Appendix B contains music that can be used for further study. Look for suggestions for further analysis and review.

Appendix C contains a clean copy of *all* the part-writing and melodic harmonization examples found in this guide for you to work on independently.

Appendix D contains an index of contextual listening aural examples.

Look for this symbol 🎵, alerting you to questions with **aural prompts**.

Access audio at
http://barronsbooks.com/ap/mtheory/

Here are other things you will find within each chapter:

- Every vocabulary word listed in the front of each chapter is defined within the context of the chapter material. The **vocabulary term** is in boldface the first time it's used in the chapter.
- The lightbulb 💡 icon signals an important tip. Read this material carefully.
- **IF–THEN** information connects the many layers of music—to spiral back and transfer concepts from task to task.
- At the conclusion of every chapter is a summary, a synopsis of the critical content of each chapter.

WHAT IS THE COMMON PRACTICE PERIOD?

Throughout this guide you will see reference to the Common Practice Period, or common-practice style. This broadly references the compositional techniques and the harmonic language of music from 1650 to 1850. This includes the Baroque, Classical, and Romantic eras of music history.

SIGHT-SINGING

Sight-singing is an important component of musicianship because it is a method of training your brain to recognize and understand the relationships between notes. The use of solfege syllables is a way to automatically recognize those relationships. Because sight-singing is such an important facet of this course and the AP exam process, it is important that you use a **consistent** method for singing—whether it is singing the scale degree numbers or a solfeggio system.

SOLFEGGIO

Solmization is a system of designating notes by the **solfege** (*So-Fa*) syllables. **Solfeggio** is the term for the method of sight-singing using these syllables. One of the primary reasons the use of a solfeggio system is encouraged is the ease of singing syllables over numbers. Singing accidentals or altered pitches is also made easier through the use of syllables. Any solfeggio method, movable-*Do,* fixed-*Do*, *Do*-based minor, or *La*-based minor, has it strengths. **In this guide we will use the movable-*Do* system, where *Do* always represents tonic ($\hat{1}$), *So* always represents dominant ($\hat{5}$), and *Ti* is always the leading tone ($\hat{7}$).** The movable-*Do* and other solfeggio systems are discussed in more detail in Chapter 4. We continue to use the movable-*Do* system not only in singing scales and melodies but also with intervals and the relationship between scale degrees. If you are using another system of sight-singing, you are encouraged to continue to do so. The use of scale degree numbers and names will help to reconcile these systems with each other. In this guide, solfege syllables will be bold and italicized.

Music Fundamentals

1

- Aspects of Sound
  - Pitch–Wavelength
  - Dynamics–Wave Height
  - Timbre–Waveform
  - Articulation–Envelope
  - Duration
- Piano Keyboard
  - Octave Designation
  - Half Step
  - Whole Step
  - Chromatic
  - Enharmonic
- Accidental
  - Flat
  - Sharp
  - Natural
  - Double Sharp
  - Double Flat
  - Cautionary Accidental

- Clefs
  - G Clef
    - Treble Clef
  - F Clef
    - Bass Clef
  - C Clef
    - Alto Clef
    - Tenor Clef
  - Neutral Clef
- Grand Staff
- Notation
  - Accidental
  - Note Head
  - Stem
  - Flag
  - Beam
  - Bar Line
  - Double Bar Line
  - Final Bar Line
  - Ledger Lines
  - Measure
  - Staff
  - Staves
  - System

ASPECTS OF SOUND

Let's begin by defining the aspects of sound—properties that are fundamental to the elements of sound and music. Most of these elements have two labels. The first (shown in bold in the following box) is familiar to us in music; the second (underlined) is the scientific term studied in physics.

Sound has:
- **PITCH** (also known as FREQUENCY) = <u>WAVELENGTH</u>
- **DYNAMIC** (also known as AMPLITUDE) = <u>WAVE HEIGHT</u>
- **TIMBRE** (also known as TONE COLOR) = <u>WAVEFORM</u>
- **ARTICULATION** = <u>ENVELOPE</u>
- **DURATION**

Pitch–Frequency–<u>Wavelength</u>

In physics there are two useful measurements that tell you something about the sound wave. One measurement is the *distance* between one wave and the next. This is the **wavelength**, which is related to the frequency and the **pitch** of the sound. *Frequency* is the rate of vibration measured in "times per second," called Hertz. When a violinist plays her A string, the string vibrates back and forth 440 times per second, or 440 Hertz (Hz). The higher the frequency, the higher the pitch and the shorter the wavelength.

Dynamics–Amplitude–<u>Wave Height</u>

The other measurement is the size of each individual wave: its "height" or "intensity" rather than its length. This is the *amplitude* of the wave, and it determines the loudness of the sound. In the study of music, **wave height** is referred to as **dynamic**.

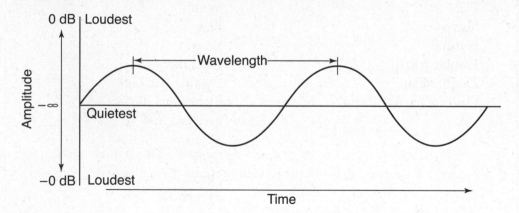

Timbre–Tone Color–<u>Waveform</u>

Waveform refers to the shape and form of the sound wave as it moves in distance and frequency. The shape of the waveform produces unique qualities of sound called timbre. **Timbre** (pronounced "TAM-ber") is made up of more than one frequency, often involving *harmonics* or *overtones*. We hear each mixture of frequencies and overtones not as separate sounds but as the unique coloring or character of each voice or musical instrument. The basic frequency and its overtones determine the timbre of a sound.

Articulation–Envelope

An **envelope** of sound is composed of a sound's *attack, sustain,* and *release*. We know this as **articulation**; it is the manner in which we begin the note, sustain it, and end the note.

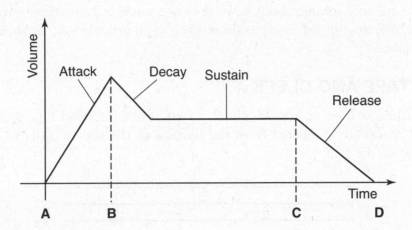

This is how sound is engaged.

1. **Attack:** Sound begins at **A** and reaches its peak at level **B**.
2. **Sustain:** The sound drops slightly in level (decay at **B**) and remains steady until **C**.
3. **Release:** When the sound source is removed at **C**, the sound decays to a point of silence at **D**.

Duration

Duration is the length of time sound and silence lasts. We will tackle the issues of note lengths and rhythm in the next chapter. Sound, whether it is consonant or dissonant, musical or noise, has a *proportional relationship* between note lengths as well as note pitch.

In its simplest terms a musical note has two aspects of sound: pitch and duration. An *XY*-graph of proportional notation demonstrates these elements in relation to the *first* note.

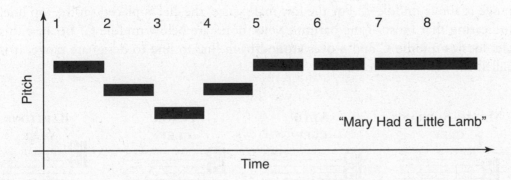

In relation to the first pitch, the second pitch is lower *but* the same length as note 1. Notes 5, 6, and 7 are the same pitch as note 1, but note 7 is twice as long as notes 1, 5, and 6. In listening to music we are constantly asking our ear to hear duration and pitch, and almost always in relation to something specific.

When we look at music we see all five aspects of sound notated on the musical score. We are very specific about how we notate pitch and duration, but there is a considerable amount of interpretation involved in articulation, dynamics, and, often, timbre.

THE STAFF AND CLEFS

Most music is written on a **staff** (plural, *staves*) of five lines and four spaces. The lines and spaces are numbered **from the bottom to the top** in order to indicate their place on the staff.

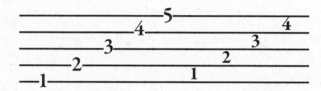

Each line or space is named for a letter of the alphabet using only letters A through G. Once you arrive at G you start over again with A.

The names of the lines and spaces are determined by the **clef** that is used. Clefs originally conformed to vocal ranges:

- Soprano (highest female voice)
- Mezzo soprano (moderately high female voice)
- Alto (low female voice)
- Tenor (high male voice)
- Baritone (low male voice)

There is one clef sign, the **C clef** (which looks like 𝄡), that is used for all of these vocal ranges, but is moved from line to line to show where **middle C** is located. The purpose of moving the clef is to eliminate excessive ledger lines. For the high female voice, middle C is going to be low on the staff because most of the soprano's range is above middle C. For the low male voice, the clef is placed on the top line, indicating that most of the baritone voice notes are below middle C. Because this clef locates middle C and moves around from line to line to designate range, it is called the **movable C clef**.

| **Soprano** | **Mezzo-Soprano** | **Alto** | **Tenor** | **Baritone** |
| CLEF | CLEF | CLEF | CLEF | CLEF |

The alto and tenor clefs are still used today by some instruments. The viola plays in alto clef and the bassoon and trombone frequently use the tenor clef. Both of these clefs are utilized in AP questions.

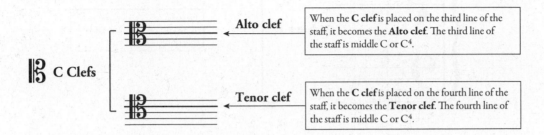

Alto clef → When the **C clef** is placed on the third line of the staff, it becomes the **Alto clef**. The third line of the staff is middle C or C[4].

Tenor clef → When the **C clef** is placed on the fourth line of the staff, it becomes the **Tenor clef**. The fourth line of the staff is middle C or C[4].

When music was mostly a single line of melody (monophonic), this system of notation of vocal ranges worked just fine; however, when music became increasingly more complex, using more layers of music with multiple lines being sung or played at the same time (polyphonic), one clef for all female voices *above* middle C and one clef for all male voices *below* middle C evolved. The upper voice clef symbol still moved from line to line—this time indicating where *G above middle C* (commonly considered the middle of the female voice range) was located. The clef began as a stylized or fancy cursive G. When the "G" clef is placed on the second line of the staff (the clef curls around the second line), it is then referred to as the **treble clef**.

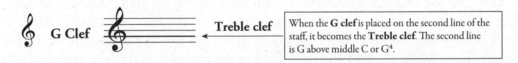

Treble clef → When the **G clef** is placed on the second line of the staff, it becomes the **Treble clef**. The second line is G above middle C or G[4].

Likewise, the lower voice clef symbol also moved from line to line and indicated where *F below middle C* (commonly considered the middle of the male voice range) was located. It began as a fancy cursive letter F, and when placed on the fourth line of the staff (with the two dots above and below the fourth line), it is then referred to as the **bass clef**.

Bass clef → When the **F clef** is placed on the fourth line of the staff, it becomes the **Bass clef**. The fourth line is F below middle C or F[3].

The Grand Staff

The **grand staff** combines both treble and bass clefs and is used by the piano as well as for notating both female voices (treble clef) and male voices (bass clef) in chorale or hymn style. When multiple staves are connected together by bar lines, a bracket, or a brace, it is called a **system**. Staves within a system may utilize different clefs.

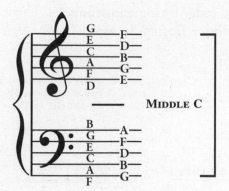

MIDDLE C

> The grand staff is a system of two staves: the top staff uses the treble clef and the bottom staff uses the bass clef.

OCTAVE DESIGNATION

Another way to label the notes of the grand staff is related to where they occur on the piano keyboard. There are eight Cs on the piano; *each C begins a new octave.* All pitches within that octave are labeled with the same number. The lowest C on the piano is C^1, middle C is C^4, and the last note on the piano is C^8. The first two notes on the far left are simply labeled A and B. The following illustration indicates octave designation on the piano keyboard as it relates to location on the grand staff.

LEDGER LINES

When you are reading one staff only, the notes that are above or below the staff require the use of ledger lines. These small lines extend the staff while still keeping the 5 lines and 4 spaces intact. In this way the treble and bass clefs actually overlap.

It is important to note when reading in the treble clef that notes that use ledger lines below middle C could also be written in the bass clef, and those reading above middle C in the bass clef could also be written in the treble clef.

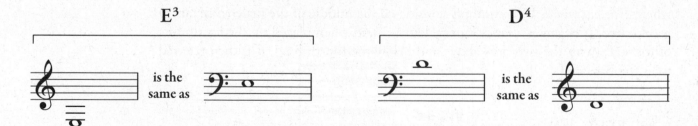

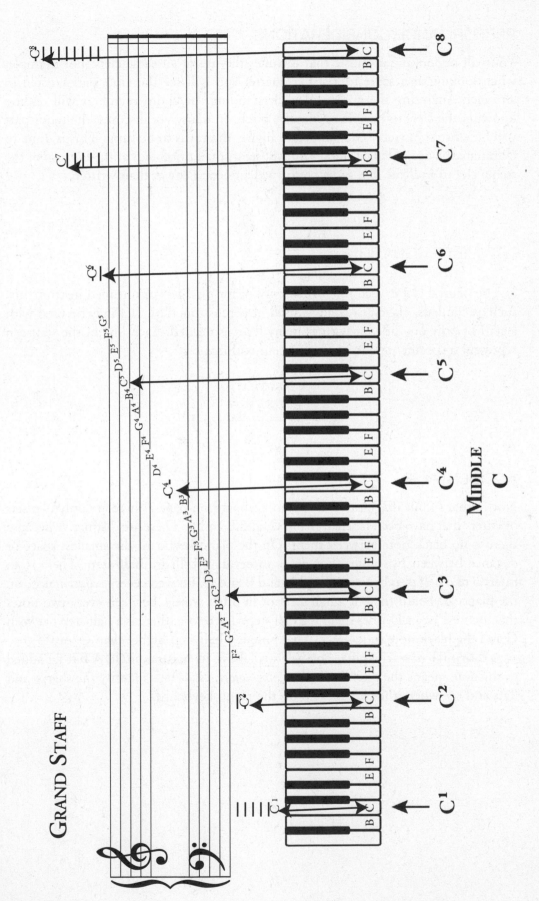

PERFORMANCE CONSIDERATIONS

You will be looking at music that includes the use of all these clefs. For example, when looking at a score to a string quartet you will see the viola part written in alto clef. Analyzing the notes and understanding the chord members will require knowing the clefs to be able to identify pitch. In many vocal scores, the tenor part will be written in treble clef, an octave higher than it is to be sung. This is done to eliminate the use of ledger lines. You will see a small number 8 at the bottom of the treble clef to indicate it is to be performed an octave lower than written.

The neutral clef is used for *rhythm only,* or for pitchless or untuned instruments, such as cymbals, claves, or triangle used in percussion. This clef may be used with a staff of only one line, or with as many lines as needed. Each line of the staff can represent a specific percussion instrument within a set.

NEUTRAL
CLEF

ACCIDENTALS

Notice that in our diagram of the piano keyboard on page 7 there are only two sets of letters that have been labeled: B and C, and E and F. These are distinctive because there is no black note between them. On the piano keyboard the smallest space or distance between two notes (known as **interval**) is called a **half step**. There is an interval of a half step between E and F, and B and C. Between every *adjacent* note on the piano keyboard there is a half step, or in other words, between every two notes that are next to each other there is a half step. Therefore, there is a half step between C and the black note to its right. That note is a half step higher than C, or C♯.

A **sharp** (♯) *raises* the pitch one half step above its natural pitch. A **flat** (♭) added to the note means the pitch is one half step *lower*. Now let's identify the sharps and flats and see where they are located on the piano keyboard.

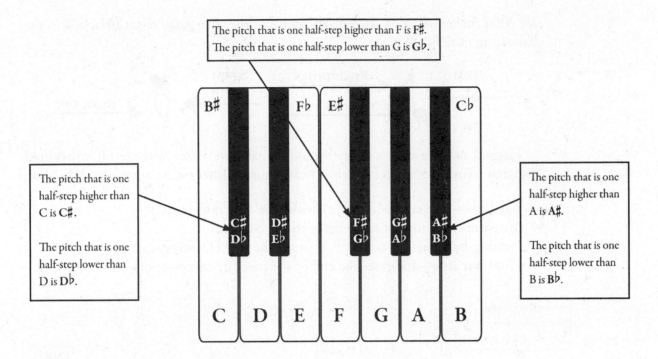

Keyboard illustration courtesy of Mary Elizabeth.

Notice that each of these pairs of pitches (C♯ / D♭, F♯ / G♭, A♯ / B♭) are the same key on the piano. They sound alike but have two different names. A♯ is the **enharmonic equivalent** of B♭. If we are referring to the pitch that is one half step higher than A, it is A♯. If we refer to a pitch that is one half step lower than B, it is B♭. The same thing applies to E–F and B–C, the pitches that have no black keys between them. The pitch that is a half step higher than E is E♯. Looking at the diagram of the keyboard we see that the note a half step higher than E is F; therefore, E♯ and F are enharmonic equivalents. Other enharmonic equivalents are B♯ = C, C♭ = B, and F♭ = E. Two half steps equal one **whole step**. Two white notes that *do* have a black note between them are one whole step apart.

The music symbol that means to raise a pitch by two half steps is the **double sharp** (✗). The **double flat** (♭♭) lowers the pitch by two half steps. We use a double sharp to raise a note one half step if that note is already sharp, and a double flat to lower a note that is already flat without changing the letter name. The musical symbol that cancels out a flat or a sharp is a **natural** (♮).

NOTATION

As previously discussed, a note is a musical symbol that represents pitch and duration. The **note head** is the body of the note. The **stem** is part of a note that is common to all note types *shorter in duration than the whole note*. The **flag** is part of the note that is common to all note types *shorter in duration than a quarter note*. The more flags on the note stem, the shorter the duration of the note.

A note head placed *below the middle line* of the musical staff has the *stem going up* and is attached to the right of the note head. Likewise, a note head placed on *the third line or above* on the musical staff has the *stem going down*, attached to the left of the note head.

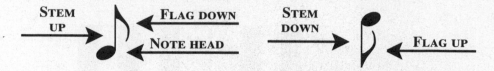

Flagged notes usually convey an individual note value, but are often **beamed** together to indicate units of time or beat groups. Other music notation symbols are

Bar line—the vertical line that divides the staff into measures
Measure—the unit of space between the bar lines
Double bar line—two lines that signal the end of a section of music
Final bar line—indicates the end of the piece or composition

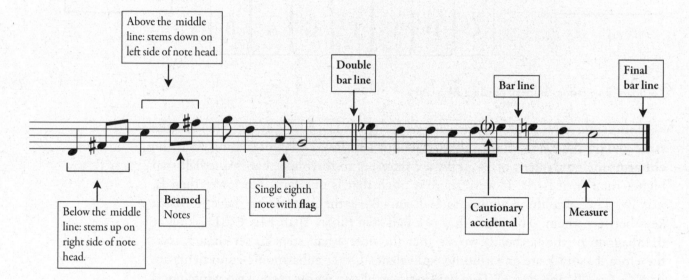

> **When accidentals are added to a pitch they are always notated to the left of the note head.** Accidentals carelessly written are a common problem on the AP exam. Be accurate!

Accidentals carry into other octaves in the same measure, but it's a good idea to specify each accidental when you change octaves. If there is an accidental early in a measure, it is wise to use a **cautionary accidental** in parentheses for later placement of the same accidental. Though a bar line does technically cancel an accidental, specifying the desired accidental in the new measure is advisable.

Chapter Summary

- The aspects of sound are **pitch** (wavelength), **dynamic** (wave height), **timbre** (waveform), **articulation** (envelope), and **duration**.
- Most music is written on a staff of five lines and four spaces.
- Labeling the pitch names of the lines and spaces of the staff depends on the clef used. **Clef designates range**.
- The purpose of using different clefs is to eliminate excessive ledger lines.
- **Movable C clef** designates the location of middle C (C^4).
- **Alto clef** and **tenor clef** are the most commonly used C clefs.
- The **G clef** designates G *above* middle C (G^4) and when placed on the second line is called the **treble clef**.
- The **F clef** designates F *below* middle C (F^3), and when placed on the fourth line of the staff, it is called the **bass clef**.
- The **grand staff** is a system of two staves—the top staff uses the treble clef and the bottom staff uses the bass clef.
- The **neutral clef** is used for rhythm only, or for pitchless or untuned instruments such as triangle, cymbals, or tambourine.
- Because there are only seven letters used in the musical alphabet and notes sound in multiple octaves, we can specify which octave by using a numeric system.
- There are eight Cs on the piano. Middle C is designated at C^4.
- **Ledger lines** are small lines that extend the staff while still keeping the five lines and four spaces intact.
- The smallest space or distance between notes (known as **interval**) is called a **half step**.
- A **sharp** (♯) added to a note means to raise the pitch one half step.
- A **flat** (♭) added to the note means the pitch is one half step lower.
- When accidentals are added to a pitch they are always notated to the left of the note head.
- A♯ and B♭ are the same pitch on the keyboard. They sound alike but have two different names. This is called **enharmonic** or **enharmonic equivalent**.
- The musical symbol that cancels out a flat or a sharp is a **natural** (♮).
- The music symbol that means to raise a pitch by two half steps while retaining the same letter name is the **double sharp** (𝄪). The double sharp is also used to raise an already sharped pitch one half step.
- The **double flat** (𝄫) lowers the pitch by two half steps while retaining the same letter name. The double flat is also used to lower an already flattened pitch one half step.
- Parts of a musical note include the note head, stem, flag, and beam.
- A note head placed below the middle line of the musical staff has the stem going up and is placed to the right of the note head. Likewise, a note head placed on the middle line and above on the musical staff has the stem going down, placed to the left of the note head.

Practice Exercises

Questions 1–7 are based on the following excerpt from a Mozart string quartet.

Quartet No. 14 in G Major

Wolfgang Amadeus Mozart
(1756-1791)
K. 387

1. The first note in the viola part is

   (A) F♯
   (B) G
   (C) E
   (D) A

2. The notes played by the violin II and viola on the downbeat of measure 2 are

   (A) unison
   (B) the same pitch name, but the viola plays an octave lower
   (C) the same pitch name, but the viola plays an octave higher
   (D) different pitch names

3. The viola is playing in what clef?

   (A) Tenor
   (B) Alto
   (C) Treble
   (D) G clef

4. What marking at the beginning of this excerpt indicates amplitude?

   (A) ♩

   (B) *f*

   (C) Allegro vivace assai

   (D)

5. The accidentals found in the first two measures of this excerpt are

   (A) D♯ and F♯
   (B) F♯ and G♯
   (C) C♯ and A♯
   (D) D♯ and G♯

6. A three-note chromatic pattern is found in what measure(s)?

   (A) Violin I second and fourth measures
   (B) Viola second measure
   (C) Cello second measure
   (D) Both in the cello second measure and violin I in the fourth measure

7. If this piece were performed by a woodwind quartet, what would be the primary change you would hear?

   (A) Amplitude
   (B) Pitch
   (C) Timbre
   (D) Envelope

8. The enharmonic equivalent of F♭ is

   (A) E♯
   (B) F♯
   (C) E
   (D) F

9. The tenor clef is positioned on the

   (A) second line of the staff
   (B) third line of the staff
   (C) fourth line of the staff
   (D) fifth line of the staff

10. The movable C clef designates the location of

   (A) C³
   (B) C⁴
   (C) G⁴
   (D) F³

11. What clef is used for rhythm only, or for untuned instruments?

   (A) Treble clef
   (B) Tenor clef
   (C) Tunable clef
   (D) Neutral clef

12. When a pitch is lower or higher than the lines of the staff we generally

   (A) change octaves
   (B) transpose
   (C) add beams
   (D) add ledger lines

13. The distance between any two pitches is called

   (A) a step
   (B) a leap
   (C) an interval
   (D) a skip

14. There is a half step between which two pairs of white notes on the piano keyboard?

   (A) E–F and B–C
   (B) C–D and F–G
   (C) E–F and G–A
   (D) D–E and B–C

15. The pitches A♯ and B♭ are

   (A) intervallic equivalents
   (B) enharmonic equivalents
   (C) chromatic equivalents
   (D) frequency equivalents

ANSWER KEY

1. **B**	6. **A**	11. **D**
2. **B**	7. **C**	12. **D**
3. **B**	8. **C**	13. **C**
4. **B**	9. **C**	14. **A**
5. **D**	10. **B**	15. **B**

ANSWERS EXPLAINED

1. **(B)** The first note in the viola part is G, specifically G⁴, meaning the G above middle C.

2. **(B)** The violin and viola are both playing an A; however the violin II is playing the A above middle C (A⁴) and the viola is playing the A *below middle C* (A³).

3. **(B)** The viola plays in alto clef establishing the middle line as middle C. The viola is the alto voice instrument of the orchestra, and like the alto vocal range, middle C is approximately the middle of the usable range.

4. **(B)** Amplitude refers to volume, or dynamic—how loud or how soft. The dynamic marking at the beginning is *f*, indicating to play forte, meaning loud.

5. **(D)** The accidentals found in the first two measures are the D♯ in the violin I and the G♯ in the cello and viola.

6. **(A)** A three-note chromatic pattern is found in two places in this excerpt, in measure 2 (m2) and measure 4 (m4), both in the violin I part.

7. **(C)** If this piece were performed by a woodwind quartet it would look different because it would be transposed into different keys for the woodwind instruments, but you would definitely *hear* a change in the timbre.

8. **(C)** The note a half step lower than F (F♭) is E.

9. **(C)** The tenor clef is positioned on the fourth line of the staff. Remember you always count the lines of the staff from the bottom.

10. **(B)** The movable C clef determines where C is, and middle C is C⁴, the fourth C on the piano from the bottom. (There are eight Cs on a full keyboard.)

11. **(D)** Neutral clef is for untuned percussion or any rhythm-only line.

12. **(D)** When a pitch is higher or lower than the five lines and four spaces of the staff we add ledger lines.

13. **(C)** The distance between any two pitches is called an interval. In this chapter we discussed the interval of a half step and a whole step.

14. **(A)** There is a half step between the white notes E and F and B and C on the piano keyboard.

15. **(B)** The pitches A♯ and B♭ are enharmonic equivalents.

Rhythm, Meter, and Metric Organization

2

- Alla Breve
- Anacrusis
- Bar Line
- Beat
- Beat type
     Compound
     Simple
- Changing Meter (Multimeter)
- Common Time
- Dot, Double Dot
- Dotted Rhythm
- Duplet, Triplet
- Duration
- Downbeat
- Hemiola
- Irregular Meter

- Meter
     Asymmetrical Meter
     Duple
     Triple
     Quadruple
- Note Value
- Rhythm
- Subdivision
- Syncopation
- Tempo
- Tie
- Time Signature (Meter Signature)

NOTATING RHYTHM

Music is sound and silence in time. Throughout the history of Western music, composers have represented sounds with symbols called notation. It is our written musical language. Music notation does not indicate the exact duration of sound; instead, it shows how long one note lasts *in relation* to others. It is a common mistake to simply say "the whole note gets four beats" or "a quarter note gets one beat." It does *sometimes*—but not always. What is *always* true is that two half notes equal a whole note and two quarter notes equal the duration of a half note. The following illustration shows the *relationship of durational symbols*, usually called the note tree.

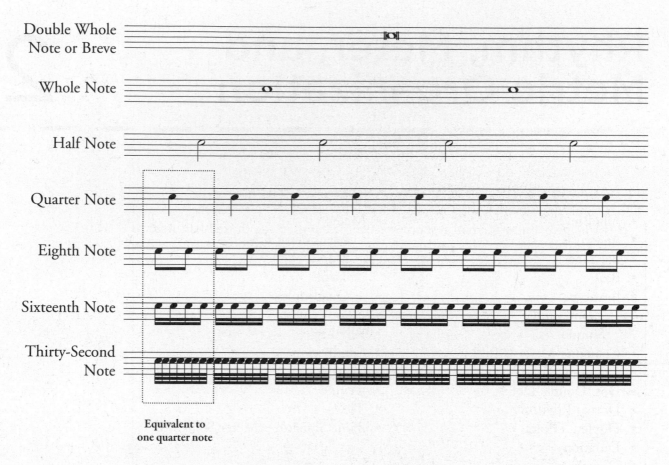

This illustration shows the *relationship of the equivalent rests*—the rest tree.

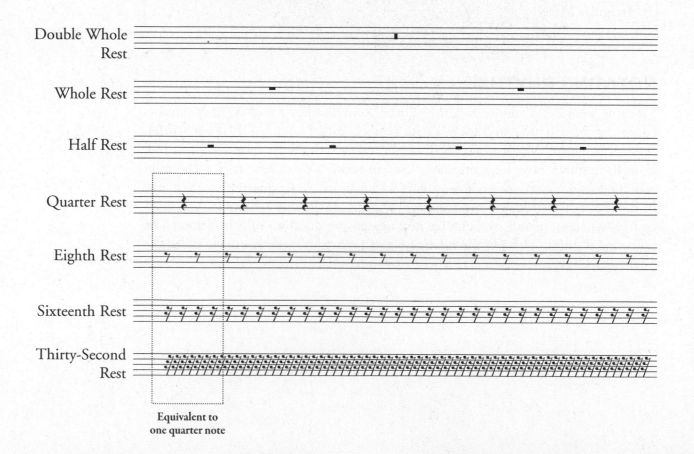

The Dot and the Tie

The dot and the tie are two symbols that extend the length or duration of a note. They both serve the same purpose (to make durations longer), but visually look much different. The **dot** is used to extend the value of a *single* note by one-half of its original value. If the half note receives two beats for example, the dotted half note has the value of three beats. If the value of the half note is one beat, then the dotted half note receives one and a half beats. The quarter note divides equally into two eighth notes. A dotted quarter note divides into three eighth notes. A second dot (**double dot**) lengthens the dotted note value by half the length of the first dot. The dot and double dot apply to rests as well as to notes.

If the half note and the half rest receive two beats, then the dotted half note or rest has a value of three beats and the doubly dotted half note or rest equals three and a half beats.

While the dot increases the value of a single note or rest, the **tie** combines the durational values of two or more notes of the same pitch using a curved line. Ties allow us to extend the duration of a pitch beyond a single measure.

METRIC ORGANIZATION

In its widest sense, rhythm is the flow of music through time. Rhythm is basic to life and is the lifeblood of music, too. Rhythm and meter are very often misunderstood and can frequently be an area of confusion. Let's begin by defining the basic terminology.

- **Duration**—the length of time sound (or silence) occurs
- **Beat**—a regular, recurring pulsation that divides music into units of time
- **Meter**—the organization of beats into regular groups of two, three, and four (usually with strong and weak beats) and how the beat is subdivided
- **Subdivision**—the division of the beat into two or three equal parts
- **Rhythm**—series of durations, often varying, of sound and silence
- **Tempo**—the speed of the beat

Meter is the organization of musical time into recurring patterns of strong and weak beats. Each complete pattern is a measure. The patterns group into

duple (two beats per measure)	*or*	**strong**	weak	
triple (three beats per measure)	*or*	**strong**	weak	weak
quadruple (four beats per measure)	*or*	**strong**	weak	**less** strong weak

Additionally, the *number of subdivisions per beat* provides more information about the meter.

The meter signature (or time signature) at the beginning of a musical score establishes the grouping of the beats and the nature of the subdivision of the beat.

Simple meter refers to the beat being divided equally into *two* parts.

whole = **2** halves; half = **2** quarters; quarter = **2** eighths; eighth = **2** sixteenths

Compound meter refers to the beat being divided equally into *three* parts.

*Compound meter normally has a **dotted note** as the beat.*

dotted half = **3** quarters   **dotted** quarter = **3** eighths
dotted eighth = **3** sixteenths

Here is an **IF–THEN** chart to help determine meter.
The numbers in this chart refer to the *top* number in the time signature.

	Duple	Triple	Quadruple
Simple	2	3	4
Compound	6	9	12

IF the top number is a 2 or a 6, **THEN** you have duple meter.
IF the top number is a 3 or a 9, **THEN** you have triple meter.
IF the top number is a 4 or a 12, **THEN** you have quadruple meter.
IF the top number is 2, 3, or 4, **THEN** you have simple meter.
IF the top number is 6, 9, or 12, **THEN** you have compound meter.

Simple Meter

"What you see is what you get" represents a time signature in **simple meter**. The top number represents the number of beats per measure and the bottom number represents the fractional equivalent of the note that is the beat. There will never be a time signature with a 7 on the bottom or a 10 on the bottom because there is no such thing as a "seventh note" or a "tenth note." Therefore:

- A time signature of $\frac{2}{16}$ or $\frac{2}{8}$ or $\frac{2}{4}$ or $\frac{2}{2}$ is Simple **Duple**.
  The beat note is:

- A time signature of $\frac{3}{16}$ or $\frac{3}{8}$ or $\frac{3}{4}$ or $\frac{3}{2}$ is Simple **Triple**.
  The beat note is:

- A time signature of $\frac{4}{16}$ or $\frac{4}{8}$ or $\frac{4}{4}$ or $\frac{4}{2}$ is Simple **Quadruple**.
  The beat note is:

> **TIP**
>
> Sometimes $\frac{3}{8}$ or $\frac{3}{4}$ *at a very fast tempo* treats each measure as a **single** compound beat. Thus far, the AP exam has not used this type of meter.

You may also see other time signatures that represent simple meter. For example, c, called common time, is frequently used to represent $\frac{4}{4}$, and ¢, sometimes called "cut time" or **alla breve**, is a substitute for $\frac{2}{2}$.

Compound Meter

If in compound meter the beat is normally a dotted note, there is no fraction that represents a dotted quarter ♩. or dotted half note ♩. ; therefore, in **compound meter** the time signature represents the *subdivision* and not the beat. For example, a $\frac{9}{4}$ time signature represents triple compound meter. There are nine quarter notes (or the durational equivalent) per measure. The beat note is the dotted half note.

You would conduct in three. Each dotted half note receives one beat and the beat is divided equally into three parts (quarter notes).

- A time signature of $\frac{6}{16}$ or $\frac{6}{8}$ or $\frac{6}{4}$ or $\frac{6}{2}$ is Compound **Duple**.
  The beat note is:

- A time signature of $\frac{9}{16}$ or $\frac{9}{8}$ or $\frac{9}{4}$ or $\frac{9}{2}$ is Compound **Triple**.
  The beat note is:

- A time signature of $\frac{12}{16}$ or $\frac{12}{8}$ or $\frac{12}{4}$ or $\frac{12}{2}$ is Compound **Quadruple**.
  The beat note is:

Asymmetrical Meters

The term **asymmetrical** means *not* symmetrical or *not equal*, and refers to meters that have beat units of *unequal length*. The most common asymmetrical meters have 5 or 7 as the top number. An asymmetrical meter such as ⅞ could mean 2 + 3 + 2, which might make the beat units within one measure a quarter note–dotted quarter–quarter note, or 3 + 4 (or 3 + 2 + 2) would be dotted quarter–quarter note–quarter note. How do you know which it is? When listening to music, the pattern of strong and weak beats informs the ear. When looking at music, the beaming of the notes clarifies the beat and informs the eye. *Correct notation reinforces the beat unit.* Sometimes when the same division groupings occur for several measures, the composer will indicate such in the meter signature. In the following example, the time signature would be ⅞.

Triplets and Duplets

In simple meter the regular division of a note value is always in *two* equal parts. An irregular division occurs when it is divided into an odd number of parts (*three, five,* or *seven*). This type of division requires a bracket and a number, or simply the number, if the notes are beamed. The most common division is the **triplet**—dividing a regular duration into three.

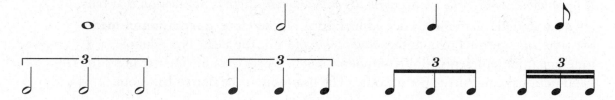

This can also be explained as borrowing the beat unit from compound meter by imposing a triplet into simple meter. Likewise, in compound meter, the beat is normally a dotted note and divides into *three* equal parts. Therefore, a simple division of a *dotted* note occurs when two notes divide the beat instead of three. This type of division also requires a bracket and the number 2 and is called a **duplet** or a **tuplet**.

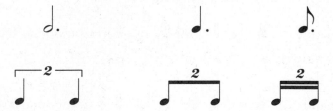

This can also be explained as borrowing the beat unit from simple meter by imposing duplets into compound meter.

Downbeats and Upbeats

The downbeat is what we commonly call the first beat of the measure. This label refers to the fact that in every conducting pattern the first beat is always down. Not all music begins on the downbeat. Some songs begin on a beat that *precedes* the first beat. This is called the **anacrusis**, or pick-up note(s). In music that begins with an anacrusis, the last measure is incomplete so as to balance metrically with the pick-up note(s)—the anacrusis and the last measure will equal one complete measure. Melodically an anacrusis is very often *So* leading to *Do* on the downbeat. In the following example of *Air in F Major* by Bach, notice that the melody begins on beat four and is *So* to *Do* in the key of F Major. The last measure of this excerpt has only three beats and repeats back to the beginning where the anacrusis is beat four.

Air in F Major
Notebook for Anna Magdalena Bach, 1725

Johann Sebastian Bach
(1685-1750)
BWV Anh 131

Syncopation is the rhythmic displacement of the expected strong beat created by dots, rests, ties, accent marks, and dynamics. Syncopation also occurs when the emphasis or stress is in between the beats or on a normally weak beat. Because syncopation emphasizes a beat (or part of a beat) other than the one expected, it creates a conflict with the established grouping of beats. It is an interruption of the regular flow of rhythm. It can also be the placement of stress, accents, or even longer durations where they would not normally occur.

The Entertainer

Scott Joplin
(1868-1917)

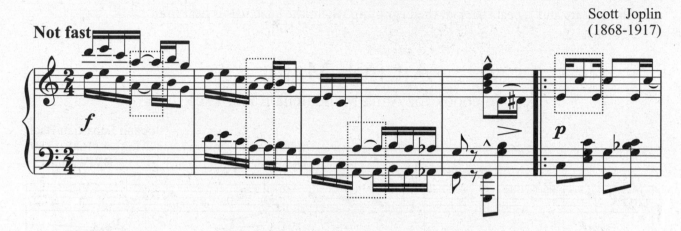

This is a style of music called "ragtime," popular during the turn of the twentieth century that features syncopation. This example uses the *tie* to add length and therefore *stress on the upbeat*, and it also uses a syncopated rhythm to create *stress in between the beats*.

Hemiola or **hemiolia** was used in the Common Practice Period as a special type of syncopation in triple meters, in which the beat is temporarily regrouped into twos as in this example from a piano sonata by Franz Schubert.

Piano Sonata in B♭ Major

excerpt from Third Movement

Franz Schubert
(1797-1828)
D. 960

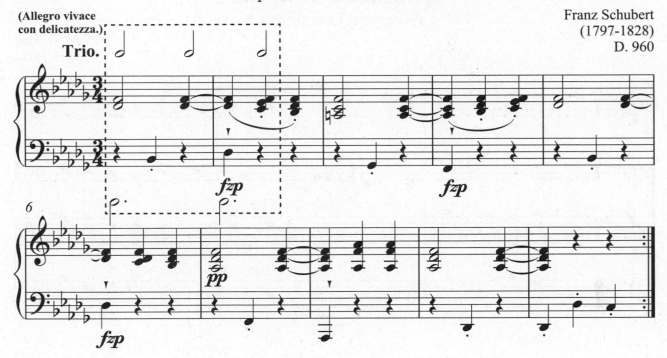

Notice in the upper staff the rhythm is temporarily grouped into units of two because of the half-note rhythm and the use of ties across the bar line, even though the time signature is ¾.

A more modern application of hemiola, sometimes called cross rhythm, is a metric device where the rhythmic relation of three notes occurs in the time of two. It consists of superimposing two notes in the time of three (duplet), or three in the time of two (triplet).

RHYTHMIC NOTATION GUIDELINES

When writing music, the stem can be attached to the note head on the right side extending upward, or on the left side extending downward. For pitches on the *middle line and above* on the staff, the stems go downward. For pitches *below the middle line*, the stems extend upward. When drawing notes with single flags, the flag goes on the right side of the note head regardless of whether the stem is up or down. Rhythmic patterns should be grouped with the beam to indicate beat units. When beaming pairs or multiples of notes you will determine the stem direction by the note that is the farthest from the middle line. The ability to notate rhythms correctly will also improve your ability to sight sing rhythms quickly and accurately.

REVIEW

Unquiet Thoughts
Ayres and Lute Songs I

John Dowland
(1563-1626)

- This very early music (written in the sixteenth century) has four *staves* for four vocal parts connected into one *system*. The top two staves are for the two female voices and the bottom two staves are for the two male voices.
- The third staff is designated as the tenor part with the treble clef and the number 8 below indicating the tenor will sing an octave lower than written. It is written this way to avoid using ledger lines. If the tenor part was written in bass clef it would look like this

- The time signature is $\frac{2}{1}$, which is **simple duple meter**. There are two beats per measure and *the whole note gets one beat*. One measure in this time signature contains two whole notes, or the equivalent of two whole notes.
- The second measure is an interesting one rhythmically. Let's look again at the tenor's line. The second measure is **syncopated** because the emphasis is *in between* the beats. This upsets the "normal" duple meter and makes it asymmetrical in this measure. The bass line, however, continues with straight two beats per measure (subdivided into two parts). Because of the way these are notated, the beat units of these measures look like the example on the next page.

Chapter Summary

- Rhythmic notation does not indicate the exact duration of sound; instead it shows how long one note lasts in relation to others.
- Music is metrically defined by the groupings or organization of the beat into **duple** (two beats per measure), **triple** (three beats per measure), or **quadruple** (four beats per measure).
- The number of subdivisions per beat provides more information about the meter. **Simple meter** refers to the beat being divided equally into two parts.
- Simple meter signatures you are most likely to encounter include:

Simple duple		$\frac{2}{8}$ $\quad$ $\frac{2}{4}$	$\frac{2}{2}$
Simple triple	$\frac{3}{16}$	$\frac{3}{8}$ $\quad$ $\frac{3}{4}$	$\frac{3}{2}$
Simple quadruple	$\frac{4}{16}$	$\frac{4}{8}$ $\quad$ $\frac{4}{4}$	$\frac{4}{2}$

- **Compound meter** refers to the beat being divided equally into three parts.
- Compound meter always has a **dotted note** as the beat.
- When the time signature is simple meter, the top number represents the number of beats per measure and the bottom number represents the fractional equivalent of the note that is the beat.
- In compound meter the time signature represents the division of the beat and not the beat.
- Compound meter signatures you will most likely encounter are:

Compound duple	$\frac{6}{16}$	$\frac{6}{8}$	$\frac{6}{4}$
Compound triple	$\frac{9}{16}$	$\frac{9}{8}$	$\frac{9}{4}$
Compound quadruple	$\frac{12}{16}$	$\frac{12}{8}$	$\frac{12}{4}$

- Not all music begins on the downbeat. Some songs begin with an upbeat that precedes the first beat. This is called the **anacrusis**, or pick-up. In music that begins with an anacrusis, the last measure is incomplete so as to balance metrically with the pick-up.
- **Syncopation** is the rhythmic displacement of the expected strong beat by using dots, rests, ties, accent marks, and dynamics that create a conflict with the established grouping of beats.
- **Hemiola** was often used in the Common Practice Period as a special type of syncopation in triple meter, in which the beat is temporarily regrouped into twos instead of threes.

Practice Exercises

Questions 1–3 are based on an excerpt from the hymn tune "Blessed Assurance."

Blessed Assurance

Phoebe Palmer Knapp
(1839-1908)

1. The meter of this piece can best be described as

   (A) compound duple
   (B) simple quadruple
   (C) simple triple
   (D) compound triple

2. The note that receives one beat in this meter is the

   (A) dotted half note
   (B) half note
   (C) dotted quarter note
   (D) eighth note

3. The first three notes are

   (A) equivalent to a beat and a half
   (B) equivalent to a quarter note
   (C) an anacrusis
   (D) considered the downbeat

4. Compound meter always

    (A) has three beats per measure
    (B) has a dotted note as the beat
    (C) has complicated rhythms
    (D) subdivides into two equal parts

5. The correct way to beam this ⅜ rhythm below into a two-measure rhythm is

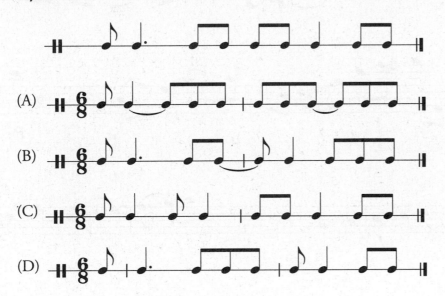

Viola Sonata in G Minor
Solo Part

Henry Eccles
(1670-1742)

6. The musical example above represents the opening line of four different movements of a sonata by Eccles. Identify the meter of each movement *and* the note value that receives one beat.

Grave: _____

Courante: _____

Adagio: _____

Vivace: _____

Questions 7–9 refer to the excerpt below from the hymn tune "Woodworth" by W. B. Bradbury.

Woodworth

William B. Bradbury
(1816-1868)

7. What is the meter of this hymn tune?

   (A) Compound triple
   (B) Simple triple
   (C) Simple duple
   (D) Compound duple

8. The note that gets one beat in this meter is the

   (A) half note
   (B) dotted half note
   (C) quarter note
   (D) dotted quarter note

9. Because the first two eighth notes are the anacrusis, the last measure of this hymn tune will contain what durational value?

   (A) 𝅝·

   (B) 𝅗𝅥· + 𝅗𝅥

   (C) 𝅗𝅥· + ♩

   (D) 𝅗𝅥 + 𝅗𝅥

Questions 10–11 refer to this excerpt by Bach.

Gib dich zufrieden und sei stille
Be Thou Contented
(Soprano and Bass parts)

Johann Sebastian Bach
(1685-1750)
BWV 315

10. This selection includes all of the following **except**

    (A) an anacrusis
    (B) syncopation
    (C) hemiola
    (D) simple meter

11. The last measure has only three beats because

    (A) the ending is designed to be abrupt
    (B) it is really not the end because it repeats
    (C) syncopation displaces the rhythm
    (D) the last measure and the anacrusis combine to create one metrically correct measure

ANSWER KEY

1. **D**	5. **A**	8. **B**
2. **C**	6. **See Answers**	9. **B**
3. **C**	**Explained.**	10. **C**
4. **B**	7. **D**	11. **D**

ANSWERS EXPLAINED

1. **(D)** The meter of this example is compound triple. The top number of the time signature is 9, which tells us the time signature represents the subdivision of the beat or nine eighth notes.

2. **(C)** In compound meter, look at the bottom number in the time signature. The beat note is going to be the next larger duration with a dot. Since this time signature has an 8 as the bottom number (representing the eighth note as the subdivision duration), the beat note is the next duration larger, quarter note + the dot $\frac{3}{\text{♩.}}$.

3. **(C)** The first three notes are the anacrusis (pick-up notes). In this meter the beat is the dotted quarter note, so three eighth notes are equal to one beat. The anacrusis is before the downbeat—in this case, on beat 4 of the measure.

4. **(B)** Compound meter always has a dotted note as the beat.

5. **(A)** The purpose of beams is to indicate clearly the units (beats) of the meter. How do you arrive at the correct answer? First of all, the example has a total of twelve eighth notes—the shortest duration notated. In two measures that would be six eighth notes per measure $\frac{6}{8}$ time signature. Because this meter is compound, three eighth notes are beamed together to clearly indicate the beat.

6. **Grave:** Common time or $\frac{4}{4}$ is simple quadruple. There are four beats per measure and the quarter note gets one beat.
   Courante: The time signature is $\frac{3}{4}$, simple triple meter. The quarter note gets one beat.
   Adagio: The time signature is $\frac{3}{2}$, also simple triple meter; however, in this movement the half note (designated by the number 2 on the bottom of the time signature) gets one beat.
   Vivace: The time signature is simple triple. (Remember that *any* time signature with a 3 as the top number will be simple triple.) The eighth note gets one beat and each beat subdivides into two sixteenth notes.

7. **(D)** The meter is compound duple—two beats per measure with each beat dividing into three equal parts.

8. **(B)** The dotted half note gets one beat in this meter.

9. **(B)** The anacrusis is equivalent to one quarter note, leaving the remaining five beats for the last measure.

10. **(C)** This example contains an anacrusis, syncopation in the bass clef (left hand) measure 3, and is simple meter. It does NOT include an example of hemiola.

11. **(D)** The last measure has three beats because the anacrusis is a quarter note combined with the last measure to equal one full measure in common time. Because the anacrusis is an incomplete measure, it is never numbered. Measure 1 is always *after* the anacrusis.

Scales, Keys, and Modes

3

- Accidental
- Blues Scale
- Circle of Fifths
- Chromatic, Chromaticism
- Diatonic
- Diatonic Scale/Chord Names
    - $\hat{1}$ Tonic
    - $\hat{2}$ Supertonic
    - $\hat{3}$ Mediant
    - $\hat{4}$ Subdominant
    - $\hat{5}$ Dominant
    - $\hat{6}$ Submediant
    - $\hat{6}$ Raised Submediant
    - $\hat{7}$ Subtonic
    - $\hat{7}$ Leading Tone
- Key
- Key Signature
- Major and Minor Pentachord
- Major Tetrachord
- Major (Ionian)
- Minor
    - Harmonic Minor
    - Melodic Minor (ascending/ descending)
    - Natural Minor (Aeolian)
- Modes
    - Ionian
    - Dorian
    - Phrygian
    - Lydian
    - Mixolydian
    - Aeolian
    - Locrian
- Modality
- Movable-Do Solfeggio System
- Parallel Key (parallel major or parallel minor)
- Pentatonic Scale
- Relative Key (relative major or relative minor)
- Scalar Variance
- Scales/Keys/Modes
- Tonal
- Tonality
- Tonic
- Whole-Tone Scale

CHROMATIC, MAJOR, AND MINOR SCALES

Scales are an ordered collection of pitches in whole- and half-step patterns. The word *scale* comes from the Latin word *scalae* meaning "stairs" or "ladder."

The Chromatic Scale

The **chromatic scale** is a *symmetrical* scale with all pitches spaced a half step apart. The chromatic scale is written using sharps for the ascending scale and the *enharmonic equivalent* flats for the descending scale.

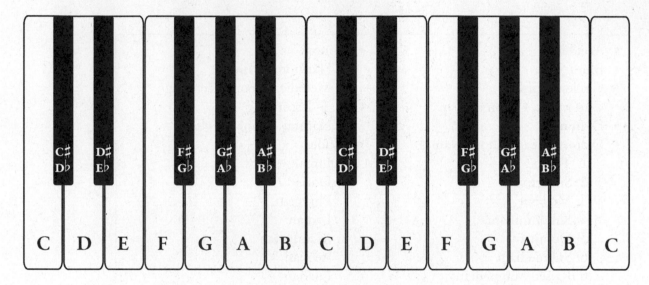

Keyboard illustration courtesy of Mary Elizabeth

Use sharps ascending: C C♯ D D♯ E F F♯ G G♯ A A♯ B C

And flats descending: C B B♭ A A♭ G G♭ F E E♭ D D♭ C

The Major Scale Pattern

A **major scale** is created using a pattern of whole and half steps. In contrast to the chromatic scale, the major scale is *asymmetrical,* meaning the pattern is a combination of whole and half steps. **All major scales share the same pattern.**

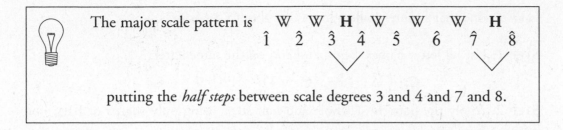

putting the *half steps* between scale degrees 3 and 4 and 7 and 8.

This divides the scale into two four-note groups called tetrachords. Each tetrachord consists of the pattern **W W H** (the **major tetrachord**), and is also connected by a whole step.

The major scale will start and end on the same note name (tonic) and use all seven letter names. In order to correctly "spell" the scale according to the pattern of whole and half steps, either all sharps or all flats are used, not a mixture of sharps and flats.

Let's build a major scale beginning on G.

STEP 1: Use all letter names; begin and end on the same letter.

STEP 2: Apply the pattern of whole and half steps using only sharps or flats, not both.

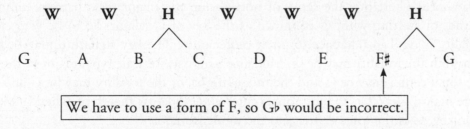

STEP 3: The accidental needed to correctly construct the scale is one sharp—F♯.

STEP 4: The major scale pattern produces the key signature with one sharp for the key of **G Major.**

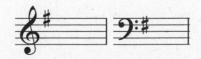

Let's do one that's more challenging. How about G♯ Major?

STEP 1: Use all letter names; begin and end on the same letter.

G♯ A B C D E F **G♯**

STEP 2: Apply the pattern of whole and half steps using only sharps or flats, not both.

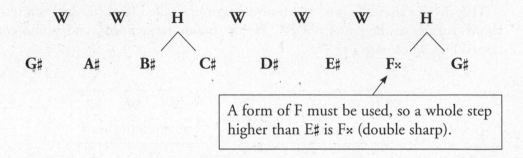

A form of F must be used, so a whole step higher than E♯ is F✕ (double sharp).

STEP 3: The accidentals needed to correctly construct the G♯ Major scale are one double sharp—F✕ and 6 sharps—C♯, G♯, D♯, A♯, E♯, B♯. This *is* a viable key; however, it's normally written **enharmonically** as A♭ major!

STEP 4: The major scale pattern does not produce a standard key signature for the key of **G♯ Major**. So is G♯ Major a viable key? Sure it is. We just don't have a recognizable standard key signature for it. So what exactly is a key? A **key** is a specific series of pitches based on a pattern of whole and half steps that define a **tonality**—the principle of organizing a composition around that key note or tonic. Keys may be defined as major or minor (or possibly pentatonic or a church mode—coming later), referred to as **modality**, and are named after their tonic or keynote. Therefore, the series of notes using the major scale pattern centered around, or starting with, G is known as the key of G Major. So to be very clear: Tonality is used in reference to pitch center only. The key signature may be two sharps but the tonality may be G. Modality is an issue of scale type, major or minor. The tonal center may be G and the mode minor, or the tonality may be G and the mode major. *Key* refers to both tonal center *and* modality; therefore, when G Major is the key, G is the tonal center and the mode is major.

There are fifteen major scales all together; however, there are three scales that are **enharmonic**. This means sounding the same but written or notated differently. Here are the enharmonically equivalent major scales:

	1̂	2̂	3̂	4̂	5̂	6̂	7̂	8̂
B and Cb	B	C#	D#	E	F#	G#	A#	B
	Cb	Db	Eb	Fb	Gb	Ab	Bb	Cb
			∨				∨	
			H				H	

	1̂	2̂	3̂	4̂	5̂	6̂	7̂	8̂
F# and Gb	F#	G#	A#	B	C#	D#	E#	F#
	Gb	Ab	Bb	Cb	Db	Eb	F	Gb
			∨				∨	
			H				H	

	1̂	2̂	3̂	4̂	5̂	6̂	7̂	8̂
C# and Db	C#	D#	E#	F#	G#	A#	B#	C#
	Db	Eb	F	Gb	Ab	Bb	C	Db
			∨				∨	
			H				H	

KEY SIGNATURES

The **W W H W W W H** pattern generates the major scale, and the pitches that are altered to create that pattern become the key signature. The key signature is a form of "shorthand" that dispenses with the writing of accidentals (sharps and flats) for the notes affected by the pattern. The **key signature** written at the beginning of every staff shows which pitches are to be sharp or flat consistently throughout the piece, and helps determine the key or tonal center (tonality).

Sharps and flats, when used in key signatures, are found in a specific order. The sequence or order of sharps is **F C G D A E B**; the order of flats is the same, only backward: **B E A D G C F**.

PLACEMENT OF KEY SIGNATURES ON THE GRAND STAFF

The key signature is always written on the staff between the clef and the meter signature. The placement of sharps on the staff alternates direction in a "**down** first–then **up**" pattern.

Because *accidentals are not notated on ledger lines*, the sharp on A creates an exception to using the "down–up" pattern (the sharp that would fall on a ledger line in the treble clef is written an octave lower) with two "downs" in a row in both treble and bass clefs. The placement of flats on the staff alternates direction in an "**up** first–then **down**" pattern in both treble and bass clefs.

IDENTIFYING THE KEY FROM THE KEY SIGNATURE

Your first choice is to memorize, but the easiest way to figure out the major key from the key signature is

- For sharps—the last sharp in the key signature is *Ti* or scale degree 7; therefore, the name of the key is up one half step.
- For flats—the last flat in the key signature is *Fa* or scale degree 4; therefore, since the flat keys are a fourth apart, the name of the key is the next to the last flat in the key signature. The last flat in the key signature is also the name of the *next* flat scale.

THE CIRCLE OF FIFTHS

The Circle of Fifths demonstrates the relationship of the tonal centers to each other. Each key signature that requires sharps appears around the circle to the right (clockwise), with each key a fifth higher. The key signatures that require flats appear around the circle to the left (counter-clockwise), each a fifth lower. Although you *must* memorize the major keys and the key signatures, it's important to remember that it is the major scale **pattern** that generates the major key signatures and *not* the other way around.

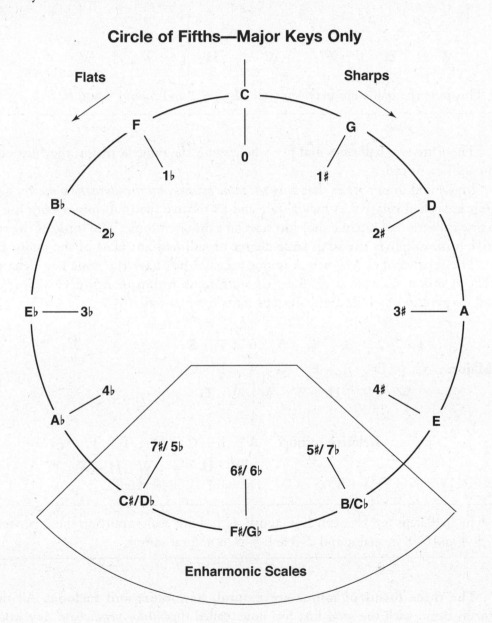

Circle of Fifths—Major Keys Only

The Minor Scale Pattern

The natural minor scale has a pattern of whole and half steps that is different from the major scale. **There are three forms of the minor scale, and all are derived from this natural minor pattern.**

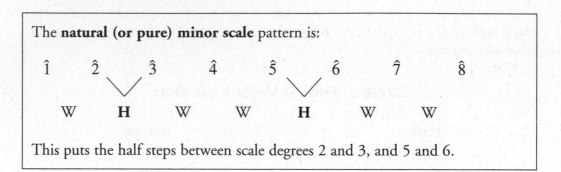

The **natural (or pure) minor scale** pattern is:

$\hat{1}$ $\hat{2}$ $\hat{3}$ $\hat{4}$ $\hat{5}$ $\hat{6}$ $\hat{7}$ $\hat{8}$

W   H   W   W   H   W   W

This puts the half steps between scale degrees 2 and 3, and 5 and 6.

There are two half steps and five whole steps, the same as major; they just occur in a different order.

Major and minor scales that *have the same pitches and therefore the same key signature* are called **relative**. A major scale and its relative (natural) minor both use the same collection of pitches; they just start on a different tonic. **The tonic of the relative minor scale is the sixth scale degree or submediant (*La*) of the major key.**

The relative of C Major is A minor because they have the same key signature. The A minor scale starts on the *sixth scale degree* (submediant) of C Major. The minor pattern of whole and half steps starts there as well.

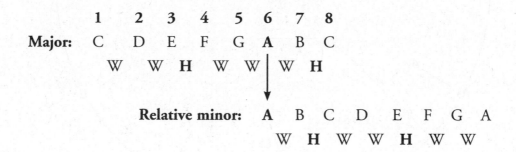

	1	2	3	4	5	6	7	8
Major:	C	D	E	F	G	A	B	C
		W	W	H	W	W	W	H

Relative minor: A   B   C   D   E   F   G   A
W   H   W   W   H   W   W

The half steps are between E–F and B–C in both scales, putting them between 3–4 and 7–8 in major and 2–3 and 5–6 in natural minor.

The three forms of minor are natural, harmonic, and melodic. All three forms begin with the *same* first five notes called the *minor pentachord* (five notes), but from scale degree 5 up to tonic, each form of the minor scale is different. The minor pentachord differs from the major pentachord by one pitch—the third scale degree is lowered one half step.

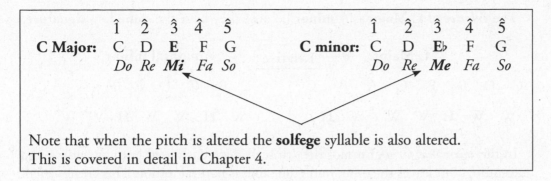

Note that when the pitch is altered the **solfege** syllable is also altered.
This is covered in detail in Chapter 4.

The natural minor is called *natural* to differentiate from the artificial forms of the scale.

In the *natural* or *pure* form of the minor scale there are no alterations from the key signature. **The half step between 2 and 3 is what gives the minor scale its characteristic sound.** Another striking difference between major and natural minor is that the *whole step* between 7 and 8 fails to lead to the tonic with the same intensity as the half step in major. For this reason the term *leading tone* is not used in natural minor.

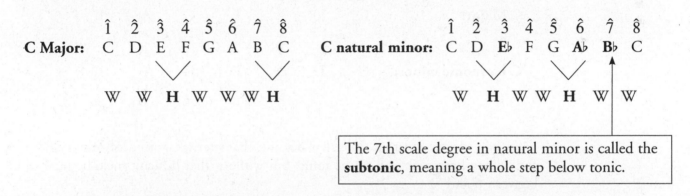

The 7th scale degree in natural minor is called the **subtonic**, meaning a whole step below tonic.

Major and minor keys with different key signatures but with the *same tonic* are called *parallel*. When comparing natural minor to its parallel major, the 3rd, 6th, and 7th scale degrees are lowered.

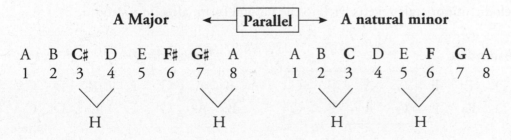

A Major and **A minor** are *parallel* because they have the **same tonic**.

The *relative* of **C Major** is **A minor** because they have the **same key signature.**

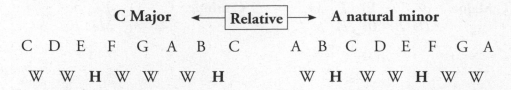

In the *harmonic form* of minor the 7th scale degree is raised both ascending and descending, but leaves the other notes the same as natural minor. This creates a half step below the tonic so that the 7th scale degree once again *leads to tonic* or **Do**, providing a more convincing harmonic pull to tonic while retaining the characteristic color of minor.

As the name implies, during the Common Practice Period composers used this form of minor most often when harmonizing melodies. The interval between $\hat{6}$ and $\hat{7}$ is now larger than a whole step (i.e., a step and a half), making it difficult to sing melodically.

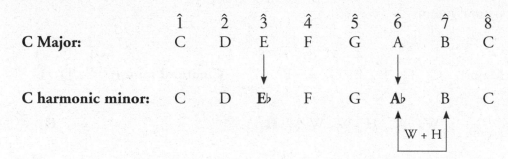

So how do we create a scale that has the characteristic sound of minor and a convincing harmonic pull to the tonic, but without that difficult melodic interval between $\hat{6}$ and $\hat{7}$?

We start with the minor pentachord, then **raise *both* the 6th and the 7th scale degrees**, of course! This is called the *melodic form of minor.* The upper tetrachord (last four notes) is the same as major. Because the 6th and 7th scale degrees are raised in order to go more smoothly and convincingly **UP** to the tonic, these scale degrees will only be raised when the melody (or scale) is ascending. The descending melodic minor scale reverts back to the natural form, affecting $\hat{7}$ and $\hat{6}$.

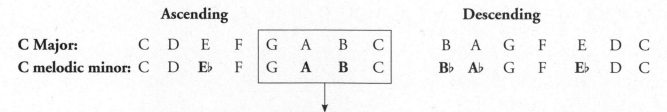

The upper tetrachord of the ascending scale (last four notes) is the same in ascending melodic minor as the parallel major. Therefore, if you hear the minor pentachord but the last four notes of the scale sound like major, then you are in melodic minor.

Now let's compare all three forms of minor:

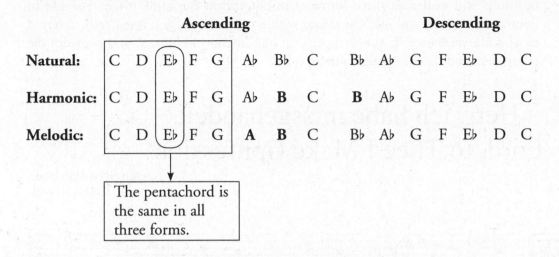

	Ascending	Descending
Natural:	C D Eb F G Ab Bb C	Bb Ab G F Eb D C
Harmonic:	C D Eb F G Ab **B** C	**B** Ab G F Eb D C
Melodic:	C D Eb F G **A B** C	Bb Ab G F Eb D C

The pentachord is the same in all three forms.

Circle of Fifths—Minor Keys Only

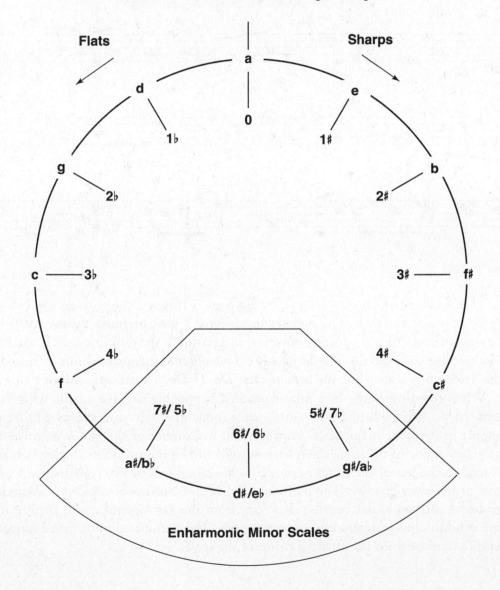

Flats

Sharps

a
0
d — 1b
g — 2b
c —— 3b
f — 4b
a#/bb — 7#/ 5b
d#/eb — 6#/ 6b

e — 1#
b — 2#
3# —— f#
c# — 4#
g#/ab — 5#/ 7b

Enharmonic Minor Scales

When studying music in a minor mode it is important to note that many compositions will utilize all three forms of minor within the same piece. The use of natural, harmonic, and melodic minor within one composition is generally referred to as **scalar variance**. It simply opens up our "menu of choices" and provides the composer (and listener) with more options.

Herr, ich habe missgehandelt
Lord, to Thee I Make Confession

Johann Sebastian Bach
(1685-1750)

This harmonization of a chorale by Bach in A minor demonstrates the occurrence of scalar variance. The melody in measure 1 uses **melodic minor** with the raised 6th and 7th scale degree; however, in measure 2 the alto line uses F natural. Continuing with the alto line in measure 3 we observe the **natural minor** form of the descending scale while the bass line has ***Do-Ti-Do***, a **harmonic minor** pattern.

When notating music in a minor mode it is possible to have a scale with flats *and* sharps. This will not occur in a major modality—flats and sharps will never appear in the same major scale. However, the occurrence of sharps (or naturals) in a flat key is one of the signals that help us to identify a minor mode. Accidentals are placed to the left of the notes as needed—the raised 6th or 7th scale degree is *not* part of the key signature. The harmonic and melodic forms of minor are **artificial scales** or **altered scales** because they vary from the key signature and require the use of additional accidentals to create the scale. The natural minor is called **natural** to differentiate from the artificial forms of the scale.

The Full Circle of Fifths—Major and Relative Minor

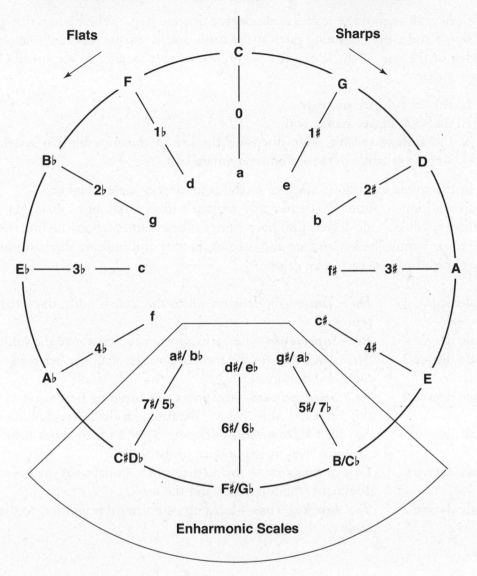

See Appendix A for more helpful information on the Circle of Fifths.

Scales are one of the first things we learn as performers; however, music doesn't always use complete scales. Melodies often contain segments of scales. **Learn to identify, sing, and notate major scales and all forms of minor scales.**

SCALE DEGREE NAMES

We call each step of the scale a **scale degree** or scale step. When you write, play, or sing a scale, the beginning pitch is the **tonic** and is usually repeated one octave higher at the end of the scale. It is helpful to be able to refer to the members of the scale by

1. the scale degree **number**,
2. the scale degree **name**, and
3. the **solfege** syllable. (We discussed the use of the movable-*Do* system of singing syllables in the introductory material.)

In this guide we will use all three methods to identify scale members.

In addition to numbers, customarily written with a caret above them ($\hat{1}$), and solfege syllables, scale degrees also have names. These names reflect the function of the tones within the key and are also used to identify and indicate the harmony of the chords built on each scale degree.

Scale degree $\hat{1}$ ***Do* = *Tonic***—the tone on which the scale is built, the tonal center

Scale degree $\hat{2}$ ***Re* = *Supertonic***—the prefix *super*, meaning above the tonic

Scale degree $\hat{3}$ ***Mi* = *Mediant***—in the median position, halfway between tonic and dominant

Scale degree $\hat{4}$ ***Fa* = *Subdominant***—the prefix *sub*, meaning below, refers to this pitch as a fifth "below" the tonic, or the lower dominant

Scale degree $\hat{5}$ ***So (Sol)* = *Dominant***—refers to a perfect fifth above tonic, the pitch next in importance to the tonic

Scale degree $\hat{6}$ ***La* = *Submediant***—the median pitch, in between the lower dominant (subdominant) and the tonic

Scale degree $\hat{7}$ ***Ti* = *Leading Tone***—leads upward toward resolution to the tonic

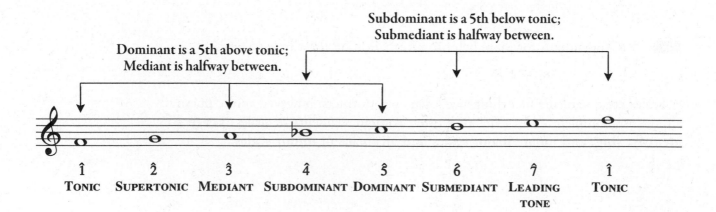

Major Scale

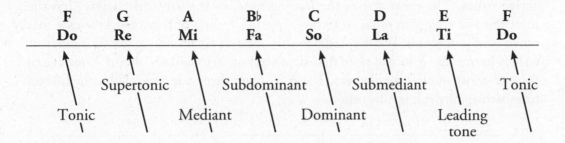

Minor Scales

In the natural minor scale the 7th scale degree is a whole step below tonic; it is *not* a leading tone. This scale degree is called the **subtonic**, meaning (one whole step) below the tonic.

The **parallel natural minor scale** is F minor and has a key signature of four flats:

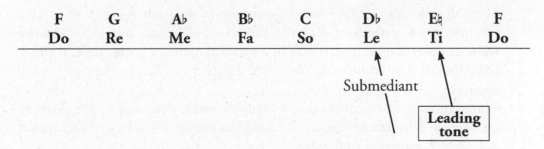

In the harmonic form of minor the 7th scale degree is raised; it *is* a leading tone as it is one half step below the tonic and once again leads to *Do*.

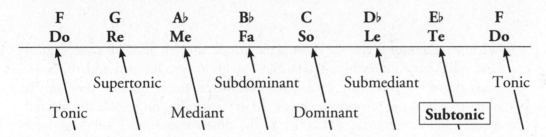

In the melodic form of minor the **raised submediant** is the name of the 6th scale degree and the 7th scale degree is still the leading tone. All other scale degree names are the same in minor as they are in major.

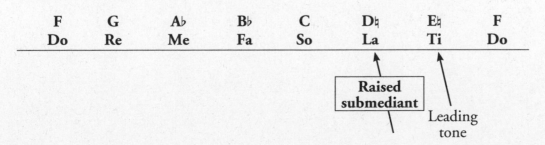

Certain pitches in the scale sound stronger or more stable than others. The strongest, most stable pitch is, of course, the tonic. Scale degrees $\hat{4}$, $\hat{6}$, and $\hat{7}$ are **active tones**. The most active, the leading tone, or the 7th scale degree, has the most musical energy to move to resolve. It is this feeling of tension and release that moves music forward. We will refer to this chart often in talking about melody as well as harmony. You will note that the two most active tones, $\hat{4}$ and $\hat{7}$, resolve to the two most stable scale degrees, $\hat{1}$ and $\hat{3}$. The other scale tones align themselves from strong to weak in this order:

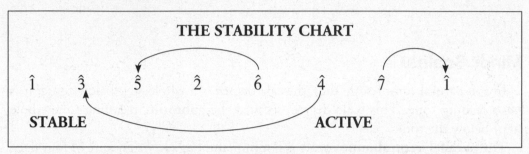

THE STABILITY CHART

$\hat{1}$ $\hat{3}$ $\hat{5}$ $\hat{2}$ $\hat{6}$ $\hat{4}$ $\hat{7}$ $\hat{1}$

STABLE   **ACTIVE**

Courtesy of Dr. Blaise Ferrandino, Texas Christian University, Fort Worth, Texas.

- Within the **major** scale, the most active tones, the 4th and 7th scale degrees, have half-step relationships to the most stable tones, the 3rd and the tonic. Scale degrees 1 and 3 are considered **resolution tones** because they are the notes to which the active tones move. In other words, you resolve the instability of $\hat{4}$ and $\hat{7}$ by moving a half step to the closest stable tones—the subdominant (***Fa***) moves down to the mediant (***Mi***) and the leading tone (***Ti***) resolves upward to tonic (***Do***).
- The 6th scale degree (***La***) resolves down a whole step to the 5th (***So***). This is especially true in minor because there is a half step between $\hat{6}$ (***Le***) and $\hat{5}$ (***So***). The 2nd scale degree (***Re***) resolves downward to the tonic.
- The resolution is always a **diatonic** step away. (Diatonic means **within the scale**, or notes that occur naturally in a standard major or minor scale, without being modified by accidentals other than the sharps or flats in the relevant key signature.)
- Chromatic notes or accidentals are even less stable than any of the diatonic scale tones. They create tension that wants to resolve a half step to the nearest scale degree, either up or down.

PENTATONIC, WHOLE-TONE, AND BLUES SCALES

Pentatonic Scale

As the name implies, this scale has five tones (not including the octave) in contrast to the **heptatonic** scale such as the major scale that has seven. Pentatonic scales are very common and are found all over the world. There are five rotations of the anhemitonic (containing *no half steps* and therefore *no* active tones) pentatonic scale taking five consecutive pitches from the Circle of Fifths and then rearranging the order so that they fit within one octave. Any member of the pentatonic scale may serve as the tonic; thus, five "modes," or rotations, are possible.

C–D–E–G–A–(C) = the most common
D–E–G–A–C–(D)
E–G–A–C–D–(E)
G–A–C–D–E–(G)
A–C–D–E–G–(A)

Whole-Tone Scale

The whole-tone scale is hexatonic, as it has six notes (not including the octave)—each pitch a whole step apart. In relationship to a major scale, the whole-tone scale is $\hat{1}$–$\hat{2}$–$\hat{3}$–$\flat\hat{5}$–$\flat\hat{6}$–$\flat\hat{7}$ if you are using flats; or enharmonically in sharp keys it is $\hat{1}$–$\hat{2}$–$\hat{3}$–$\#\hat{4}$–$\#\hat{5}$–$\#\hat{6}$. This is an **artificial scale** because the altered notes do not represent a standard key signature and therefore accidentals are required to create the pattern.

Enharmonically this could also be: C–D–E–G♭–A♭–B♭–C
C–D–E–F♯–G♯–A♯–C

Blues Scale

This is a six-note scale, not counting the octave (hexatonic), that does not have a second or sixth scale degree but includes the flatted fifth *and* the fifth. It is generally associated with a slower, jazzy song style of lamentation known as "the blues." The lowered notes are referred to as "blue notes." In relationship to the major scale, the blues scale is $\hat{1}$–$\flat\hat{3}$–$\hat{4}$–$\flat\hat{5}$–$\hat{5}$–$\flat\hat{7}$.

C–E♭–F–G♭–G–B♭–C

CHURCH MODES

The term **mode** is synonymous with **scale**. A church mode is a scale with a different pattern of whole and half steps from major or minor.

> There are six commonly used diatonic modes, sometimes called church modes. The **Ionian** mode has the *same pattern as the major scale* and the **Aeolian** mode has the *same pattern as the natural minor scale*. The other four commonly used modes are related to either Ionian or Aeolian.

Dorian, **Phrygian**, and **Aeolian** are related to each other as *minor modes*. Dorian is similar to natural minor (Aeolian) with a raised 6th scale degree, while Phrygian is related to the natural minor with a lowered 2nd scale degree. **The tonic triads of these three modes are minor.** What creates the different sound of Dorian from Aeolian, for example, is of course the pattern of whole and half steps. Let's compare C Phrygian and C Dorian to C Aeolian.

C Phrygian: C–D♭–E♭–F–G–A♭–B♭–C   (Natural minor + ♭2)

C Aeolian: C–D–E♭–F–G–A♭–B♭–C   **Natural minor**

C Dorian: C–D–E♭–F–G–A–B♭–C   (Natural minor + ♯6)

Lydian, **Mixolydian**, and **Ionian** are related to each other as *major modes*. Lydian is similar to major (Ionian) with a raised 4th scale degree, while Mixolydian is similar to major with a lowered 7th scale degree. **The tonic triads of these three modes are major.** Now we will compare C Mixolydian and C Lydian to C Ionian.

C Mixolydian: C–D–E–F–G–A–B♭–C   (Major + ♭7)

C Ionian: C–D–E–F–G–A–B–C   **Major**

C Lydian: C–D–E–F♯–G–A–B–C   (Major + ♯4)

A seventh mode, the **Locrian** mode, is used less than the other modes and has a **diminished tonic triad**; therefore, it is unlike either major or minor. It is generally considered to be minor based with a ♭2 and a ♭5. It is the lowered 5th scale degree that creates the diminished tonic triad.

C Aeolian   C D E♭ F G A♭ B♭ C
C Locrian   C **D♭** E♭ F **G♭** A♭ B♭ C   (natural minor + ♭2, ♭5)

Another way of looking at these modes is a rotation of all natural notes so that each mode starts on a different diatonic note of the C Major scale. This creates *seven scales with all natural notes*, with each diatonic mode beginning on a different scale degree.

Here is a mnemonic device to help you remember the natural note modes and their order.

	All <u>natural</u> notes	create this	mode.
1	C D E F G A B C	**I**	(**I**onian) = major
2	D E F G A B C D	**D**on't	(**D**orian) = natural minor + ♯**6**
3	E F G A B C D E	**P**lay	(**P**hrygian) = natural minor + ♭**2**
4	F G A B C D E F	Loud	(**L**ydian) = major + ♯**4**
5	G A B C D E F G	**M**usic	(**M**ixolydian) = major + ♭**7**
6	A B C D E F G A	**A**t	(**A**eolian) = natural minor
7	B C D E F G A B	**L**unch	(**L**ocrian) = natural minor + ♭**2** and ♭**5**

➡ For further information, including identifying modal key signatures, see Appendix A.

It is significant to note here that when studying melodies there are a number of factors that determine the key, or tonality. The key signature is just one of those factors. *Look at the music* and not just the key signature.

- Which note seems to be the center or main tone? Looking at the end of the music, not just the beginning, generally will reinforce this concept. Look at the final melodic pattern. Music will usually end on ***Do*** or tonic.
- We have spent some time discussing the patterns of whole and half steps that create scales. Doesn't it make sense that because there are seven letters used in our musical alphabet that there are a possibility of seven patterns, each generating a different key signature? Having all seven patterns is indeed the full menu of scalar choices, although we commonly use Aeolian (minor) and Ionian (Major).

- **Music often moves around from key to key**, from major to minor or from mode to mode, often while maintaining the original key signature. I like to compare this to "playing in our neighbor's yard." We generally don't wander far away from home (tonic), but exploring other neighboring areas is interesting and gives us more to experience than what is only in "our yard." Remember when we built the major scale on G♯? Usually when music moves from one key to another it moves close by (to keys that have many notes in common). But sometimes a composer may want to simply move up or down a half step. So, if the original key is centered around G and we move up a half step, we are now centered around G♯—hence, the use of F double sharp as an accidental (the leading tone one half step below G♯).

- The use of accidentals is a *huge* clue. If we are in a major mode the use of accidentals signals a move to a new key, if only for a short visit. If we are in a minor mode, the accidentals provide information as to what form of minor is used, or that we have moved to a new key center.

- Look for significant half-step relationships that may point to a change in tonality, key, or mode. Accidentals once again are clues. We will commonly see an accidental *leading* upward. This means the note has been raised so that it has more intensity or pull to the next note, generally a half step above. Here the word *leading* is also a clue because that's what leading tones do—they *lead* us to tonic. So what we may be seeing with an accidental is a **leading tone relationship—in another key**.

- The world would be boring indeed if there were only vanilla ice cream. I want *all* the flavors! In music that means looking outside the key signature to find all the "flavors" that may be hiding in the music.

REVIEW

Sonata for Piano with Horn, Op. 17

Ludwig van Beethoven
(1770-1827)

- The excerpt above demonstrates several elements previously discussed in our first three chapters. This is an example of three staves connected into one system. The top staff is for the solo instrument, in this case, the horn. The bottom two staves, connected by a bracket, are for the piano.
- Notice that the key signature for the horn is different from the key signature for the piano. This is discussed in a later chapter. What we do know thus far is that the horn part is written in the key of C Major and the piano part is written in the key of F Major.
- Note that in the piano part *both* the right hand and the left hand are playing in treble clef because both are *above middle C.*
- The time signature is common time or $\frac{4}{4}$. The meter is simple quadruple. The anacrusis in the horn part is a dotted eighth and sixteenth note (it is also *So* leading to *Do* in C Major). The accompaniment part enters in the second measure with a three eighth-note anacrusis.
- The last note played by the horn is C^2, notated in the bass clef to avoid using all those ledger lines that would be required if it stayed in treble clef. How many ledger lines, you ask? The answer is eight!
- Notice the melody line uses correct placement of stems up or down, while the piano left hand notates all three notes with one stem, regardless of placement on the staff, to show all notes are to be played at the same time with the same hand.
- There is an F♯ in the fourth measure that is not part of the key signature in C Major. It has an accidental (the sharp is placed to the left of the note head), a chromatic pitch that is a half step higher than F leading to the G.
- All five aspects of sound are notated in this one four-measure example. (Remember the anacrusis is never counted as a measure because it comes *before* measure 1.) We can see pitch (wavelength), dynamic (wave height), articulation (envelope), timbre (waveform), and durations, including rests.

This is a lot of information! You're becoming a thinking musician already.

Chapter Summary

- **Scales** are an ordered collection of pitches in whole- and half-step patterns.
- The **chromatic scale** is a symmetrical scale with all pitches spaced a half step apart.
- The **major scale pattern** is:

W	W	H	W	W	W	H
$\hat{1}$	$\hat{2}$	$\hat{3}$	$\hat{4}$	$\hat{5}$	$\hat{6}$	$\hat{7}$	$\hat{8}$

  Here the half steps are between scale degrees $\hat{3}$ (*Mi*) and $\hat{4}$ (*Fa*), and $\hat{7}$ (*Ti*) and 8 (*Do*).
- In music, notes you play that are within the scale are called **diatonic**. Any notes you play that are outside the scale are **chromatic** notes.
- The **W W H W W W H** pattern generates the major scale, and the pitches that are altered to create that pattern become the key signature.
- The **key signature** written at the beginning of every staff shows which pitches are to be sharped or flatted consistently throughout the piece and indicates the key or tonal center.
- Sharps and flats are in a specific order when placed in the key signature.
- The sequence or order of sharps is **F♯ C♯ G♯ D♯ A♯ E♯ B♯**. The order of flats is the same, only backward: **B♭ E♭ A♭ D♭ G♭ C♭ F♭**.
- A **key** is a specific series of notes based on a pattern of whole and half steps that define a tonality—the principal of organizing a composition around that keynote or tonic. Keys may be defined as major or minor and are named after their tonic or keynote.
- The natural (or pure) minor scale pattern is: **W H W W H W W**. Here the half steps are between scale degrees $\hat{2}$ and $\hat{3}$, and $\hat{5}$ and $\hat{6}$.
- There are three forms of minor: **natural**, **harmonic**, and **melodic**.
- In the natural or pure form of the minor scale there are no alterations from the key signature.
- In the harmonic form of minor the 7th scale degree is raised but leaves the other notes the same as natural minor.
- The melodic form of minor begins with the minor pentachord and raises *both* the 6th and 7th scale degrees in the ascending scale, but reverts back to the natural minor form of the scale when descending.
- The term **relative major** and/or **relative minor** refers to denoting a major and minor key that have the same key signature. A major scale and its relative (natural) minor both use the same collection of pitches; they just start on a different tonic. The tonic of the relative minor scale is the 6th scale degree (*La*) of the major key.
- Major and minor keys with different key signatures but with the same tonic are called **parallel**.
- The **Circle of Fifths** demonstrates the relationship of the tonal centers (keys) to each other with each key a fifth apart.
- **Solmization** is a system of designating notes by the *solfege* (*Sol-Fa*) syllables. **Solfeggio** is the term for the method of sight-singing using these syllables.

- The standard solfege syllables are:

Do	*Re*	*Me Mi*	*Fa*	*So(l)*	*Le La*	*Te Ti*	*Do*
$\hat{1}$	$\hat{2}$	$\hat{3}$	$\hat{4}$	$\hat{5}$	$\hat{6}$	$\hat{7}$	$\hat{1}/8$

- **Scale degree names** are used to identify and indicate the harmony of the chords built on each scale degree. Scale degree names are $\hat{1}$ *Tonic,* $\hat{2}$ *Supertonic,* $\hat{3}$ *Mediant,* $\hat{4}$ *Subdominant,* $\hat{5}$ *Dominant,* $\hat{6}$ *Submediant,* $\hat{7}$ *Leading tone.*
- In the natural minor scale the 7th scale degree is a whole step below tonic and is called the **subtonic**.
- In the melodic form of minor the 6th scale degree is referred to as the **raised submediant**.
- The **pentatonic scale** has five tones (not including the octave) in contrast to the heptatonic scale, such as the major scale that has seven. There are five rotations of the anhemitonic (containing no half steps) pentatonic scale taking five consecutive pitches from the Circle of Fifths and then rearranging the order so that they fit within one octave. Most commonly C–D–E–G–A–(C).
- In relationship to a major scale, the **whole-tone scale** is $\hat{1}$–$\hat{2}$–$\hat{3}$–$\flat\hat{5}$–$\flat\hat{6}$–$\flat\hat{7}$ or $\hat{1}$–$\hat{2}$–$\hat{3}$–$\sharp\hat{4}$–$\sharp\hat{5}$–$\sharp\hat{6}$.
- In relationship to the major scale, the **blues scale** is $\hat{1}$–$\flat\hat{3}$–$\hat{4}$–$\flat\hat{5}$–$\hat{5}$–$\flat\hat{7}$.
- There are six commonly used diatonic modes, sometimes called **church modes**. The **Ionian mode** has the same pattern as the major scale and the **Aeolian mode** has the same pattern as the natural minor scale. The other four modes can be derived from Ionian or Aeolian.
- **Dorian** is similar to natural minor (Aeolian) with a raised 6th scale degree, while **Phrygian** is natural minor with a lowered 2nd scale degree. Therefore, when relating to minor key signatures, Dorian mode adds one sharp and Phrygian mode adds one flat.
- **Lydian** is major (Ionian) with a raised 4th scale degree, while **Mixolydian** is major with a lowered 7th scale degree. Therefore, when relating to major key signatures, Lydian mode adds one sharp and Mixolydian mode adds one flat.

Practice Exercises

Questions 1–3 are based on the string section parts from this concerto grosso by Corelli.

Concerto Grosso, Op. 6, No. 8
("Christmas Concerto"—excerpt of string section parts)

Arcangelo Corelli
(1653-1713)

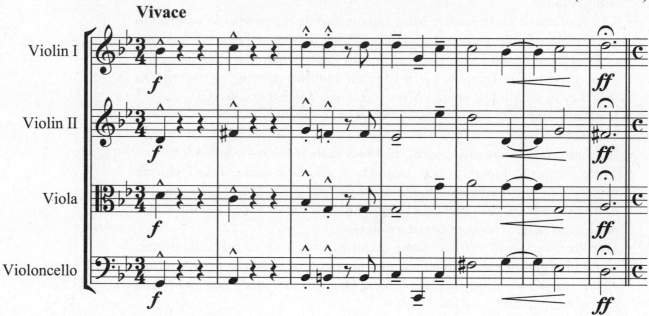

1. Noting the change of time signature at the end, the meter of this passage changes from

    (A) simple triple to simple quadruple
    (B) compound triple to simple duple
    (C) simple triple to compound triple
    (D) simple triple to simple duple

2. This excerpt features all of the following **except**

    (A) a form of syncopation called hemiola
    (B) an anacrusis
    (C) tenor clef
    (D) note values lengthened by the use of dots and ties

3. This excerpt is in what key?

    (A) D minor
    (B) G minor
    (C) B♭ Major
    (D) C Major

Questions 4–6 are based on *English Suite II: Gigue*.

English Suite II: Gigue

Johann Sebastian Bach
(1685-1750)
BWV 807

4. The meter of this selection by Bach is:

   (A) compound duple
   (B) simple duple
   (C) simple triple
   (D) compound triple

5. This example features all of the following **except**

   (A) an anacrusis
   (B) scalar variance
   (C) a passage in A melodic minor
   (D) hemiola

6. The anacrusis and downbeat are what scale degrees?

   (A) $\hat{5}$–$\hat{1}$
   (B) $\hat{1}$–$\hat{4}$
   (C) $\hat{1}$–$\hat{1}$
   (D) $\hat{1}$–$\hat{5}$

Look at the following excerpt and answer **Questions 7–9**.

Contrapunctus XII
Canon alla Ottava

Johann Sebastian Bach
(1685-1750)
BWV 1080

7. Which scale is used in this excerpt?

   (A) F Major
   (B) A harmonic minor
   (C) D harmonic minor
   (D) D melodic minor

8. The bass line in measure 5 is all of the following **except**

   (A) an imitation of the first phrase that was played by the right hand
   (B) syncopated
   (C) it includes a leading tone
   (D) an octave lower than the melody in measure 1

9. All of the following are true about the meter of this selection **except** the

   (A) meter represents the subdivision of the beat
   (B) meter is compound triple
   (C) duration that receives one beat is the sixteenth note
   (D) duration that receives one beat is the dotted eighth note

10. The relative key of A Major is

    (A) A minor
    (B) F minor
    (C) F♯ minor
    (D) C Major

11. Which of the following is a Mixolydian scale?

    (A)

    (B)

    (C)

    (D)

12. Which of the following pitches is <u>not</u> diatonic in B Major?

    (A) C♯
    (B) A♯
    (C) E
    (D) E♯

13. The notes D♯, A, and B are all contained in which of the following pairs of scales?

    (A) E Major and C♯ harmonic minor
    (B) B Major and D melodic minor
    (C) D Major and B harmonic minor
    (D) E Major and E harmonic minor

14. Another name for cut time is:

    (A) common time
    (B) ²/₄
    (C) alla breve
    (D) ⁴/₄

15. If A♯ is the raised submediant in minor, what is the key signature of the relative major key?

    (A) Seven sharps
    (B) Four sharps
    (C) Two sharps
    (D) No sharps or flats

Questions 16–20 are fill in the blanks.

So oft ich meine Tobackspfeife
Aria—Soprano Part

Johann Sebastian Bach
(1685–1750)
BWV 515

16. What two keys are used in the excerpt above and what is the relationship between them?

_____ and _____; _____

Piano Sonata, Op. 2, No. 1

Ludwig van Beethoven
(1770-1827)

17. What is the key of this melody by Beethoven?

_____

18. Does this example contain an anacrusis? Yes or No. Identify the solfege.

_____

19. What is the scale degree name for the E♮ in measures 2 and 3?

_____

20. What rhythmic figure is used to indicate a compound subdivision of the eighth note?

_____

ANSWER KEY

1. **A**	5. **D**	9. **C**	13. **D**
2. **C**	6. **A**	10. **C**	14. **C**
3. **B**	7. **C**	11. **B**	15. **B**
4. **A**	8. **B**	12. **D**	

Questions 16–20. **See Answers Explained.**

ANSWERS EXPLAINED

1. **(A)** The meter in this example changes from simple triple to simple quadruple.

2. **(C)** The excerpt contains an example of hemiola in measures 5 and 6 because, for those two measures, the notes are grouped in beats of two instead of three. Both ties and dots are used to lengthen duration. Although an anacrusis does not *begin* this phrase, the eighth note at the end of measure 3 is considered an anacrusis into the next measure. The viola is in alto clef, not tenor clef.

3. **(B)** This excerpt is in G harmonic minor. The F♯ (occurring in the violin II as well as the cello part) confirms the tonic by leading to G.

4. **(A)** The meter of this example is compound duple. The top number of the time signature is 6, which tells us the time signature represents the subdivision of the beat. In compound meter the beat note is going to be the next larger duration with a dot. Since this time signature has an 8 as the bottom number (representing the eighth note as the subdivision duration), the beat note is the next duration larger with a dot. The time signature $\frac{6}{8}$ is best notated like this: $\frac{2}{\text{♩.}}$. The top number, 2, indicates two beats per measure. The dotted quarter note, ♩., is the duration that is equivalent to one beat.

5. **(D)** This excerpt does not contain an example of hemiola. It *does* have an anacrusis, a passage in A melodic minor in the bass clef fourth measure (F♯–G♯–A), and it does demonstrate scalar variance. In a minor mode, all three forms of minor are frequently used. In this case, we are primarily seeing A harmonic minor, evidenced by the consistent use of G♯, but the melodic pattern of (F♯)–G♯–A is only visible once in the left hand.

6. **(A)** The anacrusis and downbeat pitches are $\hat{5}$ to $\hat{1}$ in the key of A minor.

7. **(C)** This example is clearly in D harmonic minor. In both the treble and bass clefs, the C♯ is consistently used to lead to *Do* with no other forms of minor present.

8. **(B)** The left hand is imitating the first measure that the right hand played an octave higher, which includes the leading tone (C♯). The melody is *not* syncopated.

9. **(C)** The duration that receives one beat is the dotted eighth note, *not* the dotted sixteenth note. The time signature $\frac{9}{16}$ represents the subdivision of the

beat—three dotted eighth notes each dividing into three sixteenth notes—compound triple meter.

10. **(C)** The relative key of A Major is the minor key with the same key signature—F♯ minor. The relative minor tonic is the sixth note of the major scale: A B C♯ D E Ⓕ♯ G♯ A.

11. **(B)** The Mixolydian scale refers to a mode similar to the major scale (Ionian) but with a lowered 7th scale degree. Since all four responses begin on D, the D major scale would have two sharps (F♯ and C♯). Since C♯ occurs on the 7th scale degree it would be lowered to C♮. Since there is no key signature, the natural sign is not used.

12. **(D)** The key of B Major has five sharps: F♯ C♯ G♯ D♯ A♯. The note that is *not* diatonic is E♯.

13. **(D)** D♯, A, and B are all contained in both E major and E harmonic minor. D♯ is the leading tone in both E major and E minor.

> E Major: E F♯ G♯ **A B** C♯ **D♯** E
> E harmonic minor: E F♯ G **A B** C **D♯** E

14. **(C)** Another name for cut time is *alla breve* or $\frac{2}{2}$; the meter is two beats per measure (duple) with the half note as the beat unit, which divides equally into two parts (simple) $\overset{2}{}$.

15. **(B)** If A♯ is the raised submediant, then tonic is C♯ (melodic) minor. The relative key (having the same key signature) is E Major. The key signature of E Major is four sharps.

16. This one eight-measure melody contains two phrases. The first phrase is in D minor and the second in F Major. Because D minor and F major are relative keys, they use the same collection of pitches and the same key signature. You certainly could not say the first four measures are centered around F, or that the last four are centered around D—that's why we say "it is the music that will determine the tonality," not the key signature. The key signature is a clue and the best place to start. Also notice that the two phrases begin with an identical melodic pattern and rhythm.

17. The scale of this excerpt is F harmonic minor.

18. Yes, this melody begins with an anacrusis. The solfege is:

19. The E natural is the raised 7th scale degree, the leading tone, and pulls the ear to confirm F as the tonal center.

20. The triplet is used in measures 2 and 4 to divide an eighth note into three sixteenth notes instead of the regular two sixteenth notes.

AURAL UNIT 1
Multiple-Choice Questions
for Chapters 1–3

Directions: Each of the questions or incomplete statements below is followed by four suggested answers or completions. Select the best answer in each case and circle your answer on the page. In this unit, you will see a treble clef icon, 𝄞, which indicates when music will be played. **Questions 1–7** ask you to identify pitch patterns that are played. In each case, the question number will be announced. You will have **10 seconds** to read the choices; then you will hear the musical example played twice, with a brief pause between playings. Remember to read the choices for each question after the number is announced.

1. Which of the following pitches are sounded? (Notice that two answers begin with a m2 and two answers begin with a M2.)

(A)
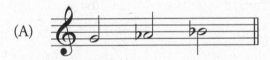

(B)

(C)
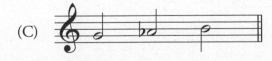

(D)

Pitch pattern, played twice. 𝄞

2. Which of the following pitches are sounded?

(A)

(B)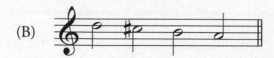

(C)

(D)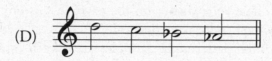

Pitch pattern, played twice.

3. Which of the following pitches are sounded?

(A)

(B)

(C)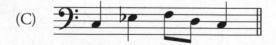

(D)

Pitch pattern, played twice.

4. Which of the following pitches are sounded?

(A)

(B)

(C)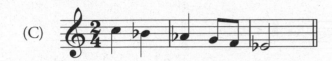

(D)

Pitch pattern, played twice.

5. Which of the following scale patterns is played?

(A)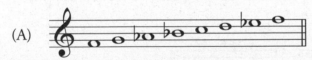

(B)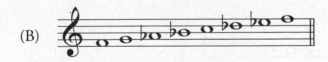

(C)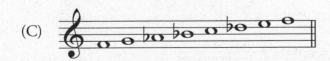

(D)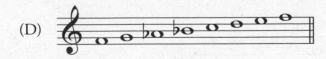

Pitch pattern, played twice.

6. Which of the following scale patterns is played?

(A)

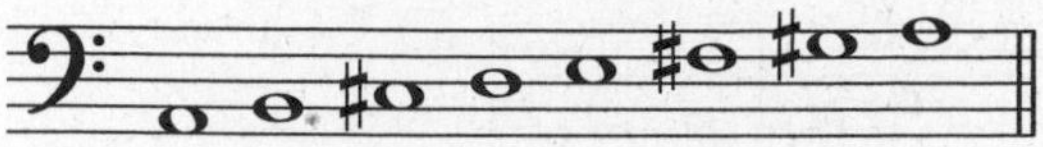

(B)

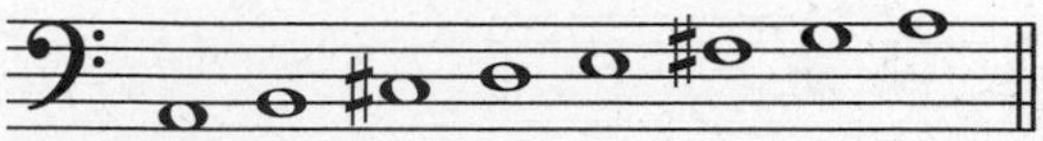

(C)

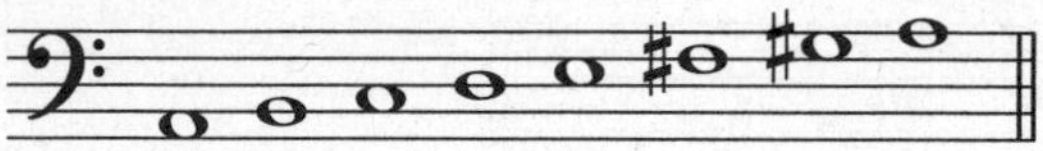

(D)

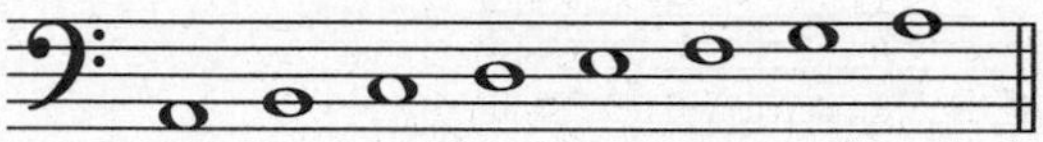

Pitch pattern, played twice.

7. The next four patterns represent modes that all begin on D. Which of the following modal scale patterns is played? (Can you identify all four modes?)

(A)

(B)

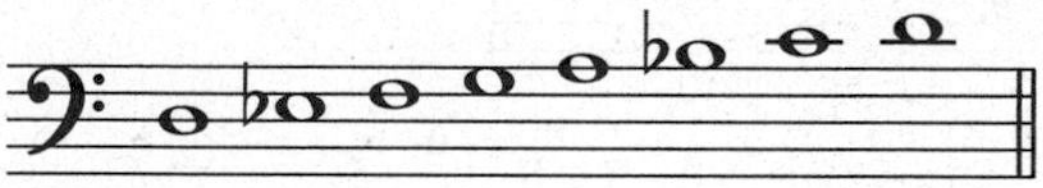

(C)

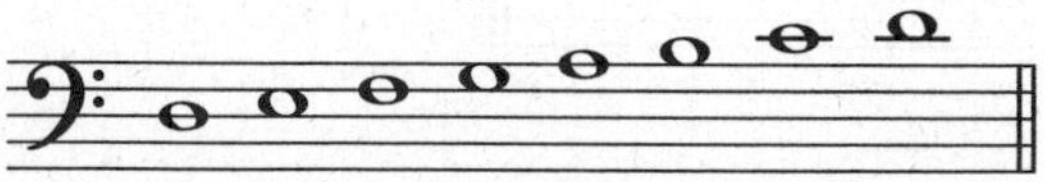

(D)

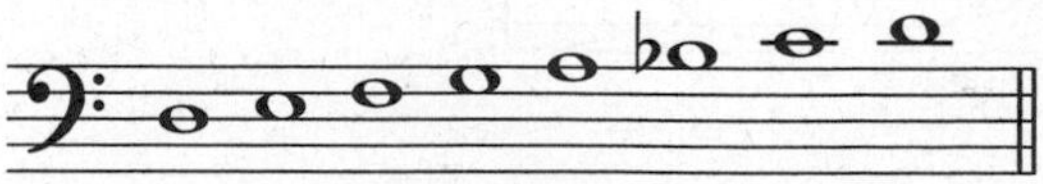

Pitch pattern, played twice.

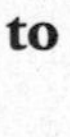

Go on to the next group of questions.

TRACK 2 **Questions 8–9** ask you to identify rhythm as it is performed within a melody. After the question is announced you will have ten seconds to read the question. It is important that you read the choices carefully before the aural example is given. Each example will be played twice with a brief pause between playings. Now listen to the music and answer **Questions 8–9**. Identify the rhythm that correctly matches the example that is played.

8. Which of the following represents the **rhythm** that is sounded?

Rhythm pattern, played twice.

9. Which of the following represents the **rhythm** that is sounded?

(A)

(B)

(C)

(D)

Rhythm pattern, played twice.

Go on to the next group of questions.

Questions 10–12 are based on an excerpt that will be played three times. The score is printed correctly below; however, what you will hear has several errors in either pitch or rhythm. The questions ask you to identify those errors. Before listening to the excerpt for the first time, please read **Questions 10–12** carefully and look at the score.

10. In measure 1, there is an error in the

    (A) pitch in the treble staff
    (B) pitch in the bass staff
    (C) rhythm in the treble staff
    (D) rhythm in the bass staff

11. In measure 2, there is an error in pitch on beat:

    (A) 1 treble clef
    (B) 1 bass clef
    (C) 4 treble clef
    (D) 4 bass clef

12. In measure 3, there is an error in

    (A) rhythm in the treble staff
    (B) rhythm in the bass staff
    (C) pitch in the bass staff
    (D) pitch and rhythm in the treble staff

Now listen to the music for the first time and answer **Questions 10–12.**

The excerpt will now be played a second time.

The excerpt will now be played a third time.

Go on to the next group of questions.

> **Questions 13–20** are based on an excerpt containing two sections of a piano sonata by Mozart. Each section contains two phrases. The first section will be played twice, followed by the complete excerpt played twice. Before listening to Section 1 for the first time, read **Questions 13–18**.

13. The first note of the melody is what scale degree?

    (A) $\hat{1}$
    (B) $\hat{3}$
    (C) $\hat{5}$
    (D) $\hat{7}$

14. The modality of this excerpt is best described as being in

    (A) major
    (B) melodic minor
    (C) Dorian mode
    (D) natural minor

15. The meter of this excerpt is

    (A) simple duple
    (B) simple triple
    (C) compound duple
    (D) compound simple

16. The predominant one-measure rhythmic pattern of this excerpt is

    (A)

    (B)

    (C)

    (D)

17. The first section ends with what scale degree pattern in the melody?

    (A) $\hat{3}\ \hat{2}\ \hat{1}$
    (B) $\hat{1}\ \hat{7}\ \hat{1}$
    (C) $\hat{1}\ \hat{2}\ \hat{1}$
    (D) $\hat{5}\ \hat{7}\ \hat{1}$

18. The first section ends with what scale degree pattern in the bass?

    (A) $\hat{4}\ \hat{5}\ \hat{1}$
    (B) $\hat{5}\ \hat{5}\ \hat{1}$
    (C) $\hat{1}\ \hat{7}\ \hat{1}$
    (D) $\hat{5}\ \hat{1}\ \hat{1}$

The first section will now be played the first time. 𝄞

The first section will now be played a second time. 𝄞

Now read **Questions 19–20** before listening to **both sections** of the excerpt.

19. Compared to the first section, all of the following are true of the second section **except** the

    (A) melody begins on a higher pitch
    (B) bass line plays arpeggios
    (C) melody is played with the left hand while the right hand is the accompaniment
    (D) melody of the first section returns at the end

20. Which of the following statements is true of the second section?

    (A) It is slightly shorter than the first section.
    (B) It is exactly the same length as the first section.
    (C) It is slightly longer than the first section because of an added coda.
    (D) It seems longer than the first section because the meter changes.

The entire excerpt will now be played for the first time. 𝄞

Review all your answers as the entire excerpt is played a final time. 𝄞

This concludes the Aural Multiple-Choice Questions for Chapters 1–3.

ANSWER KEY

1. **D**	6. **A**	11. **D**	16. **A**
2. **B**	7. **A**	12. **D**	17. **A**
3. **C**	8. **A**	13. **B**	18. **B**
4. **B**	9. **B**	14. **A**	19. **C**
5. **D**	10. **B**	15. **C**	20. **C**

ANSWERS EXPLAINED

1. **(D)** The pattern played was two whole steps: Answers (B) and (D) both began with a M2 so the other two could be eliminated after the first hearing. Confirm the correct answer with a second listening.

2. **(B)** The pattern played was the descending D Major scale pattern.

3. **(C)** Answers (A) and (B) began in stepwise motion. Answers (C) and (D) both began with a skip of a third—answer (C), the m3, and (D), the M3. The pattern played began with a **m3** from **C–E♭**. (It is important to note that the clef has changed.)

4. **(B)** Two answers start on C and proceed in a descending pattern to end on E♭, one answer starts on C and descends to E natural, and one answer starts on C and descends to F. Each pattern begins with a different interval. The first interval played was a **m3** and the pattern was from *So* to *Mi* in F Major.

5. **(D)** In the scale pattern questions you want to be able to recognize what type of scales are given as answers and then match what you hear with what you see. If you cannot recognize the complete scale pattern, then look for something you *do* recognize and *can* identify, such as the beginning intervals or the ending interval. In this example all four answers began with the same first four notes—that of the F minor scale. Therefore, the upper four notes determine what form of minor, or in this case, one modal scale pattern. Answer (A) is F Dorian, (B) is F natural minor (Aeolian), (C) is F harmonic minor, and (D) is F melodic minor. What was played was melodic minor with the raised 6th and 7th scale degrees. Because no key signature is given, no accidentals are needed to raise the 6th and 7th scale degrees.

6. **(A)** In this example, you must recognize the change of clef. Notice both Questions 5 and 6 begin on the first space of the staff so it is easy to overlook the change of clef because these questions look so similar. What was played was the A Major scale.

7. **(A)** The modal scales are more often a visual question, but here is an opportunity to practice interval pattern identification. Identifying the intervals between just the first three pitches in each answer would have been enough to determine the correct answer. Listening holistically, answer (A) is the D Mixolydian scale (Major + ♭7) and was the answer played. (B) is Phrygian (minor + ♭2). (C) is

Dorian (minor + raised 6th scale degree), and (D) is Aeolian, the natural form of the D minor scale.

8. **(A)** Once again, look for same and different when you are reading the answers and remember that *pitch does not matter*—just rhythm.

9. **(B)** Notice that both (A) and (D) have the same rhythm in the first measure and (C) and (D) have the same rhythm in the last measure, but (B) was the rhythm that was played—the only answer beginning with the dotted-eighth and sixteenth notes.

Questions 10–12 are error-detection questions based on the excerpt that was **played**, shown below. This is different than what you looked at as the excerpt was played.

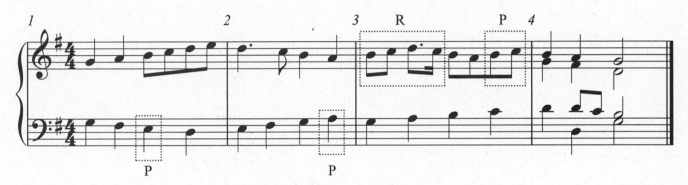

10. **(B)** The error is the E on beat 3. What is printed is ***Do–Ti–Do–↓So***, but what is played is a descending scalewise pattern: ***Do–Ti–La–So***.

11. **(D)** The error in measure 2 is in the pitch in the bass clef on beat 4. What is written is ***La–Ti–Do–↓So***, but what is played is ***La–Ti–Do–Re***.

12. **(D)** In measure 3 there are two errors—both in treble clef. The dotted-eighth and sixteenth notes should be on beat 1 and the melody on beat 3 and 4 is ***Mi–Re–Do–Re*** instead of what was played—***Mi–Re–Mi–Fa***.

13. **(B)** The first note of the melody is $\hat{3}$ or ***Mi***.

14. **(A)** The modality of this excerpt is major.

15. **(C)** The meter is compound duple—the time signature is $\substack{6 \\ 8}$. Notice there is a clue to the meter in the next question. The choices are all compound duple! (It pays to read them all.)

16. **(A)** The rhythm heard most often throughout the first section begins with the dotted eighth and sixteenth notes (answer (A) or (D)). The correct answer is (A).

17. **(A)** The first section is eight measures long and ends with the most common phrase ending for a melody: ***Mi–Re–Do*** ($\hat{3}$–$\hat{2}$–$\hat{1}$).

18. **(B)** The first section also ends with the most common phrase ending for the bass line: *So–So–Do* ($\hat{5}$–$\hat{5}$–$\hat{1}$). This information will be reinforced in Chapter 4, "Aural Skills."

19. **(C)** In the second section the melody begins on *So*, scale degree 5, the bass line plays arpeggios, and the melody does return at the end of the second section. The melody continues in the right hand and does *not* shift to the bass clef.

20. **(C)** The second section is slightly longer than the first section (ten measures). After the melody returns, a two-measure ending (coda) is added for a more final conclusion.

Aural Skills Part I: Fundamentals and Singing

4

- Aural Skills
- Solfege
- Solfege Syllables
- Movable-*Do*

- Sight-Singing
- Melodic Dictation
- Harmonic Dictation
- Melodic Patterns

Music is a process of communication. In language we hear words. We reproduce the words we hear. We read and write words of others. We use words to write our own original thoughts and ideas.

"Aural skills" refers to the process of identifying, producing, and notating the elements of music that we *hear*. Aural skills are a very important part of this course and therefore of the exam. Preparing yourself for the aural skills portion of the AP music theory exam is an ongoing process from day one. It begins with overcoming the fear of hearing your own voice! For those of you who are vocalists, you have an edge here—make sure you use it. For those of you who are instrumentalists, it's time to strip away anxiety and let loose! The sight-singing portion of the exam is frightening to many students, mainly because they have not prepared well enough by not singing enough. Many are anxious because as musicians we are performers, and this aspect of the exam requires us to perform (for some, with an unfamiliar instrument—our voice). In this chapter we look at all the aspects of aural skills and help you find your inner AP Music Theory voice.

> In the AP music theory classroom, our language is music. We sing or perform. We read the music of others and notate what we hear. We use the language of music to write our own original compositions.

AURAL SKILLS COMPONENTS OF THE AP MUSIC THEORY EXAM

Let's begin by understanding *exactly* what is going to be on the **aural portion of the exam** and what skills are required to successfully accomplish each section.

1. There Will Be Notating on One Staff!

The free-response section includes two melodies that will be performed either by instrument or by voice, and students are expected to write down both the pitch and rhythm accurately. This is called **melodic dictation**.

- As with the sight-singing portion, the melodic dictation will have one melody in treble clef and one melody in bass clef.
- One melody will be in simple meter and one will be in compound meter.
- One melody will be in a major key and one will be in a minor key.
- The melody will be played three times for the first example and four times for the second example with time in between to notate.

What Skills Are Required for Successful Melodic Dictation?

- Recognizing the key center or tonality
- Recognizing the meter and understanding the rhythms
- Understanding the relationship of the pitches to the tonal center
- Recognizing familiar melodic and rhythmic patterns and their placement in the measure
- Being able to correctly draw note heads, stems, dots, beams, and flags that correspond to rhythm and pitches, including accidentals, on the staff corresponding to placement in the tonality
- One of the keys to successful melodic dictation is being able to reproduce the melody you hear in your head (audiation). Listen to the melody as if you were to be asked to sing it back. It is oversimplification to state, "If you can hear it, you can notate it," but you definitely will have difficulty notating the phrase successfully if *you can't retain the melody.*

2. There Will Be Notating on the Grand Staff!

Going one step deeper into hearing, identifying, and notating is the skill of **harmonic dictation**. This process requires you to listen to a four-part harmonization of six to eight chords. The first chord is given to you. The student must then write down the melody (soprano) and the bass line *and* give the Roman numeral chord symbol and inversion (if needed) for each chord. There will be two harmonic dictations.

- Both will be approximately the same length, both will be played on a piano, but one will be more challenging than the other.
- One will be in a major key and one will be in a minor key.
- The more challenging harmonic dictation usually (but not always) includes chromatic (secondary) harmony.

What Skills Are Required for Successful Harmonic Dictation?

- Understanding the relationship of chords to the tonal center
- Discriminating between chord qualities and recognizing inversions
- Recognizing familiar melodic patterns (*linear* movement) in the melody and bass and their placement within the example
- Recognizing and notating cadences
- Understanding the "norms" of the common-practice style

3. There Will Be Identification, Error Detection, and Score Analysis!

The multiple-choice portion of the exam has two parts. Part A uses recorded music that requires the student to:

- Identify from four possible choices such things as scales, modes, interval quality, chord quality, and rhythm. These questions are usually played on piano.
- Listen to a two-, three-, or four-part harmonization played by piano and recognize mistakes in the score in pitch and rhythm. This is called error detection.
- Listen to short excerpts from various genres (ranging from chamber music, to full orchestra, jazz band, or solo voice) and answer multiple-choice questions based on the aural presentation.

What Skills Are Required for Successful Score Analysis?

- Recognizing the key
- Recognizing the meter and understanding the rhythms
- Understanding the relationship of the pitches to the tonal center
- Recognizing cadences and non-chord tones
- Recognizing and undestanding form and texture
- Recognizing and understanding performance considerations including timbre, dynamic, articulation, tempo, and style
- Recognizing harmonic progression and relationship of key centers
- Understanding the "norms" of the common-practice style

4. There Will Be Singing!

The final portion of the exam is **two sight-singing examples** that must be sung and recorded. These recordings are evaluated by exam graders called "readers" who meet every summer in June with the sole purpose of grading the free-response section of the AP Music Theory exam.

- **One melody will be in treble clef and one will be in bass clef.** Most students are linear readers—meaning they have spent the last five to six years reading only one clef. You must become fluent with reading and writing both treble and bass clef and *practice* singing daily in both clefs.
- **One melody will be in simple meter and one will be in compound meter.** Once again, students who have not read much music in $\frac{6}{8}$ time may become anxious at this prospect.
- **One melody will be in a major key and one melody will be in a minor key.** The melody in minor will usually reflect what music does in minor—it will have scalar variance. You may sing a leading tone in one measure, followed by the use of a subtonic in the next measure, and end with a melodic minor passage. That's what real music does.
- **Melody 2 is usually more complex than melody 1.**
- **You will have 75 seconds to prepare and practice, and 30 seconds to record your performance.**

What Skills Are Required for Successful Sight-Singing?

- Recognizing the key
- Recognizing the meter and understanding the rhythms
- Understanding the relationship of the pitches to the tonal center
- Being able to reproduce the melody while maintaining the tonal center

---

TIP

To be successful in the aural skills portion of the AP exam one must connect what the ears **hear** and the eyes **see** with what the brain **knows** is common and the "norm" for this period of music. It is not enough to be able to recognize a melodic minor scale when you see it—you must also be able to reproduce the sound by singing what you see. And the reverse skill would be to recognize that what you are hearing is a melodic minor scale and then be able to notate what you hear.

SINGING

In this chapter we focus on singing, so let's begin by discussing systems used for sight-singing. You may sing using numbers, or simply a neutral syllable like "lah" or "dah"; however, the use of singing with a system of solfege syllables is the most common choice. Sight-singing is a method of training your brain to understand the *relationship* between notes within a specific scale or tonality. The solfege syllables are a tool to make recognizing those relationships automatic. You are learning to sing (and hear) each note according to its role in the key. You will hear (and sing) notes in relationship to the preceding note or in relation to the tonic.

One commonly used method of solfeggio is called **movable-*Do***. Movable-*Do* means that regardless of what key you are in, the tonic (first note of the scale) is always "*Do*."

Whether singing the G Major scale or the C Major scale using the movable-*Do* system, the solfege remains the same even though the pitches are different. This reinforces the fact that the major scale pattern of whole and half steps remains the same and sounds the same.

Movable-*Do*

$\hat{1}$	$\hat{2}$	$\hat{3}$	$\hat{4}$	$\hat{5}$	$\hat{6}$	$\hat{7}$	$\hat{8}$
G	A	B	C	D	E	F♯	G
Do	*Re*	*Mi*	*Fa*	*So*	*La*	*Ti*	*Do*
C	D	E	F	G	A	B	C

> With movable-*Do*, the solfege, like the numbers, are the same from scale to scale.

This is in contrast to a solfeggio system called **fixed-*Do***. The fixed-*Do* system attaches solfege syllables that remain with the pitch regardless of key; C is always *Do*, D is always *Re*, and so forth. In fixed-*Do*, G is always *So*; therefore, the G Major scale would start on *So*.

Fixed-*Do*

$\hat{1}$	$\hat{2}$	$\hat{3}$	$\hat{4}$	$\hat{5}$	$\hat{6}$	$\hat{7}$	$\hat{8}$
G	A	B	C	D	E	F♯	G
So	*La*	*Ti*	*Do*	*Re*	*Mi*	*Fa*	*So*

> For most who use the fixed-*Do* system, chromaticism does not affect the syllable. All "Fs" are sung ***Fa.***

There are also two prevalent systems for singing in a minor mode. ***Do-*** based minor is the movable-*Do* system in minor. The tonic (first pitch of the scale) is ***Do*** just like in Major, but because the C minor scale differs from the C Major scale, the solfege syllables are also different. (See more on page 85.)

Another system of singing in minor is called ***La-***based minor. This system reflects the fact that the relative minor of any major scale uses the same pitches starting on the sixth scale degree or ***La.*** The system is very prevalent in choral music to facilitate moving from a major key to the relative minor.

Major	C	D	E	F	G	A	B	C
	Do	*Re*	*Mi*	*Fa*	*So*	*La*	*Ti*	*Do*
Parallel minor	C	D	E♭	F	G	A♭	B♭	C
Do-based	*Do*	*Re*	*Me*	*Fa*	*So*	*Le*	*Te*	*Do*

Major	C	D	E	F	G	A	B	C
	Do	*Re*	*Mi*	*Fa*	*So*	*La*	*Ti*	*Do*
Relative minor	A	B	C	D	E	F	G	A
La-based	*La*	*Ti*	*Do*	*Re*	*Mi*	*Fa*	*So*	*La*

Any solfeggio method, movable-*Do*, fixed-*Do*, ***La-***based, or ***Do-***based minor, has its strengths. In this guide we will use the movable-*Do* system for both major and minor, where ***Do*** always represents tonic ($\hat{1}$), ***So*** always represents dominant ($\hat{5}$), and ***Ti*** is always the leading tone ($\hat{7}$). If you are using another system of sight-singing, you are encouraged to continue to do so. The use of scale degree numbers and names will help to reconcile these systems with each other. In this guide, solfege syllables will be bold and italicized.

Chapter 3 presented information on major and minor scales and the organization of pitches into keys. Now we are ready to sing those scales and couple this information with the skill of notating.

Singing Warm-Ups in Major

 "Hear–Sing–Notate" will be our motto! Listen to scales and scale patterns. Play them on any instrument. Sing them. Notate scales in every key. **Hear–Sing–Notate!**

Starting with the pattern of whole and half steps that generate the major scale (**W W H W W W H**) we attach solfege syllables to each note representing the degrees of the scale. Let's review:

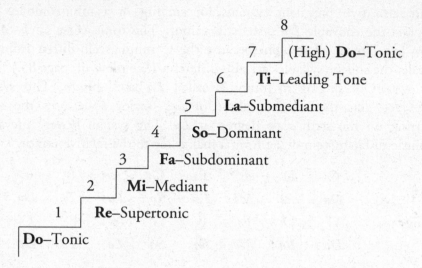

8
7   (High) **Do**–Tonic
6   **Ti**–Leading Tone
5   **La**–Submediant
4   **So**–Dominant
3   **Fa**–Subdominant
2   **Mi**–Mediant
1   **Re**–Supertonic
Do–Tonic

Here are the basic scale patterns, shown here in F Major, that are important for you to be able to recognize—when you **hear** it, when you **sing** it, and when you **notate**:

1. F Major **scale:**   F Major **tonic arpeggio:**

FM: Do Re Mi Fa So La Ti Do   FM: Do Mi So Do So Mi Do ↓So Do

2. Diatonic **ascending intervals:**

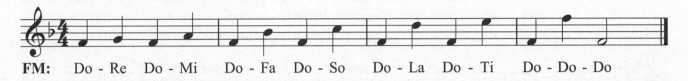

FM: Do - Re   Do - Mi   Do - Fa   Do - So   Do - La   Do - Ti   Do - Do - Do

3. Diatonic **descending intervals:**

FM: Do - Ti   Do - La   Do - So   Do - Fa   Do - Mi   Do - Re   Do - Do - Do

4. Scale in thirds:

FM: Do Mi Re Fa Mi So Fa La So Ti La Do Ti Re Do

5. Arpeggiated chords:

Practice jumping octaves when the range becomes difficult.

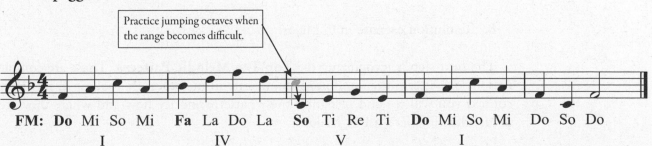

FM: **Do** Mi So Mi **Fa** La Do La **So** Ti Re Ti **Do** Mi So Mi Do So Do

     I   IV   V   I

6. Adding the **V⁷**:

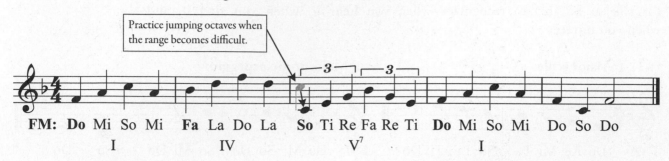

Practice jumping octaves when the range becomes difficult.

FM: **Do** Mi So Mi **Fa** La Do La **So** Ti Re Fa Re Ti **Do** Mi So Mi Do So Do
   I   IV   V⁷   I

7. This exercise is called the **scale degree finder**. It is helpful to quickly go through the scale and "find" the pitch you need. It also contains the tonic triad and common diatonic intervals. Each measure starts with **Do**, this time in D Major. It's a great warm-up exercise before sight-singing.

DM: **Do-Re** Do-Re **Mi** Do-Mi So-Mi Do-Mi-So **Fa** Do-**So** Do-So **La** Do-Do **Ti** **Do-Do**

Here's another great warm-up exercise using the tonic triad and the individual **resolutions of the tendency tones**: *Fa* resolves down to *Mi*; *La/Le* resolves down to *So* (more important in minor when there is a half step between 6 and 5); *Ti* resolves upward to *Do*; *Re* resolves to *Do*; and particularly in the bass—*So* resolves to *Do*.

Skips within a melody are often one of these fragments moving to another one of these fragments connected by stepwise motion. Sing as one continuous line.

Do Mi So Mi Do Fa - Mi La - So Ti - Do Re - Do So Do

8. Resolution exercise in C Major:

The next step is recognizing the **Top Ten Melodic Patterns**. These are combinations or patterns that are found abundantly in melodies. By looking at music in context you will see and recognize these patterns; notice how and where they are used. This time let's use G Major.

The Top Ten Melodic Patterns in G Major

The most common **ending** of melodies

The 2nd most often used melodic ending

Variation of *Re-Ti-Do*

The most often used anacrusis (pick-up note)

1. Mi Re Do   **2.** Re Ti Do   Ti Re Do   **3.** ↓So Do

All or part of the steps of a scale, going up or down

Tonic triad **ascending** or **descending**

4. Do Re Mi Fa So   So Fa Mi Re Do   **5.** Do Mi So   So Mi Do

All or part of a scale in thirds

Low *So* ascending up to Tonic (also a common ending)

Fi (#4) is the most often used **altered** note and resolves to *So*

6. Do Mi Re Fa   **7.** ↓So La Ti Do   **8.** So Fi So   Fa Fi So

The most common **Bass** line ending

Split octave *So-So-Do* is also a very common ending

The second most often used **Bass** ending

9. So down to Do   So So Do   So So Do   **10.** Fa So Do

Review in Major

Here is a simple hymn tune in G Major. It is in simple triple meter with a one beat anacrusis on *So*. Look for the Top Ten Melodic Patterns—they will occur in all four parts, not just the melody. Solfege all four parts and sing!

Azmon

Carl G. Glaser
(1784–1829)

What stands out?
- Melodic ending is *Do-Re-Do*.
- Bass ends in *Fa-So-Do*.
- Anacrusis is *So-Do*.
- Whenever there is a skip larger than a third it is usually *from Do* or *So* or *to Do* or *So*.
- In the melody, there is mostly stepwise motion or skipping up or down by thirds.

Minor Scale Review

Before singing in minor, let's review the forms of the minor scale. There are three forms of minor: natural, harmonic, and melodic. All three forms begin with the *same* first five notes called the minor pentachord, but scale degrees 6 and 7 are different, depending on the form of minor. The minor pentachord differs from the major pentachord by one pitch—the third scale degree is lowered one half step.

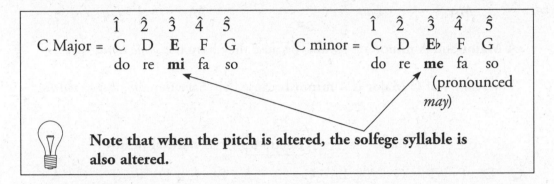

C Major = C D **E** F G
　　　　 do re **mi** fa so

C minor = C D **E♭** F G
　　　　 do re **me** fa so
　　　　　　　　 (pronounced *may*)

　　　Note that when the pitch is altered, the solfege syllable is also altered.

Major and minor keys with different key signatures but with the same tonic are called **parallel.**

When comparing natural minor to its parallel major, the 3rd, 6th, and 7th scale degrees are lowered, so the solfege syllables on $\hat{3}$, $\hat{6}$, and $\hat{7}$ are altered as well. Using the movable-*Do* solfege system for sight-singing in minor reinforces the concept of *Do* as the center of the tonality (tonic).

In the *natural* or *pure* form of the minor scale there are no alterations from the key signature.

C Major = C D E F G A B C
　　　　 Do Re Mi Fa So La Ti Do

C natural minor = C D **E♭** F G **A♭ B♭** C
　　　　　　　 Do Re **Me** Fa So **Le Te** Do

The 7th scale degree in natural minor is called the subtonic, meaning a whole step below tonic.

Another prominent element is that four of the scale degrees are exactly the same when comparing major and parallel minor—*Do*, *Re*, *Fa*, and *So*. This once again helps to establish consistency when singing. Whether in major or minor, *Do* to *So* **sounds the same.** It should—it's the same interval.

Here is one more comparison:

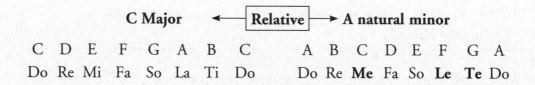

	A Major	←	Parallel	→	**A natural minor**

$\hat{1}$	$\hat{2}$	$\hat{3}$	$\hat{4}$	$\hat{5}$	$\hat{6}$	$\hat{7}$	$\hat{8}$		$\hat{1}$	$\hat{2}$	$\hat{3}$	$\hat{4}$	$\hat{5}$	$\hat{6}$	$\hat{7}$	$\hat{8}$
A	B	**C♯**	D	E	**F♯**	**G♯**	A		A	B	C	D	E	**F**	**G**	A
Do	Re	**Mi**	Fa	So	**La**	**Ti**	Do		Do	Re	**Me**	Fa	So	**Le**	**Te**	Do

Pronounced: *Mee*   *Lah Tee*   *May*   *Lay Tay*

A Major and **A minor** are *parallel* because they have the *same tonic*.

The *relative* of **C Major** is **A minor** because they have the *same key signature*.

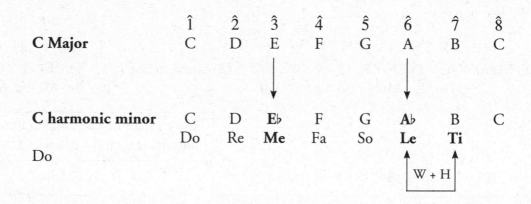

	C Major	←	Relative	→	**A natural minor**

C	D	E	F	G	A	B	C		A	B	C	D	E	F	G	A
Do	Re	Mi	Fa	So	La	Ti	Do		Do	Re	**Me**	Fa	So	**Le**	**Te**	Do

In the **harmonic form** of minor the 7th scale degree is raised both ascending and descending, but leaves the other notes the same as natural minor. This creates a half step below the tonic so that the 7th scale degree once again *leads to tonic*.

	$\hat{1}$	$\hat{2}$	$\hat{3}$	$\hat{4}$	$\hat{5}$	$\hat{6}$	$\hat{7}$	$\hat{8}$
C Major	C	D	E	F	G	A	B	C
			↓			↓		
C harmonic minor	C	D	E♭	F	G	A♭	B	C
	Do	Re	**Me**	Fa	So	**Le**	**Ti**	Do
Do						↑	↑	
						W + H		

> ***Do*** is always tonic.
> ***Re*** is always supertonic.
> ***Fa*** is always subdominant.
> ***So*** is always dominant.
> ***Ti*** is always leading tone.

The minor scale, with *both* **the 6th and the 7th scale degree raised**, is the **melodic form of minor**. The upper tetrachord (last four notes) is the same as major. Because the 6th and 7th scale degrees are raised in order to go more smoothly and convincingly *up* to the tonic, these scale degrees will only be raised when the melody (scale) is ascending. The descending form of the melodic minor scale reverts back to the natural form.

	Ascending								Descending						
C Major	C	D	E	F	G	A	B	C	B	A	G	F	E	D	C
C melodic minor	C	D	E♭	F	G	A	B	C	B♭	A♭	G	F	E♭	D	C
	Do	Re	**Me**	Fa	**So**	**La**	**Ti**	**Do**	Te	Le	So	Fa	**Me**	Re	Do

The upper tetrachord (last four notes) is the same in melodic minor as the parallel major. Therefore, **IF** you see the melodic form of minor, **THEN** your last four notes are sung like major.

Singing Warm-Ups in Minor

Now let's go back and put those sight-singing exercises into the parallel minor.

1. F **natural** minor scale and F minor tonic arpeggio:

2. Diatonic ascending intervals, **harmonic minor**:

FM: Do - Re Do - **Me** Do - Fa Do - So Do - **Le** Do - **Ti** Do - Do - Do

3. Diatonic descending intervals: **natural minor**:

fm: Do - **Te** Do - **Le** Do - So Do - Fa Do - **Me** Do - Re Do - Do - Do

4. Scale in thirds, **melodic minor**. (This is slightly different because raising $\hat{6}$ and $\hat{7}$ leads to *Do*, and the natural minor form is used for the descending line.)

> The descending scale goes back to natural minor.

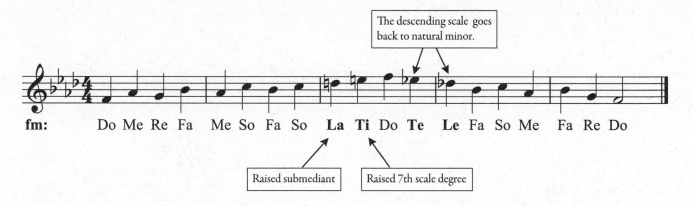

fm: Do Me Re Fa Me So Fa So **La Ti** Do **Te Le** Fa So Me Fa Re Do

> Raised submediant

> Raised 7th scale degree

5. Arpeggiated chords, **harmonic minor**:

> Practice jumping octaves when the range becomes difficult.

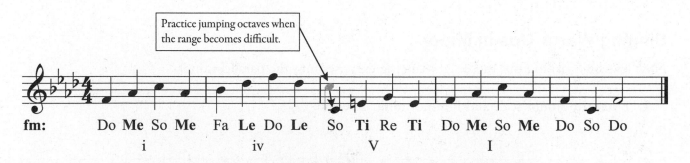

fm: Do **Me** So **Me** Fa **Le** Do **Le** So **Ti** Re **Ti** Do **Me** So **Me** Do So Do

    i   iv   V   I

> Note that the dominant triad and dominant 7th chord (in this case arpeggio) are the same in F Major *and* in F harmonic minor.

6. Adding the **V⁷** chord:

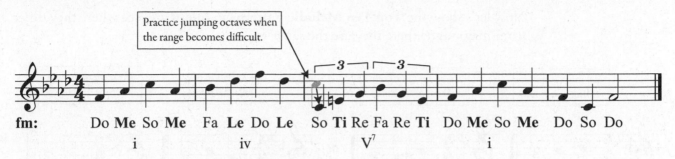

Practice jumping octaves when the range becomes difficult.

fm: Do **Me** So **Me**   Fa **Le** Do **Le**   So **Ti** Re Fa Re **Ti**   Do **Me** So **Me**   Do So Do

       i   iv   V⁷   i

7. Scale degree finder in **D harmonic minor**:

dm: Do-**Re** Do-Re **Me** Do-Me So-Me Do-Me-So **Fa** Do-**So** Do-So **Le** Do-Do **Ti** **Do-Do**

Scale degree 3 (*Me*) and scale degree 6 (*Le*) are what differ from major. The leading tone is the same in both.

8. Resolution exercise in **C harmonic minor**:

cm: Do   Me   So   Me   Do   Fa - Me   Le - So   Ti - Do   Re - Do   So   Do

The Top Ten Patterns in G Minor

Now let's show the **Top Ten Melodic Patterns** in minor and see where they differ from major and where they are the same.

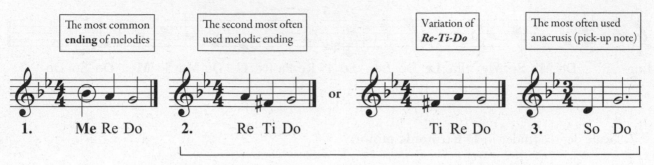

The most common **ending** of melodies

The second most often used melodic ending

Variation of *Re-Ti-Do*

The most often used anacrusis (pick-up note)

1. **Me** Re Do
2. Re Ti Do or Ti Re Do
3. So Do

SAME IN MAJOR AND MINOR

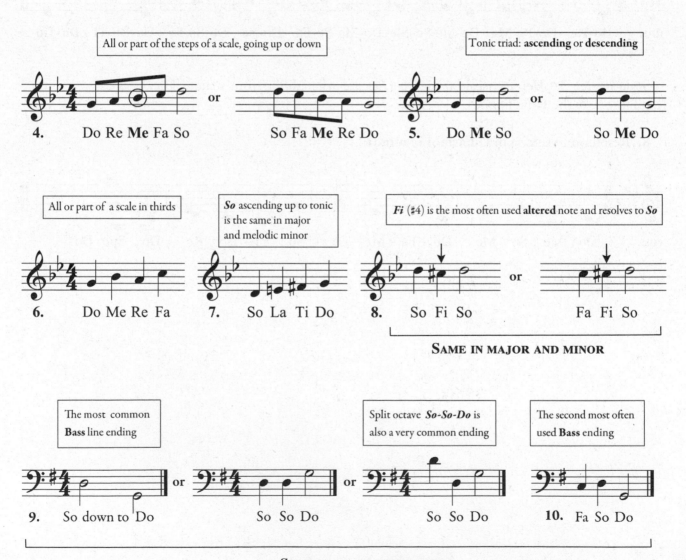

All or part of the steps of a scale, going up or down

Tonic triad: **ascending** or **descending**

4. Do Re **Me** Fa So or So Fa **Me** Re Do
5. Do **Me** So or So **Me** Do

All or part of a scale in thirds

So ascending up to tonic is the same in major and melodic minor

Fi (♯4) is the most often used **altered** note and resolves to *So*

6. Do Me Re Fa
7. So La Ti Do
8. So Fi So or Fa Fi So

SAME IN MAJOR AND MINOR

The most common **Bass** line ending

Split octave *So-So-Do* is also a very common ending

The second most often used **Bass** ending

9. So down to Do or So So Do or So So Do
10. Fa So Do

SAME IN MAJOR AND MINOR

The Chromatic Scale in Solfege

Now that we have practiced in the major and minor form of the scale, let's review the whole menu of solfege choices—**the chromatic scale!**

doh	DO	C		C	DO	doh
tee	TI	B		B	TI	tee
lee	LI	A♯		B♭	TE	tay
lah	LA	A		A	LA	lah
see	SI	G♯		A♭	LE	lay
so	SO	G		G	SO	so
fee	FI	F♯		G♭	SE	say
fah	FA	F		F	FA	fah
mee	MI	E		E	MI	mee
ree	RI	D♯		E♭	ME	may
ray	RE	D		D	RE	ray
dee	DI	C♯		D♭	RA	rah
doh	DO	C		C	DO	doh

Notice that in this example of the C chromatic scale, when the pitches are the same (such as the pitch D or *Re*) the solfege is the same whether ascending or descending. The differences occur in the solfege just like in notation, because of enharmonic spellings. Although C♯ and D♭ are the same pitch, C♯ must be a variation of *Do* (*Di*) and D♭ is a variation of *Re* (*Ra*). The note that is a half step higher than *Fa* is *Fi*; the note that is a half step lower than *So* is *Se*.

Ten Sight-Singing Tips

Now—practice singing! Here are a few suggestions to help develop your skill for sight-singing.

1. Check the clef.
2. Check the key signature. Is the melody major or minor?
3. Check out the time signature.
4. Consider the range and determine where to set *Do*. If the given pitch is uncomfortable, you may move *Do* to any pitch.

5. Always know where the tonic pitch (***Do***) is and be able to return to it even if you get lost.
6. Sing a warm-up exercise such as the scale degree finder or the resolution exercise.
7. Look for familiar melodic patterns.
8. Use a pencil to circle all the tonics or write the solfege (use just one letter per syllable) for a section or chunk that is not stepwise or easily recognizable.
9. Sing up the scale to find pitches you are unsure of or for difficult intervals, or use the scale degree finder.
10. Practice the melody out loud—use all seventy-five sections of practice time to sing.

Evaluating Your Sight-Singing

This guide does not include recorded examples of what these melodies "should" sound like. The practice melodies will be most effective if you employ the sight-singing *process* by

- limiting your time while looking and practice singing each melody,
- then performing each melody straight through without stopping.

Once you have gone through the process of sight-singing each of these melodies, you will need to play them on the piano or an instrument of your choice to at least hear the correct pitches. You sight-sing *once*—after that it's called practice. After you have "performed," go over your mistakes and figure out what is correct. Observe the patterns and look carefully at the rhythms. It would be very helpful to record yourself singing the examples and perhaps go over them with your teacher, especially for the sight-singing in the Practice Exams. Circle the places on the page where you made mistakes. Don't forget to include holding out the last note full value.

Melodies to Practice Singing

1A.

1B. Here is the same melody in the **parallel harmonic minor**. *Do* is the same (F). In this example, the only difference between the two melodies is A♭ (*Me*).

2A. Exercise #2A is in the key of E♭ Major putting *Do* on the first line.

2B. This is the same melody in the **relative minor** key (C is *Do*) *and* in the **bass clef**.

3A. Here is a melody in compound meter.

3B. If we sing the same melody in **F melodic minor** (the parallel minor) we hear (and see) the similarity between it and major when ascending from **So** up to **Do**. Because of the raised 6th and 7th it is exactly the same.

HINT: Any of these melodies that are in major can be sung in the parallel minor. Any melodies that are in minor try singing in the parallel major. For extra practice, rewrite them in the relative minor or relative major.

4.

5. This melody is in E harmonic minor. E is **Do** and the raised 7th scale degree (**Ti**) is D♯.

 Count carefully and take your time. Accuracy is more important than speed.

6.

HARMONIC MINOR SCALE PATTERN

 Remember to hold notes full value, especially the *last note*.

7.

Practice as often in bass clef as you do in treble clef. This example is a **bass line** that might accompany a melody.

8.

9.

Look for familiar patterns: Do   Ti La   So   Fa Mi Re   Do

 Instead of writing in all the solfege, consider circling *only the tonic* notes.

10.

HINT: Look for familiar melodic patterns in the music.

11.

12.

13.

14. Note the similarities and differences when the same melody is written in the
parallel minor key.

MELODIC MINOR

Remember to take a full, relaxed breath. No tension.

15.

16.

17. This exercise contains four accidentals—the **maximum** number of accidentals that will be used in sight-singing on the AP exam.

18. Here is a melody that does not start on *Do*; however, in recent years, all sight-singing melodies have started and ended on *Do*.

19. This is the same melody in the parallel harmonic minor. Sing the lowered 3rd and 6th scale degree—the leading tone is raised and therefore is the same pitch as in major.

Sing with confidence!

20.

21.

Look at the rhythm very closely and count accurately.

22.

23. Notice that the melody returns to low ***Do*** for the bottom pitch and descends scalewise for the top pitches.

24.

End the phrase after the A♭, and take a breath.

 Maintain a steady tempo throughout. Don't rush!

25.

➡ There is more information, discussion of scoring procedures, and additional melodies for practice in Chapter 22, "Strategies for Sight-Singing."

Let's sing!

Harmonic Organization I: Intervals, Triads, and Seventh Chords

5

- Counterpoint
- Harmony
- Intervals
    - Compound Interval
    - Consonant Interval
    - Diatonic Interval
    - Dissonant Interval
    - Enharmonic Interval
    - Half Step
    - Harmonic Interval
    - Inversions of Intervals
    - Interval Quality
        - Perfect (P)
        - Major (M)
        - Minor (m)
        - Augmented (A or +)
        - Diminished (dim or °)
        - Doubly Augmented
        - Doubly Diminished
    - Melodic Interval
    - Numerical or Interval Quantity
    - Simple Interval
    - Tritone
    - Whole Step
- Triads
    - Augmented (A or +)
    - Diminished (dim or °)
    - Major (M)
    - Minor (m)
    - Inversions of Triads
        - Root Position
        - First Inversion (1st Inversion)
        - Second Inversion (2nd Inversion)
- Seventh Chords
    - Major Major (MM)
    - Major-Minor Seventh (Mm, Dominant 7th Chord)
    - Minor Seventh (mm)
    - Diminished minor (Half-Diminished Seventh, ⌀7)
    - Diminished Diminished (Fully-Diminished Seventh, °7)
    - Inversions of Seventh Chords
        - Root Position
        - First Inversion (1st Inversion)
        - Second Inversion (2nd Inversion)
        - Third Inversion (3rd Inversion)
- Unison

Harmony refers to the way notes are simultaneously sounded creating a *vertical* element to music. A single melody line or linear voice added to another line or voice is called **counterpoint**. This combination of voices, each significant by itself, creates this "note against note." It is unique to music to be able to comprehend two things being "said" at the same time. While a composer may weave together two or three (or more) melodies (linear), he also recognizes what combining those melodies creates harmonically (vertical). In the next three chapters we learn how chords are constructed and how they follow each other (progression) through a musical composition. As a melody progresses, it gives clues for harmonizing in a multitude of convincing ways. We'll begin by putting notes together—two at a time.

INTERVALS

> The ability to identify intervals aurally and visually is a critical building block of AP Music Theory. It is based on recognition of scales and key signatures. Interval knowledge leads to chords and chord knowledge leads to the understanding of harmonic function. Intervals will aid you in voice leading, composition, and transposition as well as sight-singing and dictation.

An **interval** is the distance between two pitches. Intervals are **melodic**—sounding one after another as in a melody, or **harmonic**—two pitches sounding at the *same* time. **We describe exact interval size by quantity (size) and quality**. Quantity is expressed by a number and is determined by simply counting the distance between one letter name and the next letter name. Remember to always count the bottom note as "1."

From a line to a line (or space to space) is always an odd number and from a line to space is always an even number.

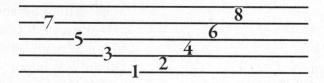

Identifying Interval Quality

<table>
<tr><td>**TIP**

In this guide all **perfect** intervals will be labeled using the uppercase **P** and **major** intervals will be labeled using uppercase **M**.</td></tr>
</table>

All intervals built from the tonic up to notes within a major scale are either **major** or **perfect**. The perfect intervals are unison (sometimes called prime) (P1), perfect fourth (P4), perfect fifth (P5), and perfect eighth or octave (P8); therefore, the major intervals are major second (M2), major third (M3), major sixth (M6), and major seventh (M7). Unisons, fourths, fifths, and octaves can never be major or minor, and seconds, thirds, sixths, and sevenths are never perfect.

Intervals in a major scale, in this case F Major:

PERFECT UNISON	MAJOR 2ND	MAJOR 3RD	PERFECT 4TH	PERFECT 5TH	MAJOR 6TH	MAJOR 7TH	PERFECT OCTAVE
P1	M2	M3	P4	P5	M6	M7	P8

Intervals built from the tonic to notes within the natural minor scale include major, minor, and perfect. **A minor interval is one half step smaller than major.**

Intervals in the F natural minor scale:

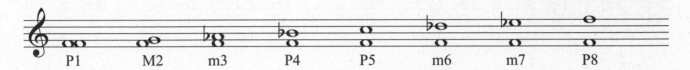

So now let's look at the intervals side by side and compare:

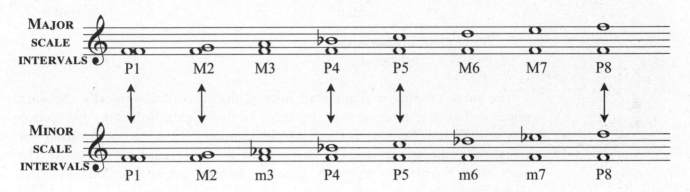

Notice that the **perfect** intervals are the same in major or minor. The intervals that are different are the third, sixth, and seventh. As discussed in Chapter 3, scale degrees 3, 6, and 7 give major or minor their characteristic sound. **The intervals from 1̂–3̂, 1̂–6̂, and 1̂–7̂ are major in a major tonality and minor in a minor tonality.**

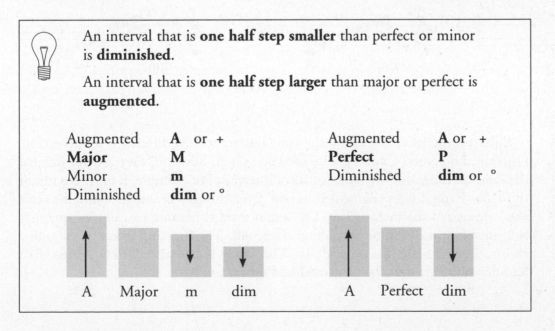

An interval that is **one half step smaller** than perfect or minor is **diminished**.

An interval that is **one half step larger** than major or perfect is **augmented**.

Augmented	**A** or +
Major	**M**
Minor	**m**
Diminished	**dim** or °

Augmented	**A** or +
Perfect	**P**
Diminished	**dim** or °

A   Major   m   dim

A   Perfect   dim

Here are some major and perfect intervals transformed into diminished and augmented intervals. Notice what happens when the accidental is on the bottom note.

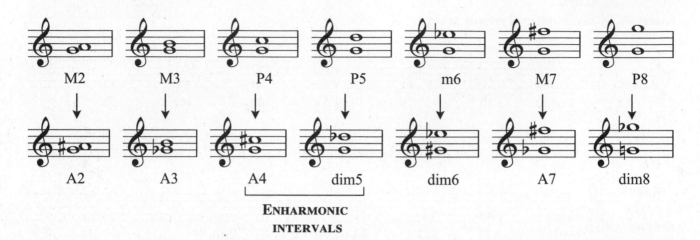

ENHARMONIC
INTERVALS

The most prominent diminished interval that occurs **diatonically** (between notes within the same key or tonality) is the diminished fifth that occurs between *Ti* and *Fa* in major and harmonic minor. This interval **inverted** (by transferring the upper note an octave lower) is the augmented fourth. The augmented fourth is commonly called a **tritone** because it contains three whole steps.

Ti to *Fa* in major or harmonic minor.

> **TIP**
>
> In this guide all **diminished** intervals will be labeled **dim** or ° and **augmented** intervals will be labeled **A** or +.

Enharmonic intervals sound the same but are spelled differently and therefore function differently. C♯ and D♭ are the same pitch; however, they are not notated the same on the staff. The same is true of intervals. For example, F to A♭ is a minor third, but F to G♯ is an augmented second. Even though A♭ and G♯ sound the same you cannot call the interval F to G♯ a minor third because its numeric quantity is 2; therefore it has to be some kind of second. The function refers to the pull a chromatic note has either up or down. The A♭ has a natural pull to G because flats lead downward, where the G♯ would lead upward to A♮.

Examples of Enharmonic Intervals:

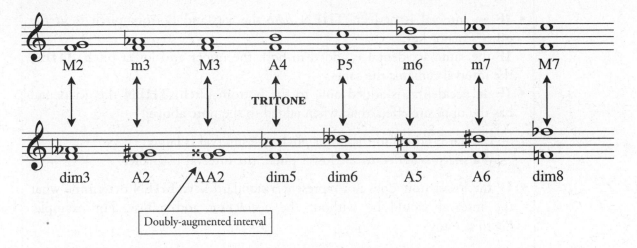

Doubly-augmented interval

When a major or perfect interval is made one **whole step** larger, without changing the letter names of the pitches, it is called **doubly augmented**. When a minor or perfect interval is made one **whole step** smaller without changing the letter names of the pitches it is called **doubly diminished**. These intervals will usually require the use of the double flat or the double sharp sign.

IF–THEN Intervals

A great way to learn to identify or "spell" intervals that also reinforces key signatures and scales is by thinking of the interval *in the key of the bottom note*. Ask yourself, "**IF** the bottom note is tonic of a *major* key, **THEN** is the top note *diatonic* (found within the notes of the scale) in the key (of the bottom note)?"

- **IF** the top note *is* in the major key of the bottom note, **THEN** it is major or perfect.
- **IF** the top note is a half step *lower* than the diatonic note would be, **THEN** it is a minor or diminished interval.
- **IF** the top note is a half step *higher* than the diatonic note would be, **THEN** it is an augmented interval.

More IF–THEN Considerations

- **IF** an interval is perfect, **THEN** *both* the top and bottom pitch is in the other's major key.
- **IF** the same accidental is added to both the upper and lower pitch, **THEN** the interval remains the same.
- **IF** an accidental is added only to the bottom pitch, **THEN** the accidental has the opposite effect than when added to the note above:

  - If a flat is added to the lower pitch, the interval is larger.
  - If a sharp is added to the lower pitch, the interval is smaller.

- **IF** the lower note does not represent a standard key, **THEN** determine what the interval would be without the accidental and adjust. For example: G♯ to E = m6.

  - Because G♯ is not a standard key signature we determine that G to E = M6 and because the bottom note is sharp, it reduces the quality by one half step to m6.

- Remember that **IF** you are spelling intervals *below* a given pitch, **THEN** you must still associate the top note to the major key of the bottom note. You cannot change the given note.

Intervals that are one octave or smaller in quantity are called **simple intervals**. Intervals that are larger than an octave are called **compound intervals**. The most common are the ninth, tenth, eleventh, and twelfth, which correspond to an octave plus a second, third, fourth, and fifth.

- Compound intervals are reduced to a simple interval by subtracting seven. For example: a major ninth (–7) reduces to a major second.
- To expand a simple interval to compound, add seven. For example: a minor third (+ 7) becomes a minor tenth.
- The *quality* of the interval does not change when reducing or expanding.

MAKING SIMPLE INTERVALS COMPOUND

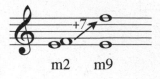

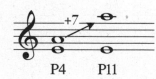
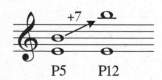

m2   m9   M3   M10   P4   P11   P5   P12

As mentioned earlier, intervals are **inverted** by transferring the lower note an octave higher or by transferring the higher note an octave lower:

- Major intervals invert to minor intervals.
- Augmented intervals invert to diminished intervals.
- Perfect intervals invert to perfect.
- A second inverts to a seventh.
- A third inverts to a sixth.
- A fourth inverts to a fifth.

> **The Rule of Nine:** When any simple interval is inverted, the sum of the ascending and descending intervals must add up to nine.

**INVERTING INTERVALS
WITH THE RULE OF NINE**

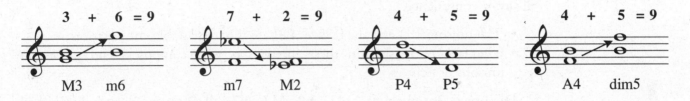

$3 + 6 = 9$ $7 + 2 = 9$ $4 + 5 = 9$ $4 + 5 = 9$

M3   m6   m7   M2   P4   P5   A4   dim5

Strategies for Difficult Intervals

Let's look at a few examples and develop a strategy for identifying and building intervals that are a little more difficult.

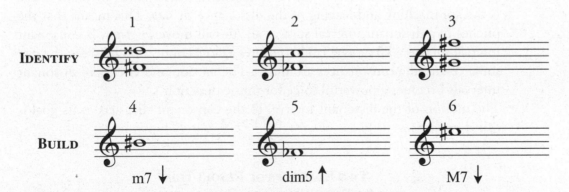

IDENTIFY — 1, 2, 3

BUILD — 4, 5, 6

m7 ↓   dim5 ↑   M7 ↓

There are two methods to identify difficult intervals: (1) invert and identify or (2) cover up one or both of the accidentals to determine *what you know for sure*—then adjust accordingly. In the first example the quantity is a sixth. Use the second method and cover up the double sharp on the top pitch. What note is a M6 (diatonic) in the key of F♯ Major? Answer: D♯. Therefore, since a double sharp makes the interval larger, the answer is A6 (a half step larger than major). Do the same thing for example 2. By removing the flat, the interval is a P5. By adding a flat on the bottom, the interval is made larger. F♭ to C would be an A5. Or, invert interval 2 by placing the F♭ **above** the C, creating a dim4. The inversion of a dim4 is an A5.

For example 3, invert the G♯. F♯ to G♯ is a M2 so the inversion is m7. Use the same methods for constructing intervals. To find a m7 below B♯ (example 4), remove the sharp and determine what pitch is a m7 below B♮. Answer: C♯. Therefore, by adding a sharp to the top pitch, you must also add a sharp to the lower pitch to maintain the quality of the interval. A m7 below B♯ is C×. In example 5, a P5 above F♭ is C♭. Therefore, to create a diminished fifth the upper note is lowered to C♭♭. In example 6, invert and find a m2 **above** E♯. Still not sure? Take away the sharp sign. What is a m2 above E♮? Answer: F. Therefore, by adding a sharp to both the top and bottom pitch you maintain the same interval quality and quantity—a m2 above E♯ is F♯; therefore, an F♯ inverted is a M7 below E♯.

Intervals are classified as either **consonant** (stable) or **dissonant** (unstable—the impression of activity or tension). **Consonant intervals** are the P1, P5, P8, M3, m3, M6, m6, and sometimes the P4, depending on context. Melodically a P4 is always a consonance.

- The unison (P1) and the octave (P8) are the most stable consonances.
- The lack of tension in these intervals is why composers end pieces on unisons or octaves.

Dissonant intervals are M2, m2, M7, m7, all augmented and diminished intervals, and sometimes the P4 (which is generally **considered a dissonance when used harmonically above the bass**).

- In Chapter 3 we saw that $\hat{2}$, $\hat{4}$, $\hat{6}$, and $\hat{7}$ function as active tones that tend to lead to $\hat{1}$, $\hat{3}$, and $\hat{5}$. The division of the scale into *active* and *stable tones* relates directly to consonance and dissonance of intervals.
- A fundamental characteristic of the treatment of dissonances in tonal music is the approaching and leaving of the dissonance *by step*. This means that the pitches in a dissonant interval such as an A4 will move *by step* to a consonant interval such as a P5 or a M3. This ensures a close connection between the dissonance and the consonances around it. The tension and energy of dissonant intervals becomes a powerful force for music direction.
- The motion of the dissonant interval to the consonant that acts as its goal is called *resolution*.

TWO EXAMPLES OF RESOLUTION
OF A DISSONANCE TO A CONSONANCE

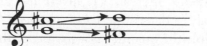   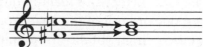

A4 resolves to m6   dim5 resolves to M3

REVIEW

Aurelia

Samuel Wesley
(1810–1876)

| Chord Number: | 1 | 2 | 3 | 4 | 5 | 6 | 7 | 8 | 9 | 10 | 11 | 12 | 13 |

Notice that within any four-part composition there is a possibility of six intervals between voices. Those intervals are between:

A–S   (Alto and Soprano)
T–S   (Tenor and Soprano)
T–A   (Tenor and Alto)
B–S   (Bass and Soprano)
B–A   (Bass and Alto)
B–T   (Bass and Tenor)

For practice, let's identify all the intervals found in this four-measure phrase and see what is revealed about intervals within a composition. Fill in the chart below and circle the intervals that are considered **dissonant**. Answers follow.

Chord #	1	2	3	4	5	6	7	8	9	10	11	12	13
A–S	M3												
T–S	M6												
T–A	P4												
B–S	M3												
B–A	P8												
B–T	P5												

Answers:

Chord #	1	2	3	4	5	6	7	8	9	10	11	12	13
A–S	M3	M3	M3	P4	M3	M3	m3	P1	m3	M6	P5	(dim5)	M3
T–S	M6	M6	M6	m6	M6	M6	P5	P4	(m7)	P5	m3	(m7)	M6
T–A	P4	P4	P4	m3	P4	P4	M3	P4	P5	(m7)	m6	M3	P4
B–S	M3	M3	M3	(P4)	M3	M6	M6	m6	P5	M3	P8	(m7)	M3
B–A	P8	P8	P8	P8	P8	(P4)	(A4)	m6	M3	P5	(P4)	M3	P8
B–T	P5	P5	P5	M6	P5	P8	(M2)	m3	M6	M6	M6	P8	P5

Observations:

There are seventy-eight intervals in these thirteen chords! The circled intervals are dissonant. Notice that the majority of these dissonances occur at the end of the phrase and all the dissonant intervals (except one) resolve to a consonant interval. For example, in chord 7 the A4 resolves to a m6 and the m7 in chord 9 resolves to a P5. Chord 12, the penultimate chord, has three dissonant intervals creating intensity in the music right before the end of the phrase. Also note that all the dissonant intervals contain one or BOTH of the most active scale members *Fa* (G) and *Ti* (C♯). If we isolate the most active chord (12), we see that the active notes resolve correctly with *Fa* (G) resolving down by step to *Mi* (F♯) and *Ti* (C♯) resolving upward to *Do* (D). Why is the P4 circled in chords 4, 6, and 11 and not in the other places the P4 occurs? The answer is that in common-practice style, the interval of a fourth *against the bass* was considered dissonant. This is important to remember and is discussed in future chapters.

TRIADS

A chord is a group of pitches that forms a single harmonic idea. The use of chords is the basic foundation of harmony. **A triad is a three-note chord (built like a snowman) made up of two intervals stacked in thirds.**

The lower note of the chord is called the **root**, the middle note is the **third** because it is an interval of a third above the root, and the upper note is called the **fifth**, a fifth above the root.

Building Triads

A triad is two intervals—both thirds, stacked on top of each other, snowman style. The Common Practice Period uses this type of **tertian harmony** (harmony built on thirds). A triad actually contains three separate intervals. From the root to the third is one interval—a third. From the third to the fifth is the second interval—another third. The two outside tones, the root and the fifth, also create an interval—a fifth.

HOW TO BUILD A TRIAD

1. Build the "snowman" in thirds above the root. **Tertian harmony thirds will either be all lines or all spaces.**
2. Identify the quality of the lower third as major or minor.
3. Identify the quality of the fifth (between the root of the triad and the fifth) as perfect, diminished, or augmented.
4. Identify the chord with the pitch name letter (the root of the "snowman").
5. Identify the quality of the triad:

   - **M3 + P5 = major triad** (or M3 + m3)
   - **m3 + P5 = minor triad** (or m3 + M3)
   - **m3 + dim5 = diminished triad** (or m3 + m3)
   - **M3 + A5 = augmented triad** (or M3 + M3)

HOW TO BUILD A TRIAD

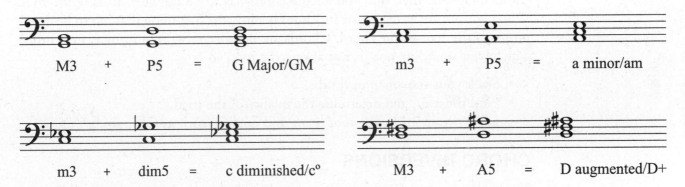

If you know what the **major triad** is, then you can easily adjust the third and the fifth to create the other chord qualities.

- From major, raise the fifth to create an augmented triad.
- From major, lower the third to create a minor triad.
- From major, lower the third *and* the fifth to create a diminished triad, or lower only the fifth from the *minor triad.*

The key to this method is *knowing* what the **Major** triad is!

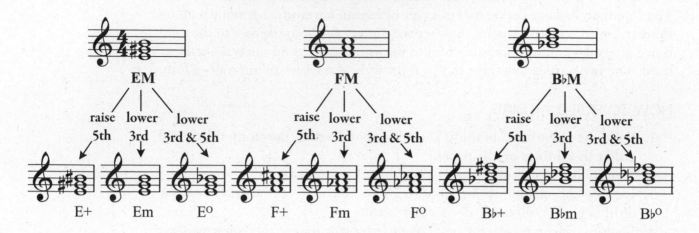

➡️ See Appendix A for more information on visually identifying major chords.

Recognizing Triads

Once you are comfortable with building triads in all qualities, it's time to look at real music and recognize chords in context. Much of the music we study in AP Music Theory has four parts, or voices. When we have four parts and only three chord members, then one note of the chord has to be doubled, usually the root. When you are analyzing music for chord quality, the first thing that has to be determined is the root of the chord. Chords are not always written in nice, neat order. The lowest sounding note is **not** always the root, so

- Stack your snowman in thirds.
- Find the root, and determine the quality of the triad.
- Label the chord by the root name and quality (such as GM, gm, g°, or G⁺).

CHORD INVERSIONS

Triads that have a chord member *other than the root* as the lowest sounding voice (the bass) are called **inversions**. When you move the position of any of the chord members, an interval **inverts**. Any member of the chord may sound in the bass. Since there are three notes in a triad, there are three possible positions.

- Root position—the root of the chord is in the bass.
- First inversion—the third of the chord is in the bass.
- Second inversion—the fifth of the chord is in the bass.

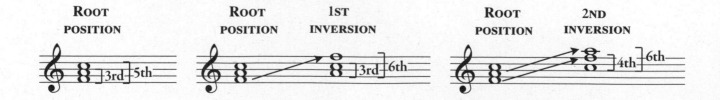

When a chord is in root position the intervals above the bass note (the root) are a third and a fifth. When a chord is in first inversion the intervals above the bass are a third and a sixth. When a chord is in second inversion, the bass note is the fifth of the chord and the intervals above the bass are a sixth and a **fourth**. Yes, the fourth above the bass in the second inversion triad is a dissonant interval and must be handled with care. If you go back to the interval exercise we did on *Aurelia* you will notice that chords 4, 6, and 11, which have the P4 against the bass, are all second inversion chords. We will revisit this information again when discussing chord symbols and inversions, but for now let's move on to the discussion of chords with four different notes—seventh chords.

SEVENTH CHORDS

A **seventh chord** contains four notes—the root, third, fifth and an **added seventh**. Because this arrangement of tones contains an interval of a seventh, which is a dissonant interval, all seventh chords are considered dissonant (unstable).

Building and Recognizing Seventh Chords

Given the types of triads combined with the types of sevenths, there are sixteen possibilities of seventh chords. Although other types are possible, five types of seventh chords are most often used in common-practice music and are prevalent on the AP Music Theory exam.

Five Basic Seventh Chords

- Major seventh (Major triad, Major seventh—**MM7**) or M3, m3, M3
- Dominant seventh or Major-minor seventh (Major triad, minor seventh—**Mm7**) or M3, m3, m3
- Minor seventh (minor triad, minor seventh—**mm7**) or m3, M3, m3
- Half-diminished seventh (diminished triad, minor seventh—**dim m7**) or m3, m3, M3
- Fully-diminished seventh (diminished triad, diminished seventh—**dim dim7**) or m3, m3, m3

Let's build these five seventh chords on G:

	MAJOR 7TH	DOMINANT 7TH	MINOR 7TH	HALF-DIMINISHED 7TH	FULLY-DIMINISHED 7TH
Triad+7th Quality:	M+M7	M+m7	m+m7	dim+m7	dim+dim7

With a four-note chord you must first stack the pitches in snowman style to be able to identify the root of the chord, then you must identify the quality of the triad and the quality of the seventh. Sometimes it is difficult to rearrange the four chord members into a snowman.

Try these helpful hints:

- Remember that a seventh inverts to a second, so find the two notes that are a second apart—the root of the chord is the **higher** of the two notes.
- Another way to "stack the snowman" is by memorizing the combinations. As with triads, there are only seven combinations of letter names:

Triads: C–E–G   D–F–A   E–G–B   F–A–C   G–B–D   A–C–E   B–D–F

Seventh chords: C–E–G–B   D–F–A–C   E–G–B–D   F–A–C–E   G–B–D–F   A–C–E–G   B–D–F–A

If you have spent time identifying intervals, then triads and seventh chords are just an extension of that information. Seventh chords are also found in root position and inverted. Because there are four notes, there are four possible chord positions:

THE FOUR POSITIONS OF G⁷

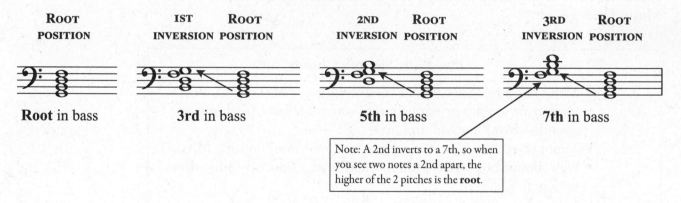

ROOT POSITION	1ST INVERSION ROOT POSITION	2ND INVERSION ROOT POSITION	3RD INVERSION ROOT POSITION
Root in bass	**3rd** in bass	**5th** in bass	**7th** in bass

Note: A 2nd inverts to a 7th, so when you see two notes a 2nd apart, the higher of the 2 pitches is the **root**.

The **intervals above the lowest sounding note—(the bass)** that are created when a seventh chord is inverted will be discussed in more detail in Chapter 6. At this point we want to simply recognize a seventh chord, identify the note that is the root of the chord, determine the quality of the triad and the seventh, and determine the inversion if appropriate.

In order to apply this information, let's go back to the chorale on page 109 and identify the chords, quality, and inversions within the first phrase.

REVIEW

STEP 1: Identify the key. The key is D Major. Let's begin.

STEP 2: Create the chord stack by putting the chord members in "snowman style" and identifying the root of the chord by putting it on the bottom of the stack. Identify the notes that are doubled by putting them side by side in the stack. **Circle the notes that are in the bass**—this will tell you the inversion. If it's a seventh chord—just keep stacking.

Aurelia

Samuel Wesley
(1810–1876)

STEP 3: What do we know now? Based on the chord stack and the circles we know that chord numbers 1 (also 2, 3), 5, 12, and 13 are in root position. All the triads in root position have the root of the chord doubled in this example. Chord numbers 4 and 11 are in second inversion. In these two chords the fifth of the chord has been doubled. Chord numbers 7, 12 and 9, 10 are seventh chords (7 and 12 are the same chord, and 9 and 10 are the same chord). Of these four seventh chords, only one (12) is in root position. Chord number 7 has the seventh of the chord as the lowest sounding note, while 9 and 10 are first inversion seventh chords. Chord 8 is a first inversion triad. Chord numbers 1, 5, 6, 8, 11, and 13 are D Major chords—tonic in this key. It is the chord most often used.

STEP 4: Determine the **root**, **quality**, and **inversion** of each triad or seventh chord.

1, 2, 3 _____

4 _____

5 _____

6 _____

7 _____

8 _____

9, 10 _____

11 _____

12 _____

13 _____

FOR YOUR INFORMATION

We will mention at this point the chord symbols used for chords and inversions. Although it is *not* tested on the exam, many students are familiar with this way of labeling chords and often find it helpful when learning the concepts of chord identification and inversion. In chord symbols a root position G Major triad is simply written G. The G Major triad with an added minor seventh is written G⁷. The G minor triad is written Gm. The G Major chord in first inversion is labeled G/B and the G Major chord in second inversion is labeled G/D. The pitch after the slash indicates the lowest sounding pitch in the chord. If there is no slash the chord is in root position. Chord symbols are placed **above the staff**.

Here's what the chord symbols would look like added to our "Aurelia" example:

Aurelia

Samuel Wesley
(1810–1876)

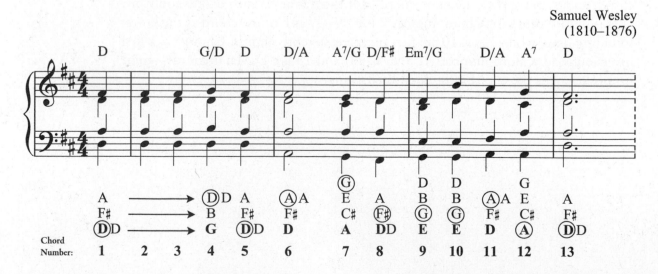

Here are the answers to Step 4:

1(2, 3) = D Major triad in root position
    4 = G Major triad in second inversion
    5 = D Major triad in root position
    6 = D Major triad in second inversion
    7 = A Major triad with m7 (Mm7 chord)
        The seventh of the chord is in the bass. (Yes, that would be third inversion.)
    8 = D Major triad in first inversion
9(10) = E minor triad with m7 in first inversion (mm7 chord)
    11 = D Major triad in second inversion
    12 = A Major triad with m7 in root position (Mm7 chord)
    13 = D Major triad in root position

➡️   For additional study, see *Abide With Me* (or any other hymn tunes available in **Appendix B**) as well as the full chorale of *Aurelia*.

Do an analysis of the chords by stacking like a snowman with the root on the bottom. Label the chord with letter name and quality. *Circle the note that is in the bass.* Note that some chords are inverted.

Chapter Summary

- An **interval** is the distance between two notes. Intervals are **melodic** (sounding one after another as in a melody), or **harmonic** (two notes sounding at the same time.
- We describe exact interval size by **quantity** (size) and **quality**.
- Diatonic intervals above the tonic in a major scale are P1, M2, M3, P4, P5, M6, M7, P8.
- When the quantity remains the same, an interval that is one half step smaller than major is **minor**.
- When the quantity remains the same, an interval that is one half step **smaller** than perfect or minor is **diminished**.
- When the quantity remains the same, an interval that is one half step **larger** than major or perfect is **augmented**.
- **Enharmonic** intervals *sound the same but are spelled differently.*
- The only diatonic augmented or diminished interval is the augmented fourth or diminished fifth. The augmented fourth is commonly called a **tritone**.
- When a major or perfect interval is made *one whole step larger*, without changing the letter names of the pitches, it is called **doubly augmented**. When a minor or perfect interval is made *one whole step smaller* without changing the letter names of the pitches it is called **doubly diminished**.
- Intervals are **inverted** by transferring the lower note an octave higher or by transferring the higher note an octave lower.
- Intervals that are one octave or smaller are called **simple intervals**.

- Intervals that are larger than an octave are called **compound intervals**. The most common are the ninth, tenth, eleventh, and twelfth, which correspond to an octave plus a second, third, fourth, and fifth.
- **Consonant intervals** are the P1, P5, P8, M3, m3, M6, m6, and sometimes the P4, depending on context.
- **Dissonant intervals** are M2, m2, M7, m7, all augmented and diminished intervals, and sometimes the P4, which is generally considered a dissonance when used harmonically above the bass.
- The motion of the dissonant interval to the consonant that acts as its goal is called **resolution**.
- A **triad** is a three-note chord made up of two intervals stacked in thirds. The lower note is called the **root**, the middle note is the **third** because it is an interval of a third above the root, and the upper note is called the **fifth**, a fifth above the root.

  – M3 and P5 = major triad
  – m3 and P5 = minor triad
  – M3 and A5 = augmented triad
  – m3 and dim5 = diminished triad

- If you know what the major chord is, then you can easily adjust the third and the fifth to create the other chord qualities.

  – From major, raise the fifth of the chord to create an augmented chord.
  – From major, lower the third to create a minor chord.
  – From major, lower the third *and* the fifth to create a diminished chord, or lower only the fifth from the *minor chord*.

- Triads that have a chord member *other than the root* as the lowest sounding voice (the bass) are called **inversions**.

  – **Root position**—when the root of the chord is in the bass
  – **First inversion**—when the third of the chord is in the bass
  – **Second inversion**—when the fifth of the chord is in the bass

- **A seventh chord** contains four notes—the root, third, fifth, and seventh. Because this arrangement of tones contains an interval of a seventh, which is a dissonant interval, all seventh chords are dissonant (unstable).
- **Five basic seventh chords:**

  – Major seventh (Major triad + Major seventh)
  – Dominant seventh or Major-minor seventh (Major triad + minor seventh)
  – Minor seventh (minor triad + minor seventh)
  – Half-diminished seventh (diminished triad + minor seventh)
  – Fully-diminished seventh (diminished triad + diminished seventh)

Practice Exercises

Questions 1–7 are based on phrase 1 of the hymn "Aberystwyth."

Aberystwyth

Joseph Parry
(1841–1903)

1. The key of this excerpt is

    (A) G Major
    (B) G minor
    (C) E minor
    (D) B minor

2. Identify the chord and inversion of chord 1.

    (A) B minor in root position
    (B) E minor in first inversion
    (C) E minor in second inversion
    (D) G Major in first inversion

3. What chord member is doubled in chord 1?

    (A) The root is doubled.
    (B) The third is doubled.
    (C) The fifth is doubled.
    (D) No note is doubled.

4. What chord member does the alto sing in chord 3?

    (A) The third of an E minor triad
    (B) The fifth of an E minor triad
    (C) The root of a B Major triad
    (D) The root of a B Major seventh chord

5. All of the following are true of chord 2 **except**

    (A) It is a B Major triad with an added seventh in the tenor (after the beat).
    (B) It has *So* in the bass.
    (C) D♯ is the third of the chord and the leading tone in E harmonic minor.
    (D) It contains an interval of a P4 against the bass.

6. Chord 4 would be identified as an E minor chord

    (A) in root position
    (B) in first inversion
    (C) in second inversion
    (D) with an added seventh

7. Chord 5 would be identified as a B Major

    (A) seventh chord
    (B) triad in root position
    (C) chord in first inversion
    (D) chord in second inversion

Questions 8–16 are based on the string parts from this *Concerto Grosso* by Corelli. We have seen this example before; however, this time we will look at interval, chords, and inversions.

Concerto Grosso Op. 6, No. 8

("Christmas Concerto"—excerpt of string section parts)

Arcangelo Corelli
(1653–1713)

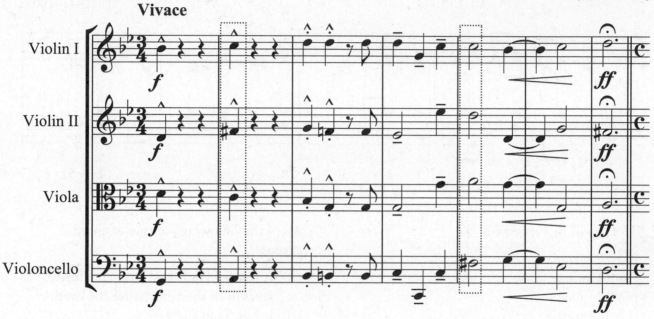

8. The key of this example is

(A) B♭ Major
(B) G minor
(C) G Major
(D) D minor

9. The F♯ in this example would be identified as the

(A) supertonic
(B) subtonic
(C) leading tone
(D) mediant

10. The chord on the downbeat of measure 2 is

(A) an A Major chord in root position
(B) an A minor chord in root position
(C) a D Major chord in second inversion
(D) an F♯ diminished chord in first inversion

11. The interval between the notes in first and second violin in this chord (m2, beat 1) is

(A) P4
(B) P5
(C) dim5
(D) A4

12. The interval between the cello and the viola (in the same chord) is a compound interval. This interval reduces to

    (A) M2
    (B) M3
    (C) m3
    (D) P4

13. The chord at the fermata is a

    (A) D Major triad
    (B) D Major triad with an added seventh
    (C) G Major triad
    (D) G minor triad

14. The viola plays what chord member in the chord at the fermata?

    (A) The root of the chord
    (B) The third of the chord
    (C) The fifth of the chord
    (D) The seventh of the chord

15. What position is the chord at the fermata?

    (A) Root position
    (B) First inversion
    (C) Second inversion
    (D) Third inversion

16. The chord immediately preceding the fermata is identified as

    (A) E♭ Major in root position
    (B) E♭ minor in root position
    (C) C minor in first inversion
    (D) A minor in first inversion

17. Which of the following is not a minor sixth interval?

    (A)
    (B)
    (C)
    (D)

18. All of the following are true of this chord **except**

    (A) It's a major chord with an added m7.
    (B) It's in first inversion.
    (C) The root of the chord is E.
    (D) The fifth of the chord is G.

19. All of the following intervals are enharmonic equivalents **except**

    (A) M2 and dim3
    (B) M7 and m2
    (C) dim5 and A4
    (D) m6 and A5

20. The difference between a half-diminished seventh chord and a fully-diminished seventh chord is the

    (A) quality of the triad
    (B) third is lower in half-diminished
    (C) fifth is lower in fully-diminished
    (D) quality of the seventh

ANSWER KEY

1. **C**	6. **A**	11. **C**	16. **C**
2. **C**	7. **B**	12. **C**	17. **C**
3. **C**	8. **B**	13. **A**	18. **C**
4. **B**	9. **C**	14. **C**	19. **B**
5. **D**	10. **D**	15. **A**	20. **D**

ANSWERS EXPLAINED

1. **(C)** This excerpt is in E harmonic minor. The raised seventh scale degree (D♯) is used consistently throughout.

2. **(C)** Chord 1 is an E minor in second inversion. The chord is E–G–B with the B in the bass.

3. **(C)** The fifth is doubled. The fifth (B) occurs in the bass and in the tenor.

4. **(B)** The alto sings the fifth of an E minor chord (B or *So.*)

5. **(D)** Chord 2 does not contain an interval of a P4 against the bass.

6. **(A)** Chord 4 is an E minor chord in root position.

7. **(B)** Chord 5 is a B Major triad in root position.

8. **(B)** G minor.

9. **(C)** The leading tone. In G harmonic minor the raised seventh scale degree (leading tone) is F♯.

10. **(D)** An F♯ diminished chord in first inversion. The chord is F♯–A–C and the A (the third of the chord) is in the bass.

11. **(C)** The interval between F♯ and C is a diminished fifth.

12. **(C)** The reduced interval is a m3. The bass is an A and the viola is playing C. The compound interval is a m10.

13. **(A)** D-Major triad.

14. **(C)** The viola is playing A, the fifth of the chord.

15. **(A)** It is a root position triad, meaning the root of the chord, D, is in the bass.

16. **(C)** The chord preceding the fermata is a C minor triad in first inversion. The chord is C–E♭–G and the E♭ is in the bass.

17. **(C)** A to F♯ is a major sixth.

18. **(C)** The example chord is a major triad with a minor seventh. The chord is C–E–G–B♭ with the E in the bass making it a first inversion seventh chord. The root of the chord is C, not E.

19. **(B)** A Major seventh inverts to a minor second, but it is not an enharmonic equivalent. The examples that are enharmonic equivalents are M2 and dim3 (F–G is the same as F–A♭♭), dim5 and A4 (F♯–C is the same as G♭–C), m6 and A5 (F–D♭ is the same as F–C♯).

20. **(D)** The difference is the seventh. The half-diminished and fully-diminished seventh chords have the same quality triad (diminished) but the half-diminished has a minor seventh (dim m7) and the fully-diminished seventh chord has a diminished seventh (dim dim7). Therefore, in the fully-diminished seventh chord the seventh is a half step lower.

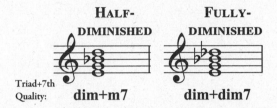

HALF-DIMINISHED   **FULLY-DIMINISHED**

Triad+7th Quality: **dim+m7**   **dim+dim7**

Harmonic Organization II: Chords in Diatonic Context

6

- Harmonic Function
- Roman Numerals
    - Diatonic Triads in Major
    - **I ii iii IV V vi vii°**
    - Diatonic Triads in Minor
    - **i ii° III III⁺ iv V VI vii° VII**
- Inversions of Triads
    - Root Position   **V**
    - First Inversion   **V⁶**
    - Second Inversion **V⁶₄**
- Inversions of Seventh Chords
    - Root Position   **V⁷**
    - First Inversion   **V⁶₅**
    - Second Inversion **V⁴₃**
    - Third Inversion   **V⁴₂ or V²**
- Figured Bass
- Realization of Figured Bass

TRIADS IN A DIATONIC CONTEXT

Now we are ready to combine two concepts: chord qualities and how they relate to the diatonic scale. In tonal music the **harmonic function** of a triad is associated with the scale degree on which it is built. In G Major the chord built on the tonic note (G) is called the tonic triad (G–B–D). The quality of this triad is major. Similarly, we refer to the triads built on each note of the scale by their scale degree name. In analyzing music it became necessary to find a way to label triads with their quality and their function (their placement within the key). Thus began the use of Roman numerals to identify and label chords. Major triads are indicated with uppercase Roman numerals (such as **I**, **IV**, or **V**) and minor triads are indicated with lowercase numerals (such as **ii**, **iii**, or **vi**). For the diminished triad a small circle is added to lowercase numerals (**vii°**). For the augmented triad, the plus sign is added to the uppercase Roman numeral (**III⁺**). Please note that the **III⁺** is rarely, if ever, used on the AP exam.

Diatonic Triads in Major

The example below, in G Major, shows the triad, quality, scale degree name, and Roman numeral analysis. Because the scale pattern of W–W–H–W–W–W–H is the same for every major scale, likewise, the stacking of the notes creates the same intervals and, therefore, the same qualities of triads in every major key. These triads are **diatonic** because they use pitches found only in that key. Note that when showing Roman numeral analysis (which indicates function *within a specific key*), the key is always indicated at the beginning of the analysis. Use uppercase for major and lowercase for minor.

In this example, accidentals are used.

DIATONIC TRIADS
IN THE KEY OF G MAJOR

	TONIC	SUPERTONIC	MEDIANT	SUBDOMINANT	DOMINANT	SUBMEDIANT	LEADING TONE
GM:	I	ii	iii	IV	V	vi	vii°
Triad Quality:	M	m	m	M	M	m	dim

> Throughout this discussion of diatonic chords we consider the major, minor, and diminished triads built on G as the root, to observe where each chord occurs and how it functions. In a major tonality there are only three places where a major triad occurs—on **I**, **IV**, and **V**. With this information we then know that the G Major triad (G–B–D) will be I (tonic) in G Major, IV (subdominant) in D Major, and V (dominant) in C Major. Where will the **G minor** chord occur? In a major tonality a minor chord occurs on **ii**, **iii**, and **vi**; therefore, G minor (G–B♭–D) will occur as the supertonic (ii) in F Major, the mediant (iii) in E♭ Major, and the submediant (vi) in B♭ Major. There is only one diminished triad in any given major tonality; therefore, **G diminished** (G–B♭–D♭) will occur on the seventh scale degree (**vii°**) in only one key—A♭ Major. There are no augmented chords in major.

Diatonic Triads in Minor

The example we use is in E minor, the relative minor of G Major. Because the key signature is the same as G Major (therefore, the same pitches are used), the chords have the same qualities as those found in G Major, *just on a different scale degree.* The *relative major* chord symbols have been placed above for comparison. First let's look at chords in *natural minor.*

DIATONIC TRIADS
IN THE KEY OF E NATURAL MINOR

For comparison:

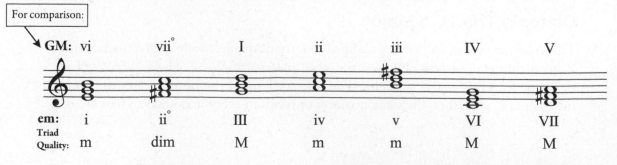

	GM:	vi	vii°	I	ii	iii	IV	V
	em:	i	ii°	III	iv	v	VI	VII
Triad Quality:		m	dim	M	m	m	M	M

Remember that the chord built on the 7th scale degree in natural minor is called the *subtonic triad.* It is a *major* chord—a whole step below tonic. The VII is just as common as the vii° in minor.

After the initial comparison of the natural minor to major, we turn immediately to the harmonic form of minor. It is used most often for *harmonizing* in a minor key and is the form of minor *most prominent on the AP exam.* In harmonic minor the *7th scale degree is raised,* creating a half step below tonic so that the 7th scale degree once again *leads to tonic* or **Do**. This provides a more convincing harmonic pull to tonic while retaining the characteristic color of minor.

- The chords that are different from natural minor are only the chords that contain scale degree 7.
- **Remember to "raise the seventh scale degree in minor!"**

DIATONIC TRIADS
IN THE KEY OF E HARMONIC MINOR

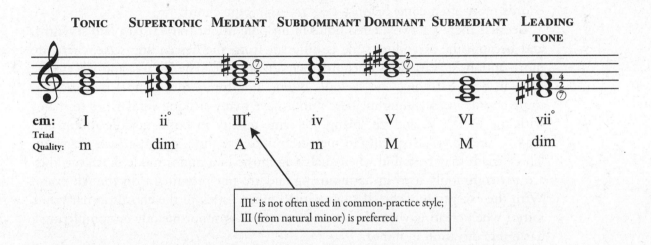

III⁺ is not often used in common-practice style; III (from natural minor) is preferred.

In a minor tonality the minor chord takes center stage. Where does our target chord occur? **G minor** will function as tonic (**i**) in G minor and subdominant (**iv**) in D minor. Obviously, the G Major chord functions differently in minor than it does in major. Based on this information we know that the G Major triad will occur as **V** or **VI**, so G Major will be the dominant chord (**V**) in the key of C minor and **VI** (submediant) in B minor. The diminished triad (G–B♭–D♭) occurs on $\hat{2}$ (supertonic) in F minor; the Roman numeral chord symbol is **ii°**. In harmonic minor we find the augmented triad for the first time. The G augmented (G–B–**D♯**) occurs in only one minor key—where G is the mediant. That key is E minor. However, during the Common Practice Period (CPP), the mediant ($\hat{3}$) was harmonized more often with **III** (natural minor) than with **III⁺** (harmonic minor).

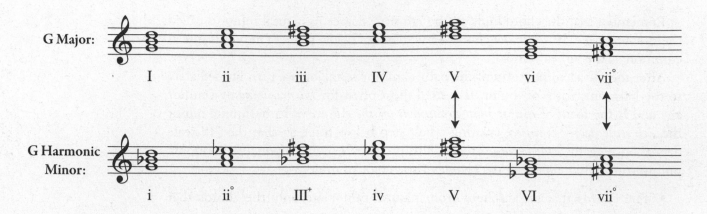

When we compare the qualities of triads found diatonically in major to those in the harmonic minor scale, we find that the **dominant triad (major)** and the **leading-tone triad (diminished)** *are the same quality in both.* The V and vii° triad both contain the leading tone (which we already know leads to tonic) so these two chords most often come before—*lead to*—the tonic chord.

Because there are two altered notes in melodic minor (raised sixth and seventh), and because the ascending scale is different from the descending scale, there are more options or variations of chords that are possible. The III⁺, V, and vii° are the same in both harmonic and melodic minor. It is interesting to note that the diatonic chords in ascending melodic minor have many striking similarities to major with the **ii**, **IV**, **V**, and **vii°** being the same quality in both melodic minor and major. Altered triads specific to melodic minor are those that use scale degree 6. These triads may be found when analyzing music in a minor mode; however, they are *not* commonly used in harmonizing and are not prominent on the AP exam. With the exception of the III from natural minor, stick to the chords in harmonic minor when creating your own harmonization of a minor melody or completing a harmonic dictation in minor.

The prominent triads in a minor mode (reflecting all three forms) are:

i   ii°   III   iv   V   VI   vii° or VII

➤ Check out Appendix A to do a side-by-side comparison of diatonic triads and seventh chords.

DIATONIC SEVENTH CHORDS

Now let's build seventh chords diatonically in major and harmonic minor, discuss the chord symbols, and compare. We continue to use G as our tonic, first in major.

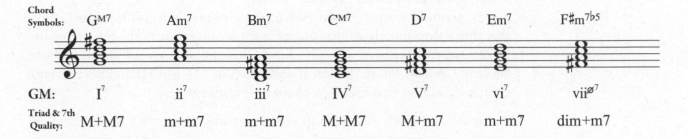

Chord Symbols:	G^{M7}	Am^7	Bm^7	C^{M7}	D^7	Em^7	$F\sharp m^{7\flat5}$
GM:	I^7	ii^7	iii^7	IV^7	V^7	vi^7	$vii^{\varnothing7}$
Triad & 7th Quality:	M+M7	m+m7	m+m7	M+M7	M+m7	m+m7	dim+m7

- The quality of the seventh is the same as the quality of the triad in all but **V** and **vii°**.
- When a minor seventh is added to a triad, the chord symbol is *superscript ^{7}* ($m7$ or $^{-7}$).
- When a major seventh is added to a triad, the chord symbol is *superscript ^{7}* (^{M7} or ^{Maj7}).
- When a minor seventh is added to a diminished triad (dim m), the chord is called *half-diminished*. The superscript $^{\varnothing7}$ with the *diminished circle slashed*, is added to the Roman numeral ($viii^{\varnothing7}$).
- With lead-sheet chord symbols, small case m after the letter refers to the quality of the triad. When the superscript 7 is added, it always means a *minor* seventh (Gm^7 is a G minor triad with an added minor 7th, and G^{M7} means a G Major triad with an added M7. The half-diminished seventh chord is referred to as a minor triad with a lowered 5th ($\flat5$) and an added minor 7th ($Gm^{7\flat5}$).

Now let's look at the seventh chords that are diatonic in the **G harmonic minor scale**.

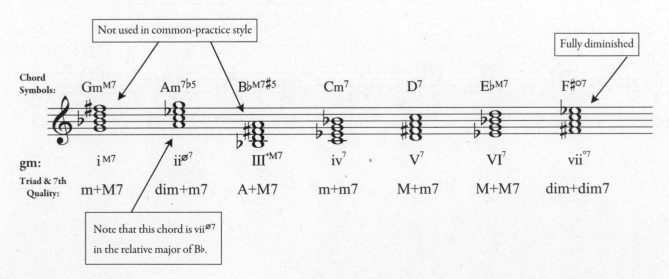

	Not used in common-practice style						Fully diminished
Chord Symbols:	Gm^{M7}	$Am^{7\flat5}$	$B\flat^{M7\sharp5}$	Cm^7	D^7	$E\flat^{M7}$	$F\sharp^{\circ7}$
gm:	i^{M7}	$ii^{\varnothing7}$	III^{+M7}	iv^7	V^7	VI^7	$vii^{\circ7}$
Triad & 7th Quality:	m+M7	dim+m7	A+M7	m+m7	M+m7	M+M7	dim+dim7

Note that this chord is $vii^{\varnothing7}$ in the relative major of B♭.

- The *fully-diminished* seventh chord (diminished triad *and* diminished seventh) occurs on the leading tone in harmonic minor; because it is *fully*-diminished, the diminished circle is not slashed.
- It is significant that the V⁷ (dominant seventh) chord is exactly the same in major and in the parallel harmonic minor.
- The supertonic seventh chord in harmonic minor is half-diminished. Note that this is the same chord that occurs as the leading tone in the relative major.
- There are two types of seventh chords that are *not* one of the Five Basic Seventh Chords: the mM7 (on **i**) and the Aug M7 (on **III⁺**). These seventh chords are almost never used in common-practice style.

There are many triads and seventh chords on the menu now. Some are commonly used, some rarely used, and some are never used on the AP exam. So the question to ask is **"Where do I use this information and what chords should be used?"** You will apply this information when doing harmonic dictation (FR 3 or 4), when harmonizing a melody (FR 7), and when analyzing chords visually and aurally. Let me be very specific!

In major, use: I   ii   ii⁷   IV   V   V⁷   vi   vii°   vii°⁷

In **F Major** these chords are:

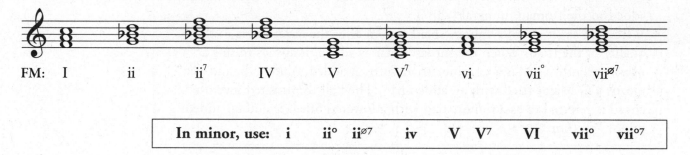

FM: I   ii   ii⁷   IV   V   V⁷   vi   vii°   vii°⁷

In minor, use: i   ii°   ii°⁷   iv   V   V⁷   VI   vii°   vii°⁷

In **F harmonic minor** these chords are:

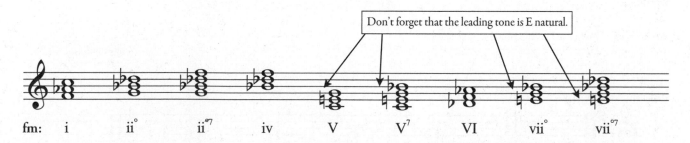

Don't forget that the leading tone is E natural.

fm: i   ii°   ii°⁷   iv   V   V⁷   VI   vii°   vii°⁷

What do we observe?

- The V, V^7 and vii° chords are the same in both major and minor!
- The half-diminished seventh chord occurs on the leading tone in major (vii$^{\varnothing 7}$) and the supertonic in minor (ii$^{\varnothing 7}$).
- The *only* place a fully-diminished seventh chord occurs is on the leading tone in minor (vii°^{7}).
- We are *not* using the I^7 or i^7, the III chord (at all), the IV^7 or iv^7, vi^7 or VI^7. It's not necessary. It's not common. It's not characteristic of the period and/or style.

INVERSION SYMBOLS

Now that we know how to label chords in a diatonic context using Roman numerals, let's consider how we can label the triads that are inverted. A root-position triad has a third and a fifth above the bass. This is implied but not written in the Roman numeral (with no superscript). You *could* see this chord symbol as I($^5_3$).

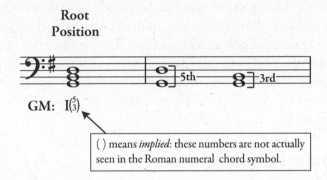

( ) means *implied*: these numbers are not actually seen in the Roman numeral chord symbol.

From our earlier discussion we know the third of a chord is in the bass in a first inversion triad. The interval of a sixth above the bass identifies the root of the chord in first inversion. The inversion symbol is a superscript Arabic number *6* placed to the right of the Roman numeral. Another way to explain this is that the chord symbol *I⁶* indicates a tonic triad with the third of the chord as the lowest sounding note (in the bass), creating the interval of a sixth between the bass note and the root.

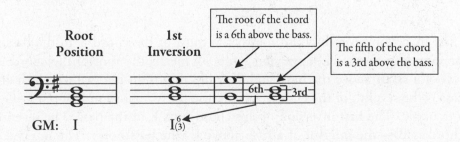

In second inversion we know that the fifth of the chord is the lowest sounding note; the intervals above the bass are a sixth and a fourth. The note a fourth above the bass is the root. The inversion symbol for a second-inversion triad is superscript $^6_4$ added to the chord symbol. The chord symbol V^6_4 indicates a dominant triad in second inversion.

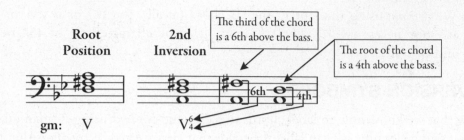

In seventh chords the inversion symbols represent *three* notes above the bass—some are written in the symbol; others are "understood" to be there, or implied, but are not written. A seventh chord in root position has the intervals of a third, a fifth, and a seventh above the bass. The only number written is the superscript ^{7}, the $^{\varnothing 7}$, or the $^{\circ 7}$ added to the Roman numeral to indicate the added interval. For example, V^7 means the dominant triad with an added seventh or ii^7 means the supertonic triad with an added seventh.

ROOT POSITION 7TH CHORD

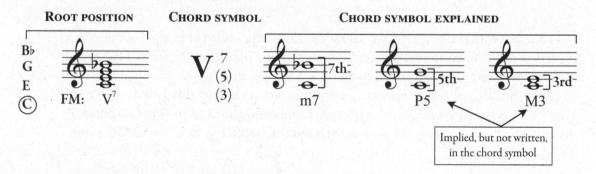

A first inversion seventh chord means the third of the chord is in the bass (the lowest sounding tone). The inversion symbol $^6_5$ means the root of the chord is an interval of a **sixth** above the bass, and the note that is an interval of a fifth above the bass is the seventh of the chord. We will use the V^7 chord in FM (C–E–G–B♭) as an example. The first inversion of this chord puts E in the bass. The seventh of the chord is B♭—the interval of a fifth above E (the bass note). The interval of a third above the bass is the fifth of the chord. It is implied but not written in the inversion symbol.

1st Inversion 7th chord

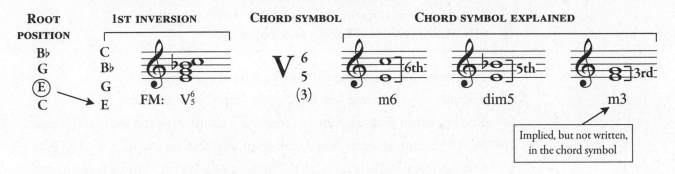

The seventh chord in **second inversion** has the Roman numeral chord symbol in this example of V$_3^4$, indicating there is an interval of a fourth above the bass (the root) and an interval of a third above the bass (the seventh of the chord). The interval of a sixth above the bass (the third of the chord) is implied but not written in the chord symbol.

2nd Inversion 7th chord

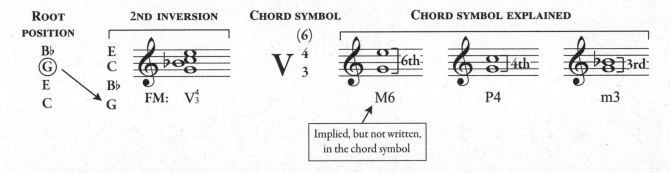

The **third inversion** of a seventh chord has a Roman numeral chord symbol of V$_2^4$, or possibly V². The pitch that is an interval of a fourth above the bass is the third of the chord. In a third inversion chord, the seventh of the chord is in the bass and the root is the interval of a second above the bass. The interval of a sixth above the bass (the fifth of the chord) is implied but not written.

3rd Inversion 7th chord

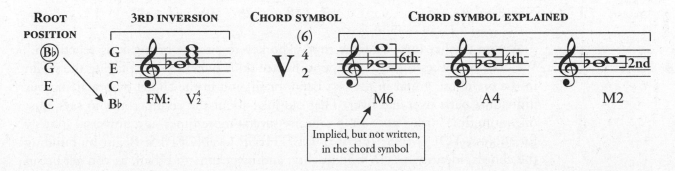

> 💡 An easy way to remember the inversion symbols is to think of all of them connected like a phone number I call the
> **INVERSION HOTLINE: 664-765-4342**

^{6} —First inversion triad (the third of the chord is in the bass)

$^6_4$ —Second inversion triad (the fifth of the chord is in the bass)

^{7} —Root-position seventh chord (a four-note chord with the root in the bass)

$^6_5$ —First inversion seventh chord (the third of a seventh chord is in the bass)

$^4_3$ —Second inversion seventh chord (the fifth of a seventh chord is in the bass)

$^4_2$ —Third inversion seventh chord (the seventh of a seventh chord is in the bass)

Let's go back to *Aurelia* one more time and label the chords with Roman numerals and inversions. In D Major the diatonic chord symbols are:

D	Em (Em^7)	F♯m	G	A (A^7)	Bm	C♯° (C♯$^{m7♭5}$)
I	**ii (ii^7)**	**iii**	**IV**	**V (V^7)**	**vi**	**vii° (vii^{ø7})**

Now we can transfer the information we have already gathered to create the harmonic analysis using the Roman numerals and inversion symbols.

Aurelia

Samuel Wesley
(1810-1876)

A wise teacher once told me that "The key to success in music is repetition." We become successful with our performance skills (whether it is playing the violin in the orchestra, guitar in the jazz band, or singing in the choir) by practicing our individual parts over and over. That old joke about the conductor who says "just one more time" (then goes on to rehearse several more times) is a universal strategy for success. YOU MUST PRACTICE THESE CONCEPTS. Begin by building the chords, identifying the root, quality, and inversion; and then, as you get better at that process, begin transferring the information to Roman numerals with inversions. The more you practice, the faster you will go and the easier it will become. You are practicing the language.

Here is a new chorale for more practice. Identify the chords with circled notes by leaving out the pitches that are circled. More later. Something you don't know? Just label that chord with chord name, quality, inversion, and continue.

Eventide

William H. Monk
(1823-1889)

This is a diminished triad in first inversion. **What do we know for sure?** This chord is **not** found in E♭M. It is the leading tone triad in B♭ Major!

FIGURED BASS

During the Common Practice Period (CPP) composers and performers used a system of reading music from "shorthand" of the bass line and figures (mostly numbers and accidentals) beneath the bass. This shorthand style of reading music is called **figured bass**. The numbers represent the intervals above the bass that create the chords. Figured bass consists of the bass line and the figures below; however, the voicing of the chord, the melody, and the linear movement of each line was determined by the performer. In the days of Bach, figured bass was used much as a lead-sheet in pop music notation (with chord symbols above the melody line) is today. Keyboard players (often harpsichord or organ) looked at the bass line and the figures and knew what chords to play above them and improvised the harmonization. A chord with no figures beneath is a root-position triad; you may see the figures ⅗. A triad in first inversion has the Arabic number 6 indicating that the interval of a sixth above the bass is the root of the chord. There is also an interval of a third above the bass, but it is "implied," not written. A chord in second inversion has the numbers ⁶⁄₄ placed with the 6 on top of the 4, indicating that these two intervals are found above the bass note. The note an interval of a fourth above the bass is the root of the chord. Sound familiar? Figured bass and inversion symbols are very similar but do not serve the same purpose. The purpose of figured bass is to indicate intervals above a given bass line. The purpose of inversion symbols is to indicate the lowest sounding note within a chord.

Realizing Figured Bass

Here is an example of figured bass using root position chords and inversions. From this, we do a **realization of the figured bass** (writing out the chords) to create a chord stack and the Roman numeral symbols.

Any pitch in the bass that has the figures ⅗, or *no figures* at all beneath it, means a root-position triad. In our example, chord numbers 1, 3, 5, and 9 are root-position G Major triads (I). Chord number 8 is also root-position, but the triad is built on D, which is V in the key of GM. Chord 2 has an F♯ in the bass as well as an A in the chord (third above) and a D (sixth above). The pitch that is a sixth above the bass (D) is the root. This triad is V⁶. Chord 6 has a C in the bass and a figured bass symbol of 6. The root of the chord is an interval of a sixth above the bass note (A). The chord is A–C–E, a minor triad in first inversion built on the supertonic (ii⁶). Chords 4 and 7 have the figures ⁶⁄₄, meaning that there is an interval of a sixth and an interval of a fourth above the bass. The pitch that is a fourth above the bass is the root.

These are the *realized* pitches above the bass according to the figured bass symbols. For many students, this is difficult to remember or keep in their head as they try to do harmonic analysis or compose a part-writing exercise. So, I use what I call the **chord stack**, which is essentially the chord "menu" of available pitches.

CREATING THE CHORD STACK

Creating the *chord stack* simply places the pitch names in snowman style, determines the root, and leads you to the correct Roman numeral. Circling the pitch that is the bass note leads you to the correct inversion. This was first introduced on page 115 and is discussed further in Chapter 8.

Chord Stack

G:	I	V⁶	I	IV⁶₄	I	ii°⁶	I⁶₄	V	I
	D	A	D	Ⓖ	D	E	Ⓓ	A	D
	B	Ⓕ	B	E	B	Ⓒ	B	F#	B
	Ⓖ	D	Ⓖ	C	Ⓖ	A	G	Ⓓ	Ⓖ

ALTERED NOTES IN THE CHORD STACK

If notes within the chord are altered by scalar variance or mode mixture, then figured bass symbols would include slashes or plus signs to indicate raising a pitch, or flats, sharps, or naturals with the number to tell the performer to raise the interval of a sixth above the bass or lower the seventh, for example. If the note a *third above the bass* in a root-position chord is to be raised, the figured bass would be only the accidental. It may be a sharp sign, meaning to raise a natural, or it may be a natural sign, meaning to raise a flat. The number 3, indicating an interval of a third, is *not* needed. Inversion symbols do *not* include slashes, plus signs, accidentals, or other symbols.

> What do figured bass symbols tell you that the inversion symbols don't? Figured bass, unlike inversion symbols, tells you when a pitch is altered and *how* it is altered. Inversions tell you what chord member is in the bass; the quality of the chord represented by the Roman numeral **implies** any altered pitches.

Here is a figured bass example in G minor using seventh chords and altered chord members. To realize the figured bass, we create the chord stack and determine the Roman numerals.

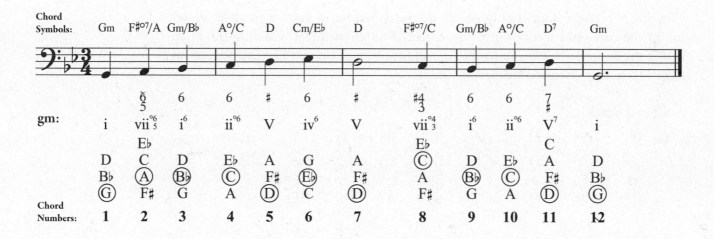

Chords 1, 5, 7, 11, and 12 are in root position. In chord 2, the 6̆ tells you the pitch that is the interval of a sixth above the bass is raised (F♯). The F♯ is the leading tone in G harmonic minor. It is a first inversion, fully-diminished, leading-tone seventh chord. Chord 5 is in root position and the interval of a third above the bass is raised, shown by the sharp sign in the figured bass. Chord 8 is also a fully-diminished, leading-tone seventh chord, this time in second inversion. The ♯4 (F♯) is the root of the chord. Notice that the sharp sign in the figured bass is not part of the Roman numeral chord symbol. Chord 11 is a root-position V⁷ chord. The ♯ below the 7 indicates that the note a third above the bass is raised (F♯ is the leading tone in G harmonic minor, making the quality of the triad major).

Chapter Summary

- In tonal music the **harmonic function** of a triad is associated with the scale degree on which it is built.
- Qualities of **diatonic triads** in a major key are:

M	m	m	M	M	m	dim
tonic	supertonic	mediant	subdominant	dominant	submediant	leading tone
I	ii	iii	IV	V	vi	vii°

- The harmonic form of minor is used most often for **harmonizing** in a minor key. Qualities of diatonic triads in harmonic minor are:

m	dim	$\left[\begin{array}{c} \text{A} \\ \text{mediant} \end{array}\right.$	$\left.\vphantom{}\right]$	m	M	M	dim
tonic	supertonic			subdominant	dominant	submediant	leading tone
i	ii°	III⁺		iv	V	VI	vii°

- The chord built on the seventh scale degree in natural minor is called the **subtonic triad**. It is a major chord—a whole step below tonic. The subtonic and the major mediant (III) are commonly used triads from natural minor.

  - **III** (from the natural minor form of the scale) is more common than III⁺.
  - **VII** (also from natural minor) is just as common as vii° in minor.

- When we compare the qualities in the diatonic major and harmonic minor scales we find that the dominant chord (major) and the leading-tone chord (diminished) are the same quality in *both*.
- When a chord is in first inversion, the note that is the interval of a sixth above the bass is the root, therefore the inversion symbol is a superscript Arabic number 6 placed to the right of the Roman numeral.
- When a chord is in second inversion, the intervals above the bass are a sixth and a fourth. The note that is a fourth above the bass is the root. The inversion symbol for a second inversion triad is superscript $^6_4$ added to the Roman numeral chord symbols.
- A **seventh chord** contains four notes: the root, third, fifth, and seventh. Because this arrangement of tones contains an interval of a seventh, which is a dissonant interval, all seventh chords are dissonant (unstable).
- **Five Basic Seventh Chords:**

  - Major seventh (major triad + major seventh)
  - Dominant seventh (major triad + minor seventh)
  - Minor seventh (minor triad + minor seventh)
  - Half-diminished seventh (diminished triad + minor seventh)
  - Fully-diminished seventh (diminished triad + diminished seventh)

- A seventh chord in first inversion has the third of the chord in the bass, the root of the chord is the interval of a **sixth** above the bass, and the added seventh is the interval of a **fifth** above the bass. The inversion symbol is $^6_5$.

- A seventh chord in second inversion has the fifth of the chord in the bass, the root of the chord is the interval of a **fourth** above the bass, and the added seventh is a **third** above the bass. The inversion symbol is $\frac{4}{3}$.
- A seventh chord in third inversion has the seventh of the chord in the bass and the root of the chord is a **second** (the inversion of a seventh) above. The inversion is commonly written $\frac{4}{2}$ but sometimes simply ^{2}.
- An easy way to remember the inversions is the **"Inversion Hotline"**: **664-765-4342**.
- The **fully-diminished seventh chord** (diminished triad and diminished seventh) occurs on the leading tone in harmonic minor.
- It is significant that the **V**^{7} chord (major triad with minor seventh) is exactly the same in major and harmonic minor and *only* occurs on the dominant.
- **Figured bass** consists of the bass line and the Arabic numbers under the bass line (figures) that represent the intervals above the bass to be played. The voicing of the chord and the linear movement of each line is determined by the performer.
- The purpose of inversion symbols is to indicate the lowest sounding note within a chord.
- The Arabic numbers used in inversions indicate the same thing when used as part of figured bass—**intervals above the bass**—but the added accidentals, slashes, or plus signs that may be part of figured bass are *not* included in inversions.
- Chords to use when harmonizing are:

In major, use:	I	ii	ii^7	IV	V	V^7	vi	vii°	vii$^{\varnothing 7}$

In minor, use:	i	ii°	ii$^{\varnothing 7}$	iv	V	V^7	VI	VII	vii°	vii$^{°7}$

Practice Exercises

Questions 1–2 refer to the excerpt below by Mozart.

Andantino

Wolfgang Amadeus Mozart
(1756–1791)

1. This excerpt reflects what two tonalites?

   (A) E♭ Major and C minor
   (B) G minor and B♭ Major
   (C) E♭ Major and B♭ Major
   (D) B♭ Major and B♭ minor

2. What is the signal that you have changed tonal center?

   (A) The change from A♭ to A natural
   (B) The opening note is G
   (C) The final chord is B♭ Major
   (D) Both A and C

Questions 3–6 refer to *He Leadeth Me*.

He Leadeth Me

William B. Bradbury
(1816–1868)

3. The key of this hymn tune is

   (A) A minor
   (B) D minor
   (C) D Major
   (D) B minor

4. This hymn has four phrases. How does the analysis between phrase 1 and phrase 2 differ?

   (A) Both phrase 1 and 2 begin with a I_4^6 chord but end differently.
   (B) Phrase 1 ends with dominant and phrase 2 ends with tonic.
   (C) Phrases 1 and 2 both end with tonic but begin differently.
   (D) Phrases 1 and 2 both end with dominant.

5. EVERY phrase

   (A) begins with a tonic chord anacrusis
   (B) begins with a dominant chord anacrusis
   (C) ends with a tonic chord
   (D) is the same length

6. The chord in the dotted box (the same in both places) functions as

   (A) ii
   (B) IV
   (C) iii
   (D) vi

Since we are comparing phrases, it is interesting to note that:

- Phrases 1 and 2 *begin* with the same melody.
- Phrases 3 and 4 *begin* with the same melody.
- Phrases 2, 3, and 4 have one measure that is exactly the same in all four parts (in brackets).
- Phrases 1 and 3 end exactly the same.
- Phrases 2 and 4 end exactly the same.

Questions 7–12 refer to the *String Quartet No. 18 in E minor.*

String Quartet No. 18 in E minor

Gaetano Donizetti
(1797–1848)

7. The harmonic analysis of measures 1 and 2 would best be identified as

    (A) i–V–i
    (B) i–IV–i
    (C) i–v–i
    (D) i–iv–i

8. Violin I has what type of scale passage in measures 2 and 3?

    (A) E melodic minor
    (B) E harmonic minor
    (C) A melodic minor
    (D) A Major

9. The two eighth note chords in measure 3 (within the box) would be correctly analyzed as

    (A) vii°–i
    (B) V–i
    (C) V$^6_5$–I
    (D) V$^6_5$–i

10. The harmonic analysis of the chords within the box in measures 7 and 8 would best be identified as

    (A) V$^4_3$–i–V
    (B) V$^6_5$–I–V^7
    (C) V$^6_5$–i–V
    (D) V$^4_3$–I–V^7

11. The third of the chord is played by what voice in measure 10?

    (A) Violin I
    (B) Violin II
    (C) Viola, upper voice
    (D) Viola, lower voice

12. The last three chords of this excerpt are most like what other chords in this piece?

    (A) Measure 4
    (B) Measures 5 and 6
    (C) The first three chords
    (D) There are no other chords like it.

Questions 13–20 pertain to this string quartet by Haydn.

String Quartet, Op. 20, No. 3 in G minor

(Franz) Joseph Haydn
(1732-1809)

13. In G minor, chord 1 is a

    (A) fully-diminished leading-tone chord in first inversion
    (B) leading-tone triad in first inversion
    (C) major triad in second inversion
    (D) dominant seventh chord in second inversion

14. The quality of chord 2 is

    (A) diminished
    (B) minor
    (C) half-diminished
    (D) fully-diminished

15. Chords 1, 2, and 3 all have the same note in the bass. The opening key is G minor. The correct Roman numeral analysis of these three chords is

    (A) vii⁶–vii°⁷–V⁷
    (B) vii°⁶–vii°⁶₅–V⁷
    (C) vii°⁶–vii°⁶₅–V⁶₅
    (D) vii°⁶–vii°⁶₅–V⁴₃

16. In chord 4, what note is the accidental?

    (A) A natural
    (B) E natural
    (C) B natural
    (D) F natural

17. What is the quality of chord 4?

    (A) Major
    (B) Minor
    (C) Diminished
    (D) Augmented

18. Chord 5 would best be identified as

    (A) E♭ Major triad
    (B) C Major in first inversion
    (C) C minor triad in root position
    (D) C minor triad in first inversion

19. Chord 4 is **not** in our original key of G minor, but chord 5 functions as the

    (A) supertonic
    (B) subdominant
    (C) submediant
    (D) mediant

20. What is the relationship between chords 4 and 5?

    (A) Leading-tone triad to tonic in the key of C minor
    (B) Dominant triad to tonic in the key of C minor
    (C) Leading-tone triad to tonic in the key of C Major
    (D) Dominant triad in the key of B♭ major

ANSWER KEY

1. **C**	6. **D**	11. **C**	16. **C**
2. **D**	7. **D**	12. **C**	17. **C**
3. **C**	8. **B**	13. **B**	18. **D**
4. **B**	9. **D**	14. **D**	19. **B**
5. **D**	10. **A**	15. **D**	20. **A**

ANSWERS EXPLAINED

1. **(C)** The excerpt reflects the keys of E♭ Major and B♭ Major.

2. **(D)** Both the change from A♭ to A natural and the final chord being B♭ Major signals the change of tonality.

3. **(C)** The key is D Major.

4. **(B)** Phrase 1 ends with a dominant triad and phrase 2 ends with a tonic triad.

5. **(D)** Every phrase is the same length.

6. **(D)** The chord is B–D–F♯ which is a minor triad that functions as the submediant (vi) in D Major.

7. **(D)** The harmonic progression of measures 1 and 2 is i–iv–i.

8. **(B)** Violin I plays a scale passage in E harmonic minor.

9. **(D)** The correct analysis is V_5^6–i.

10. **(A)** The harmonic progression is V_3^4–i–V.

11. **(C)** Viola upper voice is playing the G that is the third of the E minor chord.

12. **(C)** The last three chords are most like the first three chords. What is different is the voicing of the viola and the cello.

13. **(B)** Chord 1 is the leading-tone triad in first inversion (vii°⁶).

14. **(D)** Chord 2 is F♯–A–C–E♭ with the A in the bass. It is fully-diminished.

15. **(D)** The correct analysis is vii°⁶–vii°$_5^6$–V$_3^4$.

16. **(C)** The accidental is B natural (alto clef!).

17. **(C)** The chord (B–D–F) is diminished.

18. **(D)** Chord 5 is spelled C–E♭–G with the E♭ in the bass making it a C minor triad in first inversion.

19. **(B)** Chord 5 is the subdominant in C minor (iv).

20. **(A)** The relationship between chords 4 and 5 is leading tone to tonic in the key of C minor. The B natural would be the leading tone ($\hat{7}$) in the key of C minor. A diminished chord *only* functions as a leading tone (in major or minor) or as a supertonic in a minor tonality. The purpose of chord 4 is to intensify chord 5—the C minor triad.

Harmonic Organization III: Function and Cadences

7

- Chord Function
  - Tonic Function (T)
  - Subdominant Function (S)
  - PreDominant Function (PD)
  - Dominant Function (D)
  - T–S–D–T

- Cadences
  - Authentic
    - Perfect Authentic (PAC)
    - Imperfect Authentic (IAC)
  - Half (HC)
    - Phrygian Half (PHC)
  - Plagal (PC)
  - Deceptive (DC)
- Resolution Tones
- Tendency Tones

CHORD FUNCTION

Function refers to the placement of the chord within the key. You can also think of function as the "job" of that chord. The G Major chord will have a different role when it is the tonic in G than when it is the dominant in C. Refer back to the material found in Chapter 3 regarding stable and active notes within the scale and review this information to find out *why*.

Certain pitches in the scale sound stronger or more stable than others. The strongest most stable pitch is, of course, the tonic. Scale degrees 4, 6, and 7 are **active tones**. The most active, the leading tone, or the 7th scale degree, has the most musical energy to move to resolve. It is this feeling of tension and release that moves music forward. We will refer to this chart* often in talking about melody as well as harmony. **You will note that the two most active scale degrees, 4 and 7, resolve to the two most stable scale degrees, 1 and 3.** The other scale tones align themselves from strong to weak in this order:

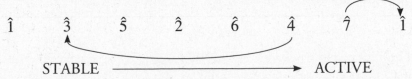

$$\hat{1} \quad \hat{3} \quad \hat{5} \quad \hat{2} \quad \hat{6} \quad \hat{4} \quad \hat{7} \quad \hat{1}$$

STABLE ——————————→ ACTIVE

*Courtesy of Dr. Blaise Ferrandino, Texas Christian University, Fort Worth, Texas.

- Within the major scale, the most active tones, the 4th and 7th scale degrees, have **half-step** relationships to the most stable tones, the 3rd and the tonic. These are called **tendency tones** because they have the tendency to resolve by half step. Scale degrees 1 and 3 are considered **resolution tones** because they are the notes *to which* the active tones move. In other words, you resolve the instability of $\hat{4}$ and $\hat{7}$ by moving a half step to the closest stable tones—$\hat{4}$ (*Fa*) moves to the $\hat{3}$ (*Mi*) and the $\hat{7}$ (*Ti*) resolves to tonic $\hat{1}$ (*Do*). The resolution is always a **diatonic** step away.
- Within the minor scale the 6th scale degree (*Le*) resolves down a half step to $\hat{5}$ (*So*). The leading tone (*Ti*) again resolves upward to *Do*.

Now that we are stacking up notes into chords, the amount of tension within the chord (instability or degree of activity) is determined by the stability or activity of its members. Just by looking at this chart we can tell that the tonic chord is the most stable chord because $\hat{1}$–$\hat{3}$–$\hat{5}$ are at the far left of the chart. Compare that to a chord that contains *both* $\hat{4}$ and $\hat{7}$ (vii° and V⁷). The leading-tone triad and dominant seventh chords are very "active" chords, with the most active members wanting to resolve. Quite simply, that is why in common-practice style music the vii° and V⁷ chords generally progress to the tonic chord.

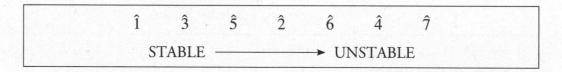

Now let's compare a single **major chord** (G–B–D) in three very different functions. As **tonic** (**I**) in G Major (chord members $\hat{1}$–$\hat{3}$–$\hat{5}$), the chord is very stable. As **subdominant** (**IV**) in D Major ($\hat{4}$–$\hat{6}$–$\hat{1}$) the chord has two members moving toward the right of the chart but one member all the way to the left ($\hat{1}$), which reduces the level of activity of the $\hat{4}$ and $\hat{6}$. The **dominant triad** (**V**) in C Major ($\hat{5}$–$\hat{7}$–$\hat{2}$) has one tone to the far right ($\hat{7}$), one in the middle, and one moving toward stable—producing a more active chord than IV. We are comparing the same chord to a different FUNCTION. Using this stability chart we can determine which chords function as part of the same group or family.

Here are our families according to **FUNCTION**:

Tonic	Subdominant or Predominant	Dominant
I i and vi VI	IV iv and ii ii°	V and vii°

So what about the mediant (iii, III, or III⁺) chord? It is really a "chameleon" chord, changing dramatically depending on what chord member is doubled and what chords are around it. The iii chord contains $\hat{3}$ and $\hat{5}$, both fairly stable tones, but also $\hat{7}$, the *most* active tone; therefore, this chord often functions both as tonic and as dominant. The mediant chord (III in natural minor) is found occasionally on the AP Music Theory exam, primarily in identification. It is **not** used in harmonic dictation, realizing figured bass, or in part writing from Roman numerals. Therefore, in this guide there is little mention of the role of the mediant chord.

The tonic family chords (I and vi) are the most stable and therefore are most often a goal or "destination." Dominant family chords (vii and V) are the most active and move music forward with energy to resolve (most often to a member of the tonic family). The leading-tone triad contains *both Ti* and *Fa*—the tendency tones that need to be resolved—and is most often in first inversion (vii°⁶). The subdominant family (chords IV, iv, ii, ii°) are generally considered transition chords. Their "job" is to transition or connect stable and active chords. Many times, especially in the Common Practice Period, the subdominant family chords come before dominant family chords and therefore are often referred to as *predominant*. In common-practice style, harmonies progressed in this T–S–D–T fashion.

Doubling of chord members will impact the function of a chord. The first choice for most chords is to double the root of the chord. In second inversion ($^6_4$) chords, double the fifth of the chord. Double the third if you have a reason, such as doubling the third of a minor chord to avoid parallelism or to achieve a smooth linear motion.

How is function altered when a seventh is added? A seventh chord is always more active, first and foremost because it has the interval of a seventh (or a second if inverted), which is a dissonant interval creating more tension and need to resolve. The dominant seventh chord, V⁷, zooms ahead to a very active position because the note added is *Fa* giving the V⁷ chord BOTH *tendency* tones (the leading-tone triad is the other chord with both *Ti* and *Fa*). The V⁷ is more active than V, and the vii⁰⁷ and vii°⁷ (both half-diminished and fully-diminished) are more active than the leading-tone triad. The other commonly used seventh chord is the ii⁷ or ii⁰⁷. Both the supertonic triad and the supertonic seventh chord are considered predominant function while the ii⁷ has even more dissonant energy and intensity to resolve to V.

CADENCES

When speaking or writing, our thoughts are punctuated with commas to represent a pause in ideas, but not a complete statement, while other marks are used to recognize the end of a sentence or completed thought. When you come to the end of a musical phrase, the natural feeling of rest or release of tension is called **cadence**.

Rhythm often slows down when it comes to a resting place, so you should expect to see changes as you approach the cadence.

> **A cadence is the harmonic, melodic, and rhythmic conclusion to a phrase.** The cadence also helps to establish the tonal center. *It is the proof we need to confidently determine the key.*

- **Authentic Cadence**—The most common **phrase-ending** chord progression uses the dominant chord (V) to set up the tension and the tonic (I or i) for the release. The dominant–tonic progression is enhanced or intensified by using the V^7 chord instead of the triad. The added dissonance gives it a stronger pull to tonic.
  - **Perfect Authentic (PAC)**—The *perfect authentic cadence* is a concluding cadence that requires both dominant and tonic chords to be in **root position**. The term *authentic* refers to the harmonic progression of V–I. The tonic chord must also double the root of the chord in the soprano creating the *perfect* interval (octave) between the bass and soprano.
  - **Imperfect Authentic (IAC)**—The *imperfect authentic cadence* is a weaker authentic (V–I) cadence that has either chord inverted, or has a chord member other than the root in the soprano of the tonic chord. A cadence utilizing the leading tone (vii° or vii°^{6}) to tonic progression is also considered an imperfect authentic cadence.
- **Plagal Cadence (PC)**—A slightly weaker progression using the subdominant (IV) to tonic to provide the resting point. Although it is an effective cadence, it isn't as strong as the authentic cadence. The plagal cadence is often called the "Amen cadence" as it is traditionally the progression used when singing "Amen" at the end of hymns.
- **Deceptive Cadence (DC)** (or interrupted)—An ending progression where the dominant chord is unexpectedly resolved to the submediant (VI or vi) instead of the tonic.
- The **Half Cadence (HC)**—Ends on the dominant (V). It is an unresolved tension used especially in the middle of a melody, an inconclusive cadence that typically ends on a root position V. The half cadence, since it is unresolved, acts like a comma would in a sentence and must be followed by another phrase that completes (resolves) the musical thought.
  - **Phrygian Half Cadence (PHC)**—A specific kind of half cadence that occurs in harmonic minor. The dominant chord is preceded by the minor subdominant in first inversion (iv^6). The descending bass line (from $\hat{6}$ to $\hat{5}$ or solfege *Le* to *So*) is approached from above by a half step and is characteristic of the Phrygian mode with its half step from $\hat{2}$ to $\hat{1}$.

Cadences

Perfect Authentic Cadence = **PAC**

- **Dominant to Tonic**
  V–I or **V–i**
  OR
  V⁷–I or **V⁷–i**
- Both chords in ROOT position and the tonic chord doubles the root in soprano

Imperfect Authentic Cadence = **IAC**

- **V–I** **V–i** **vii°⁶–I** or **i**
  OR
  V⁷–I **vii°⁷–I** **vii°⁷–i**
- Either chord is inverted, tonic chord has $\hat{3}$ or $\hat{5}$ in soprano or leading-tone substitutes for V

Plagal Cadence = **PC**

- **"Amen" cadence** **IV–I** or **iv–i**

Deceptive Cadence = **DC**

- **V–vi** or **V–VI**

End with tonic function chord I or vi

Half Cadence = **HC**

- Ends with **V** or **V⁷**
- Commonly preceded by IV, ii, ii⁶ (Predominant harmony), and I$^6_4$ or i$^6_4$

Phrygian Half Cadence = **PHC**

- Occurs in harmonic minor: **iv⁶–V** (*Le* half step down to *So* in bass)

Here are examples of all types of cadences in various keys:

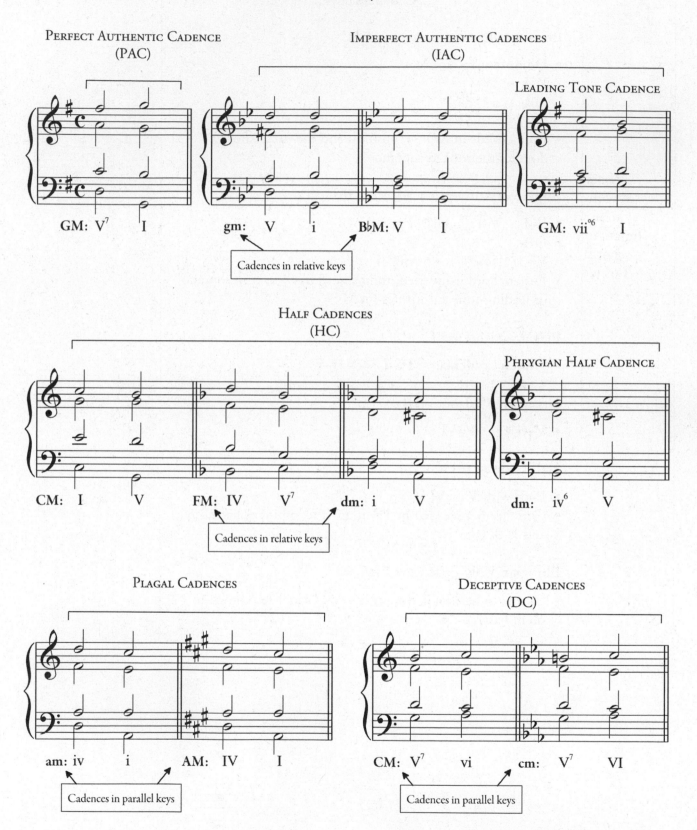

REVIEW

Let's look at the cadences and "connect a few more dots" in the familiar hymn tune "Aurelia."

Aurelia

Samuel Wesley
(1810–1876)

DM: I   IV⁶₄   I   Imperfect Authentic Cadence in D Major → I⁶₄   V⁷   I

Half Cadence in D Major → V

Imperfect Authentic Cadence in E minor → V⁶   i

Perfect Authentic Cadence in D Major → I⁶₄   V⁷   I

The first cadence is *imperfect* authentic because the soprano is singing the third of the chord instead of the root. The I$_4^6$ chord before the V^7 chord is dominant function with the fifth of the chord doubled, reinforcing the dominant (*So*). The V^7 chord correctly resolves the seventh of the chord, *Fa*, downward to *Mi* in the soprano, and *Ti* in the alto resolves upward to *Do*. The second cadence is a half cadence because the phrase ends with the V. At this point when we find something we cannot identify in the key we simply determine the quality and the root (use chord symbols, not Roman numerals) and see IF and HOW it might relate to the chord after it. The chord right before the half cadence is a G♯–B–D chord; it is a diminished triad with G♯ as the root. What do we know for sure? A diminished chord functions as a leading tone and leading tones (*Ti*) resolve to tonic (*Do*). The G♯ chord is not in the key of D Major, but the cadence chord (V) is. The G♯ chord is from A Major, our cadence chord, and is used to add intensity (more on this in Chapter 12).

The third cadence ends with an E minor chord that is supertonic in our key of D Major. There is *no* cadence that ends with supertonic; therefore, we must be in a different key. The chord prior to the E minor contains a D♯, the leading tone in E minor. **Remember: A viable cadence is the proof we need to confidently determine the key.** Therefore, the third cadence is an imperfect authentic cadence (V^6–i) in the key of E minor. The final cadence is perfect authentic in our original key of D Major.

Notice in our two authentic cadences in D Major that the chord progression is I$_4^6$–V^7–I. The bass line for both cadences is *So-So-Do*. The soprano for cadence 1 is *So-Fa-Mi* (IAC) and *Do-Ti-Do* (PAC) for the final cadence.

Hearing *So-So-Do* in the bass commonly produces the I$_4^6$–V^7–I cadence, and when paired with *Mi-Re-Do*, or as in this example *Do-Ti-Do* and *So-Fa-Mi* in the soprano, it is confirmed. Use this knowledge to help you when listening to progressions. It's the norm.

The first measure is an example of using the IV chord to *prolong tonic function*, and not as subdominant or predominant function. Notice the bass line stays on the same pitch (this is called a pedal); the D is a common tone occurring in both the I chord and the IV, with the subdominant chord in second inversion. The alto and tenor voices move up to the neighbor above and back down.

Did you notice the return of the *same melody* at the end? Measures 1 and 2 are the same melody as measures 13 and 14. Measure 13 is also the same harmonic progression as 1; however, the harmony in measure 14 is different from measure 2.

We also notice that generally the bass line and the soprano move by step, skip, and leap, and are more disjunct than the alto and tenor. In this example the bass seems to stay on the same pitch frequently and also moves upward by step. The alto and tenor seem to "hang around" the same pitch—the alto seems to center around D and the tenor seems to center around A.

This is what music in common-practice style looks like and sounds like. The progressions found here in *Aurelia* are standard common-practice style progressions. The AP exam expects you to be able to identify, notate, and hear what is representative of this style. For more practice, go back to page 135 and identify the cadences in "Eventide."

Chapter Summary

- **Function refers to the placement of the chord within the key.**
- Within the major scale, the most active tones, the 4th and 7th scale degrees, have **half-step** relationships to the most stable tones, $\hat{3}$ and the tonic. These are called **tendency** tones because they have the tendency to resolve by half step.
- The amount of tension within the chord (instability or degree of activity) is determined by the stability or activity of the chord members.
- Here are the families according to function:

Tonic	Subdominant or Predominant	Dominant
I i and vi VI	IV iv and ii ii°	V and vii°

- In common-practice style, harmonies progressed in "**T–PD–D** resolving to **T**" fashion.
- Function is altered when a seventh is added, the more a chord is inverted, and when you consider what chord member is doubled.
- The more a chord is inverted, the weaker its function or the more it functions like another chord.
- Doubling of chord members will impact the function of a chord. As a **general** rule for doubling, your first choice is to double the root of a chord, and second choice is to double the fifth. Double the third in a minor triad to avoid parallelism or to achieve a smooth linear motion.
- **A cadence is the harmonic, melodic, and rhythmic conclusion to a phrase.** The cadence also helps to establish the tonal center. *It is the proof we need to confidently determine the key.*
- Cadences end with only three chords: I (i), vi (VI), or V (v).

  - Cadences ending with tonic function with the tonic chord are perfect authentic (PAC), imperfect authentic (IAC), and plagal (PC).
  - The cadence ending with tonic function but with the submediant chord [vi (VI)] is the deceptive cadence (DC).
  - Cadences that end on the dominant are the half cadence (HC) and the Phrygian half cadence (PHC).

Practice Exercises

Questions 1–6 pertain to this excerpt from Sonata No. 6 by Beethoven.

Piano Sonata No. 6, Op. 10, No. 2
(Second Movement)

Ludwig van Beethoven
(1770–1827)

1. The harmonic interval between the notes in the top and bottom staff in the anacrusis is a

   (A) m6
   (B) M6
   (C) P8
   (D) P4

2. In measure 1 and measure 3 the occurrence of the E natural leading to the F signals that the opening of this melody is in the key of

   (A) F Major
   (B) F minor
   (C) Eb Major
   (D) Bb Major

3. All of the following are also indicators of the opening tonality **except** the

   (A) F minor arpeggio in measure 2
   (B) unison nature of the beginning of the excerpt
   (C) key signature
   (D) anacrusis to the down beat is *So-Do*

4. At the end of the phrase the tonality shifts to the

   (A) key of the dominant
   (B) key of the subdominant
   (C) parallel major key
   (D) relative major key

5. The cadence within the box at measure 7 is best identified as

   (A) perfect authentic in Ab M
   (B) imperfect authentic in Fm
   (C) half cadence in Ab M
   (D) half cadence in Eb M

6. The appropriate Roman numeral chord symbols at the cadence are

   (A) V–i
   (B) V⁷–I
   (C) I⁶₄–V⁷
   (D) IV–V

Questions 7–9 are based on the following excerpt by Corelli.

Concerto Grosso, Op. 6, No. 8
("Christmas Concerto"—excerpt of string section parts)

Arcangelo Corelli
(1653–1713)

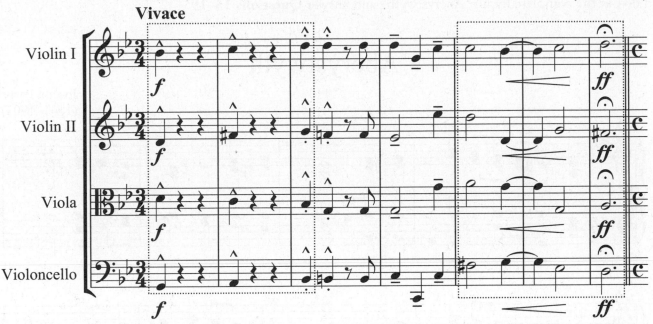

7. The chord progression for the first three chords is

   (A) i–V$^4_3$–i
   (B) i–vii°^{6}–i
   (C) i–ii–i
   (D) i–vii°^{6}–i^6

8. The second chord progression can be identified as

   (A) V^6–I–IV–V
   (B) V$^6_5$–i–iv–V
   (C) V$^6_5$–i–iv^6–V
   (D) V$^6_5$–i–iv^6–V^7

9. The cadence at the fermata can be identified as

   (A) perfect authentic
   (B) Phrygian half
   (C) deceptive
   (D) plagal

10. What is required to *confidently* determine the key?

   (A) Cadence
   (B) Key signature
   (C) Accidentals
   (D) A tonic chord

11. The leading tone chord most often is in

    (A) root position leading to V
    (B) first inversion leading to I or I⁶
    (C) second inversion leading to V
    (D) root position leading to IV

12. Cadences *end* on only what three chords?

    (A) I, IV, V in major (i, iv, V in minor)
    (B) I, ii, V in major (i, ii°, or V in minor)
    (C) I, V, vi in major (i, V, VI in minor)
    (D) I, ii, IV in major (i, ii°, iv in minor)

Look at the complete hymn "Aberystwyth." and answer **Questions 13–19**.

Aberystwyth

Joseph Parry
(1841–1903)

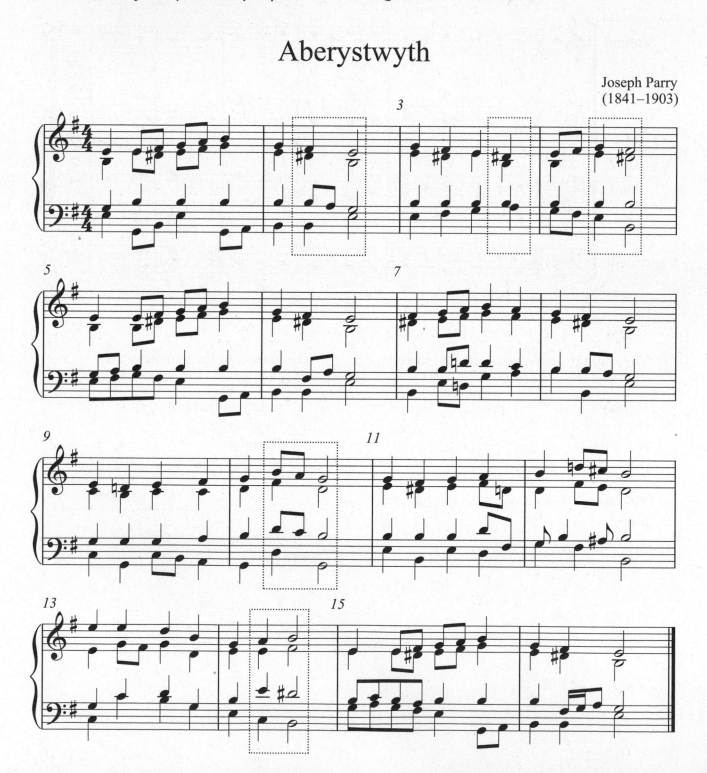

13. Cadence 1 (measure 2) can be identified as

    (A) perfect authentic in E minor
    (B) imperfect authentic in E minor
    (C) a half cadence in G Major
    (D) a deceptive cadence in G Major

14. The cadence at measure 4 can be identified as

    (A) Phrygian half
    (B) half
    (C) imperfect authentic
    (D) deceptive

15. The chord in measure 3 is all of the following except

    (A) third inversion of a seventh chord
    (B) resolves to i^6
    (C) V^4_3
    (D) V^4_2

16. The cadence in measure 10 is best described as

    (A) a half cadence in the key of the tonic
    (B) a half cadence in the key of the dominant
    (C) a perfect authentic cadence in the key of the relative major
    (D) an imperfect authentic cadence in the key of the subdominant

17. Measure 12 briefly implies the key of

    (A) D Major
    (B) D minor
    (C) B minor
    (D) E minor

18. The chord progression for measure 14 is best analyzed as

    (A) $iv–V^7–i$ in B minor
    (B) $IV–ii^6–i$ in B minor
    (C) $i–iv–V$ in E minor
    (D) $i–iv^6–V$ in E minor

19. The cadence in measure 14 is

    (A) plagal
    (B) deceptive
    (C) half
    (D) Phrygian half

20. All of the following progressions could be examples of imperfect authentic cadences **except**

    (A) $V^6–I$
    (B) $IV–I$
    (C) $vii^{o6}–I$
    (D) $V^7–I$

ANSWER KEY

1. **C**	6. **B**	11. **B**	16. **C**
2. **B**	7. **D**	12. **C**	17. **C**
3. **B**	8. **C**	13. **A**	18. **D**
4. **D**	9. **B**	14. **B**	19. **D**
5. **A**	10. **A**	15. **C**	20. **B**

ANSWERS EXPLAINED

1. **(C)** Both the right and left hand are in bass clef; therefore, the interval is a P8.

2. **(B)** The opening key is F (harmonic) minor.

3. **(B)** The key signature of four flats, the anacrusis of **So** leading to **Do**, plus the tonic arpeggio in measure 2 are all conclusive evidence that the key is F minor.

4. **(D)** The phrase ends in A♭ Major—the **relative** major key. This is confirmed by the absence of E natural, the return of E♭, and by the conclusive cadence.

5. **(A)** The cadence is a perfect authentic cadence in A♭ Major.

6. **(B)** The analysis of the last two chords is V⁷–I.

7. **(D)** The progression in G minor is i–vii°⁶–i⁶. Notice that the bass line ascends scalewise by step. The progression is definitely a norm for the style (vii°⁶–i⁶) with the leading tone chord in first inversion resolving to a first-inversion tonic chord.

8. **(C)** Be careful to correctly identify seventh chords and the inversions. As demonstrated here, this is often the only difference between answers.

9. **(B)** The cadence is a Phrygian half cadence. Once you have identified the progression as iv⁶–V it's a "no-brainer." Aurally the clue is the bass line descending by step from above to the dominant.

10. **(A)** The cadence is what allows us to confidently determine the key. It is the final piece of evidence. Look for all the clues, not just the key signature.

11. **(B)** The leading-tone chord is found most often in first inversion and resolves to I/I⁶ (or i/i⁶).

12. **(C)** **Cadences *end* in only I (i), V, or vi (VI).** PERIOD! If your phrase ends on ii, iii, or IV, then you have changed key centers. The tonic function chords (I and vi) are the destination chords and therefore are the ending chords of four out of six cadences. The other two cadences end on V.

13. **(A)** Cadence 1 is perfect authentic in E minor. The chord progression is i⁶₄–V(V⁷)–i. The bass line is **So-So-Do** and the melody is **Me-Re-Do**.

14. **(B)** Cadence 2 is a half cadence in E minor. The progression is i–V.

15. **(C)** The chord in measure 3 is the dominant seventh chord in third inversion (V_2^4). It resolves to I^6 because otherwise it would not correctly resolve the seventh of the chord. The V^7 chord is *So-Ti-Re-Fa* with *Fa* in the bass. As you know, *Fa* must resolve to *Mi* (you can also think of it as the seventh of the chord resolving down by one step); therefore, the chord following V_2^4 *must* be a I^6 so that *Mi* is in the bass.

16. **(C)** Measure 10 ends with a G Major chord. That would be III in our original key of E minor. Since III is not a viable cadence chord we look at the chord preceding the GM chord and note that it is D Major with an added seventh. Since G Major is the relative major of E minor the phrase has shifted to G ending with a perfect authentic cadence.

17. **(C)** Measures 11 and 12 briefly imply the key of B minor. The addition of C♯ might make us think of D Major; however A♯ is not in the key of D Major, but *is* in the key of B minor. The cadence provides the evidence we need (V^7–i) in the key of B minor.

18. **(D)** Measure 14 sees the return of D♯ and also E minor. The correct harmonic analysis is i–iv⁶–V in E minor.

19. **(D)** The cadence in measure 14 is therefore a Phrygian half cadence.

20. **(B)** The progression IV–I is a plagal cadence; all the others *could* be examples of imperfect authentic since we do not know the pitch in the soprano.

AURAL UNIT 2
Multiple-Choice Questions
for Chapters 5–7

Directions: Each of the questions or incomplete statements below is followed by four suggested answers or completions. Select the best answer in each case and circle your answer on the page. In this unit you will see a treble clef icon, 𝄞, which indicates when music will be played. **Questions 1–6** ask you to identify pitch patterns that are played. In each case, the question number will be announced. You will have **ten seconds** to read the choices; then you will hear the musical example played twice, with a brief pause between playings. Remember to read the choices for each question after the number is announced.

Now listen to the music for **Questions 1–6** and identify the pitch patterns that are played.

1. Which of the following pitch patterns is played?

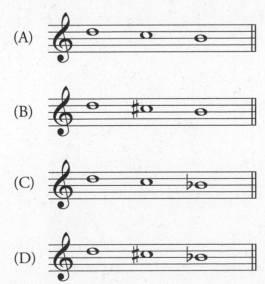

Access audio at
http://barronsbooks.com/ap/mtheory

Pitch pattern, played twice. 𝄞

2. Which of the following intervals is played?

(A)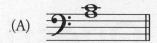

(B)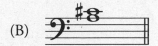

(C)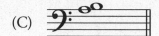

(D)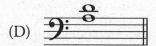

Pitch pattern, played twice.

3. Which of the following triads is played?

(A)

(B)

(C)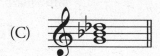

(D)

Pitch pattern, played twice.

4. Which of the following triads is played?

(A)

(B)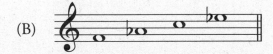

(C)

(D)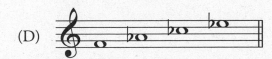

Pitch pattern, played twice.

5. Which of the following pitch patterns is played?

(A)

(B)

(C)

(D)

Pitch pattern, played twice.

6. Which of the following pitch patterns is played?

(A)

(B)

(C)

(D)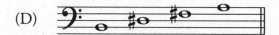

Pitch pattern, played twice.

Go on to the next group of questions.

For **Questions 7–8** you will be asked to listen to a three-chord ending progression and identify which cadence, containing two chords and beginning with a tonic triad, is played. The cadence will be played twice. Now listen to the music for **Questions 7–8** and identify the cadence that is played.

7. Which of the following three-chord progressions in Major is played? (**cadence** identification)

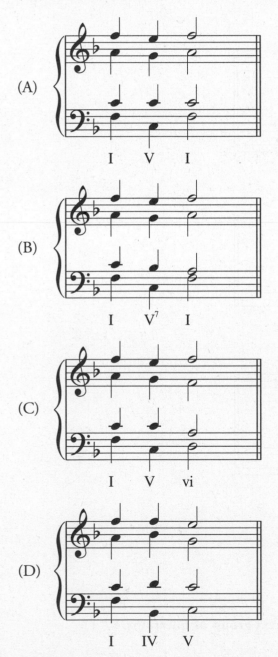

(A)   I   V   I

(B)   I   V⁷   I

(C)   I   V   vi

(D)   I   IV   V

Cadence, played twice.

8. Which of the following three-chord progressions in minor is played? (**cadence** identification)

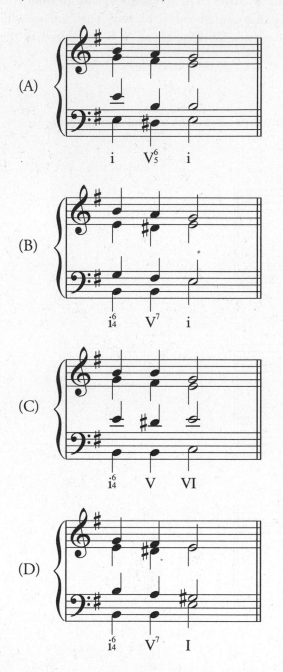

Cadence, played twice.

Go on to the next group of questions.

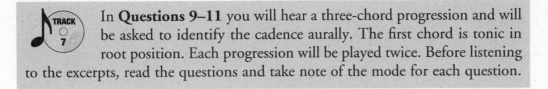

In **Questions 9–11** you will hear a three-chord progression and will be asked to identify the cadence aurally. The first chord is tonic in root position. Each progression will be played twice. Before listening to the excerpts, read the questions and take note of the mode for each question.

9. The cadence is correctly identified in minor as

 (A) perfect authentic
 (B) deceptive
 (C) PAC with Picardy third
 (D) Phrygian half cadence

Progression, played twice.

10. The cadence is correctly identified in major as

 (A) perfect authentic
 (B) deceptive
 (C) imperfect authentic
 (D) half cadence

Progression, played twice.

11. The cadence is correctly identified in minor as

 (A) perfect authentic
 (B) deceptive
 (C) PAC with Picardy third
 (D) Phrygian half cadence

Progression, played twice.

Go on to the next group of questions.

TRACK 8 **Questions 12–16** are based on an excerpt that will be played four times. The score is printed correctly below; however, what you will hear has several errors in either pitch or rhythm. The questions ask you to identify those errors. Before listening to the excerpt for the first time, please read **Questions 12–16** carefully and look at the score.

12. In measure 2, there is an error in the

   (A) rhythm in the treble staff
   (B) rhythm in the bass staff
   (C) pitch in the treble staff
   (D) pitch in the bass staff

13. In measure 3, there is an error in the

   (A) rhythm in the treble staff
   (B) rhythm in the bass staff
   (C) pitch in the treble staff
   (D) pitch in the bass staff

14. In measure 5, there is an error in the

   (A) rhythm in the treble staff
   (B) rhythm in the bass staff
   (C) pitch in the treble staff
   (D) pitch in the bass staff

15. In measure 6, which beat(s) contains a pitch error?

   (A) 1
   (B) 2
   (C) 3
   (D) Beats 1 and 2

16. Measure 7 has an error in

   (A) pitch in the treble staff
   (B) pitch in the bass staff
   (C) pitch and rhythm in the bass staff
   (D) just rhythm in the bass staff

Now listen to the excerpt for the first time and answer **Questions 12–16.**

The excerpt will now be played a second time.

The excerpt will now be played a third time.

The excerpt will now be played a final time.

Go on to the next group of questions.

Questions **17–21** are based on an excerpt from an instrumental piece. You will hear the selection played two times. Before listening to the excerpt for the first time, read **Questions 17–21**.

17. The accompaniment in the opening section can best be described as

  (A) arpeggiated
  (B) a pedal
  (C) chordal homphony
  (D) Alberti bass

18. The opening solo instrument is the

  (A) clarinet
  (B) flute
  (C) English horn
  (D) bassoon

19. After the opening solo section, the interval between the first two notes played by the French horn is

  (A) M3
  (B) P4
  (C) P5
  (D) m6

20. After the horn call, the strings enter using what performance marking?

  (A) Pizzicato
  (B) Arco
  (C) Tremolo
  (D) Forzando

21. The mode of this excerpt is

  (A) major
  (B) minor
  (C) pentatonic
  (D) Phrygian

The excerpt will now be played for the first time. 𝄞

The excerpt will now be played a second time. 𝄞

Go on to the next group of questions.

Questions 22–25 are based on a short excerpt in two sections for Baroque orchestra. You will hear the first section played once, followed by the entire excerpt played twice. Before listening to Section 1, read **Questions 22–24**.

22. The meter type is

    (A) compound duple
    (B) simple triple
    (C) compound triple
    (D) simple quadruple

23. The cadence at the end of the first section is

    (A) imperfect authentic
    (B) perfect authentic
    (C) half
    (D) Phrygian half

24. This excerpt is based on which of the following scales?

    (A) Pentatonic
    (B) Whole tone
    (C) Major
    (D) Minor

Section 1 will now be played. 𝄞

Before listening to the entire excerpt, please read **Question 25**.

25. Which of the following elements change in the second section compared to the first section?

    (A) Meter
    (B) Tempo
    (C) Timbre
    (D) Harmonic progression

The entire excerpt will now be played. 𝄞

Review your answers to **Questions 22–25** as the entire excerpt is played a final time. 𝄞

This concludes the Aural Multiple-Choice Questions for Chapters 5–7.

ANSWER KEY

1. **C**	6. **A**	11. **C**	16. **B**	21. **B**
2. **B**	7. **D**	12. **C**	17. **B**	22. **D**
3. **B**	8. **A**	13. **B**	18. **C**	23. **B**
4. **C**	9. **B**	14. **D**	19. **C**	24. **C**
5. **C**	10. **A**	15. **C**	20. **A**	25. **C**

ANSWERS EXPLAINED

1. **(C)** The methods of correctly answering a question like this are (1) to look at the three pitches from note to note and determine the melodic interval, (2) to look at the three pitches as a unit and identify pattern, or (3) a combination of the two. I like the combo deal. Answers (B) and (C) are easily identified as patterns. (B) is a descending major scale pattern and (C) is a descending natural minor scale pattern; however, (A) and (D) are not recognizable patterns. Identify what you can visually—write what you *see*. For example: (A) M2 m2, (D) m2 A2. The answer is (C), descending natural minor scale.

2. **(B)** The interval is a M3.

3. **(B)** A minor triad is played. With the time given between the aural examples, identify what you see and let your ear confirm it. This one is a little more difficult because both (B) and (D) are minor triads. The correct answer is the one in root position.

4. **(C)** Major triad in first inversion: (1) Listen for quality and (2) Is the root in the bass? When the root is inverted, the P5 becomes a P4.

5. **(C)** If you look at this measure *holistically*, you will see a major triad with a minor seventh.

6. **(A)** A diminished triad with a diminished seventh or fully-diminished seventh chord is played.

7. **(D)** This is a half cadence. (The clue is **Do-Fa-So** in the bass and **Do-Do-Ti** in the soprano.)

8. **(A)** This is an imperfect authentic cadence. It has the dominant to tonic sound but the leading tone is in the bass. The melody is **Me-Re-Do** in harmonic minor.

9. **(B)** This is a deceptive cadence in minor. The bass moves up by step from **So** to **Le**. The submediant triad is in the tonic family and shares two of the same pitches.

10. **(A)** The cadence is perfect authentic. This is a *root position* cadence of I–V⁷–I with **Do-Ti-Do** in the soprano. It is a standard PAC, but not as common as I$_4^6$–V⁷–I containing **So-So-Do** in the bass.

11. **(C)** The cadence is a PAC with the Picardy third. The third of the tonic triad is raised (inner voice) to make the final chord major tonic with **Me-Re-Do** in soprano and **So-So-Do** in bass.

Questions 12–16: Error Detection. This was played.

12. **(C)** The second measure is played higher by a third than what is written.

13. **(B)** The third measure has a dotted-quarter and eighth-note pattern in the bass staff.

14. **(D)** In measures 4–6, the bass line continues to descend by step. It does not move up then leap down. When you are looking at the score, "anticipate" places where errors might occur; always look at the places where the music skips or leaps. Look at rests and unusual or unique rhythms (different from other rhythms around it) for places for possible errors.

15. **(C)** In measure 6 the melody leaps up to **Do** from **So** and then returns to **So**.

16. **(B)** In measure 7 the bass line pitch is ascending (**Mi-Fa-So-Do**) by step and does not leap up as written (**Mi-Do-Ti-Do**).

17. **(B)** The accompaniment is a pedal—a continuously sustained pitch under the melody.

18. **(C)** The solo instrument is the English horn, a double-reed woodwind instrument in the oboe family.

19. **(C)** The interval is a perfect fifth (P5). This horn call is sounded three times.

20. **(A)** After the horn call, the strings enter plucking the strings. This is called pizzicato.

21. **(B)** The excerpt is in minor.

22. **(D)** The meter is simple quadruple.

23. **(B)** The cadence at the end of the first section is perfect authentic in major.

24. **(C)** This excerpt is based on a major scale.

25. **(C)** The difference is the timbre. The melodic material is the same, as is the harmonic progression, meter, and tempo.

Harmonic Composition Part I: Fundamentals

8

- Simple Part-Writing Rules
- "The Road Map" Technique
- Counterpoint, Contrapuntal
- Crossed Voices
- Doubling Chord Members
- Overlapping Voices
- Motion
    - Contrary Motion
    - Similar Motion
    - Parallel Motion
    - Oblique Motion
- Part Writing to the Roman Numerals
- Realization of Figured Bass
- Resolution Rules
- Spacing Between Voices
- Vocal Ranges
- Voice Characteristics
    - Conjunct
    - Disjunct
    - Static

In this chapter we review the basic principles of voice-leading for four voices in the style of the Common Practice Period and the guidelines for realizing figured bass. Tackling the part-writing portion of the AP exam is a major hurdle. Part writing includes recognizing and applying so many concepts that it is an *ideal* way to put all our knowledge to use. **Part writing** requires knowledge of melody, interval, triads, seventh chords, cadences, non-chord tones, figured bass, chromatic harmony, resolution tendencies, and counterpoint as well as progressional norms for the Common Practice Period.

My approach to part writing is from the viewpoint of the melody—starting with the relationship of two lines (**counterpoint**) between the bass, which is given, and the melody, which you have to compose. This process does not rely on lots of rules (some believe there are as many as eighty part-writing "rules"); however, it *does* rely on creating a great melody that works with the bass line. What we are creating are four distinct and independent voices for four different characters. Our job as the composer is to create a fabulous single melody line that works. We will begin with what I call:

THE SIMPLE PART-WRITING RULES

RULE 1

Know the vocal ranges and stay within the heart of each range.

The soprano is always written with the stem up and the alto with stems down regardless of placement on the staff. The tenor is always written with the stem up and the bass with stems down, regardless of placement on the staff.

The functional range that each voice may use is confined to the **heart** of the range. To keep it simple, remember it this way: The soprano and tenor range is from **C** to **G**; the alto and bass range is the opposite—from **G** to **C**. Here it is on the grand staff:

Although we realize that the soprano can and does sing above G⁵, she doesn't have to. Taking her up to A♭ and A is certainly acceptable—much higher is just not necessary. So try and stay within this range, knowing that each voice has at least a whole step in either direction for extreme range.

RULE 2

Write for four different voices; they are individual characters.

Know the **contrapuntal** character (linear or horizontal movement) of each voice. The bass line is given to you. Either the bass is written and the figured bass implies the chords and linear movement of each voice (FR 5) or the chord symbols with inversions are given and you must fill in the notes of the bass dictated by the symbols (FR 6). In either case, **the bass is a given**. In part-writing from the chord symbols, you do have the freedom to determine what octave your bass moves in after the first chord. The bass is the most *disjunct* (moving by skips and leaps) and is often the most disjunct at the cadence. **The soprano is always the melody.** As discussed in depth in Chapter 9, the melody has only one climax point and works toward the climax and then away. The melody most often moves by step (conjunct motion), but sometimes it moves by skip or leap; therefore, it is considered somewhat disjunct. The melody always has an intended goal in mind—usually the tonic, and moves forward in anticipation of that goal.

Her (remember the melody is always the soprano) most frequent endings are ***Mi-Re-Do***, or ***Re-Ti-Do***. The alto and the tenor are as **static** as possible—moving very little. As a matter of fact the word *tenor* comes from the word *tenere*, which means "to hold." So if you write an alto or a tenor line that stays on the same note all the way through, you win the grand prize for common-practice style! Write a good melody and everything else is easy (well, let's say easier).

RULE 3   Motion is the key to successful counterpoint.

Motion refers to the direction the melody moves *in relation to the bass line*. There are four types of motion. **Contrary motion** moves the melody in the opposite direction of the bass. If the bass moves up, the melody moves down. Contrary motion is desirable and used most often in four-part voice leading. **Oblique motion** is when one voice remains on the same note and the other moves in either direction. If the bass is repeating a note, the melody has the option to move either up or down. The third form of motion is **similar motion**, when the bass and the soprano move in the same direction but at different intervals. A fourth form of motion, known as **parallel motion**, where the soprano and bass move in the *same direction and at the same interval*, can be the undoing of good part writing. Never write a parallel octave or parallel fifth between the bass and the soprano (or between any other two voices). Just don't do it! Why are parallel fifths and eighths to be avoided? The reason is a linear one. Parallelism confuses the distinction between the four independent voices or lines, particularly when you have *perfect* parallels. We are writing *four distinct and independent voices* for four different characters. When parallelism occurs the ear cannot distinguish those four voices; instead they sound like three voices or even two. When any two voices move in the same direction at the same interval, they sound as one, giving us three voices instead of four. The lines will often surrender their individuality for the purpose of bringing the voices together for a unified conclusion at the cadence; otherwise, write four clearly defined voices. A good melody uses four types of motion (contrary, oblique, similar, and, with discretion, parallel motion), but features contrary motion most often.

RULE 4   Don't confuse the ear!

The first way you can confuse the ear is by writing **crossed voices**. This means that you cannot write the soprano voice lower than the alto, or the alto voice lower than the tenor. It confuses the ear because it cannot separate the lines. Remember the goal is to write four distinctly separate lines.

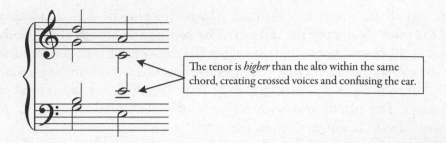

The tenor is *higher* than the alto within the same chord, creating crossed voices and confusing the ear.

The second way to confuse the ear is to **overlap** the voices. This simply means that you don't want to write one voice higher than another voice **has been** in the previous chord. Overlap is between two chords.

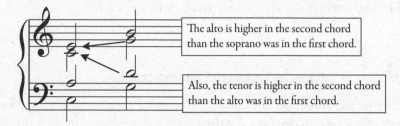

The alto is higher in the second chord than the soprano was in the first chord.

Also, the tenor is higher in the second chord than the alto was in the first chord.

In the example above, we not only have overlapping voices but we have parallel octaves between the bass and the alto (C to G). Overlapping may happen because one (or in this case two) of the voices takes over the "character" or the role of another voice. In our example the soprano is clearly singing in alto territory in the first chord, which creates an identity crisis, and the problem continues in the bass. The bass jumps up into the tenor range and we have not allowed enough room for our other voices to compensate. Remember that if the bass is given we have no control over it, but we *can* control the other three. If the bass is in a high range, then the soprano is usually in the high end of her range. It was the **parallel motion** that was the egregious error in this example. A better voicing of the first chord would have been

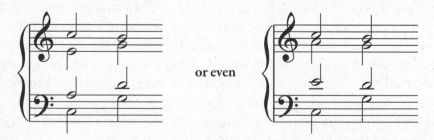

or even

RULE
5   Spacing is an issue.

The soprano and the alto must be within an octave of each other, and the alto must be within an octave of the tenor. Therefore, the soprano, alto, and tenor have an available range of two octaves. *It doesn't matter how far the tenor is from the bass.*

Writing the melody first often determines how high the tenor will be. If the soprano is high, the tenor will also be high, otherwise there will be spacing issues between two of the voices. Don't hesitate to write the tenor above C⁴—the tenor should be "singing" in that range for much of the time.

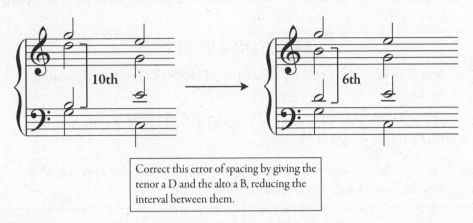

Correct this error of spacing by giving the tenor a D and the alto a B, reducing the interval between them.

RULE 6

Double the root first, the fifth second, and the third with a reason.

When you have a three-note chord (triad) and four available voices, one chord member will be doubled. The first choice in doubling is the root of the chord, especially if it is a major chord. The second choice would be to double the fifth of the chord. Avoid doubling the third of the chord except for minor chords with a reason. For example, when V goes to vi, double the third in the vi chord to avoid parallelism. The more a chord is inverted, the less it sounds like itself and the more it sounds like something else, particularly when considering the doubling. A chord in second inversion *should double the fifth*—strengthening the pitch that reinforces $^6_4$ function—passing, pedal, or cadential. **Never double a tendency tone**, most often the leading tone (*Ti*) and the seventh of the V⁷ chord (*Fa*), but also include any tone that must be resolved such as chromatic passing tones.

General Rules for Doubling

- Your first choice is to double the root of a chord especially if it is in root position.
- Double the fifth of a $^6_4$ chord or double the fifth as your second choice for root position chords.
- Double the third *with reason* (voice leading) or in some instances in minor chords, such as the ii⁶ to reinforce *Fa*, and doubling the third of the vi chord, especially when V goes to vi to avoid parallelism.
- Include all four members of a seventh chord; however, when V⁷ goes to I (in a root position cadence) it is very common to **omit** the fifth of the tonic triad.

When composing four-part harmony, try to move your voices to the nearest chord members—the line or movement of the voice is often more important than whether to double the root.

RULE
7 Resolutions

There are three rules of resolution. Memorize them and learn to apply the concepts.

RESOLUTION RULES

RULE 1: **IF** V goes to I (i) or VI (vi), **THEN** *Ti* resolves upward to *Do*.

RULE 2: **IF** vii°/vii°⁷ OR V⁷ goes to I (i) or VI (vi), **THEN** *Ti* resolves to *Do* AND *Fa* resolves to *Mi*.

RULE 3: **IF** you have a seventh chord of *any* kind, **THEN** the seventh of the chord resolves downward, or holds until it can.

PART WRITING AS A GAME

Just for fun, let's relate the part-writing concepts to a game:

- The playing field is the grand staff.
- The players are SATB.
- The playing area for each player is the vocal range.
- The player's positions are

  S: the star player, or the melody; her position moves in contrary motion to the bass line.
  A and T: lend support to the melody and the bass and move as little as possible on the playing field.
  B: given to us, the established foundation with whom S, A, and T must move.

- The playbook is the chord progression and/or figured bass. It tells us what choices we have in moving the players across the playing field.
- Our goal is to successfully move our players across the playing field while avoiding parallel fifths and octaves, overlapping or crossed voices, inappropriately doubled chord members, and unresolved chordal sevenths.

FOUR PART-WRITING EXAMPLES FROM FIGURED BASS AND ROMAN NUMERAL

When I teach part writing I begin with only tonic chords and inversions. Our "menu" of choices is greatly reduced—there are only three notes on the menu! Let's begin with a figured bass example in C minor.*

EXAMPLE 1: Figured Bass in C minor

STEP 1: Determine the Roman numerals and create the road map.

The **road map** is the visible reminder of the menu of chord member choices, appropriate doublings, and resolutions. Write the Roman numeral chord symbols below the figured bass (FB); *never* attach your chord symbols to the same line as the FB symbols. The **chord stack** (with the root of the chord on the bottom in "snowman" style) is written below. If done correctly, this step can eliminate a multitude of mistakes when examples are more difficult. It is super simple to learn with only one chord.

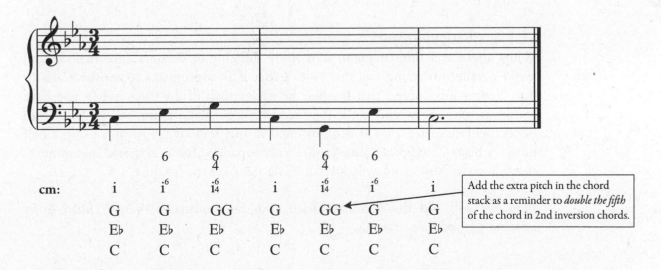

Add the extra pitch in the chord stack as a reminder to *double the fifth* of the chord in 2nd inversion chords.

There are no resolutions to consider since this is only the tonic triad.

---

*This progression and the others in this chapter are courtesy of Dr. Blaise Ferrandino, Texas Christian University, Fort Worth, Texas.

STEP 2: Write the melody.

Look at the bass line and observe the shape, recognizing the bass line has ascending and descending lines. Try to create a melody that moves in contrary or oblique motion to the bass line.

STEP 3: Fill in the alto and tenor at the same time.

STEP 4: Check your work.

When there is a limited menu it is more difficult to create a nice melody and avoid parallel fifths and eighths. Notice that it is appropriate to move the tenor into "ledger line" range; that is where he sings much of the time. When you have common tones between chords it is acceptable to make them half notes instead of rearticulating the tone as demonstrated in our melody. However, using a half note for beats 2 and 3 in $\frac{4}{4}$ time creates a syncopation that is not used in common-practice style. Also avoid syncopation using ties over the bar line.

Now we will add the dominant triad and the dominant seventh chord using another figured bass example.

EXAMPLE 2: Figured Bass in D Major

STEP 1: **Determine the Roman numerals and create the road map.**

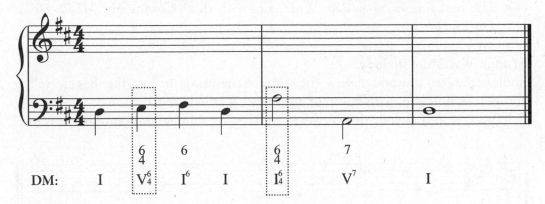

Notice in this example there are two second-inversion ($^6_4$) chords. The first chord is used to prolong tonic and creates a *passing chord* between the I and I⁶ creating the bass line **Do-Re-Mi**. The I$^6_4$ chord is used as part of the cadence. The **cadential $^6_4$ chord** can be used on a strong beat and is the *only* type of second inversion chord that should be written on beat 1 or beat 3. Now create the chord stack, note the appropriate doublings, and show resolutions.

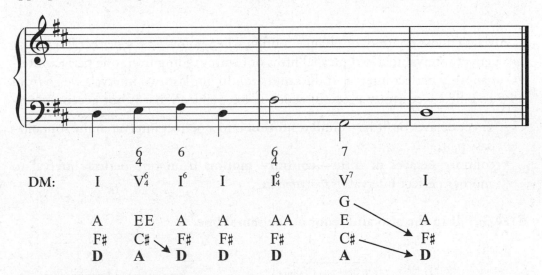

What do we know for sure?
• There are two second-inversion chords that should double the fifth of the chord.
• There is one V chord leading to a I⁶ (resolve the *Ti* to *Do*) and one V⁷ chord resolving to I (resolve both *Ti-Do* and *Fa-Mi*).

> **NOTE: Arrows are used in the chord stack to show the pitches that *must* resolve, and to which pitch.** In this guide, when the final progression is written, you will see the arrows *within the composition* as a reminder that the resolutions have indeed been written. **This is a reminder and a way to check your work.** Once you are confident that you are resolving correctly, leave out the arrows within the composition.

- The bass line is high—actually singing in tenor range much of the time. We can write a melody putting the soprano high in her range but we *must* write the tenor high to avoid overlapping with the bass.
- The bass line is **So-So-Do**. What goes with that? Commonly **Mi-Re-Do** or **Do-Ti-Do**.

STEP 2: Write the melody.
Look at the bass line and observe the shape, recognizing the bass line has ascending and descending lines with a leap of an octave. Write the NORM.

Try to create a melody that moves in contrary or oblique motion to the bass line.

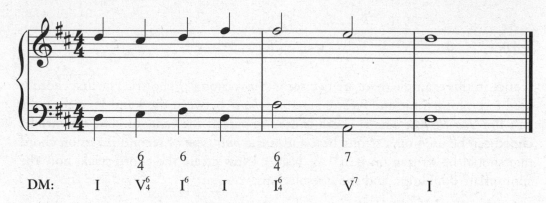

Always choose contrary or oblique motion when going *from* a perfect interval or *to* a perfect interval to avoid parallel fifths or octaves (going from one perfect interval to another perfect interval of the same size). In our last two intervals we go from a P5 to a P8 **by contrary motion**, which is acceptable. What is **not acceptable** is

- direct octaves or fifths—**similar motion** into a perfect interval in the soprano–bass pair;
- contrary octaves or fifths—**contrary motion** from one perfect interval to another perfect interval *of the same size*.

STEP 3: Fill in the alto and tenor at the same time.

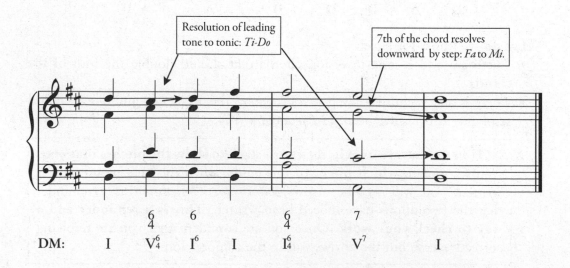

EXAMPLE 3: Part Writing to the Roman Numerals in F Major

Now we are ready to part-write from Roman numerals. The process of composing is the same; however, the bass is *not* given—just the Roman numeral chord symbols. There is one additional step after creating the chord stack—writing the bass line. We are going to use a variation of the last progression, this time in F Major.

STEP 1: Create the road map.

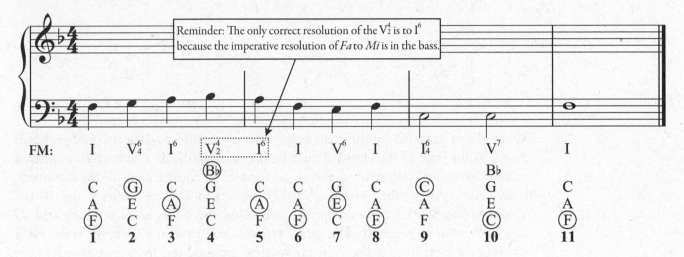

The pitches **that are circled are the notes that will be in the bass** according to the Roman numerals and inversion symbols. As you are looking at the harmonic progression of this part-writing example observe the use of the second inversion triads and remember there are very specific ways to use the $_4^6$ chord. The two used here are passing and cadential.

CONNECT THE DOTS . . .

This information about the use of second inversion chords in part-writing transfers to harmonic dictation (where we might expect to *hear* $_4^6$ chords used in a four-part chorale) *and* to harmonizing a melody (where we must once again apply this knowledge when writing the bass line and an appropriate harmonic progression like the one used here).

Now you are ready to transfer this information to the staff.

STEP 2: Write the bass line as outlined by the circled notes on the road map.

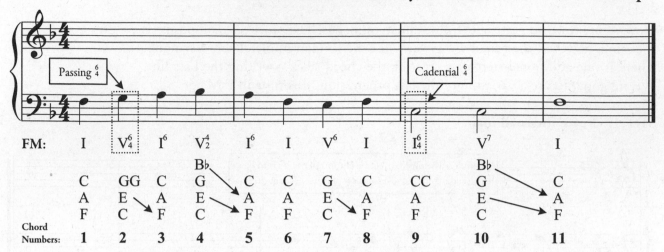

What else is revealed by the road map? In both second inversion chords (chords 2 and 9) the fifth of the chord should be the note doubled. The resolution arrows mark what notes *must* resolve, and to what note. In chords 2 and 7 the dominant triad is followed by the tonic triad, so **Ti** resolves to **Do**. In chords 4 and 10 the V⁷ chord has two resolution imperatives because the V⁷ includes both **Fa** and **Ti** and both *must* be resolved. The arrow reminds you that in whichever voice **Fa** is written, the next note is also "already written" because the *resolution must occur in the same voice*. It is also easy to use the road map to slash through the pitches as you are writing to clearly see that all notes are utilized and which notes have been doubled.

STEP 3: Write the melody.

Look at the bass line and observe the shape, recognizing the bass line has ascending, descending, and oblique motion. The melody will want to move in contrary motion to the bass and end with an authentic cadence.

With the cadence already determined and the outline of the motion in mind, we write the melody using only our choices from the road map, and we observe resolutions when necessary.

Here is one possible melody.

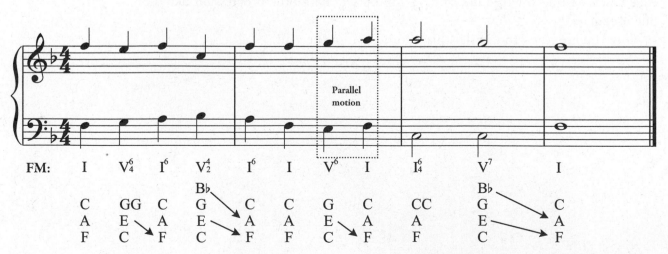

At this point we check for parallelism, noting that we have one instance of parallel motion, creating parallel thirds that are acceptable. Our melody has two large leaps, but they are the most common—from **Do** to **So** and back. The melody is high and slightly outside the "heart" of the soprano range; therefore, the alto and tenor are also high to avoid spacing errors.

STEP 4: Fill in the alto and the tenor at the same time.

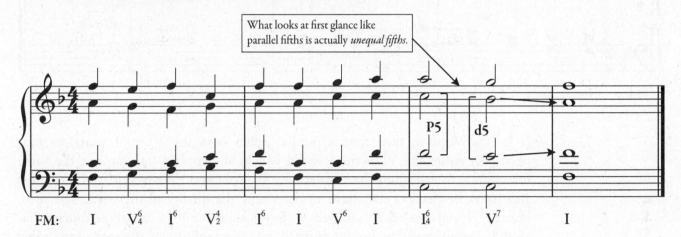

It's time to check your work. Note that in the example above the inside voices have what looks like parallel fifths in the **penultimate** (next to last) measure. These are not parallel fifths—but what we do have is a P5 to a d5 between the tenor and alto, which is extremely common.

Let's try another ending to this melody.

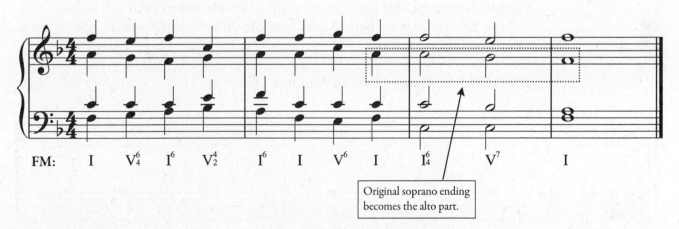

With solution 2, our original soprano ending is now in the alto, but our melody does not appear to have a climax point.

Let's try again. Here is alternate solution 3.

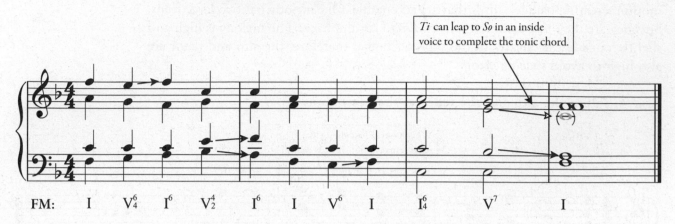

Ti can leap to *So* in an inside voice to complete the tonic chord.

FM: I   V$_4^6$ I^6 V$_2^4$ I^6 I   V^6 I   I$_4^6$ V^7 I

It is important to note that, typically, when resolving V^7 to I (both in root position), either the V^7 or the I chord will be incomplete (leaving out the fifth) for smooth voice leading. You **must** have the root and the seventh, and you must also have the third of the chord to determine the quality of the triad. The fifth, however, is not needed. In all three of our solutions the V^7 chord in the cadence has all four members and as a result of the imperative resolutions, the root of the tonic chord is tripled and the fifth of the chord is left out. As stated earlier, this is a very common occurrence particularly at the cadence when the four voices "surrender their individuality."

It is permissible at the cadence for scale degree 7 (***Ti***) to leap to $\hat{5}$ (***So***) when it's an inside voice to complete the tonic chord. In this example the leading tone (E) in the alto could have gone to C to fill out the chord at the cadence as shown by the parentheses. Again, this is acceptable only for **inside voices** (alto and tenor).

Now let's try another figured bass example, this time in A minor, adding some new figured bass symbols.

EXAMPLE 4: Figured Bass in A minor

am: $_5^6$ 6 $_4^{\cancel{6}}$ #   7
                            3   #

What do we know for sure? The G♯ in the bass line is a clue that tells us we are in **A harmonic minor**, plus we see altered figures such as $\cancel{6}$ and the sharp sign that indicate a note that is not in the key signature. There are four root position triads, one root position triad with the third raised, one first inversion triad and one first inversion seventh chord, one second inversion seventh chord, and one V^7 chord in root position.

STEP 1: Add the Roman numeral chord symbols and inversions, and write the progression below the figures.

STEP 2: Create the road map, including the resolution arrows and doubling reminders. Write in the space provided. (Answers are on page 194.)

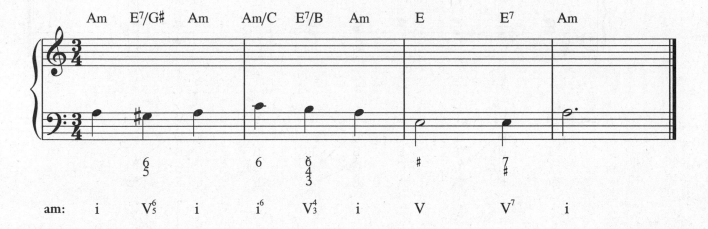

- The added symbols to the figures (♭6 and ♯) indicating accidentals are *not* part of the Roman numeral chord symbol.
- Be careful to add accidentals where needed when notating.

STEP 3: Write the melody. You're on your own to write a great melody.

STEP 4: Fill in the alto and tenor at the same time.

Because the V⁷ chord is incomplete—the 5th is omitted—the tonic chord can be complete.

am:	i	V⁶₅	i	i⁶	V⁴₃	i	V	V⁷	i

	D			D				D	
E	B	E	E	B	E	B	B	E	
C	G#	C	C	G#	C	G#	G#	C	
A	E	A	A	E	A	E	E	A	

You must be careful when resolving the tritone (in this key G# to D) in the V⁷ chord to **avoid unequal fifths**—the motion from the diminished fifth to a perfect fifth, especially in the soprano–bass pair. If you resolve correctly, this will not occur. Motion from a P5 to a dim5 is acceptable. Note that in the penultimate chord the root of the V⁷ chord (E) is doubled; therefore, the fifth of the chord (B) is left out. Because the V⁷ chord is incomplete, the final tonic chord is complete.

note to self

Did you check your work?

- Correct chord members including accidentals ✔
- Adding accidentals where needed—especially in a minor key ✔
- Resolutions ✔
- No parallel fifths or eighths ✔
- Correct spacing, including no crossed voices or overlapping voices ✔

Part writing requires knowledge of melody, interval, triads, inversions, seventh chords, cadences, figured bass, resolution tendencies, and counterpoint as well as what is typical and/or prevalent for the Common Practice Period. Practicing this skill is an ideal way to reinforce all of these concepts. All of the examples from this chapter as well as Part II can be found in Appendix C for you to compose a new melody and complete for additional practice.

Chapter Summary

- The functional range that each voice may use is confined to the heart of the range. To keep it simple, remember it this way: the soprano and tenor range is from C to G; the alto and bass range is the opposite—from G to C.

- The bass is the most disjunct (moving by skips and leaps) and is often the most disjunct at the cadence.
- The soprano is always the melody.
- The melody has only one climax point and works toward the climax and then away. The melody most often moves by step, but sometimes by skip or leap; therefore it is considered somewhat disjunct. The melody always has an intended goal in mind—usually tonic.
- The alto and the tenor are as static as possible—moving very little.
- **Motion** refers to the direction the melody moves in relation to the bass line. There are four types of motion.

    - **Contrary motion** moves the melody in the opposite direction of the bass. If the bass moves up, the melody moves down.
    - **Oblique motion** is when one voice remains on the same note and the other moves in either direction.
    - **Similar motion** is when the bass and the soprano move in the same direction but at different intervals.
    - **Parallel motion** is where the soprano and bass move in the same direction and at the same intervals.

- Never write parallel fifths or eighths. Parallelism clouds the distinction between the four independent voices, particularly when you have *perfect* parallels. When parallelism occurs the ear cannot distinguish those four voices; instead they sound like three voices or even two.
- Don't confuse the ear by writing crossed voices or overlapping voices. It confuses the ear because it cannot separate the lines.
- The goal is to write four distinct separate lines.
- Avoid spacing issues by writing the soprano and the alto within an octave of each other, and the alto within an octave of the tenor. Therefore, the soprano, alto, and tenor have an available range of two octaves.

    - It doesn't matter how far the tenor is from the bass.

- The first choice in doubling is the root of the chord, especially if it is a major chord. The second choice would be to double the fifth of the chord.
- A chord in second inversion should double the fifth—strengthening the pitch that reinforces $^6_4$ function—passing, pedal, or cadential.
- Avoid doubling the third of the chord except for minor chords with a reason.
- There are three rules of resolution.

    - Rule 1: IF V goes to I (i) or VI (vi), THEN *Ti* resolves upward to *Do*.
    - Rule 2: IF vii°/vii°7 OR V7 goes to I (i) or VI (vi), THEN *Ti* resolves to *Do* AND *Fa* resolves to *Mi*.
    - Rule 3: IF you have a seventh chord of ANY kind, THEN the seventh of the chord resolves downward, or holds until it can.

- You must be careful when resolving the tritone in the V7 chord to avoid unequal fifths—the motion from the diminished fifth to a perfect fifth, especially in the soprano–bass pair. If you resolve correctly, this will not occur.
- It is important to note that typically when resolving the root position V7 to I, particularly at the cadence, either the V7 or the I chord will be incomplete (leaving out the fifth of the chord) for smooth voice leading.

Practice Exercises

Questions 1–4 are based on the example below.

1. The cadence is

   (A) imperfect authentic
   (B) perfect authentic
   (C) half
   (D) deceptive

2. The correct chord progression for this
   example is

   (A) I–IV–V–vi–ii^6–V–I
   (B) I–ii^6–V–vi–IV–V–I
   (C) I–ii^6–V–vi–IV–V^7–I
   (D) I–IV–V–vi–ii^6–V^7–I

3. The part-writing error in measure 2 is

   (A) spacing
   (B) incorrect chord member
   (C) parallel octaves
   (D) parallel fifths

4. This error in voice leading (refer to
   Question 3) is a result of

   (A) parallel motion in two voices
   (B) spacing too wide between bass
       and tenor
   (C) oblique motion
   (D) contrary motion

Questions 5–8 are based on the example below.

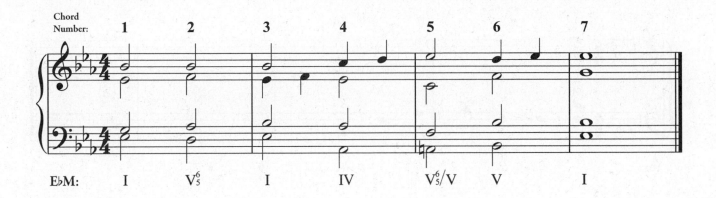

5. Chords 2 and 3 contain two voice-leading
   errors. They are

   (A) a spacing error and parallel fifths
   (B) unequal fifth and an improperly resolved
       chordal seventh
   (C) overlapping voices and an improperly
       doubled chord
   (D) a direct octave and crossed voices

6. There is a voice-leading error between
   chords 4 and 5. It is

   (A) parallel fifths
   (B) parallel octaves
   (C) direct fifth
   (D) overlapping voices

7. There are two errors between chords 5 and
   6. They are

   (A) crossed voices and an unresolved chordal
       seventh
   (B) overlapping voices and parallel fifths
   (C) an incorrect chord member and an
       unresolved chordal seventh
   (D) a spacing error and parallel fifths

8. Chords 1, 2, and 3 represent what type of
   motion between the bass and the soprano?

   (A) Contrary
   (B) Oblique
   (C) Similar
   (D) Parallel

Refer to the example below for **Questions 9–16**.

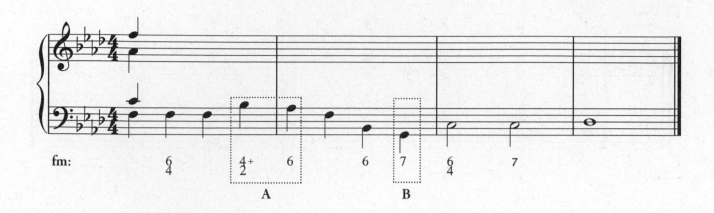

9. What type of $^6_4$ chord is used in measure 3?

   _____

10. What are the Roman numeral chord symbols for the two chords within Box A?

    _____

11. Spell the chord in Box B.

    _____

12. The chord in Box B is

    (A) half-diminished seventh chord
    (B) fully-diminished seventh chord
    (C) dominant seventh chord
    (D) a major–minor seventh chord

13. In what other key and scale degree could this chord (Box B) also function?

    _____

14. The correct Roman numeral analysis of this example is

    (A) i–iv$^6_4$–i–V$^4_2$–i^6–ii–ii^7–i$^6_4$–V^7–VI

    (B) i–iv$^6_4$–i–V$^4_2$–i^6–ii^{o6}–ii^{ø7}–i$^6_4$–V^7–VI

    (C) i–iv$^6_4$–i–V$^4_2$–i–ii^o–ii^{o7}–i$^6_4$–V–vi

    (D) i–iv–i–V$^4_2$–i^6–ii–ii^7–i$^6_4$–V^7–vi

15. The cadence is

    (A) authentic
    (B) plagal
    (C) Phrygian half
    (D) deceptive

16. All of the following could be used as the melody for the last three chords except

    (A) *Do-Ti-Do* ($\hat{1}$–$\hat{7}$–$\hat{1}$)
    (B) *Re-Ti-Do* ($\hat{2}$–$\hat{7}$–$\hat{1}$)
    (C) *Me-Re-Do* ($\hat{3}$–$\hat{2}$–$\hat{1}$)
    (D) *So-Fa-Me* ($\hat{5}$–$\hat{4}$–$\hat{3}$)

ANSWER KEY

1. **B**	6. **A**	10. **See Answers**	13. **See Answers**
2. **A**	7. **D**	**Explained.**	**Explained.**
3. **C**	8. **B**	11. **See Answers**	14. **B**
4. **A**	9. **See Answers**	**Explained.**	15. **D**
5. **B**	**Explained.**	12. **A**	16. **B**

ANSWERS EXPLAINED

1. **(B)** The last two chords are V–I. The root of the tonic chord is also in the soprano creating a *perfect* authentic cadence.

2. **(A)** The correct Roman numeral chord progression is I–IV–V–vi–ii^6–V–I. In some cases the only difference between answers is an inversion or an added seventh (or not). Be careful.

3. **(C)** The part-writing error in measure 2 is parallel octaves between the alto and bass voices.

4. **(A)** The error is a result of parallel motion in-between the bass and alto. Only the tenor stayed on the same pitch while the soprano, alto, and bass all moved ascending by step.

5. **(B)** Chords 2 and 3 contain both unequal fifths between the bass and tenor, and an unresolved seventh. The V$^6_5$ chord is B♭–D–F–A♭. The seventh of the chord, A♭, is in the tenor and should resolve downward by step to the G. Chord number 3 is an incomplete chord because the G has been left out.

6. **(A)** Chords 4 and 5 contain parallel fifths between the tenor and the alto. In this case the Roman numerals reflect what we call a secondary dominant, a concept we discuss in later chapters. Do not let this deter you from answering the question. If there is something about the example or excerpt that you don't know or are unsure of, try to answer it anyway. In many cases an example may contain complex notation or analysis but the question asked does not even pertain to that. Read the questions carefully.

7. **(D)** The two errors in chords 5 and 6 are that the spacing between the soprano and alto is too large, and there is once again parallel fifths between the tenor and the alto.

8. **(B)** The opening three chords are an example of oblique motion between the soprano and the bass. In oblique motion one voice must stay on the same pitch.

9. The third measure contains a **cadential $^6_4$ chord**, the i$^6_4$. Because the i$^6_4$ chord has *So* in the bass, it is used at the cadence as dominant function.

10. Box A has two chords: V$^4_2$–i^6. The V$^4_2$ should always resolve to i^6 or (I^6) so that the seventh of the chord (which is in the bass) can resolve correctly. The 4+ in the figured bass (you might also see ♯4 or ♮4) means to raise the pitch that is

the interval of a fourth above the bass to E♮, the raised seventh scale degree in F minor.

11. The chord in Box B is spelled G–B♭–D♭–F. Since there are no alterations noted in the figured bass it is spelled diatonically.

12. **(A)** The chord is a diminished triad (G–B♭–D♭) with a minor seventh (G–F)—a half-diminished seventh chord. In F minor that chord is the supertonic ii^{ø7}.

13. A half-diminished seventh chord also occurs diatonically as the leading-tone seventh chord in a major key. If G is the leading tone, then tonic is A♭: **vii^{ø7} in A♭ Major.**

14. **(B)** The Roman numeral chord analysis for this example is

$$\text{i–iv}^6_4\text{–i–V}^4_2\text{–i}^6\text{–ii}^{o6}\text{–ii}^{ø7}\text{–i}^6_4\text{–V}^7\text{–VI}$$

15. **(D)** The cadence is deceptive. The final two chords are V^7–VI.

16. **(B)** The chord analysis is i$^6_4$–V^7–VI. The first chord (i$^6_4$) does not contain $\hat{2}$ (*Re*).

Harmonic Progression and Harmonizing a Melody

9

- Harmonic Progression
- Common Progressions
  - Circle Progression
  - Progression by Thirds
  - Progression by Seconds
- Retrogression
- Harmonization of a Melody (FR 7)
- Harmonic Rhythm

HARMONIC PROGRESSION

Harmonic progression or "chord leading" is the process of relating chords within the scale to where they naturally lead. *Pro*gression is when the harmonies proceed from a stable beginning (tonic function), move forward through progressively more active chords (predominant and dominant function) including seventh chords, to end (resolve) once again with stability. As we discussed in Chapter 7, every chord has a function that varies depending on whether it is a triad or a seventh chord, in root position or inverted, and what note is doubled.

Chord	Leads to
I/i	any other chord
ii/ii°	V/v, vii°
III*	VI, VII, vii°
IV/iv	I/i, ii/ii°, V/v, vii°
V/v	I/i, vi/VI
vi/VI	ii/ii°, IV/iv, V/v
vii°/VII	I, i

Common Harmonic Progressions

Although **common harmonic progression** charts are frequently used in many music theory textbooks, please note that they are a broad picture of progression, and reflect chords in *root position*. This is *not* the norm because "real" music uses inversions, and inversions change the strength and the function of chords.

---

*The **mediant chord** (iii) is tricky to use because it is such a chameleon. The iii/III chord will not be used in the part-writing or harmonic dictation segments of the AP Music Theory exam.

MAJOR KEYS

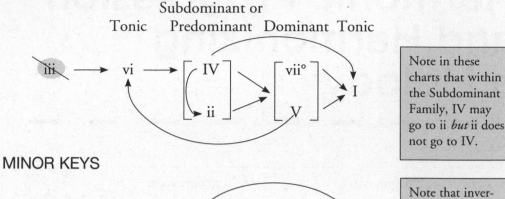

> Note in these charts that within the Subdominant Family, IV may go to ii *but* ii does not go to IV.

MINOR KEYS

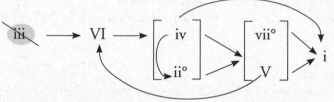

> Note that inversions and context alter the strength and role of chords diatonically.

CIRCLE PROGRESSION

Circle progression is the movement of chords where the *root* (not necessarily the bass) of each chord is a diatonic fifth above the next chord. This gives the feeling of overlapping dominants to tonic. This is the strongest motion in tonal music. All of the fifths in a full circle progression are perfect except one. Can you guess which one that is? Yes—*Fa* to *Ti* is a tritone!

I–IV–vii°–~~iii~~–vi–ii–V–I in major keys, or

i–iv–vii°(or VII)–~~III~~–VI–ii°–V–i in minor keys.

This is the complete circle progression, but please note, music generally does *not* move in just one type of progression, so you will observe music commonly using a circle progression for three or four chords—the most popular is ii–V–I, very often ii⁶–V–I (*Fa-So-Do* in the bass).

> This is a full **Circle of Fifths** progression because each chord moves to the next by the root descending a fifth.

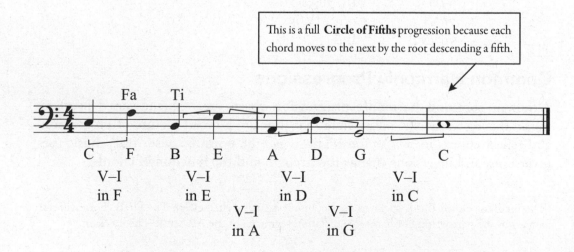

The most common use of the vii° triad is in first inversion (vii°⁶) resolving to I or I⁶. If we replace the root position leading-tone triad with vii°⁶, the inversion will be different and therefore the bass line is different—but the progression (movement of the *roots* of the chords) remains the same. Here is a more common circle progression that uses the vii°⁶ and also heightens the intensity toward the end of the phrase with the addition of two seventh chords.

CM: I   IV   vii°⁶   I⁶   ii⁶ or ii⁶₅   V   V⁷   I

PROGRESSION BY THIRDS

Progression by thirds is the movement of chords where the root of each chord is either up or down by a third. The most commonly used chain of thirds progression is

$$I–vi–IV–\ ii–\ vii°⁶–\qquad I \quad \text{in major keys, or}$$

$$I–vi–IV–\ ii–\ V–\qquad\quad I$$

$$i–VI–iv–\ ii°–\ vii°⁶\ (or\ VII)–i \quad \text{in minor keys}$$

$$i–VI–iv–\ ii°–\ V–\qquad\quad i$$

Function =   **T T PD PD D**   **T**

PROGRESSION BY SECONDS

Progression by seconds is the movement of chords where the root of each chord is either up or down to the next note in the scale. Adjacent chords with roots a second apart are responsible for many errors in part writing.

Major: I   IV   V   I   or   **Minor:**   i   VI   iv⁶   V

⌞ 2nd ⌟   ⌞ 2nd ⌟

Function =   T   PD   D   T   T   T   PD   D

> **REMEMBER**
>
> Even if the chord is inverted, the progression is based on the *root* of the chord.

How Does Inversion Affect the Function of a Chord in a Progression?

In Chapter 7 we learned that root position chords are *strong* chords. They have tonic function, dominant function, or subdominant function. Tonic function chords (I, i, vi, VI) are often **destination** chords especially when in root position. Dominant function (V, vii) chords move the harmony forward; they provide an active energy even when inverted. Subdominant function (IV, ii) are transition chords, connecting tonic to dominants; that's why they are often considered **PRED**ominant. The more a chord is inverted, the weaker its function, or the more it functions like another chord, especially when you consider what chord member is doubled. When you invert a chord you can create a smooth, connecting line by moving by step in the bass so that the inverted chord takes on a **passing** role, or by moving the bass from one pitch to the pitch a step above or below and then back. This type of inverted chord takes on a **neighbor** role. Inverted chords may serve to create an **arpeggio** in the bass line, or may hold the bass line in a **pedal** on the same note while the voices above change harmony. Because the figured bass of a second inversion triad is $^6_4$, that information tells us there is an interval of a sixth against the bass and an interval of a fourth against the bass. The interval of a sixth is a consonant interval but, in common-practice style, the interval of a ***fourth against the bass* is considered a dissonant interval** and requires special attention by normally placing it on a **weak beat** and **resolving to a consonant** in one of three roles—as a passing, pedal, or the less common arpeggiated chord.

These examples with $^6_4$ chords (on a weak beat) demonstrate the correct usage of the second inversion triad and also show the dissonant interval of a 4th above the bass *resolving to a consonant interval.*

A second inversion chord may function as a *passing chord* so that the bass line moves in stepwise motion, passing between chords that have the bass a third apart. Notice the passing $^6_4$ is on a weak beat within the measure, passing between two of the same chords.

The IV$^6_4$ chord is often used near the beginning of a phrase to extend or *prolong tonic* function in a *pedal* $^6_4$ chord. When the subdominant chord is in second inversion, *Do* is in the bass. This creates a pedal in the bass—three chords in a row with the same note (*Do*). **Second inversion chords will usually double the fifth of the chord** so all three chords have *Do* in the bass and *Do* doubled, creating a strong tonic function. Notice how similar the I and the IV chords are. They have one note in common and the other two are adjacent (neighbors). They are both major in quality in a major key and minor in quality in a minor key. This type of $^6_4$ chord is also called a *neighbor* $^6_4$ or an *auxiliary* $^6_4$ because of the way the upper voices move one step up or down and back, or in an ascending or descending pattern.

Another type of second inversion chord is the *arpeggiated* $^6_4$, which is used to create an arpeggio between the bass notes on either side. Like the passing and pedal $^6_4$ chords, the arpeggiated $^6_4$ chord should be on a weak beat.

The **cadential** $^6_4$ chord is the only second inversion chord found on a **strong beat**. In the I$^6_4$, the fifth of the chord is *So*, and because it is in the bass and usually doubled as well, the I$^6_4$ **prolongs dominant function** when it precedes V at the cadence (I$^6_4$–V–I), the most common cadential ending. In this progression the interval of a fourth above the bass resolves downward to a third above the bass and the interval of a sixth resolves to a fifth above the bass.

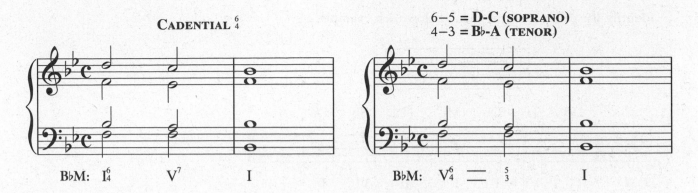

You may even see the harmonic analysis written an alternate way. Instead of the I^6_4–V–I Roman numeral analysis, you may see both chords as dominants (because they both *function* as dominants), showing the intervals in the figured bass moving downward by step (6–5 and 4–3). This is acceptable on the AP exam.

Let's take a closer look at three of these used in a harmonic progression.

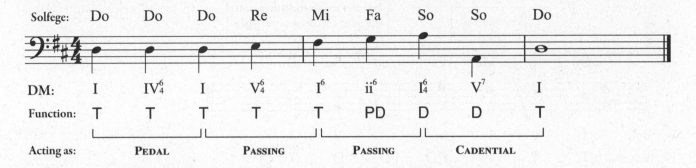

The four types of second inversion chords—passing, pedal, arpeggiated, and cadential—are all recognized uses of the $^6_4$ chord. This information is tested on the AP exam, particularly in the free-response (FR) section where you are required to write a bass line to harmonize with a given melody (FR 7). Many students make serious mistakes by using a $^6_4$ chord anywhere, with no reason or purpose. Be careful!

You must fully understand the uses of $^6_4$ chords and *not* just arbitrarily use them. Using $^6_4$ chords inappropriately is considered an *egregious* mistake (a conspicuously bad or offensive mistake).

The next five progressions have *function* identified above, chord symbol below, and the solfege of the bass note. One of the best things you can do is **sing bass lines** and recognize the connection between the bass line and the chord symbol. Learn what looks and sounds characteristic.

Identify the cadence in the blank below each example.

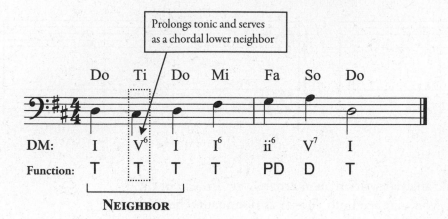

1. _____

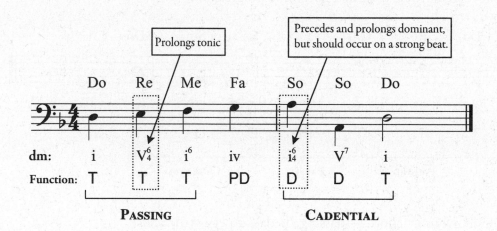

2. _____

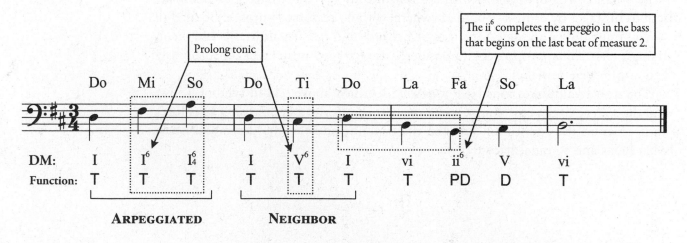

3. _____

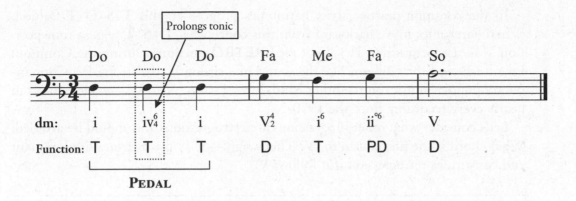

4. _____

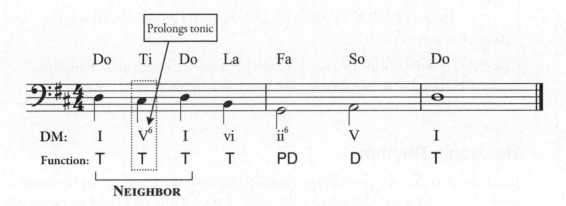

5. _____

1. Authentic
2. Authentic
3. Deceptive
4. Half
5. Authentic

> We cannot determine whether the authentic cadences are perfect or imperfect because we have not written the soprano.

PROgression vs. RETROgression

We have been talking about harmonic **PRO**gression—when the harmonies move from increasing tension (unstable) then resolve back to stable.

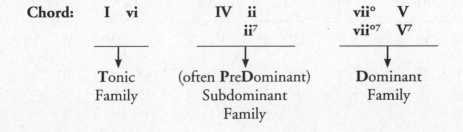

In the common-practice style, harmonies progress in this **T–S–D–T** fashion. When harmonies move backward from this concept: **T–D̄–S̄–T** (e.g., a root position V to a root position IV) it is called **RETROgression**. During the Common Practice Period they did not like the sound of a strong V to a strong IV. Contemporary popular music, on the other hand, loves a strong V to IV—made famous in nearly every recording from the 1950s.

Let's consider what other progressions are **retro**gressions and should be avoided. What chord is the first cousin to IV? That's right—ii⁶ is also a strong subdominant and constitutes retrogression if it follows V.

Here are the DO NOTs of Retrogression:

Do NOT follow V with IV, ii⁶, or ii⁶₅.

Do NOT follow vi (VI) with I (i). Why? The tonic chord is more stable, less tense than VI.

Do NOT follow ii with IV. Yes, they are both subdominant and often function as predominant, but they are not equal in tension.

Harmonic Rhythm

Just how often should you change chords? The underlying change of harmony is derived by noting the changing of the *roots* of the chords regardless of inversion. The rate at which harmony changes is called **harmonic rhythm**. There are no rules for harmonic rhythm. You can extend one harmony over several measures, or you can change chords frequently within the same measure.

In FR 7 (harmonization of a melody) *you* establish the harmonic rhythm by determining when and how the harmony moves. On the FR 7 portion of the AP exam, your harmonic rhythm should move in mostly quarter notes, but you may use note values ranging from half notes to eighth notes. Using eighth notes, though, is *not* necessary.

FUNDAMENTALS OF MELODIC HARMONIZATION
Major Scale Harmonization

If the *bass line* is an ascending major scale, what **chords above it would that** *imply*? In some cases, you have two or more commonly used choices.

Solfege	Do	Re			Mi	Fa		So		La		Ti		Do
Chord Symbol	I	ii	V⁶₄	vii°⁶	I⁶	IV	ii⁶	V	V⁷	vi	IV⁶	V⁶	V⁶₅	I
									F				F	
	S	L	Ⓡ	F	S	D	L	R	R	M	D	R	R	S
	M	F	T	R	Ⓜ	L	Ⓕ	T	T	D	La	T	Ⓣ	M
	Ⓓ	R	S	T	Ⓓ	F	R	Ⓢ	S	Ⓛ	F	S	S	Ⓓ

The bass note is not always the root because some chords are inverted.

After making some choices, the progression might look like this in G Major:

Now let's use an ascending scale as the **melody** and see what harmony might be *implied.*

The note in the bass is circled in the chord stack, reinforcing the inversion found in the Roman numeral chord symbol.

When we *hear* a complete chord progression without knowing what the symbols are, as in harmonic dictation, we want to listen to the bass line—it's a clue to knowing what the chord is. The bass line, along with chord quality and knowledge of how chords relate to each other (harmonic progression), implies possible chords. Conversely, when we *see or hear just the melody*, that also implies possible chords with which to harmonize. These are overlapping skills. Connect the dots.

The Process of Harmonizing a Melody

Harmonization of a melody is tested on the AP exam in Free Response 7. You will be given a melody (eight measures usually in a major key in Common Time) that contains four cadences. The first phrase is harmonized for you including the Roman numeral chord symbols. You are to complete the remaining three phrases including viable cadences, the Roman numeral chord symbols including inversions where appropriate, and the bass line. You do *not* write the alto and the tenor voice. This requires the understanding of counterpoint, interval, harmonic progression, cadences, chord symbols, and inversions.

Here is the process:

STEP 1: Identify the notes of the melody with either scale degree numbers or solfege.

STEP 2: Do the cadences *first*. You can earn as many as four points (out of eight) just by creating appropriate cadences.

- Cadences end with I (i) vi (VI) or V *only*; therefore, the chord symbols at the fermata(s) should only be a I, vi, or V (i, VI, or V in minor).
- Use *root* position chords for the final two chords in each of your cadences.

STEP 3: Use the same process we used to create an implied progression from the bass line to create a viable progression that goes with the melody. Remember these hints:

Keep **I**t **S**imple for **S**uccess (KISS).

- Do not invert needlessly.
- Do not use seventh chords excessively.
- Do not use root-position vii° chords.
- Do not use non-chord tones excessively in your bass line.
- Do not use second inversion triads ($\frac{6}{4}$ chords) **unless you understand the function**.

You could harmonize every diatonic note in the melody with I, IV, and V⁷.

Adding the vi or VI gives you every chord you need to write any cadence.

						F	$\hat{4}$		
S	$\hat{5}$	D	$\hat{1}$	R	$\hat{2}$	M	$\hat{3}$
M	$\hat{3}$	L	$\hat{6}$	T	$\hat{7}$	D	$\hat{1}$
D	$\hat{1}$	F	$\hat{4}$	S	$\hat{5}$	L	$\hat{6}$
I		**IV**		**V V⁷**		**vi**	

Your other choices are ii (usually ii⁶) and ii⁷. (Use ii°⁶ or ii°⁷ *only* if you understand the context of this harmony!)

- Write the norm. Write what is "common" in common-practice style. This is an exercise in creativity, but more important, it is an exercise to determine whether you understand the norms of the era.

STEP 4: Identify any notes out of the key and what that implies. (More detail on this is provided in Chapters 12 and 13.)

STEP 5: Connect the dots. By now we should begin to see opportunities to "connect the dots" between melodic patterns and implied harmonies. This will also help you in harmonic dictation.

Here is a simple example. We will go through the process and create a harmonization.

E♭M: I V I   ii^{∘6} V I

Based on what is given, what do we know for sure? The first cadence is an imperfect authentic cadence. In measure 2 the V chord harmonizes the D; the C is used to pass smoothly between *Ti* and *So*. We will circle the notes that are *not* part of the harmony.

What chords do we have to work with?

OUR CHORD MENU ⟶

		E♭			A♭			C
B♭	C	C	E♭	F	F	G	A♭	A♭
G	A♭	A♭	C	D	D	E♭	F	F
E♭	F	F	A♭	B♭	B♭	C	D	D
I	**ii**	**ii⁷**	**IV**	**V**	**V⁷**	**vi**	**vii°**	**vii°⁷**

Identify the Cadences

The second cadence ends on *Re*, which is *not* in the tonic or the submediant chord; therefore the second cadence can only be a *half* cadence. The third cadence ends on *Do*, which is found in both the tonic and submediant triad. Since this is not the final cadence we will harmonize with a deceptive cadence. The last measure should have the most final-sounding cadence; it is what is expected, so write what is expected—the perfect authentic cadence.

CONNECT THE DOTS

In the last measure the melody is **Mi-Re-Do**, one of the most common melodic endings. Harmonize it with the most common bass line ending, **So-So-Do**, creating the progression I_4^6–V or V^7–I.

What commonly comes before the submediant (vi) in the deceptive cadence? The dominant.

With this information our harmonization thus far looks like:

The last step is to see what chords will harmonize with the remainder of the given melody. You do not have to harmonize every note; however, you must have a minimum of two different chords (or change inversion) per measure—the AP exam states to use predominantly quarter notes. You might want to pencil in the choices.

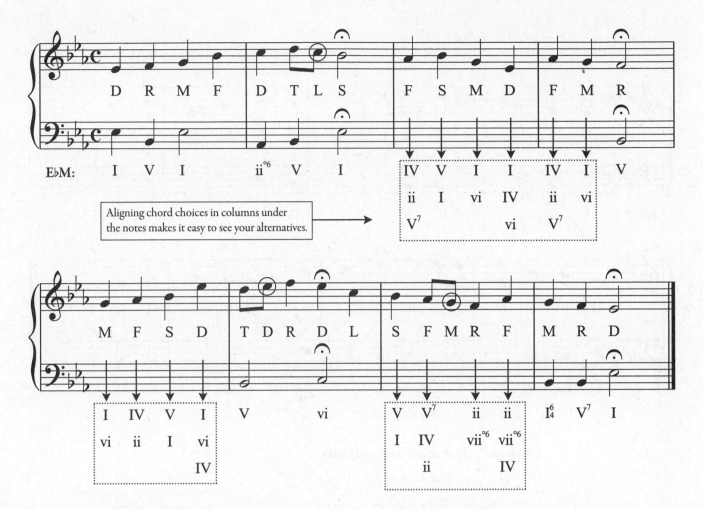

In the third measure we could harmonize both *Fa* and *So* with the V⁷ chord and *Mi* and *Do* with tonic, *but* the *Fa* resolves to *So* (it should resolve to *Mi*) in the given melody so that is not an option. In measure 4 it *does* work to harmonize *Fa-Mi* with the V⁷ chord, or harmonize *Fa* with a half note ii or IV and not harmonize *Mi*. In the fifth measure the melody line is ascending so we will try and make our bass line descending. There are several good choices available. In measure 7 we can harmonize *So* and *Mi* with tonic or *So*, *Fa*, and *Re* with the V⁷ and leave *Fa* on beat 4 to harmonize with vii°. The supertonic chord would not be a good choice after V because it creates a retrogression, especially if it's ii⁶. We could also harmonize *So* and *Mi* with the tonic chord making *Fa* a passing tone and harmonize *Re* and *Fa* with the supertonic chord.

After making some choices and trying to make the bass line move in the opposite direction of the melody (to avoid parallelism) by using appropriate inversions, we end with this harmonization. The fermata indicates the end of a phrase but also the beginning of a new phrase and the progression starts new as well.

Notice that after the fermata in measure 6 we chose to use a quarter rest since we already have two chords in that measure.

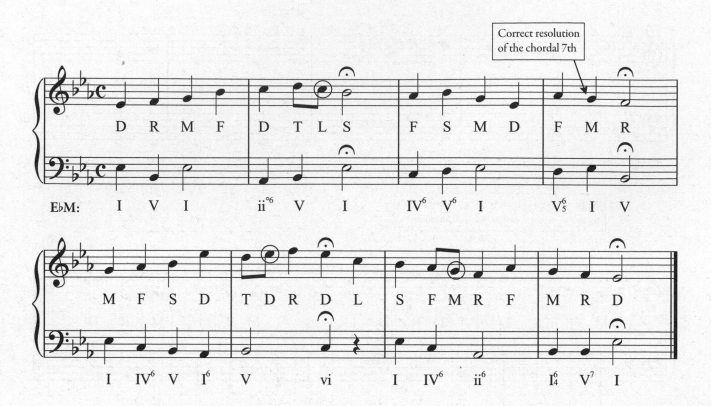

Correct resolution of the chordal 7th

Here are a few more suggestions:

- Use standard cadences.

  - I_4^6–V$^{(7)}$–I (*So-So-Do* in the bass)
  - IV–V$^{(7)}$–I (*Fa-So-Do* in the bass)
  - ii^6–V$^{(7)}$–I (*Fa-So-Do* in the bass)
  - half cadence ends on V
  - IV–I plagal
  - V–vi deceptive

> Fifty percent or more of all common-practice cadences will end with one of these three authentic cadences.

- Only three chords can end a phrase in common practice: I, V, or vi.
- Choose harmonies at the slowest possible harmonic rhythm. Keep it simple!
- Use basic primary chords: I, IV, V, or ii.

  - Do not use iii or III.
  - Stay away from vii° except in tonic expansion such as I–vii°^{6}–I^6 (*Do-Re-Mi*).

- Once you have written the cadences, you are over a third finished. Connect the dots with standard common-practice progressions such as I–vi–ii–V–I (circle progression).
- Choose to harmonize the notes of the melody that are more important—those that are longer or are on the beat.
- Keep contrary motion in mind.

➡ You will find more examples in Chapter 21, Strategies for Harmonizing a Melody.

Chapter Summary

- **Harmonic progression** or "chord leading" is the process of relating chords within the scale to where they naturally lead.
- PROgression is when the harmonies proceed from a stable beginning (tonic function), move forward through progressively more active chords (predominant and dominant functions) including seventh chords, to end (resolve) once again with stability.

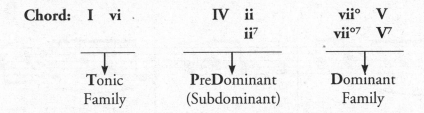

- Common progressions:

  - **Circle progression** is the movement of chords where the root (not necessarily the bass) of each chord is a diatonic fifth above the next chord.
  - **Progression by thirds** is the movement of chords where the root of each chord is either up or down by a third.
  - **Progression by seconds** is the movement of chords where the root of each chord is either up or down to the next note in the scale.

- There are four types of second inversion chords. These four types of second inversion chords—**passing**, **pedal**, **arpeggiated**, and **cadential**—are the only recognized uses of the $\frac{6}{4}$ chord.
- In the common-practice style, harmonies progress in this "T–PD–D–T" fashion. When harmonies move backward from this concept—"T–D-PD–T" (e.g., a root position V to a root position IV) it is called RETROgression.

  - Do *not* follow V with IV, ii⁶, or ii$\frac{6}{5}$.
  - Do *not* follow vi (VI) with I (i). Why? The tonic chord is more stable and less tense than VI.
  - Do *not* follow ii with IV. Yes, they are both predominant but they are not equal in tension.

- Harmonization of a melody is tested on the AP exam in Free-Response question 7 (FR 7). This requires the understanding of counterpoint, interval, harmonic progression, cadences, chord symbols, and inversions. **K**eep **I**t **S**imple for **S**uccess (KISS).

  - Do not invert needlessly.
  - Do not use seventh chords excessively.
  - Do not use non-chord tones excessively in your bass line.
  - Write what is "common" in common-practice style.

- The rate at which the harmony changes is called **harmonic rhythm**.

Practice Exercises

Questions 1–9 are based on *36 Original Dances, Op. 9, No. 3* by Schubert.

36 Original Dances, Op. 9, No. 3

Franz Schubert
(1797–1828)
D. 365

1. The harmonic rhythm in this example primarily is

   (A) every beat
   (B) every measure
   (C) twice per measure
   (D) every other measure

2. The Roman numeral chord analysis of phrase 1 is

   (A) I–IV–ii^6–V–V^7–I$^6_4$–V^7–I
   (B) I–IV–ii–V–V^7–V–V^7–I
   (C) I–IV–ii–V–V^7–I$^6_4$–V^7–I
   (D) I–IV–IV–V–V–V^7–V^7–I

3. The cadence that ends the first phrase is

   (A) plagal
   (B) half
   (C) imperfect authentic
   (D) perfect authentic

4. The chord outlined in measure 3 is a

   (A) supertonic in root position
   (B) supertonic in first inversion
   (C) subdominant
   (D) seventh chord

5. The chord outlined in measure 9 is

   (A) the mediant
   (B) the submediant
   (C) the subdominant
   (D) not in the key of A♭ Major

6. Measures 9 and 10 briefly imply the key of the

   (A) parallel minor
   (B) relative minor
   (C) dominant
   (D) mediant

7. The accidental in measure 9 could be identified as all of the following **except** the

   (A) leading tone in F minor
   (B) root of the chord
   (C) third of the chord
   (D) raised fifth scale degree (*Si*) in A♭

8. Measures 11 and 12 briefly imply the key of the

   (A) parallel minor
   (B) relative minor
   (C) dominant
   (D) subdominant

9. The type of harmonic progression of phrase 2 (measures 9–16) is

   (A) progression by seconds
   (B) progression by thirds
   (C) circle progression
   (D) a mixture

10. The process of relating chords to where they naturally lead is called

(A) harmonic progression
(B) retrogression
(C) harmonic rhythm
(D) cadential expectation

11. The rate at which harmony changes is called

(A) harmonic progression
(B) retrogression
(C) harmonic rhythm
(D) harmonic pulse

12. The following are recognized uses of second inversion chords **except**

(A) passing
(B) cadential
(C) accented
(D) pedal

13. Which of the following is <u>not</u> a viable progression in common-practice style?

(A) I–ii–IV–V–I
(B) I–vii°⁶–I–V–vi
(C) I–IV–ii–V⁷–I
(D) I–IV$^6_4$–I–IV–V

14. When harmonies within a phrase move from a strong intensity to a less strong intensity (e.g., a root position V to a root position IV) it is called

(A) progression
(B) supergression
(C) retrogression
(D) disjunct

15. Which of the following progressions maintains the tonic pitch as the bass note?

(A) I–IV⁶–vi⁶
(B) I–IV$^6_4$–I
(C) IV$^6_4$–V$^6_5$–I
(D) I–ii$^6_5$–vi⁶

Questions 16–20 refer to the melody below.

16. The meter is best described as

    (A) simple duple
    (B) compound duple
    (C) compound triple
    (D) simple triple

17. Which scale pattern is used in measures 3 and 4?

    (A) Major
    (B) Harmonic minor
    (C) Melodic minor
    (D) Pentatonic

18. Measure 1 is described as all of the following **except**

    (A) the most disjunct of the four measures
    (B) outlining the tonic triad
    (C) the most conjunct of the four measures
    (D) using the natural form of minor

19. Which harmonic pattern works best under the melody in measures 1 and 2 (presuming two chords per measure)?

    (A) i–V–ii°⁶–V
    (B) i–V–i₄⁶–V
    (C) i–VI–ii°–V
    (D) i–V–iv–i

20. A cadence occurring at the end of measure 2 would be

    (A) half
    (B) perfect authentic
    (C) plagal
    (D) deceptive

ANSWER KEY

1. **B**	6. **B**	11. **C**	16. **B**
2. **C**	7. **B**	12. **C**	17. **C**
3. **D**	8. **C**	13. **A**	18. **C**
4. **A**	9. **C**	14. **C**	19. **C**
5. **D**	10. **A**	15. **B**	20. **A**

ANSWERS EXPLAINED

1. **(B)** The harmonic rhythm (the *rate* at which harmony changes in a progression) changes every measure.

2. **(C)** The Roman numeral analysis for phrase 1 is I–IV–ii–V–V⁷–I⁶₄–V⁷–I. Let's comment about this progression. The function is T–PD–PD–D–D–D–D–T. The progression is I–IV (circle) IV–ii (third) ii–V (circle) V⁷–I⁶₄ (progression is by root so it is V–I (circle)). The type of second inversion (I⁶₄) is cadential.

3. **(D)** The cadence that ends phrase 1 is perfect authentic.

4. **(A)** The chord outlined in measure 3 is a supertonic chord in root position. In A♭ Major the supertonic is B♭–D♭–F.

5. **(D)** The chord in measure 9 is C–E♮–G–B♭, and not found diatonically in A♭ Major.

6. **(B)** Measures 9 and 10 briefly imply the key of the relative minor (F minor).

7. **(B)** The accidental is E natural. It is the leading tone in F minor, it is the third of the D♭ Major chord, and when solfeged in A♭ Major it would be *Si* (the raised $\hat{5}$ in A♭).

8. **(C)** Measures 11 and 12 imply the key of E♭ Major—the dominant. The use of the D natural, which leads to E♭, is the signal that we have temporarily left A♭ Major.

9. **(C)** The type of harmonic progression used in phrase 2 is circle progression. If we look at the roots of each of the chords (the harmony is only changing once per measure) we see:

CIRCLE PROGRESSION:
THE ROOTS MOVE IN V–I RELATIONSHIP

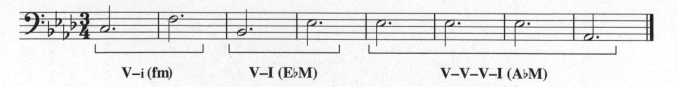

V–i (fm)   **V–I (E♭M)**   **V–V–V–I (A♭M)**

10. **(A)** Harmonic progression is the process of relating chords to where they naturally lead.

11. **(C)** The rate at which harmony changes is called *harmonic rhythm*.

12. **(C)** Accented $^6_4$ is not a type of second inversion triad. Passing $^6_4$, cadential $^6_4$, and pedal $^6_4$ are all accepted uses of second inversion triads.

13. **(A)** I–ii–IV–V–I is *not* a viable progression in common practice because ii does *not* go to IV. It is considered retrogression.

14. **(C)** When harmonies within a phrase move from strong to weaker intensity it is called *retrogression*.

15. **(B)** The tonic is maintained as the bass note in I–IV$^6_4$–I (also an example of a pedal $^6_4$).

16. **(B)** The meter in the example is compound duple (two beats per measure—each beat divides into three equal parts).

17. **(C)** The scale pattern in measures 3 and 4 is the melodic minor in E minor. Measure 3 shows the natural minor form of the scale when descending and raised 6th and 7th scaled degrees when ascending (measure 4).

18. **(C)** Measure 1 is the most disjunct (moving by skip and leap), outlines the tonic triad in E minor, and uses the natural form of minor because the D is not raised. It is the least conjunct (moving by stepwise motion).

19. **(C)** The harmonic progression that best fits this melody is i–VI–ii°–V (a circle progression). All the other answers have V as the second chord and there is no $\hat{1}$ (*Do*) in the dominant triad.

20. **(A)** The likely cadence at the end of measure 2 is the half cadence (V).

Melodic Composition

10

- Anacrusis
- Augmentation
- Conjunct
- Diminution
- Disjunct
- Elision
- Expansion
  - Internal, Cadential
- Fragmentation
- Imitation
- Leitmotif
- Literal Repetition
- Melody
- Melodic Inversion
- Mode Mixture, Modal Borrowing
- Motive, Motif
- Non-Chord Tones,
  Non-Harmonic Tones
  - Appoggiatura
  - Anticipation
  - Escape Tone (Échappée)
  - Incomplete Neighbor (Cambiata)
  - Passing Tones
    - Accented, Unaccented, and
      Chromatic
  - Neighbor Tones
    - Upper and Lower Neighbors
  - Suspension
  - Retardation
- Octave Displacement

- Phrase
- Phrase Structure
  - Symmetrical and Asymmetrical
  - Periodic Structure
    - Antecedent–Consequent
    - Parallel Period
    - Contrasting Period
    - Double Period
    - Repeated Period
    - Modulating Period
- Retrograde
- Rhythmic Displacement
- Sequence
- Transposition
- Variation

THE BUILDING BLOCKS OF MELODIC FORM

To many of us, music means melody. Melody is a series of single notes that begins, moves forward, and ends. It has direction, shape and continuity, tension and release, and expectation and arrival.

How Are Melodies Constructed?

- A melody is defined as a logical progression of pitches and rhythms—a tune. It is a linear succession of notes that *form a recognizable unit*, which is used to separate a melody from random pitches.
- Melody is the most important part of a composition and should be the most memorable.
- Melodies do not always begin on the downbeat. Sometimes the melody begins before the beat called pick-up note(s) or **anacrusis**. The anacrusis is an incomplete measure that combines with the final measure of the phrase to equal the meter.
- A good melody will use mostly stepwise motion (**conjunct**) and some skipwise (**disjunct**) motion. Most melodies rise and fall and often lead the listener **stepwise** to a climax or high point and then resolve the tension to create a feeling of comfort or relief, or may provide variety with a skip or leap.
- A good melody must have movement—moving forward with *contour* or shape of a line of music.
- The best melodies are not only centered but also somewhat contained or limited in range, usually within an octave.
- Longer melodies employ repetitions, have a distinct form, and are built from simple motifs and short melodic phrases.

How Do You Choose What Notes to Use for a Melody?

- When you are creating a melody for part writing or realizing a figured bass, the harmonic structure or chord progression presents your "menu" of note choices for the melody.
- Creating contrapuntal motion between the bass and the soprano (parallel, similar, oblique, and contrary) also impacts your choice of melody notes.
- There are four scale tones that help to define the tonality and modality of a melody:

  - The **tonic**, because it is the tonal center of the composition
  - The **mediant** defines its harmonic nature; that is, whether it is major or minor
  - The **dominant** is the fifth degree of the scale
  - The **seventh** degree of the scale positions your melody to return to the tonic; emphasizing the leading tone adds tension to a melody

- In general, you want your melody to move from *unstable to stable* tones, especially at the end of a phrase.

MELODIC STRUCTURE

Structure and form are important in any musical composition. Structure organizes the music and guides the composition through the individual components—introduction, melody, climax, development, and conclusion.

- Melodies are constructed in **phrases**. Phrases are single coherent musical thoughts that move toward a goal: the cadence. **A four-measure segment**

makes a phrase only when it concludes with a cadence. Musical phrases lead logically one to the next and also have a musical relationship to each other. This is associated once again to language where related sentences connect together into paragraphs.

  – A melodic unit that is smaller than a phrase is called a sub-phrase. It does *not* end with a cadence.

• Often, phrases occur in pairs. When the first phrase of a pair ends with a weaker cadence and the second with a stronger harmonic conclusion, then this pair of phrases together forms an **antecedent–consequent** relationship known as a **period**.

  – The most common antecedent ending is a half cadence followed by the consequent ending with a perfect authentic cadence.
  – When the two phrases making up the period begin identically, or the second phrase is a variation of the first, this structure is called a **parallel period**.
  – When the two phrases are different from each other they are called a **contrasting period**.
  – When two phrases both end with a strong cadence, there is no antecedent–consequent relationship and therefore no period. You simply have two phrases.
  – A **repeated parallel period** is just that—two phrases that form a parallel period repeated exactly.
  – A **double period** is a group of four phrases in which the only PAC appears at the conclusion of the fourth phrase. The first two phrases and the last two phrases are *paired* to form the antecedent–consequent relationship.

• When phrases are analyzed they are labeled with lowercase alphabet letters. Phrases that sound different get a different letter—*a*, *b*, *c*, and so forth—while phrases that are identical get the same letter. Phrases that are similar but not identical receive the same letter with the prime mark (′) such as **a** and **a′**, or with letters and numbers such as **a** and **a^1**, **a^2**, **a^3**.
• Phrase structure often uses charts to also represent number of measures, melodic phrase relationships, and cadence type.

$$\textbf{a} \qquad\qquad\qquad \textbf{a}^1$$

FM: ⌒ m1–8 ⌒ **HC** ⌒ m9–16 ⌒ **PAC**

This is an example of a parallel period.
• Phrase expansion refers to expanding phrases beyond normal phrase lengths by adding material to the beginning, middle, or end.

  – Material added at the beginning is called an **introduction** or prefix.
  – Expansions at the end of phrases are known as suffixes, or **cadential extensions**.
  – An **internal expansion** lengthens the phrase anywhere other than the beginning or the end.
  – **Elision** occurs when one phrase ends and the next phrase begins simultaneously with one note or chord functioning to overlap the phrases.

Let's look at a musical example and comment on the melody, phrases, and cadences.

REVIEW

Piano Sonata in A, Op. 11

Wolfgang Amadeus Mozart
(1756–1791)
K. 331

This piece has four phrases; the first two phrases (measures 1–8) create a **parallel period**. The example ends with a **cadential extension**. The first two chords in measure 16 immediately recall measure 8, and the movement of the melodic voice "wants" to go to A. When it doesn't, the melody feels interrupted through measures 17 and 18 until the final chord with A in both soprano and bass, finishing the idea in the same way that it was finished in measure 8. Harmonically, the extension prolongs the tonic before resolving with a PAC. Can you create the phrase structure chart? The answer follows.

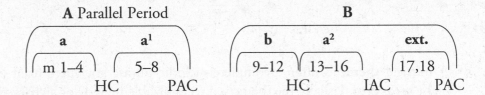

Repetition

The use of repetition is perhaps the most critical aspect of musical structure. It balances the music between the familiar and unfamiliar. A melody can be repeated in several ways.

- **Literal repetition** is exact repetition in the same voice.
- In multiple-voice compositions, the melody repeated in another part is often called **imitation** because the second part imitates the first.

REPETITION THROUGH MOTIVE

- The melodic **motive** or **motif** is a short group of notes (usually between two and eight **notes**) that is repeated throughout the melody to establish its identity and provide thematic unity. It is an important recurring musical fragment or even just a few notes in succession that have some significance to the composition. The motive may be melodic, harmonic, or rhythmic and may be repeated exactly or it may have variations; it may be transposed or altered rhythmically. The motive defines the melody and characterizes and unifies the composition. Probably the most famous motive is from Beethoven's Fifth Symphony. This motive represents "fate" knocking on the door.

- A motive thematically associated with a person, place, or idea is called a leitmotif, such as the themes representing the characters in one of Richard Wagner's operas or, more recently, in film scores, such as *Star Wars*. The leitmotif may be heard whenever that character is "on stage" or that idea is an important part of the plot. As with other motifs, leitmotifs may be changed when they return sounding quite different depending on whether the character is in love, being heroic, or dying.

This leitmotif represents the character Siegfried from Wagner's opera, *The Valkyrie*.

- A musical **theme** is often a complete melodic phrase anywhere from two to eight **measures**. Usually the theme is a recognizable melody or a characteristic rhythmic pattern. It is the main musical idea, and like the motive, it defines the composition, reinforces it through repetition, and serves as the basis for expanding and elaborating the melody often through variation.

REPETITION THROUGH VARIATION

With **variation** the original motive is used as the basis for related musical ideas. Types of variations are:

- **Melodic sequence** refers to repeating the original motive starting on a different pitch. A sequence can be exact, in which case the intervals of the original motive are retained utilizing chromatics, or inexact, where the repeated intervals are diatonic.
- **Inversion** or **melodic inversion** is the imitation of the melody performed upside-down from the original melody. It moves in the opposite direction by the same diatonic interval. For example, if the original example moved up by a third, the inversion would move down by a third. If the inverted intervals are *exact*, up a major third inverts to down a major third; this specific kind of inversion is called **mirror inversion**.
- A **retrograde** means the melody is played backward. A **retrograde inversion** plays the pitches of the original theme exactly backward and inverted.
- **Rhythmic displacement** keeps the original rhythmic structure intact but moves it to a different place in the measure. For example, instead of starting the phrase on beat 3, *you start on beat 4*. This is a very common method of variation in popular music.
- **Augmentation** is a form of **rhythmic variation** where the pitches remain the same but the rhythms are lengthened—note values are made longer.
- **Diminution** is the opposite of augmentation where the note values are shortened.
- **Expansion** adds new material typically to the end of the original phrase.
- **Modulation** refers to the act or process of changing from one key or tonal center to another. A variation may repeat exactly or alter in multiple ways but *in a different key* usually closely related to the original.

- **Mode mixture** involves combining chords from the *parallel* major or minor mode to increase harmonic resources. Mode mixture or **modal borrowing** provides more variation in harmonies by occasionally borrowing a chord from the parallel major or minor mode.
- **Ornamentation** or **embellishment** is the technique of adding or decorating the melody with non-chord tones such as passing tones, neighboring tones, and suspensions.

We now look at a more challenging example (*Minuet in G Minor*) and do an analysis of the melodic structure. Remember that cadences not only determine tonality, but are also critical when identifying phrase structure.

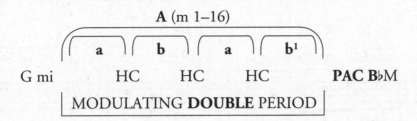

Phrases 1 and 3 begin with exactly the same melody; Phrases 2 and 4 are the same melody transposed (2 in G minor and 4 in B♭ Major); and both 2 and 4 also contain a **melodic sequence**.

Phrase 1+2: (measures 1–8) ends with HC
   in G minor—**antecedent**
Phrase 3+4: (measures 9–16) ends with a PAC
   in B♭ Major—**consequent**

} Double Parallel Period

There is periodic structure here but, because the final PAC is not in G minor but has modulated to the relative major (B♭), it is considered a **modulating** parallel double period.

Minuet in G Minor (excerpt)

From the Notebook for
Anna Magdalena Bach, 1725
BWV Anh 115

Woodworth

William B. Bradbury
(1816–1868)

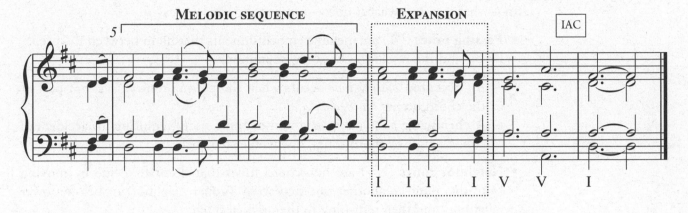

Let's look at this example in two different ways. First, consider that the example contains two phrases (measures 1–4 and 5–9), both *beginning* with the identical melody; however, this would not be considered a parallel period because there is no antecedent–consequent. Both phrases end with weak (IAC) cadences. Phrase 2 (measures 5–9) contains two sub-phrases that are asymmetrical (of unequal length). Phrase 2 also contains a melodic sequence in measures 5 and 6 (same rhythmic pattern but the melody is up an interval of a 4th) *plus* an additional measure (measure 7) that continues with the same rhythm and prolongs the tonic before the cadence.

Second, consider measures 1–4 as two phrases (measures 1–2 and 3–4) instead of one. Do these two phrases have periodic structure? The melodies are contrasting, so is this a contrasting period? The answer is no, because both phrases end with a weak (IAC) cadence. Because it could be either, the performer's interpretation of measure 2 (whether or not to make the half note a resting place) determines the phrase length.

NON-CHORD TONES

While doing harmonic analysis, you may find notes that "don't belong" in your chord. These notes that "don't belong" create a temporary dissonance against the members of the chord and are called **non-chord tones** or **non-harmonic tones** (not part of the harmony). **Non-Chord Tones** (NCTs) may occur in any voice, but are most common in the melody. Some NCTs are added as ornaments or embellishment, some are added to increase the tension, and some are used to connect chord tones together in a more pleasant melodic line. We think of non-chord tones as having three parts. The first chord tone, called the preparation, the dissonant tone (NCT) itself, and the chord tone it leads or resolves to (the resolution). The labeling of non-chord tones is one of those areas about which many music theorists "agree to disagree." Remember, you must understand the concept behind the term—what it is and what it does—not just the label.

- **Passing tones** (PT) are melodic embellishments that fill in between the preparation and the resolution by stepwise motion.

  - An **accented** *passing tone* occurs when the passing tone that is not part of the chord occurs *on the beat.*
  - A **chromatic** *passing tone* is a non-diatonic note (requiring an accidental) connecting two chord tones, one whole step apart.

- **Neighbor tones** (NT) are non-chord tones that decorate a line by moving from one pitch to another one-step above (upper neighbor) or below (lower neighbor) and then returning to the original pitch.

  - When the neighboring tone is an accidental a *half step* above or below the chord tone (but not the leading tone in minor), it is called a *chromatic neighbor.*
  - An **incomplete neighbor**, or **cambiata**, is a non-harmonic tone approached by skip or leap in one direction and resolved by stepwise motion in the opposite direction. It *occurs in a weak rhythmic position.*
  - A **neighboring group**, sometimes called a **changing tone**, consists of two consecutive non-chord tones. The first moves up by a step from a chord tone, skips down to another non-chord tone, and then resolves *to the original chord tone.* These two non-chord tones may also be called double-neighbor tones. Changing tones appear to resemble two consecutive neighbor tones: an upper neighbor and a lower neighbor with the chord tone missing from the middle.

- An **appoggiatura** is a specific kind of incomplete neighbor that leaves the preparation by leap up and then resolves down by step. **This is an accented non-chord tone because it** *occurs on the beat.*
- An **escape** tone, or **échappée**, is another form of incomplete neighbor that leaves the chord tone by step then resolves in the opposite direction by leap.
- A **suspension** occurs when a note in the preparation chord is *held over* (suspended) creating a momentary accented dissonance (on the beat) that is resolved downward by step to the resolution. Suspensions are named for the

interval numbers above the bass of the dissonant tone and the resolution. The most common types of suspension are **9–8**, **7–6**, and **4–3**.

- Suspensions are often connected to their preparation by a tie. When the suspended note is not tied to its preparation, it is called a **rearticulated suspension**.
- A **retardation** is a suspended note that *resolves upward.*
- An **anticipation** tone leaves early from the preparation chord by step to become part of the resolution chord. It anticipates the pitch to come in the next chord.

Here is an example of a melody in C Major using non-chord tones.

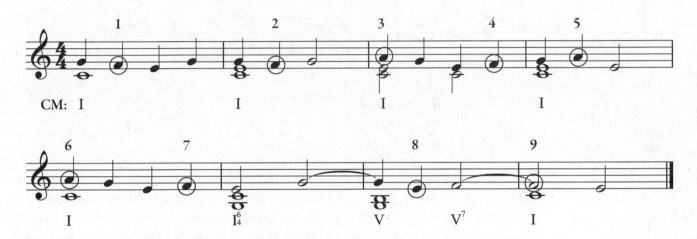

1. **Passing tone** fills in the gaps between chord tones a third apart.
2. **Lower neighbor** is one step below two of the same chord tones.
3. **Accented upper** neighbor occurs on the beat.
4. **Passing tone** fills in the gaps between chord tones a third apart.
5. **Escape tone** is unaccented—approached by step and moves away in the opposite direction by leap.
6. **Appoggiatura** is on the beat (accented) and is approached by leap and resolves in the opposite direction by step.
7. **Upper neighbor** is one step above two of the same chord tones.
8. **Incomplete neighbor** occurs on a weak beat and leaves by skip and resolves by step in the opposite direction.
9. **Suspension** (in this case 4–3) is held over from the preparation chord and resolves down by step to the chord tone.

Now go back to page 135 and see if you can identify the circled notes in "Eventide." They are non-chord tones.

Choral "O Haupt voll Blut und Wunden"

excerpt, Matthäus Passion, No. 63

Johann Sebastian Bach
(1685–1750)
BWV 244

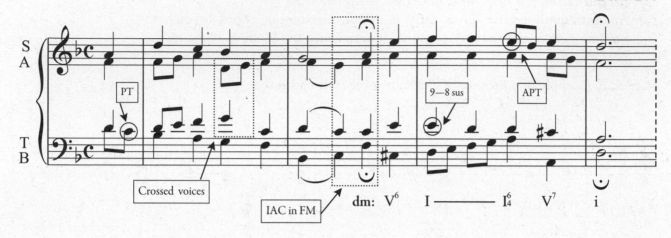

It is important to remember our earlier discussions about looking at the music and not just the key signature to determine the key and to note that music doesn't always stay in one key. In this example the first phrase is in F Major and the second phrase is in the relative minor, D minor. The cadences are the proof we need to determine the tonality.

Here is an example of an **imperfect** authentic cadence (IAC) in FM (antecedent), and a **perfect** authentic cadence (PAC) in Dm (consequent) forming a modulating contrasting period. Let's connect the dots aurally and visually—how will what we see, sound? Remembering the Top Ten Melodic Patterns, we note that Bach used *Fa-So-Do* in FM as the bass line for the first phrase (second most common bass ending) and *So-So-Do* in D minor in the second cadence (*most* common bass ending). There are several examples of NCTs, including passing tones, accented passing tone, anticipation, and a 9–8 suspension. This excerpt also includes an example of what *not* to do. Notice in the box in the first complete measure that the tenor voice is singing higher than the alto and/or alto is singing lower than the tenor—this is an example of crossed voices—a definite "no-no" on the AP exam. Now look at the whole chorale.

Choral "O Haupt voll Blut und Wunden"

Matthäus Passion, No. 63

Johann Sebastian Bach
(1685–1750)
BWV 244

This composition includes eight phrases, each ending with a fermata. Notice that Phrases 1 and 2 (measures 1–4) are identical to Phrases 3 and 4. The fifth phrase (measures 9–10) is in F Major and ends with an **imperfect authentic cadence** (vii°⁶ to I sometimes called a leading tone cadence), using a **4–3 suspension** (with a *lower-neighbor* embellishment) in the alto and an **accented upper-neighbor** tone (D) in the tenor. Phrase 6 begins with the addition of an accidental (E♭ that is in neither F Major nor D minor), retains the B♭ and later adds the F♯. The cadence proves the move to G harmonic minor with a half cadence (i–V). Phrase 7 shifts tonality again. The accidentals are a very big clue. Notice the F natural in the soprano moves down to the E, while the B♭ in the bass moves up to a C. The B♮ is retained throughout the phrase ending with a convincing cadence in C Major. Can you identify the cadence and the non-chord tones in this measure?

The final phrase is back in F Major, ends with an imperfect AC and features a 4–3 suspension in the alto. The harmonic analysis of the last two measures is **ii–I⁶–V⁴⁻³–V–I**.

Learning to play and interpret melodies using melodic and rhythmic embellishments, and understanding the structure and organization of melody, are goals musicians pursue for a lifetime.

Chapter Summary

- **Melody** is the most important part of a composition and is defined as a logical progression of pitches and rhythms.
- A good melody must have movement, contour or shape, set up and resolve tension, have a tonal center, and stay within a reasonable range.
- An interesting melody with tension and release is created by paying attention to stable and unstable tones of the diatonic scale and by using a mixture of stepwise and skipwise motion.
- Repeating and varying a main melodic theme is an effective way to create larger compositions.
- A theme or motif can be repeated in the same voice or imitated in a different voice.
- There are many ways to vary a melody including sequence, inversion, retrograde inversion, expansion, augmentation, diminution, modulation, and mode mixture.
- Musical phrases lead logically one to the next and also have a musical relationship to each other. Harmony defines phrases in the Common Practice Period.
- Often phrases occur in pairs. When the first phrase of a pair ends with a weaker cadence and the second with a stronger harmonic conclusion, then this pair of phrases together forms an **antecedent–consequent** relationship known as a period.

  - Pairs of phrases can be **parallel** (beginning with identical melodic material) or **contrasting** (beginning with different melodic material).
  - A **double period** is typically four phrases that are paired to create the antecedent–consequent relationship. The cadence at the end of phrase two is active in nature, while the strongest cadence is at the end of phrase four.

- Embellishing or ornamental notes that are *not* part of the chord create a temporary dissonance against the other members of the chord and are called **non-chord tones** or non-harmonic tones (not part of the harmony).

  - Examples of non-chord tones are **passing tones (PT)**—accented, unaccented, and chromatic; **neighbor tones (NT)**—upper, lower, and chromatic; **incomplete neighbor** or **cambiata**; **neighbor group**; **appoggiatura**; **escape tone** or **échappée**; as well as **suspension**, **retardation**, and **anticipation**.

Practice Exercises

Questions 1–8 refer to the adapted harmonization of "Was Gott tut," below.

Was Gott tut

Severus Gastorius, 1681
Adapted from harmonization in
Common Service Book, 1917

1. The cadence for this four-measure phrase is

   (A) half
   (B) imperfect authentic
   (C) perfect authentic
   (D) deceptive

2. The non-chord tone labeled 1 is an example of

   (A) a passing tone
   (B) a lower neighbor
   (C) an escape tone
   (D) suspension

3. The non-chord tone labeled 2 is an example of

   (A) a passing tone
   (B) a lower neighbor
   (C) an incomplete neighbor
   (D) suspension

4. The non-chord tone labeled 3 is an example of

   (A) an upper neighbor
   (B) a lower neighbor
   (C) an incomplete neighbor
   (D) suspension

5. The non-chord tone labeled 4 is an example of

   (A) a 7–6 suspension
   (B) a 4–3 suspension
   (C) a retardation
   (D) an anticipation

6. All of the following are true of the chord (5) in the penultimate measure except it

   (A) is a tonic chord in second inversion
   (B) functions as a passing $^6_4$ chord
   (C) is predominant function
   (D) is a seventh chord

7. The Roman numeral analysis of the last measure is

   (A) ii°⁶–V–I
   (B) ii⁰⁶₅–V–I
   (C) ii⁶₅–V⁷–I
   (D) IV⁷–V⁷–I

8. The last three chords are considered a circle progression because the

   (A) progression circles back to the tonic
   (B) roots of the chords are a P5 apart
   (C) notes in the bass are a P5 apart
   (D) cadence is a PAC

Questions 9–12 are based on Beethoven's Piano Sonata No. 6, Op. 10, No. 2

Piano Sonata No. 6, Op. 10, No. 2

Ludwig van Beethoven
(1770–1827)

9. The harmony outlined by the melody in the first four measures is

    (A) tonic
    (B) dominant
    (C) tonic and dominant
    (D) subdominant

10. The melody entering in the right hand in measure 5 is

    (A) a melodic inversion of the beginning melody
    (B) a variation of the beginning melody
    (C) an exact imitation of the beginning melody an octave higher
    (D) a melodic sequence based on the beginning melody

11. The melody enters a third time in the right hand in measure 8, this time in the key of the

    (A) dominant
    (B) relative minor
    (C) parallel minor
    (D) subdominant

12. The scale pattern presented in the boxed area at measure 17 is in

    (A) D minor
    (B) F Major
    (C) C Major
    (D) C melodic minor

Questions 13–15 are based on this excerpt from the "Hymn of Eve."

"Hymn of Eve" from *Death of Abel*
(Uxbridge)

Thomas Arne
(1710–1788)

13. The cadence in the box (measures 2 and 3) can best be described as

    (A) imperfect authentic
    (B) half
    (C) plagal
    (D) deceptive

14. The cadence in the last measure of this excerpt can best be described as

    (A) imperfect authentic
    (B) half
    (C) plagal
    (D) deceptive

15. Both of the cadences in this excerpt contain

    (A) hemiola
    (B) escape tones
    (C) Picardy third
    (D) second inversion triads

ANSWER KEY

1. **C**	5. **B**	9. **A**	13. **C**
2. **B**	6. **D**	10. **C**	14. **B**
3. **A**	7. **C**	11. **A**	15. **D**
4. **C**	8. **B**	12. **C**	

ANSWERS EXPLAINED

1. **(C)** The cadence is perfect authentic.

2. **(B)** NCT 1 is a lower neighbor (F–E–F).

3. **(A)** NCT 2 is a passing tone connecting (E–D–C), two notes a third apart.

4. **(C)** NCT 3 is an example of an incomplete neighbor. It leaves the preparation chord by leap upward and resolves down by step (leap–step in the opposite direction). Sometimes called a cambiata, this type of NCT does *not* occur on the beat.

5. **(B)** NCT 4 is a suspension. The C is the fifth of the F–A–C preparation chord. It is held over into the next beat G–B♭–D where it is *not* a chord member. The interval from the note in the bass to the NCT (G–C) is a fourth, resolving C down to B♭—a third above the bass. The interval above the bass is why it is labeled a 4–3 suspension.

6. **(D)** Chord 5 is a tonic chord in second inversion. This I_4^6 chord functions as a passing chord in predominant function. It is *not* a seventh chord.

7. **(C)** The correct Roman numeral analysis of the last measure is ii_5^6–V^7–I.

8. **(B)** The last three chords are considered a circle progression because the *roots* of the chords are a P5 apart, in this case G–C and C–F.

9. **(A)** The first four measures of *Sonata No. 6, Op. 10* are all centered around tonic harmony. The first three measures are actually the tonic arpeggio.

10. **(C)** The right hand plays the exact same melody an octave higher when it enters with the anacrusis to measure 5.

11. **(A)** When the melody enters the third time with the pick-up (anacrusis) to measure 9 it has shifted to the key of Major C, the dominant of the key of F Major.

12. **(C)** The scale pattern in measure 17 is the C Major scale. Notice that the harmony that accompanies this measure is ii^6–V–I in the key of CM.

13. **(C)** The cadence in measure 3 is a plagal cadence. The chords involved are F–A–C (IV) to C–E–C (I) in the key of C Major. The progression is IV–I_{4-3}^{6-5}.

14. **(B)** The cadence at the end of this example is a half cadence. The progression is I–V_{4-3}^{6-5}.

15. **(D)** Both cadences contain second inversion triads. In each case the cadence includes a $_4^6$ chord that includes tones that are suspended from the previous chord and resolve downward in resolution to $_3^5$ (root position).

Aural Skills Part II: Melodic Dictation

11

The Free-Response (FR) section includes two melodies that will be performed either by instrument or by voice and students are expected to write down both the pitch and rhythm accurately. **This is called melodic dictation: FR 1 and FR 2.**

- As with the sight-singing portion, the melodic dictation portion will have one melody in treble clef and one melody in bass clef.
- One melody will be in simple meter and one will be in compound meter.
- One melody will be in a major key and one will be in a minor key.
- The melody will be played three times for the first example and four times for the second example with time in between to notate.

WHAT SKILLS ARE REQUIRED FOR SUCCESSFUL MELODIC DICTATION?

- Recognizing the key
- Recognizing the meter and understanding the rhythms
- Understanding the relationship of the pitches to the tonal center
- Recognizing familiar melodic and rhythmic patterns and their placement in the measure
- Being able to correctly draw note heads, stems, dots, beams, accidentals, and flags that correspond to rhythm, and pitches on the staff corresponding to placement in the tonality
- One of the keys to successful melodic dictation is being able to reproduce the melody you hear in your head (audiation). Listen to the melody as if you were asked to sing it back. It is oversimplification to state, "If you can hear it, you can notate it," but you definitely will have difficulty notating the phrase successfully if *you can't retain the melody.*

UNDERSTANDING THE MELODY

- Know the key and any altered notes that may occur in minor from the use of scalar variance.

  - Write down the full scale if that helps you focus on the available choices.
  - Write down the leading tone in minor.

- Recognize common beginning patterns—by now this is old news.

  - *Do-Re-Mi* and *Do-Mi-So* are by far the most common patterns.

- Recognize common ending patterns.

  - ***Mi-Re-Do***
  - ***So-La-Ti-Do***
  - ***Re-Ti-Do*** and ***Ti-Re-Do***; also ***So-Ti-Do***, ***Fa-Ti-Do***, and ***Mi-Ti-Do***
  - ***Do-Re-Do*** and ***Do-Ti-Do***

- Note that at the middle of the exercise there is generally an implied half cadence.

  - Know the pitches that constitute the V⁷ chord: ***So-Ti-Re (Fa)***.
  - The melody will usually be two symmetrically related phrases in an antecedent–consequent structure of two measures each. The first phrase generally ends with an implied half cadence and the second half of the melody may start with an anacrusis.

UNDERSTANDING THE RHYTHM
Compound Meter Rhythm Menu

Many students have difficulty with the melody in § time because they often focus on the pitch so that the rhythms are overlooked. Many have difficulty identifying and notating compound meter.

Plan ahead by thinking about and writing down what possible rhythms are going to be used. You can't write down every possible combination, but you can certainly *anticipate* the most often-used rhythms. With the rhythm menu in place, much of the guesswork is gone; you have narrowed down the choices to these six one-beat rhythms (variations shown below the menu line are implied but not written in the menu).

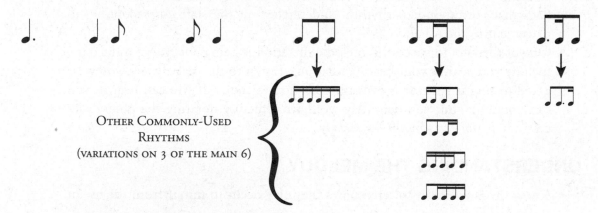

THE RHYTHM MENU

OTHER COMMONLY-USED
RHYTHMS
(VARIATIONS ON 3 OF THE MAIN 6)

These other rhythms are also commonly used in melodic dictation and represent basic division of the eighth-note pattern.

Practice Exercises

Directions: Compound meter seems to cause the most stress for students, so we begin the practice exercises with fifteen **gradually more challenging two-measure dictation exercises in ⅜ time**.

Notice that the first pitch is given as a note head only. Make sure you add the stems, flags, beams, or even dots to complete the rhythm as appropriate. In these exercises there are three examples in a row in the same key. The key is *not* given. Determining whether the example is in major or minor is part of the evaluation. Make sure you observe clef, key signature, and the first pitch. *Anticipate* what key you think it will be, *listen* with that in mind, and let your ear *confirm* what you anticipated. Some examples may imply half cadences and some, PAC. Don't forget the *rhythm menu*.

Each question number will be announced, followed by the example played three times, with a short pause between playings.

Compound Meter

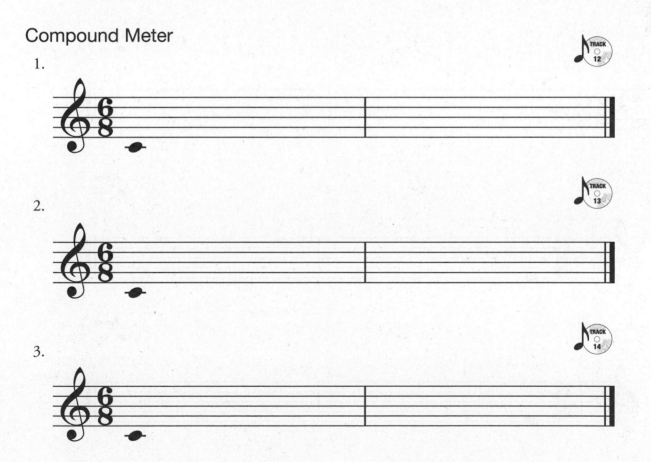

15.

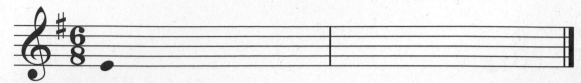

Directions: To continue our progressive preparation of melodic dictation we now have an additional eight examples that are four measures long. These examples are in **simple triple meter**. Some will imply half cadences and some, PAC.

Each question number will be announced, followed by the example played three times, with a short pause between playings.

Simple Meter

20.

21.

22.

23.

ANSWERS EXPLAINED

Compound Meter

1.

C Major:

2.

C Major:

3.

C Major:

4.

d minor

5.

d minor

6.

d minor

7.

E♭ Major

8.

9.

10.

11.

12.

13.

14.

15.

Simple Meter

16.

17.

18.

19.

20.

21.

22.

23.

Key Relationships

12

- Altered Chords
- Borrowed Chords
- Chromatic Mediants
- Closely Related Keys
- Common Chord (Pivot Chord)
- Mode Mixture

- Modulation
  - Common Chord Modulation
  - (Pivot Modulation)
  - Direct Modulation
    - Chromatic Modulation
    - Phrase Modulation
- Parallel Keys
- Picardy Third
- Temporary Tonicization

MODE MIXTURE

Mode Mixture is the harmonic technique of combining chords from a major key and the *parallel minor*, or mixing the parallel major and minor modes using the ♭3, ♭6, and ♭7 from the parallel natural minor. Harmonic interest or color is added to compositions by borrowing chords from the parallel key.

When you sing these altered scale degree pitches, the solfege syllable is also altered.

Scale degree 3 or **Mi**, ♭3 becomes **Me** (may)
Scale degree 6 or **La**, ♭6 becomes **Le** (lay)
Scale degree 7 or **Ti**, ♭7 becomes **Te** (tay)

MODE MIXTURE AND ROMAN NUMERAL CHORD SYMBOLS
BETWEEN G MAJOR AND G NATURAL MINOR

I	i	ii	ii°	iii	III	IV	iv	V	v	vi	VI	vii°	♭VII
D	D	E	E♭	F#	F	G	G	A	A	B	B♭	C	C
B	B♭	C	C	D	D	E	E♭	F#	F	G	G	A	A
G	G	A	A	B	B♭	C	C	D	D	E	E♭	F#	F

To analyze and notate chords whose quality has been altered by mode mixture:

- Adjust the Roman numeral to uppercase or lowercase to reflect the change in the third of the chord.
- If the *root of the chord is altered*, add a ♭ or ♯ before the Roman numeral to show that the chord is built on an altered pitch—such as the ♭VII in the previous example, which is the subtonic chord borrowed from the parallel *natural* minor.
- If the chord has been altered to be augmented, add the + sign; if the chord has been altered to be diminished, add the diminished (°) sign.
- As a general rule, since these mixture chords are derived from *lowered* scale degrees, resolve the chromatic alterations *down*.

Mixture Chords in Minor

We can also borrow or mix modes from the parallel major when in a minor tonality. This generally reflects the raised 7th scale degree of the harmonic form of minor that alters the dominant chord from minor v to major V and the leading tone chord from major VII to diminished vii°.

One of the most common uses of mode mixture when in minor is the practice of ending a piece with an authentic cadence using a *major* tonic. The major tonic is borrowed from the parallel for a more "authentic-sounding" ending. The third of the chord is raised to make it major. This is called **Picardy third**.

MODULATION

IF there is consistent reoccurrence of the same accidental(s), and **IF** your Roman numeral analysis presents unusual or atypical progressions in your current key, **THEN** you are most likely shifting tonal centers. **Modulation is the process of moving from one tonal center to another, with or without changing the key signature.**

It is possible to have a region of a new key, or experience a *temporary* sense of a new tonic, **tonicization**, by the occurrence of one or two non-diatonic chords, and not be completely modulated. The significant difference between modulation and temporary tonicization, or simply passing through a *region* or *area* of a new key, is the occurrence of a convincing cadence *and* significant time in the new key.

The process of modulation usually includes three stages: establishing the first key, the modulation device, and the establishment of the new tonal center. Modulation usually occurs to *closely related keys* because they have *common chords* between them. Each key has five closely related keys: the relative major or minor, the key with one more sharp or flat and its relative, and the key with one less sharp or flat and its relative. The key signatures differ by no more than one accidental.

CLOSELY RELATED KEYS

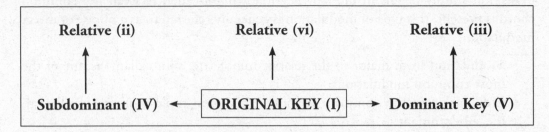

Closely Related Keys to F Major:

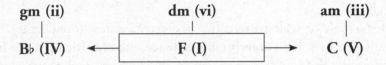

Closely Related Keys to F minor:

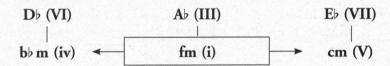

Modulation *within a phrase* is most often going to be **common chord** or **pivot modulation**.

Here is your checklist for recognizing the common chord:

- The pivot chord is diatonic to *both* keys.
- The common chord is frequently ii or IV in the *new* key.
- The common chord is where the tonality shifts (pivots) and is usually the chord just before the accidental or altered chord signaling a new key.
- The new key is established by the occurrence of an authentic cadence shortly after the modulation.
- All music before the common chord functions in the first key and all music from the common key to the cadence will function in the new key.

Any type of modulation that does not use a common chord is called **direct modulation**. If direct modulation occurs *within the phrase* it is a **chromatic modulation**. This type of modulation features a chromatically altered note *in the same voice*. It abruptly shifts from one key to another at the accidental and proceeds to cadence in the new key.

Direct modulation *between* phrases is called **phrase modulation**; a new phrase or section simply begins in the new key following a cadence. Even if a common chord is present, this type of modulation is generally referred to as a phrase or direct modulation.

- Modulation from major to the relative minor (the submediant) is one of the most common modulations.
- Modulation to the dominant is another common tonal motion as well as to the subdominant.
- The smoothest common chord modulations are those that use predominant function chords as the pivot (ii or IV in the *new* key).
- Modulation may also be made through the use of secondary dominant chromatic chords.
- Look for a scale or scale pattern that represents a new tonal center.
- Remember to look for a **convincing cadence** and **significant time in the new key**; otherwise, it is an area or region in the new key and *not* modulation.
- Notate common chord modulation recognizing the pivot chord *and* the shift to the new tonal center in this fashion.

$$\text{GM:} \quad \text{I} \quad \text{V}^6 \quad \text{I} \quad \boxed{\text{vi}}$$
$$\text{em:} \quad \boxed{\text{i}} \quad \text{ii}^{\circ 6} \quad \text{V}^7 \quad \text{i}$$

REVIEW

Piano Sonata, Op. 2, No. 1
(Third Movement)

Ludwig van Beethoven
(1770–1827)

This music example has three phrases:

1. M1–4 is in F minor and cadences with a V^6–i (**IAC**). The NCT in m4 is an appoggiatura.

2. M5–8 is in A♭ Major. The phrase modulation occurs directly after the cadence to the parallel major. This phrase also cadences with a V^6–I (**IAC**). Look carefully. The second phrase is an exact imitation in the new key.

3. M9–14 is essentially three two-measure phrases each beginning with an anacrusis; the last two measures are a cadential extension, essentially a repeat at a louder dynamic. The D in the alto in m10 is also an appoggiatura. The first two-measure phrase is loud and the cadence is V^6–I (**IAC**). The next two measures are soft in volume but the cadence intensifies because it is a root position seventh chord resolving to tonic V^7–I (**PAC**). The grace notes are appoggiaturas.

The last two measures use a **sforzando**. The *sf* (or *sfz*) means play with stress on the anacrusis notes at the volume marked (*f*). If the marking was *sff*, then that would mean play with stress at **fortissimo** volume. You might also see *sfff*. The cadence is V⁷–I (**PAC**).

Now let's look at a familiar piece and review multiple concepts, including a modulation with a common chord pivot.

Minuet in G Major

From the 1725 Notebook of
Anna Magdalena Bach

This piece in G Major is in simple triple meter with two eight-measure phrases and four four-measure phrases. Measures 1–8 and 9–16 create a parallel period.

a	a¹	b	c	d	c¹
M1–8	9–16	17–20	21–24	25–28	29–32

GM: HC   PAC   HC   PAC   HC   PAC
                                                        in   in   back in   in
                                                        DM   DM   GM   GM

Parallel Period

Let's look at Phrase 3. The harmony outlined in the first two measures (17, 18) are I–V⁶. The bass line is descending by step; the V⁶ functions as a passing chord because the F♯ does *not* resolve to **Do**—it leads to **La** (vi). We notice the inclusion of a note that is not in our key (C♯) in every measure from 20–23. Measures 23 and 24 conclude with a convincing cadence—PAC in D Major. We have modulated to D major within this phrase. The point of modulation is the vi chord in measure 19. It is our common chord—one that functions in both keys.

$$G = vi$$
$$D = ii$$

Measure 19 is our pivot chord moving us smoothly from G Major to D Major. The harmonic analysis clearly shows the point of modulation.

The music uses direct modulation back to G Major following the cadence in measure 24. What's your clue? The C natural at the end of measure 24, of course. I also think there is a strong 3-note motive using the leading tone as the lower neighbor in the melody in measures 25 and 26 that "points" to G. Note the similarity between this example and the minuet from Chapter 10 including the use of the same ascending melodic pattern (one in D Major and one in G Major), noted as **c** and **c¹** on the phrase chart, that unifies the final eight measures. Anna Magdalena Bach used these as teaching exercises for her children and we are still using them today.

Chapter Summary

- **Mode mixture** is the harmonic technique of combining chords from a major key and the *parallel minor*, or mixing the parallel major and minor modes using the ♭3, ♭6, and ♭7 from the parallel natural minor.
- Harmonic interest or color is added to compositions by borrowing chords from the parallel key.
- One of the most common uses of mode mixture when in minor is the practice of ending a piece with an authentic cadence using a *major* tonic. This is called **Picardy third**.
- **Modulation** is the process of moving from one tonal center to another, with or without changing the key signature.
- Modulation usually occurs to closely related keys because they have common chords between them.
- Modulation to the dominant is the most common tonal motion as well as to the key of the subdominant. Remember the closely related keys:

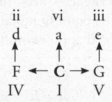

Note that the closely related keys are all diatonic to our original tonal center (C).

- Modulation to the submediant (relative minor) is also typical.
- The smoothest common chord modulations are those that use predominant function chords as the pivot.
- Modulation may also be made through the use of a secondary dominant chromatic alteration chords and would be considered *pre*dominant.
- It is possible to have a region of a new key or experience a temporary sense of a new tonic, tonicization, and not be completely modulated.

Practice Exercises

Questions 1–5 are based on this familiar piece by Mendelssohn.

Festgesang

Felix Mendelssohn-Bartholdy
Arranged and adapted by
William H. Cummings

1. Which two keys are evident in this excerpt?

   (A) F Major and D minor
   (B) F Major and C Major
   (C) C Major and C minor
   (D) C Major and A minor

2. Phrase 1 ends with what type of cadence?

   (A) Perfect authentic
   (B) Imperfect authentic
   (C) Half
   (D) Plagal

3. This excerpt is an example of a

   (A) parallel period
   (B) modulating parallel period
   (C) modulating contrasting period
   (D) perfect period

4. The circled chord on beat 1 of measure 6 functions as all of the following **except**

   (A) a D minor triad in root position
   (B) the submediant in F Major and the supertonic in C Major
   (C) the common chord pivot in the modulation to C Major
   (D) an F Major triad in second inversion

5. The A in the melody in measure 6 is best described as

   (A) an accented upper neighbor
   (B) an incomplete neighbor
   (C) a 7–6 suspension
   (D) the fifth of a D minor chord

Questions 6–10 are based on the music below, "Rustington."

Rustington

C. Hubert H. Parry
(1848–1918)

6. The cadence at the end of the first phrase (measure 4) is

    (A) imperfect authentic
    (B) perfect authentic
    (C) plagal
    (D) deceptive

7. The second phrase (measures 4–8) is a direct modulation to the key of the

    (A) relative minor
    (B) parallel minor
    (C) dominant
    (D) subdominant

8. The second phrase ends with the progression

    (A) ii^6_5 –V^6_5–V–V
    (B) vi^6_5 –ii^7–V
    (C) ii^6_5 –V^7–I
    (D) IV–V^7–I

9. The third phrase (measures 8–12) includes all of the following **except**

    (A) ending on a half cadence in F Major
    (B) several uses of suspensions
    (C) ending on an imperfect authentic cadence in C Major
    (D) a secondary dominant

10. The first two phrases (measures 1–4 and 4–8) create what phrase structure?

    (A) A parallel period
    (B) A repeated period
    (C) A modulating contrasting period
    (D) A double period

Questions 11–15 are based on String Quartet No. 13 in B♭ Major, below.

String Quartet No. 13 in B♭ Major, Op. 130

Ludwig van Beethoven
(1770–1827)

11. Measures 1–8 are an example of a parallel period because

    (A) the melodies of each phrase begin the same
    (B) there is an antecedent–consequent relationship between the phrases
    (C) the first phrase ends with a half cadence and the second phrase ends with a PAC
    (D) All of the above.

12. The modulation at measure 17 is to the

    (A) relative major
    (B) relative minor
    (C) parallel minor
    (D) parallel major

13. L'istesso tempo means

    (A) slightly less tempo
    (B) more lively
    (C) the length of the beat remains the same
    (D) with increasing tempo

14. The meter change at measure 17 is from

    (A) duple simple to triple simple
    (B) quadruple simple to duple triple
    (C) duple simple to duple compound
    (D) triple simple to triple compound

15. The melody in measures 17–24 includes all of the following **except**

    (A) upper neighboring tone grace notes
    (B) tonic and dominant arpeggiated chords
    (C) a partial major scale pattern in B♭
    (D) trills

16. The key that would <u>not</u> be closely related to the key of E Major is

    (A) C♯ minor
    (B) G♯ minor
    (C) B Major
    (D) B minor

ANSWER KEY

1. **B**	5. **C**	9. **C**	13. **C**
2. **B**	6. **A**	10. **C**	14. **C**
3. **B**	7. **C**	11. **D**	15. **D**
4. **D**	8. **C**	12. **D**	16. **D**

ANSWERS EXPLAINED

1. **(B)** The first phrase is in F Major, the second phrase begins in F (note that the melody in measures 1 and 2 and 5 and 6 are exactly the same) and modulates to C Major.

2. **(B)** Phrase 1 ends with an imperfect authentic cadence V–I with *Mi* in the soprano of the tonic chord.

3. **(B)** This excerpt is an example of a parallel period that modulates in Phrase 2—the melody of each phrase is the same and the phrases have an antecedent–consequent relationship.

4. **(D)** The circled chord is a D minor chord in root position that functions as the common chord pivot between F(vi) and C(ii).

5. **(C)** The A on beat 3 is a 7–6 suspension over the B♮ in the bass. A 7–6 suspension always occurs over a chord in first inversion. How do you know? Remember that all Arabic numbers (in this case 7–6) mean **interval**; therefore, the number 6 refers to the interval of a sixth above the bass or first inversion.

6. **(A)** The first phrase ends with an imperfect authentic cadence of ii^7–V$^4_3$–I.

7. **(C)** The second phrase begins on a C Major chord in first inversion, which functions in both F Major (as V) and C Major (as I). The B natural first appears on beat 1 in measure 5 and continues consistently throughout this phrase. The second phrase modulates to C Major, which is the dominant in our original key of FM.

8. **(C)** Because the excerpt modulates to C Major, the cadence is a perfect authentic and the progression is ii$^6_5$–V^7–I.

9. **(C)** The third phrase does *not* end with an authentic cadence in C Major. It does contain several suspensions, a secondary dominant (with the E♭), and a half cadence in F Major.

10. **(C)** The melodic structure consists of two contrasting periods; in addition, the first two phrases modulate. Phrase 1 ends with an IAC in FM, and Phrase 2 ends with a PAC in C Major. These two phrases have an antecedent–consequent relationship but the melodies are different–contrasting.

11. **(D)** Although you will rarely, if ever, see "All of the above" as an answer on the AP exam, it is important to note what elements constitute a parallel period: The melodies of each phrase begin the same and there is an antecedent–consequent

relationship between the phrases characterized by a weaker cadence at the end of the antecedent and a stronger cadence at the end of the consequent.

12. **(D)** The modulation at measure 17 is to the parallel major. The excerpt begins in B♭ minor based on the key signature and the use of the A natural functioning as the leading tone in the harmonic form. At measure 17 the key signature is reduced by 3 flats and modulates to B♭ Major, the parallel major.

13. **(C)** *L'istesso* tempo means the beat remains the same. This marking is used to indicate a change in meter but the tempo of the beat stays the same.

14. **(C)** The meter changes at 17 from duple simple to duple compound. Both sections have two beats per measure (duple), but in the opening section the beat subdivides into two parts (simple) and in the second section the beat subdivides into three equal parts (compound).

15. **(D)** Measures 17–24 include all of the following except trills. The melody alternates from a B♭ Major to an F Major arpeggio for the first six measures ending with an almost complete B♭ Major scale. Grace notes also occur in the first six measures and are actually upper neighbor tones between two identical notes.

16. **(D)** B minor is not closely related to E Major. The closely related keys to E Major are

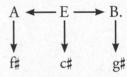

Secondary Function Harmony

- Dominant Function
- Tonicization
- Leading-Tone Relationship

- Resolutions
- Secondary Function
    - Secondary Dominant
    - Secondary Leading Tone

This chapter begins with a review of the harmonic function of the dominant family. In common-practice style, every chord has a function that depends on its location or hierarchy within the tonality. For example, an F Major chord functions differently as I in F Major, as IV in C Major, or as V in B♭ Major. This hierarchy is based on Dr. Ferrandino's scale degree stability chart as discussed in previous chapters.

Recall the stability factor: $\hat{1}$ $\hat{3}$ $\hat{5}$ $\hat{2}$ $\hat{6}$ $\hat{4}$ $\hat{7}$

Most stable   **Un**stable (Active)

The term **unstable** refers to how active or restless the note is; that is, how great is the need to move forward and resolve to a more stable note? Scale degree 7, the leading tone (**Ti**), is the most active note and wants to resolve to the most stable note—the tonic (**Do**). The subdominant pitch (**Fa**), scale degree 4, is the next most active and wants to move to mediant (**Mi**).

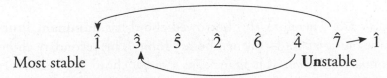

$$\hat{1} \quad \hat{3} \quad \hat{5} \quad \hat{2} \quad \hat{6} \quad \hat{4} \quad \hat{7} \rightarrow \hat{1}$$

Most stable   **Un**stable

The two most restless tones are the resolution tones: **Ti** and **Fa**. Both these pitches are found in the V[7] chord and the vii° triad.

$$\left. \begin{matrix} \hat{4} \\ \hat{2} \\ \hat{7} \\ \hat{5} \end{matrix} \right) \quad \left(\begin{matrix} \hat{6} \\ \hat{4} \\ \hat{2} \\ \hat{7} \end{matrix} \right) \longrightarrow$$

Scale degree $\hat{6}$ is the next most unstable pitch and heightens intensity of the vii°[7] even more.

$$\text{V}^{7} \qquad \text{vii}^{\circ 7}$$

The similarities of these chords puts them both in the **dominant family**—the most active function. The **pull** of $\hat{4}$ to $\hat{3}$ and $\hat{7}$ to $\hat{1}$ is why V^7 and $vii^{\circ 7}$ resolve to tonic; the chord containing all three of the most stable pitches: $\hat{1}$, $\hat{3}$, and $\hat{5}$.

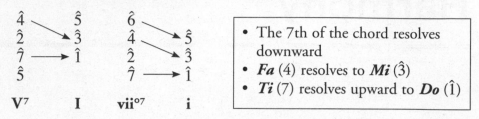

$$
\begin{array}{ll}
\hat{4} \longrightarrow \hat{5} & \hat{6} \\
\hat{2} \longrightarrow \hat{3} & \hat{4} \longrightarrow \hat{5} \\
\hat{7} \longrightarrow \hat{1} & \hat{2} \longrightarrow \hat{3} \\
\hat{5} & \hat{7} \longrightarrow \hat{1} \\
\mathbf{V^7} \qquad \mathbf{I} & \mathbf{vii^{\circ 7}} \qquad \mathbf{i}
\end{array}
$$

- The 7th of the chord resolves downward
- *Fa* (4) resolves to *Mi* ($\hat{3}$)
- *Ti* (7) resolves upward to *Do* ($\hat{1}$)

Dominant function has a very strong pull to tonic, whether that tonic is the tonal center or a **temporary tonic**. The secondary dominant function serves to heighten or intensify the pull to resolution.

SECONDARY DOMINANTS AND LEADING TONES

Recognizing Secondary Dominants and Leading Tones

Temporary **tonicization** is generally attributed to borrowing two or three chords from a closely related key to heighten the harmonic intensity and color. Very often when analyzing music, you will notice an accidental resolving upward by a half step. This is a **leading tone relationship**, and as the name implies, the accidental functions as a leading tone to a temporary tonic, not our original tonic.

The leading tone, scale degree 7, or *Ti*, no matter how you label it, is the **third** in a dominant chord or the **root** of a leading-tone chord.

$$
\begin{array}{llll}
\text{Fa} & \hat{4} & \text{La} & \hat{6} \\
\text{Re} & \hat{2} & \text{Fa} & \hat{4} \\
\boxed{\text{Ti} \quad \hat{7}} & & \text{Re} & \hat{2} \\
\text{So} & \hat{5} & \boxed{\text{Ti} \quad \hat{7}} \\
\mathbf{V^7} & & \mathbf{vii^{\circ 7}}
\end{array}
$$

Both resolve upward to *Do*. Therefore, this borrowed chord has **dominant function** (V or vii°) to its resolution chord—the temporary tonic. This secondary chord is identified as a secondary *dominant* if it analyzes as a *major* chord or a secondary *leading tone* if the chord quality is *diminished*. They are usually seventh chords, which heightens the intensity and need to resolve because both the V^7 and $vii^{\circ 7}$ contain the *tritone*. The temporary tonic chord (the resolution chord) is found within the original key. The secondary dominant or leading tone is *not* diatonic to the original key. Remember that it is the accidental that signals you are temporarily in another key. The *quality* of the secondary chord tells you whether it is a V, V^7 or a vii°, $vii^{\circ 7}$. Each has dominant function.

IF–THEN

- **IF** you have an accidental that resolves upward by a half step, **THEN** you have a leading tone relationship in a new key.
- **IF** the altered note is the *third* of the borrowed chord and analyzes as a major triad or major–minor seventh chord, **THEN** you have a chord functioning as a dominant (**V** or **V**^{7}) in another key. The temporary tonic will be the next chord (the chord it resolves to). Check to see whether the secondary chord indeed would be dominant (V) of the resolution chord. **IF** so, **THEN** you have a secondary **dominant**.
- **IF** the altered note is the *root* of a diminished triad or seventh chord, **THEN** you have a secondary chord functioning as a leading tone vii° or vii°^{7} in another key. Check to see whether the chord would indeed be vii° of the resolution chord. **IF** so, **THEN** you have a secondary leading tone.

Building and Resolving Secondary Dominants and Leading Tones

A secondary chord symbol has two parts separated by a slash. The bottom of the chord symbol represents the temporary tonic. This chord is diatonic to your key. The chord symbol above the slash represents the chord quality, inversion, and function of this borrowed chord in relation to the temporary tonic (the chord on the bottom). For example, in the key of FM: **V**^{7}**/V** is spelled **G–B♮–D–F** and is pronounced "V^7 **OF** V" (five seven OF five).

In F Major: V^7/V   V

> F resolves downward because it is the chordal 7th as well as *Fa*. B resolves to C (*Ti-Do*) in the temporary key of CM.

The B natural is the accidental that is an altered note in the key of F. The bottom Roman numeral (V in FM) is C Major (our temporary tonic). The dominant seventh chord or V^7 in CM is G–B♮–D–F and it resolves to our temporary tonic C–E–G.

Here is your checklist for *building* secondary dominants and leading tones:

1. Look at the chord symbol below the slash; that is your new tonic.
2. Spell the chord as requested above the slash including correct inversion *in the key of the new tonic*.
3. Resolve the secondary chord to the new tonic following the rules of resolution for THAT key (*Ti* goes to *Do* and *Fa* goes to *Mi*).
4. Recognize the leading-tone relationship that occurs between the altered note *Ti* and the note it leads to—*Do* in the new key.

Here are several more examples. Be sure you clearly understand *how* the correct chord is derived from the chord symbol.

vii°⁷/vi in B♭ Major (Leading-Tone Seventh **OF** vi)

- This will be a **fully-diminished** chord because vi in B♭ is G **minor**.
- The vii°⁷ of G minor is F♯–A–C–E♭.
- F♯ is the raised 7th scale degree in G minor and the altered note that signals you are temporarily out of B♭ Major. The F♯ resolves to G creating the leading-tone relationship.

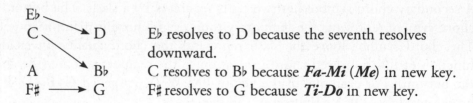

E♭		
C	→ D	E♭ resolves to D because the seventh resolves downward.
A	→ B♭	C resolves to B♭ because *Fa-Mi* (*Me*) in new key.
F♯	→ G	F♯ resolves to G because *Ti-Do* in new key.

B♭M: I   IV⁶   vii°⁷/vi   vi   ii⁶   V⁷   I

Remember that a diatonic FULLY-diminished leading-tone chord resolves to a minor tonic; however, as a secondary harmony chord, you may see a fully-diminished chord resolving to a major tonic.

V₅⁶/IV in E♭ Major (V₅⁶ **OF** IV)

- This is the dominant seventh chord in *first inversion* in the key of A♭ Major.
- The chord is spelled E♭–G–B♭–D♭ and would have G in the bass.
- The leading-tone relationship occurs between *Mi-Fa*, already a half step.

- In this case D♭ is the accidental that is not in our original key.
- The leading tone is the third of the chord and resolves to the new tonic A♭ and is in the bass.

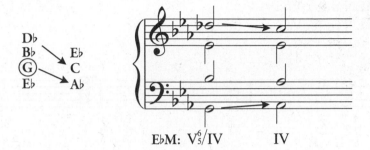

vii^{ø7}/V in D Major (Leading-Tone Seventh **OF** V)

- This a half-diminished seventh chord in root position.
- The temporary tonic is A Major.
- The leading-tone seventh chord in A Major is G♯–B–D–F♯ and is half-diminished.
- The G♯ is the accidental that signals the borrowed chord and is the leading-tone relationship resolving to A.

> Remember that a diatonic HALF-diminished leading-tone chord resolves to a MAJOR tonic.

> Remember that there are *three resolutions* in a leading-tone chord.

V$\frac{4}{2}$/iv in E minor (V$\frac{4}{2}$ **OF** iv)

- The temporary tonic is A minor.
- The dominant seventh in A minor is E–G♯–B–D.
- The chord will have D in the bass and will resolve downward to C in the bass.
- Therefore, a secondary **V$\frac{4}{2}$** will resolve to a I^6 or a i^6 so the resolution is correct.
- The correct progression and resolution would be **V$\frac{4}{2}$/iv** to **iv^6**.

Here Is Another Way to Visually Identify Secondary Harmony

IF you are in a *major* key and you analyze a chord as

- II, **THEN** think V/V
- III, **THEN** think V/vi
- VI, **THEN** think V/ii

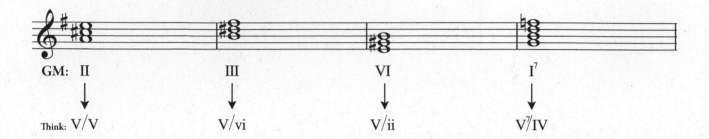

These three chords are minor (ii, iii, vi) in a major mode; therefore, an analysis of II, III, or VI is a signal to "connect the dots" and recognize *there is an accidental* creating a chromatic chord to temporarily intensify a different tonic.

- **IF** you analyze a chord in a major key as I⁷, **THEN** think V⁷ of IV.

Hearing and Notating Secondary Dominants and Leading Tones

When you hear a *Fi* ($\sharp\hat{4}$), especially if it leads to *So*, determine first if you are hearing an embellished melody note (chromatic passing tone or neighbor). If so, there is no secondary dominant. **IF** the chromatic note is an essential member of the chord that leads to a non-tonic chord, and **IF** it has dominant function (V or vii°), **THEN** you have a secondary relationship that is resolving to a temporary tonic. If used as a member of a secondary chord, *Fi* to <u>*So*</u> will always be V of <u>**V**</u> or a vii° of <u>**V**</u> because <u>*So*</u> (V) is your tonicized note.

The most common way to notate what you hear:

- Write the Roman numeral of the resolution chord (the temporary tonic) first.
- Listen to the chromatic chord for quality and inversion.
- Write that Roman numeral *in the key of the next chord.*
- Add the slash to show the secondary relationship, followed by the Roman numeral of the second chord.

Another way to say the same thing is **IF** you hear the *Ti-Do* relationship, or a *So-Do* dominant to tonic relationship, and the second chord is *not* the original tonic, **THEN** you have *secondary* dominant–tonic function.

Here is another way to **notate** it.

- Write the dominant–tonic relationship in Roman numerals, including inversions.
- Add a bracket or a line underneath *both* chords to show that you hear a secondary relationship.
- Listen for the scale degree of the temporary tonic.
- Write the Roman numeral of that scale degree under the bracket.

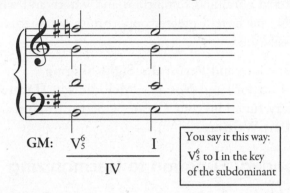

GM: V_5^6 I

IV

You say it this way:
V_5^6 to I in the key
of the subdominant

RELATING SECONDARY FUNCTION HARMONY TO OTHER SKILLS

Relating Secondary Function to Sight-Singing

When you analyze a melody for performance, one of the first things you should do is determine the mode, tonal center, and appropriate solfege or scale degree names or numbers. When a nondiatonic leading-tone relationship is present, the accidental is very often the raised 4th scale degree, or *Fi*, which resolves upward to *So*. Learn to *sing and notate* the melodic patterns of *So-Fi-So* and *Fa-Fi-So* in major and minor keys to familiarize yourself with the raised 4th scale degree and what it looks like. Also utilize various rhythmic patterns while singing the raised 4̂th. *Fi-So* is a **leading-tone relationship** that transfers to *Ti-Do* in the new (temporary) tonic.

IF–THEN

- Therefore, **IF** you have a melody that contains a *Fi-So*, **THEN** you probably have a shift of tonal center and temporary tonicization to the **key of the dominant**.
- Other common chords that tend to be tonicized are IV, vi, and ii.
  - **IF** the temporary tonic is subdominant, **THEN** the leading-tone relationship is *not* an altered note in a major tonality—it occurs between *Mi* and *Fa*. In a minor tonality, the normally ♭3 or *Me* does rise to *Mi*.
  - **IF** the temporary tonic is submediant, **THEN** the leading-tone relationship is ♯5 or *Si* to *La*.
  - **IF** the temporary tonic is supertonic, **THEN** the tonic is raised. For example, in A♭ Major the V⁷/ii chord is spelled F–A♮–C–E♭, A♮ to B♭ is the leading-tone relationship; A♮ is the raised tonic or *Di* in our original key.

Relating Secondary Function to Melodic Dictation

The concept of secondary function overlaps from one process to another. When you sing *Fi-So* you are often singing a secondary dominant or leading tone. You have seen what it looks like—you have sung it—and so it is possible that you will hear it in melodic dictation and must be able to notate the sound.

IF–THEN

IF you are **prepared** (more in later chapters on mentally preparing) for the possible occurrence of an altered note (and resolution) and **where** and **why** it might occur in a melody, **THEN** you have a greater opportunity for successfully notating it. Consider all the possibilities:

> **See** (secondary function) and **Perform = Sight-Singing**
> **Hear** (secondary function) and **Notate = Melodic** and **Harmonic Dictation**
> **Analyze** (secondary function) and **Create = Score Analysis**, **Harmonizing a Melody**, and **Part Writing**

Relating Secondary Function to Harmonizing a Melody (FR 7)

As we have already learned, an accidental resolving upward by a half step usually signals a leading-tone relationship and a temporary shift to a new tonic. The altered note, usually the raised 4th scale degree or *Fi*, would be *Ti* resolving to *Do* in our new key. Scale degree 7 (*Ti*) is the third of a dominant chord or the root of a leading-tone chord and both resolve to tonic. This commonly occurs at cadences as predominant function.

IF–THEN

Identify all the notes of the melody to be harmonized with either solfege or scale degree numbers. **IF** you have a *Fi-So* in your melody, **THEN** you may harmonize with either a secondary dominant or a secondary leading tone (I strongly recommend the V/V and *not* vii°/V).

Both the V⁷/V or the vii°⁷/V resolve to V indicating a possible half cadence, or a chord used before V (pre-dominant) in an authentic cadence. Keep it simple. Harmonize the *Fi-So* with a root position V⁷/V for *Fi* and a root position V for *So*. **IF** your melody gives you *So-Fi-So*, or *Mi-Fi-So*, **THEN** harmonize the first chord with I$^6_4$; **IF** *Fa-Fi-So*, **THEN** harmonize with ii⁶ or IV.

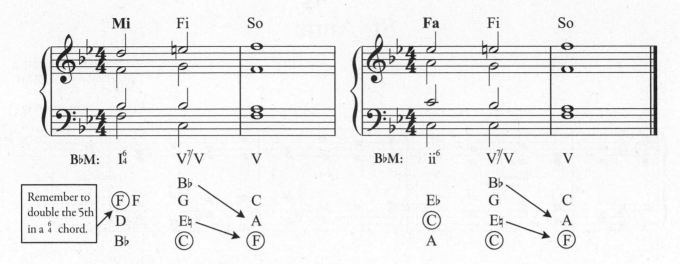

Relating Secondary Function to Harmonic Dictation

The most common melodic patterns containing an accidental or altered note are **So-Fi-So** and **Fa-Fi-So**. Prepare your ear by singing and notating these patterns in bass and treble clef in many keys. It is common for the altered note to occur in the outside voices: soprano or bass. These are the two voices that must be notated in harmonic dictation. If the **Fi** occurs in the melody, then most likely your chord is in root position. Consider the previous example of **Mi-Fi-So** or **Fa-Fi-So** when the melody is the given and you must write the bass. However, **IF** the **So-Fi-So** pattern is in the bass line and the chord quality is *major*, **THEN** you have a secondary dominant in **first inversion** because the third of the chord will be **Fi** and that note is in the bass.

	C	Fa	(4̂)				C	Do	(1̂)		
	A	Re	(2̂)	D			A	La	(6̂)	D	Re
	F♯	**Ti**	(7̂)	B			F♯	**Fi**	(♯4̂)	B	Ti
Normal Function	D	So	(5̂)	G **Do**	*Secondary*	D	Re	(2̂)	G	**So**
in G Major	V⁶₅			I	Function in C Major	V⁶₅/V	to		V	

St. Anne

William Croft
(1678–1727)

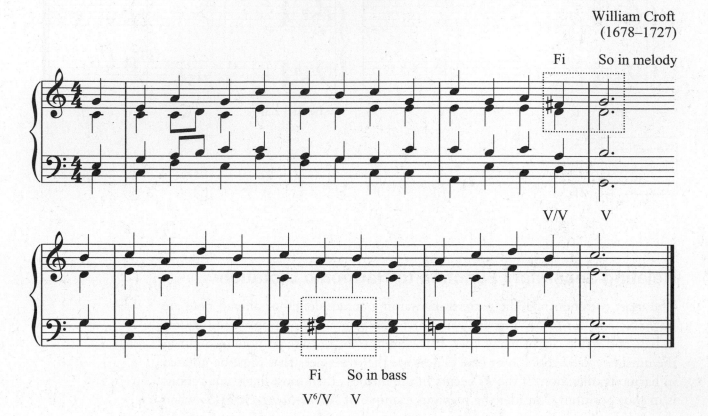

This excerpt demonstrates *Fi-So* in *both* the melody and the bass line. In measure 4 with *Fi-So* in the melody, the secondary dominant is in root position. In measure 6 the *Fi-So* in the bass gives us the progression V⁶/V–V. The phrase ends with I⁶–IV–I⁶–ii–V–I.

IF the *So-Fi-So* is in the bass line and the chord quality of the altered chord is diminished, **THEN** you would have a *root* position secondary leading chord. This is not a common occurrence in common-practice style. Leading-tone chords are most often in first inversion; therefore, secondary leading tones are as well.

	E La (6̂)			E Mi (3̂)	
	C Fa (4̂)	D So		C Do (1̂)	D Re
Normal	A Re (2̂)	B Mi		A La (6̂)	B Ti
Function in	F♯ **Ti** (7̂)	G **Do**	*Secondary*	F♯ **Fi** (4̂)	G **So**
G Major	vii°⁷	I	Function in	vii°⁷/V	to V
			C Major		

Relating Secondary Function to Part Writing and Figured Bass Realization

The issues associated with secondary harmonies when part writing are primarily understanding the chord symbols and figured bass.

- In a major key a secondary dominant or leading tone will always have an accidental.
- Figured bass symbols will also represent these altered pitches.
- In a minor key an accidental may merely be another form of minor.
- Remember that secondary function is a *relationship* between two chords, the second one being the temporary tonic.
- Make sure the chord quality of the Roman numeral symbol is the quality you have created. The most common mistake is leaving out the required accidental.
- Analyzing a chord as a major II instead of a V/V tells the exam reader that you *do* understand the chord quality and what note is the root, but you *don't* understand the **function** of that chord and how it relates to the next chord.
- The resolution tones in a secondary dominant or a secondary leading tone are based on (and must be resolved to) the temporary tonic and not the original tonic.
- If you have a complete root position secondary chord going to a root position chord, then following the rules of resolution, the temporary tonic chord will be incomplete with three roots, one third, and no fifth.
- If you want a complete resolution chord, then leave out the fifth of the secondary chord and double the root.
- Never double *Fi* (or any other accidental), when it is the leading tone of the tonicized chord.

The study of secondary dominants and leading tones is called **chromatic** harmony; therefore, it is imperative to understand that when any voice line includes chromaticism, harmonizing those non-diatonic notes requires going out of the key.

Let's look at one more example and see if we can pull all this information together.

REVIEW

Hall

Calvin Weiss Laufer
(1874–1938)

This example is in E♭ Major with a pivot modulation to the key of the sub-dominant (A♭ Major) in the third phrase and a return to the original key in the last phrase (measures 13–16). Although we have the occurrence of the D♭ in measure 11 as a signal that we have modulated, the *proof* is that if we stay in E♭ the cadence ending at 12 would be I–IV, and that is *not* a viable cadence. There are two second-ary harmony chords—one secondary dominant and one secondary leading tone. The secondary leading tone is in first inversion. The temporary tonic in both cases is dominant.

Although the melodies are not the same in each phrase, the rhythm is identical. I would call this a double period because the cadences at measures 4, 8, and 12 are all weaker cadences, while the final cadence is perfect authentic in our original key. The first phrase ends with a classic example of a plagal cadence. The second phrase ends with a half cadence intensifying the pull to B♭ with the V^7 of V and an inter-esting non-chord tone in the melody. The *escape tone* leaves by step and resolves by leap in the opposite direction. Each phrase gets progressively more active as the third phrase begins with a V^7 and modulates to A♭. The fourth phrase returns to E♭, contains the secondary leading-tone chord (***So-Fi-So*** in the tenor) and concludes with the ever popular I_4^6–V^7–I cadence.

In the measures where passing tones are labeled, the harmony is the same for the whole measure (tonic in all three measures), so the passing tones serve to embellish the line.

Chapter Summary

- **Tonicization** (temporarily shifting to a different tonic) is generally attributed to borrowing two or three chords from a closely related key to heighten the harmonic intensity and color.
- Any major or minor chord can serve as a temporary tonic. Diminished or augmented chords *cannot*. Therefore, you may have

  V/ii,   V/iii,   V/III,   V/iv,   V/IV,   V/V,   V/v,   V/vi,   V/VI

- Dominant function has a very strong pull to tonic, whether that tonic is the tonal center or a temporary tonicization. The secondary dominant family serves to heighten or intensify the pull to resolution.
- Any chord with dominant quality (Major, Mm^7, diminished, half-diminished, or fully-diminished) may function as a secondary.
- The two most restless tones are the resolution tones—*Ti* and *Fa*. Both these pitches are found in the V^7 chord and the vii° or vii°⁷ chords.
- An accidental resolving upward by a half step signals a leading-tone relationship and a temporary shift to a new tonic.
- The most common melodic patterns containing an accidental or altered note are *So-Fi-So* and *Fa-Fi-So*.
- If your accidental is a *raised* scale degree, then the note that is raised is usually the *third* of a V or V^7 or the *root* of a vii° or vii°⁷.
- If your accidental is a *lowered* scale degree, then the note that is lowered is usually the seventh of either a V^7 or vii°⁷.
- When you sing *Fi-So* you are usually singing a secondary dominant or leading tone.
- The next most common is *La-Si-La* or *So-Si-La*.
- If you have a *Fi-So* in your melody, then you may harmonize with either a secondary dominant or a secondary leading tone.
- A **half-diminished** leading-tone chord resolves to a major tonic.
- A **fully-diminished** leading-tone chord resolves diatonically to a minor tonic but may also resolve to a major tonic.
- There are **three resolutions** in a leading-tone chord.
- If the *Fi-So* pattern is in the bass line and the chord quality is major, then you have a secondary dominant in first inversion.
- The resolution tones in a secondary dominant or a secondary leading tone are based on the temporary tonic and not the original tonic.
- The study of secondary dominants and leading tones is called **chromatic harmony**; therefore, it is imperative to understand that when any voice line includes chromaticism, harmonizing those non-diatonic notes requires going out of the key.

Practice Exercises

1. The correct spelling of the V^7/V chord in D minor is

   (A) E–G–B♭–D
   (B) E–G♯–B–D
   (C) A–C♯–E–G
   (D) D–F♯–A–C

2. In B♭ Major the temporary tonic indicated in the symbol V^6_5/vi is

   (A) D–F♯–A
   (B) G–B♭–D
   (C) G–B♮–D
   (D) F–A–C

3. The appropriate Roman numeral chord symbols representing this progression in the key of D Major is

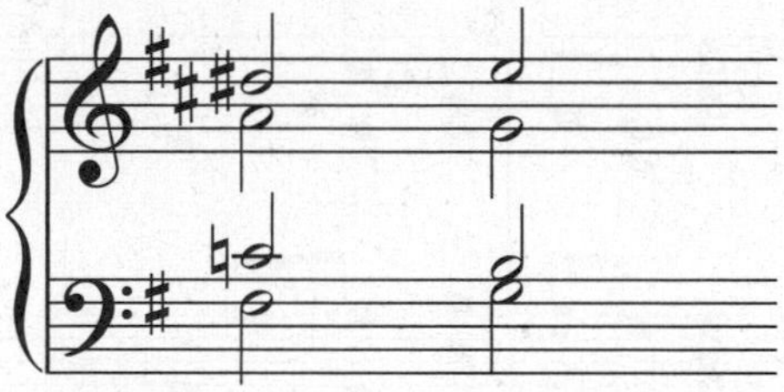

   (A) vii^{o7}/V–ii^6
   (B) V^6_5/vi–vi
   (C) $vii^{o6}_{\ 5}$/ii–ii^6
   (D) $vii^{o6}_{\ 5}$/ii–ii

4. All of the following statements about the progression in Question 3 are true **except** for which one?

   (A) It contains a fully-diminished leading-tone seventh chord.
   (B) The temporary tonic is E minor.
   (C) The secondary chord is in root position.
   (D) The third of the E minor chord is doubled to avoid unequal fifths (dim5–P5) between the bass and the tenor.

Questions 5–11 refer to "O Word of God Incarnate," below.

O Word of God Incarnate

Adapted from Felix Mendelssohn's
arrangement of "Munich"
in his oratorio *Elijah*.

5. The E♭ in the alto in measure 3 can be best described as

   (A) a suspension
   (B) an accented passing tone
   (C) an upper neighbor
   (D) an anticipation

6. The temporary tonic in measure 6 is the

   (A) supertonic
   (B) subdominant
   (C) dominant
   (D) submediant

7. When comparing measures 1–4 and measures 5–8, all the following are true **except**

   (A) the melodies are exactly the same.
   (B) measures 5–8 use different harmonizations of the same melody.
   (C) both phrases end with a PAC.
   (D) there is an antecedent–consequent relationship.

8. Measures 1–8 might be considered a

   (A) contrasting period
   (B) reharmonized repeated phrase
   (C) modulating period
   (D) repeated parallel period

9. The chords marked 1 can best be described as

   (A) V^7/ii–ii in B♭ M
   (B) vii°/ii–ii in B♭ M
   (C) iii–ii in E♭ M
   (D) vii°^{6}/ii–ii in E♭ M

10. The chords marked 2 can best be described as

   (A) V^7/V–V
   (B) ii–V
   (C) II^7–V
   (D) V^6_5/V–V

11. All of the following describe the chords marked 3 **except**

   (A) V^4_2/IV–IV^6
   (B) a dominant to tonic relationship in the key of the subdominant
   (C) a leading-tone to tonic relationship in the key of A♭ Major
   (D) a third inversion secondary dominant resolving to the temporary tonic of A♭ Major

Questions 12–15 refer to "Chorale: Gloria sei dir gesungen," below.

Chorale: Gloria sei dir gesungen
based on the melody "Wachet auf, ruft uns die Stimme?" by Philipp Nicolai

Johann Sebastian Bach
(1685–1750)
BWV 140

12. What is the most accurate description of the first two phrases of this excerpt (measures 1–5 and 6–11)?

    (A) Both phrases modulate to B♭ Major.
    (B) The first phrase ends with a half cadence using a secondary dominant, while the second phrase uses a common-chord to modulate to B♭ Major.
    (C) Both phrases end with a half cadence.
    (D) Both phrases start with a tonic chord in E♭ Major. The first phrase ends on a half cadence and the second phrase modulates to B♭ Major.

13. The V^7 of IV chord appears in what measure?

    (A) 4
    (B) 6
    (C) 9
    (D) 13

14. The progression within the box (measures 9–11) includes what type of non-chord tones?

    (A) 9–8 suspension
    (B) Accented passing tone
    (C) Chromatic lower neighbor
    (D) Both a 9–8 and 4–3 suspension and an accented passing tone

15. The Roman numeral chord analysis of the progression within the box would be

    (A) V^6_5–I–V–I
    (B) V^6_5–I^6–V–I
    (C) V^6_5/V–V^6–V/V–V
    (D) V^6_5–V^7–V–I

ANSWER KEY

1. **B**	5. **A**	9. **D**	13. **D**
2. **B**	6. **D**	10. **A**	14. **D**
3. **C**	7. **D**	11. **C**	15. **A**
4. **C**	8. **B**	12. **B**	

ANSWERS EXPLAINED

1. **(B)** The V^7 of V in the key of D minor is E–G#–B–D. The temporary tonic (V in D Major) is A Major. The dominant of A Major is E–G#–B–D.

2. **(B)** In B♭ Major the submediant triad is G–B♭–D, the temporary tonic of the progression V$^6_5$/vi.

3. **(C)** The chord progression represents the leading-tone seventh chord in the key of E minor, which is the supertonic in D Major. The chord is spelled D#–(F#)–A–C♮, with the F# in the bass. There are two accidentals in this chord—the D# is the leading tone in E minor and C natural is diatonic to E minor but *not* to D Major. Notice that the only difference between (C) and (D) is the inversion.

4. **(C)** The progression in D Major (shown below) is a fully-diminished seventh chord in first inversion temporarily leading to the supertonic (E–G–B). The resolution chord is in first inversion—doubling the third of the chord to avoid unequal fifths in the tenor. Because there are three resolutions D#–E, C♮–B, and A–G, the only "free agent" is the F#.

$$\text{vii}°^6_5/\text{ii} \qquad \text{ii}^6$$

5. **(A)** The chord is a V followed by a V^7. When analyzing something such as this, look at where the chord came from and where it is leading . . . not just the chord alone. The E♭ in the alto is a 4-3 suspension, and the F in the melody is the fifth of the chord.

6. **(D)** The temporary tonic is C–E♭–G, the submediant.

7. **(D)** When comparing measures 1–4 with measures 5–8 we see that the melody is the same while the harmony is different, specifically in measure 6, which includes harmonization with V/vi–vi. Both phrases end with a PAC; therefore, there is not an antecedent–consequent relationship.

8. **(B)** Measures 1–8 form one four-measure phrase repeated with a different harmonization on the repeat.

9. **(D)** The progression is vii°⁶/ii–ii. The temporary tonic is F–Ab–C (ii) in the key of Eb Major. The chromatic harmony is a diminished triad in first inversion E♮–G–Bb with G in the bass. The accidental E♮ in the alto voice is ***Di-Re***.

10. **(A)** V⁷/V–V is a very common cadential harmony because it is used to intensify the dominant chord. In this moment it is all about the Bb . . . and what makes Bb stronger is using its leading tone (A♮). The chromatic pitches are ***Fi-So*** in the melody (harmonized with root position chords).

11. **(C)** The progression in 3 is not a leading-tone to tonic relationship. The chromatic chord is not diminished. It *is* a secondary dominant in third inversion; therefore the resolution chord must be in first inversion (in this case IV⁶).

12. **(B)** The first phrase ends with a half cadence using a secondary dominant, while the second phrase uses a common-chord modulation to shift to Bb Major and ends with a PAC. Both phrases start in the key of Eb Major, the first phrase with a I, and the second phrase with V⁷. Phrase 1 ends with the temporary tonicization of Bb with the V of V. Phrase 2 modulates to Bb using the Eb chord on beat 3—measure 8 as the pivot—and ends with a perfect authentic cadence.

$$\left\{ \begin{array}{l} \text{Eb: I} \\ \text{Bb: IV} \end{array} \right.$$

13. **(D)** The V⁷/IV occurs in both measures 12 and 13 and resolves to the subdominant chord. The chord is Eb–G–Bb–Db (the seventh occurs on beat 4), which is the V⁷ chord in the key of Ab Major. The accidental Db is the note that signals a departure from the key of Eb, and is the chordal seventh resolving downward to the C in the tenor voice. This is a temporary tonicization as the phrase continues in Eb Major, culminating in a perfect authentic cadence in measure 16.

14. **(D)** The boxed area contains an accented passing tone (the Bb in the bass on beat 3 of measure 9) and both a 9–8 suspension (C–Bb) and a 4–3 suspension (Bb–A♮) in the alto in measure 10.

15. **(A)** The Roman numeral chord analysis is V⁶₅–I–V–I because of the modulation to Bb Major with the Eb Major chord on beat 3 of measure 8. The conclusive cadence in Bb and the longer time in this tonality is why it would be considered a move to Bb and not just a temporary tonicization.

AURAL UNIT 3
Multiple-Choice Questions for Chapters 10, 12, 13

Directions: Each of the questions or incomplete statements below is followed by four suggested answers or completions. Select the best answer in each case and circle your answer on the page. In this unit you will see a treble clef icon, 𝄞, which indicates when music will be played. **Questions 1–6** ask you to identify pitch patterns that are played. In each case, the question number will be announced. You will have **10 seconds** to read the choices; then you will hear the musical example played twice, with a brief pause between playings. Remember to read the choices for each question after the number is announced.

Now listen to the music for **Questions 1–6** and identify the pitch patterns that are played.

1. Which of the following intervals is played?

(A)

(B)

(C)

(D)

Access audio at
http://barronsbooks.com/ap/mtheory/

Pitch pattern, played twice. 𝄞

2. Which of the following pitch patterns is played?

(A)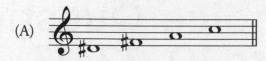

(B)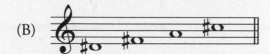

(C)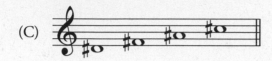

(D)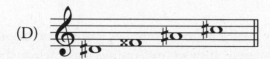

Pitch pattern, played twice.

3. In this example, your choices are four positions of the same dominant seventh chord resolving to tonic. Identify the correct answer below.

   (A) V^7–I

   (B) V^6_5–I

   (C) V^4_3–I

   (D) V^4_2–I^6

Pitch pattern, played twice.

4. Which chord progression is played?

(A) I–V$^6_5$–I
(B) I–V^7–I
(C) ii^6–vii^{o6}–I
(D) I–V$^6_5$/V–V

Pitch pattern, played twice.

In **Question 5** you are asked to identify the three chords in the second measure of a three-measure progression. Measure 1 and measure 3 are both tonic chords. You will hear the example twice.

5. The three-chord progression in measure 2 is

(A) I	ii^6–IV–V	I
(B) I	IV–V/V–V	I
(C) I	ii^6–V$^6_5$/V–V	I
(D) I	V$^6_4$–I^6–V^7	I

Progression, played twice.

In **Question 6** you are asked to identify the type of non-chord tone heard in the following four-measure excerpt. You will hear the example twice.

6. Identify what type of non-chord tone is prominent throughout this short excerpt.

(A) Appoggiaturas
(B) Suspensions
(C) Neighboring tones
(D) Passing tones

Excerpt, played twice.

Go on to the next group of questions.

Questions 7–9 are based on a repeated eight-measure excerpt of a piano sonata. You will hear the excerpt played twice. Before listening to this excerpt for the first time, please read **Questions 7–9**.

7. The meter of this excerpt is

   (A) simple duple
   (B) compound duple
   (C) simple triple
   (D) compound triple

8. This excerpt contains

   (A) trills only
   (B) triplets only
   (C) melodic sequence
   (D) both triplets and trills

9. Compared to the opening tonality, the excerpt ends in the key of the

   (A) mediant
   (B) dominant
   (C) parallel minor
   (D) subdominant

The excerpt will now be played the first time.

The excerpt will now be played a second time.

Go on to the next group of questions.

Questions 10–16 are based on an excerpt from a French opera of the nineteenth century. This excerpt has three sections. You will hear the **first two sections** played twice, the third section played once, and then the entire excerpt played once. Before listening to the first two sections for the first time, read **Questions 10–13**.

10. The meter of the opening section is

   (A) simple duple
   (B) simple triple
   (C) compound duple
   (D) compound triple

11. Which of the following is **not true** of the opening section?

   (A) The instrument(s) playing the melody change.
   (B) The melody changes amplitude.
   (C) It is a repeated parallel period.
   (D) It can be characterized as a bugle call.

12. Compared to the first section, what does **not** change in the second section?

   (A) Meter
   (B) Mode
   (C) Timbre
   (D) Tempo

13. The melodic structure of the second section is a

   (A) modulating parallel period
   (B) repeated contrasting period
   (C) repeated parallel period
   (D) modulating contrasting period

Now listen to the first two sections of this excerpt and answer
Questions 10–13. 𝄞

The first two sections will now be played a second time. 𝄞

Before listening to the third section, read **Questions 14–16**.

14. Which statement best describes the third section?

   (A) It uses a poco a poco accelerando.
   (B) It modulates.
   (C) It cadences in minor.
   (D) Both B and C.

15. Section three contains four phrases of four measures each. The end of phrase 2 contains

   (A) a half cadence
   (B) an authentic cadence
   (C) a plagal cadence
   (D) an elided authentic cadence

16. In this section, phrase 2 and phrase 4 are harmonized by

   (A) a circle of fifths progression
   (B) the bass line moving down by thirds
   (C) a descending stepwise motion in the bass
   (D) a pedal bass

Now listen to the third section of this excerpt and answer **Questions 14–16**.

The entire excerpt will now be played. Review your answers for **Questions 10–16**.

Go on to the next group of questions.

Questions 17–20 are based on a short excerpt from a baroque piece. You will hear the excerpt played two times. Before listening to the excerpt for the first time, read **Questions 17–20**.

17. The modality of this excerpt is

  (A) Lydian
  (B) minor
  (C) major
  (D) pentatonic

18. The time signature of this excerpt is most likely

  (A) $\frac{6}{8}$
  (B) $\frac{3}{4}$
  (C) $\frac{2}{4}$
  (D) **c**

19. The piece is performed by a

  (A) solo piano
  (B) woodwind trio
  (C) harpsichord and violin
  (D) solo harpsichord

20. The form of this excerpt is

  (A) theme and variations
  (B) rounded binary
  (C) ternary
  (D) rondo

The excerpt will now be played for the first time. 𝄞

The excerpt will now be played for a second time. 𝄞

Go on to the next group of questions.

TRACK 40   **Questions 21–25** are based on two short excerpts from a movement of a symphony from the classical period. The first excerpt will be played two times; the second excerpt will be played once; then the entire excerpt will be played once. Before listening to the first section for the first time, please read **Questions 21–23**.

21. What are the first three melodic pitches played by the violins?

   (A) $\hat{4}$ $\hat{5}$ $\hat{3}$
   (B) $\sharp\hat{4}$ $\hat{6}$ $\hat{5}$
   (C) $\hat{3}$ $\hat{5}$ $\hat{4}$
   (D) $\sharp\hat{5}$ $\hat{6}$ $\hat{5}$

22. The first two phrases begin with a melody played by the violins while the primary accompaniment is

   (A) pizzicato strings
   (B) arpeggiated chords by the brass
   (C) pedal point from the string bass
   (D) staccato from the woodwinds

23. Compared to the first phrase, the second melodic phrase played by the violins represents

   (A) a diminution
   (B) a literal repetition
   (C) a sequence down a third
   (D) an extended version

The first excerpt will now be played for the first time.

The first excerpt will now be played a second time.

Before listening to the second excerpt, read **Questions 24–25**.

24. Which of the following compositional devices is <u>not</u> being used in the second section?

    (A) Melodic fragmentation
    (B) Cadential extension
    (C) Syncopation
    (D) Canon

25. The excerpt ends with a

    (A) plagal cadence
    (B) half cadence
    (C) perfect authentic cadence
    (D) deceptive cadence

The second excerpt will now be played.

Now review **Questions 21–25** as you listen to the entire excerpt.

This concludes the Aural Multiple-Choice Questions for Chapters 10–13.

ANSWER KEY

1. **B**	6. **B**	11. **A**	16. **A**	21. **B**
2. **A**	7. **C**	12. **D**	17. **B**	22. **D**
3. **D**	8. **D**	13. **B**	18. **A**	23. **C**
4. **C**	9. **B**	14. **D**	19. **D**	24. **D**
5. **C**	10. **C**	15. **D**	20. **B**	25. **A**

ANSWERS EXPLAINED

1. **(B)** The interval played is a minor sixth.

2. **(A)** The pattern played is a fully-diminished seventh chord: diminished triad and diminished seventh. This one's tough. Start with *what you know for sure:* The D Major triad is D–F♯–A; therefore, D♯–F♯–A is diminished. The interval from D to C is a m7; therefore, D♯ to C is diminished.

3. **(D)** Listen for *Fa-Mi* in the bass; in this case, in C Major.

Answer D is the only answer that is *not* a root position tonic. The bass notes for all four answers would be (A) *So-Do*, (B) *Ti-Do*, (C) *Re-Do*, and (D) *Fa-Mi*.

4. **(C)** Bass line implies harmony. Listen to the bass line, identify quality, and remember that tendency tones ($\hat{4}$ and $\hat{7}$) must resolve.

Fa Mi Re Do

5. **(C)** Listen for *Fa-Fi-So* in the bass.

6. **(B)** Suspensions are the only non-chord tones in this excerpt.

7. **(C)** Simple triple meter; the time signature is $\frac{3}{4}$.

8. **(D)** This excerpt contains both triplets and trills.

9. **(B)** The phrase shifts to the key of the dominant, from C Major to G Major. The modulation occurs on the second beat of the fourth measure: C: I to G: IV. Let's look at this example:

Piano Sonata No. 3 in C Major

Franz Joseph Haydn
(1732–1809)
Hob. XVI

10. **(C)** The meter is compound duple; $\frac{6}{8}$ time signature.

11. **(A)** The opening statement played by the trumpet is a bugle call and is repeated at a louder dynamic the second time, also by the trumpet. The timbre does not change. The melody consists of two phrases that create a parallel period. Those two phrases are repeated creating a repeated parallel period.

12. **(D)** The second section is the same tempo; however, the timbre changes to flute, the meter changes to simple duple, and the mode changes to minor.

13. **(B)** The second section is a repeated contrasting period. This new melody (in minor) ends with a half cadence at the end of four measures and a PAC at the end of eight measures. The consequent phrase (measures 5–8) is a different melody than the antecedent phrase (measures 1–4).

14. **(D)** The third section has the same melody as the second section except it begins in a major key. At the end of the section, the melody shifts back to the minor key of section two and ends with a PAC.

15. **(D)** In section three, the second phrase ends with an elided authentic cadence. This actually occurs between phrases 2 and 3. The third phrase begins with the tonic harmony that ends the second phrase.

16. **(A)** In this excerpt, each (of three) sections has four phrases. In the first two sections the first two phrases are simply repeated. In the third section the first two phrases are in (B♭) Major ending with a PAC using a circle of fifth progression. The third phrase is exactly like the first phrase. The fourth phrase sequences back to minor and ends with a circle of fifths progression using the exact same minor ending as the fourth phrase of the second section.

Phrase two in B♭ Major   Phrase four in D minor

Circle of fifths progression in B♭ Major.   Circle of fifths progression ending in D minor.
Also an example of an *elided* cadence: The end of this
phrase is the beginning of the next.

17. **(B)** This excerpt is in minor.

18. **(A)** The time signature is most likely ⁶⁄₈, compound duple.

19. **(D)** The solo instrument is harpsichord.

                                                   A   B

20. **(B)** The form is rounded binary: a a   b ½a. The "a" material is an eight-measure parallel period and is repeated for the A section. When the "a" material returns at the end of the B section, only four measures are heard. Did you also hear that the return of "a" modulates?

21. **(B)** The violins are playing ♯4̂–6̂–5̂ (*Fi-La-So*). It is a consistently heard motive.

22. **(D)** In the first two phrases, the woodwinds are playing staccato accompaniment.

23. **(C)** Compared to the first phrase, the melody in the second phrase is played down a third.

24. **(D)** The second section does not contain a canon.

25. **(A)** The excerpt ends with a plagal cadence: IV–I.

Harmonic Composition Part II: The Process

14

- Creating and Using the Road Map
- Deceptive Cadence
- Doubling Notes in a Triad
- Mode Mixture
- Motion
  - Contrary Motion
  - Similar Motion
  - Parallel Motion
  - Oblique Motion
- Parallelism
- Picardy Third
- Resolution Rules
- Secondary Dominants and Secondary Leading Tones
- Unequal Fifths

Part writing requires knowledge of melody, interval, triads, inversions, seventh chords, cadences, non-chord tones, figured bass, chromatic harmony, resolution tendencies, and counterpoint as well as what is typical and/or prevalent for the Common Practice Period. Practicing this skill is an ideal way to reinforce all these concepts. In this chapter we complete our discussion of harmonic composition with seven more challenging part-writing examples and four additional exercises that are comparable to those found on the AP Music Theory exam.

PART-WRITING AND FIGURED BASS EXAMPLES

EXAMPLE 1: Figured Bass in E♭ Major*

We begin Part II with a realization of a figured bass in E♭ Major. This process requires the student to identify the figured bass symbols with the bass line, convert symbols to Roman numerals, compose the melody, and fill in the alto and tenor lines. The bass line is given.

This example uses three second inversion triads and introduces the submediant triad (vi) and the **deceptive cadence**.

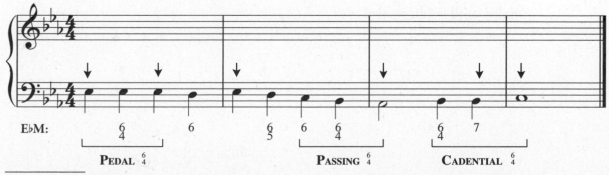

---

*Adapted from material of Dr. Blaise Ferrandino, Texas Christian University, Fort Worth, Texas.

What do we know for sure? The notes in the bass line that have no Arabic numeral figures (marked with the arrows) are *root position* triads including the last chord built on C. The chord with the figured bass 7 is a root position seventh chord. As explained earlier, figured bass symbols are numbers and/or symbols that represent the interval above the bass that are the chord members. In this example there are two first inversion triads, three second inversion triads, and one first inversion seventh chord.

STEP 1: Add the Roman numeral chord symbols and inversions.
Write the progression below the figured bass. Create the road map, including the resolution arrows and doubling reminders.

Notice that the IV$^6_4$ chord between the two tonic chords in measure 1 creates a **pedal** (oblique motion) in the bass. This type of $^6_4$ chord is sometimes called the auxiliary $^6_4$ or the neighbor $^6_4$ because the pedal in the bass will create a neighbor relationship in one of the other voices. Another important aspect of this example is the V$^6_5$ chord progressing to an inverted IV chord that provides an opportunity to put Resolution Rule 3 into action. (The chordal seventh of any seventh chord resolves down by step or *holds until it can.*) The usual resolution of the V^7 chord is to I or vi. In this example, the V$^6_5$ resolves to IV^6; therefore, the seventh of the chord (**Fa**) *cannot* resolve downward (there is no **Mi** in the IV chord), so the seventh (A♭) holds until it can resolve.

STEP 2: Write the melody.

This melody starts on *Mi* ($\hat{3}$), moves by step, reaching a peak at the cadence and extending the soprano up to E♭5. The cadence is deceptive, ending on the submediant. This progression moves toward a tonic ending but, instead, cadences with the tonic substitute (vi), "deceiving" your ears and ending in minor instead of the expected major. There is only one occurrence of parallel motion, but what is created is parallel thirds between the bass and the soprano—not a problem. Avoid additional parallelism at this spot by using contrary motion when writing the alto and tenor.

STEP 3: Fill in the alto and tenor at the same time.

Parallel thirds (between soprano and bass) are acceptable.

V and vi are adjacent chords that will create parallelism if you double the root, so double the 3rd in the submediant (vi).

STEP 4: Check your work.
- ✔ Correct chord members
- ✔ Resolutions (including holding the chordal seventh on A♭ until it can resolve to G)
- ✔ Double the fifth in ⁶₄ chords
- ✔ No parallel fifths or eighths
- ✔ Spacing

In measure 1, the G–A♭–G in the soprano and the B♭–C–B♭ in the tenor is the neighbor relationship that this type of ⁶₄ chord creates against the pedal in the bass.

EXAMPLE 2: Figured Bass in F Minor

This next example is in **F minor**; carefully observe the figured bass symbols.

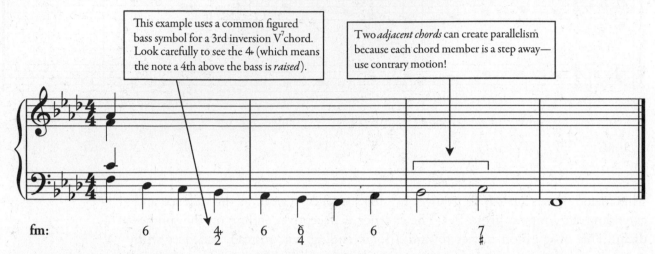

This example uses a common figured bass symbol for a 3rd inversion V⁷ chord. Look carefully to see the 4 (which means the note a 4th above the bass is *raised*).

Two *adjacent chords* can create parallelism because each chord member is a step away— use contrary motion!

fm:

STEP 1: Write the Roman numeral chord symbols and the road map.

F minor:	i	iv⁶	V	V⁴₂	i⁶	V⁶₄	i	i⁶	iv	V⁷		i
				Bb						Bb		
	C	F	F	G	C	GG	C	C	F	G		C
	Ab	Db	E♮	E♮	Ab	E♮	Ab	Ab	D	E♮		Ab
	F	Bb	C	C	F	C	F	F	Bb	C		F

- Since this is in a minor key, the half steps are between $\hat{2}$–$\hat{3}$ and $\hat{5}$–$\hat{6}$. In our resolution chart $\hat{6}$ (*Le* is Db) goes to $\hat{5}$ (*So* is C), especially in outside voices.

- Notice the stepwise descending bass line

$$\begin{bmatrix} \textbf{\textit{Do-Le-So-Fa-Me}} \\ \text{i} \quad \text{iv}^6 \quad \text{V} \quad \text{V}^4_2 \quad \text{i}^6 \end{bmatrix} (\hat{1}–\hat{6}–\hat{5}–\hat{4}–\hat{3})$$

created by the progression in measure 1.

You're on your own to follow the road map and complete this example.

STEP 2: Write the melody.
When you have finished and you have only bass and soprano, check for parallel
fifths and octaves.

Note that the V$^4_2$ resolves to i^6 and the V$^6_4$ chord in measure 2 is a passing $^6_4$ chord.
The bass line is mostly *conjunct* and ends with ***Fa-So-Do***. Here is one possible solution. That's the beauty of composition—there are many possible correct answers.
In this solution the V^7 chord at the cadence is complete; therefore, the final tonic
chord is *in*complete.

EXAMPLE 3: Part Writing to Roman Numerals in F Major

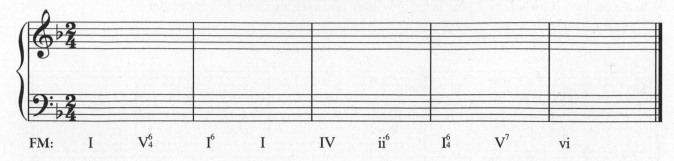

FM: I V_4^6 I^6 I   IV ii^6 I_4^6 V^7 vi

What do we know for sure? This example adds the supertonic triad and ends with a **deceptive cadence (V–vi)** that moves toward a tonic ending *but* cadences with the tonic substitute (vi), "deceiving" your ears and ending in minor instead of the expected major.

STEP 1: Create the chord stack.
Add the doublings and resolution arrows, and circle the note that is the bass note as indicated by the inversion.

STEP 2: Add the bass line.

FM: I V_4^6 I^6 I   IV ii^6 I_4^6 V^7 vi

When V goes to I or vi, ***Ti*** ($\hat{7}$) resolves to ***Do*** ($\hat{1}$). The $_4^6$ chord in measure 1 is a passing $_4^6$ prolonging tonic at the beginning. Continually try to "connect the dots"—meaning that although this is a part-writing example, it demonstrates typical harmonic progression that is expected when you harmonize a melody (FR 7) and would also be a typical progression for FR 3 or 4—harmonic dictation. Notice that the ii^6 chord is in first inversion and it comes *after* IV. The deceptive cadence chords (V–vi) are adjacent and contain pitches that are next to each other (C–D, E–F, G–A) and will create parallelism. Use contrary motion and **double the third in the vi chord.**

STEP 3: Add the melody next.

STEP 4: Add the alto and tenor voices at the same time.

One possible solution:

FM: I   V$_4^6$ I^6 I   IV   ii^6 I$_4^6$ V^7 vi

EXAMPLE 4: Part Writing to the Roman Numerals in A Minor*

am: i   V$_4^6$ i^6 ii$^{\circ6}$ i$_4^6$ V   VI   i$_4^6$ ii$_5^{\varnothing6}$ i^6 iv   i

What do we know for sure? The second measure ends with a half cadence and the final cadence is **plagal (iv–i)**. Because of the HC, you are essentially starting again in the third measure so that resolutions from V to VI from measure 2 into measure 3 are not imperative; a new phrase means a new beginning. We have included the supertonic (ii°) triad and the supertonic seventh (half-diminished) chords.

STEP 1: Complete the road map.
Include doublings and resolution reminders. Add the bass line. Do this on your own in the space provided above. The answers follow on the next page.

---

*Adapted from material of Dr. Blaise Ferrandino, Texas Christian University, Fort Worth, Texas.

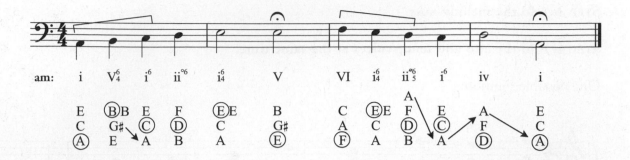

The V^6_4 in measure 1 and the i^6_4 in measure 3 are both passing $^6_4$ chords (and are on weak beats). The i^6_4 chord in measure 2 is a *cadential* $^6_4$ (positioned on a strong beat).

The seventh of the chord in the half-diminished supertonic chord (A) doesn't ever resolve to the G♯ because the usual resolution chord (V) does not follow, so **HOLD the A** in the same voice.

STEP 2: Write the melody.

There are many places where parallelism may occur because there are many chords with roots a second apart and therefore chord tones that are also adjacent. Use contrary motion whenever possible at these places.

STEP 3: Fill in the alto and tenor at the same time.

So the question is "What's more important, the line or the harmony, when it comes to doubling?" The answer is *the line*. Avoid parallelism by using contrary motion and try to use the closest chord member.

Notice that in the third chord we doubled the root, having the alto and soprano sing unison A, and then we doubled the third of the chord in the supertonic. Although there are parallel fifths between the bass and tenor as noted above, because a new phrase begins after the fermata, this is not considered to be an error. The C in the tenor that creates the parallel fifths was chosen because it leads better to the E in the next chord; however, if this was not a cadence and we had to avoid parallel fifths, the best choice would be to double the A in the tenor. Our alto sings the "A line."

EXAMPLE 5: Figured Bass Realization in G Minor*, Including a Picardy Third
The next figured bass example in G minor has a progression (V–VI where the roots are a second apart) that will create parallelism if you double the root, so **double the third in the VI**. This will also strengthen the feeling of tonic as the third of the chord is *Do*. It also includes a pedal $^6_4$ chord and a half-diminished supertonic seventh chord.

What do we know for sure? In measure 3 the chord *changes* on beat 2. The bass note does not change, but because a figure is added (6), the harmony above the C changes to the supertonic triad in first inversion. On the fourth beat the seventh is added to the V chord. The final chord features the most common form of mode mixture—the **Picardy third**. The natural sign in the figured bass means the chord is G–B♮–D, borrowing from the parallel major. The Roman numeral must reflect this as well as the use of the accidental in the composition.

STEP 1: Add the Roman numeral progression and the road map. Use the space provided above. The answers follow on the next page.

---

*Adapted from material of Dr. Blaise Ferrandino, Texas Christian University, Fort Worth, Texas.

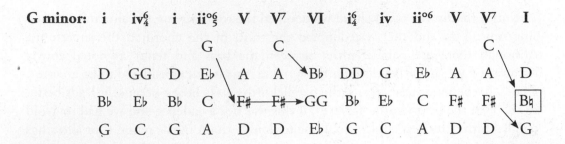

G minor:	i	iv$_4^6$	i	ii$_5^{o6}$	V	V^7	VI	i$_4^6$	iv	ii^{o6}	V	V^7	I
					G		C					C	
	D	GG	D	E♭	A	A	B♭	DD	G	E♭	A	A	D
	B♭	E♭	B♭	C	F♯	F♯	GG	B♭	E♭	C	F♯	F♯	B♮
	G	C	G	A	D	D	E♭	G	C	A	D	D	G

STEP 2: Write the melody.

STEP 3: Fill in the alto and tenor at the same time.

➡ You can find clean copies of all the part-writing and figured bass examples in Appendix C.

EXAMPLE 6: Figured Bass in D Major* Using Mode Mixture

What do we know for sure? Because there is a flat sign used in the figured bass in a *major* tonality we know that we have a *borrowed chord*. The figured bass tells us that it is a root position seventh chord and the seventh is lowered. The chord is spelled C♯–E–G–B♭, which is certainly *not* a chord found in D Major; however, it *is* found in the parallel minor—D minor. This is an example of **mode mixture**. The chord is a *fully-diminished* seventh chord borrowed from the parallel harmonic minor; it does not resolve to a D minor chord in this example—it resolves to the D *Major* tonic chord.

---

*Adapted from material of Dr. Blaise Ferrandino, Texas Christian University, Fort Worth, Texas.

STEP 1: Add the Roman numeral progression.
Continue to use the road map if this is helpful to you. You may also find it helpful to write in the required accidentals *above* the staff as a reminder.

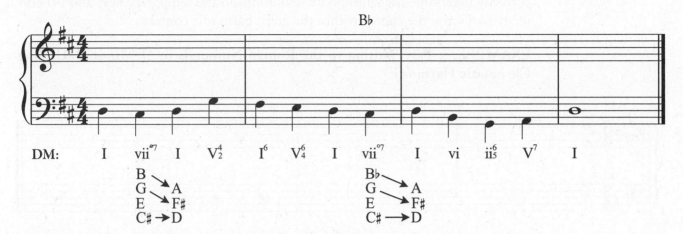

The leading tone chords will have **three resolution tones**. Note the only difference between these two chords is that the seventh in the **fully**-diminished chord is B♭, a half step lower than in the B♮ in the half-diminished chord.

STEP 2: Write the melody.

STEP 3: Fill in the alto and tenor at the same time.
Check the resolution imperatives. Remember that the arrows in the finished progression are resolution tones properly resolved.

Notice that in the boxed area there are parallel fifths between the alto and tenor. They are **unequal fifths**, which are acceptable if it is a P5 to a dim5. In the tonic triad the interval is a P5; in the vii°7 the interval is dim5. An acceptable alternative to avoid the fifth is to move the tenor to an F♯, doubling the third in the tonic triad. Unequal fifths from dim5 to P5 are *not* acceptable in common-practice style.

We were able to end with our old favorite melodic ending, *Mi-Re-Do*.

It is becoming increasingly common to see the use of secondary (chromatic) harmony particularly in FR 6, requiring the ability to (1) correctly identify the symbol and the resolution chord, (2) correctly determine the chord members, (3) correctly determine the appropriate resolutions in the temporary key, and (4) correctly part write the chords within the given harmonic context.

EXAMPLE 7: Part Writing to the Roman Numerals in D Minor, Including Chromatic Harmony

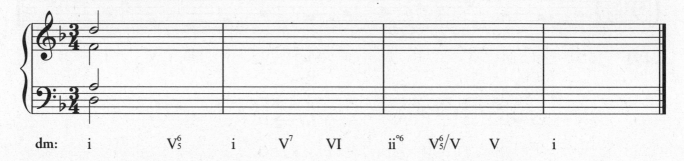

dm: i   V$^6_5$ i   V^7 VI   ii^{o6} V$^6_5$/V   V   i

STEP 1: Create the chord stack.

Add the doubling reminders and resolution arrows, and circle the notes that will be in the bass line as indicated by the inversion.

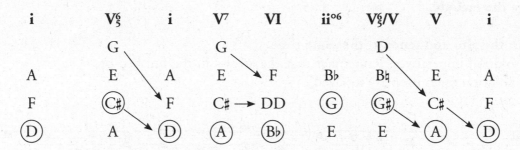

The secondary dominant is **V$^6_5$** of **V**. Our temporary tonic is the key of A major (V in our original key). The chord is spelled E–G♯–B♮–D with the G♯ in the bass ($^6_5$ inversion). There are *two* notes that are not diatonic in D minor: the G♯ and the B♮. Don't forget the accidentals! Try writing them above the staff.

Write the bass line.

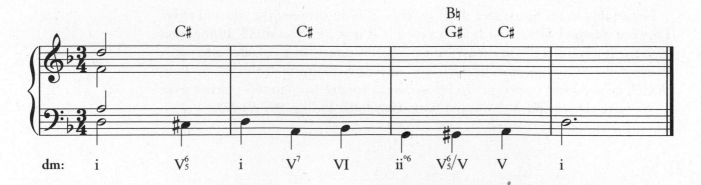

dm: i   V$^6_5$ i   V^7 VI   ii^{o6} V$^6_5$/V   V   i

STEP 2: Write the melody.

Use contrary motion where possible. Observe the resolutions, *especially* if they are used in the outer voices.

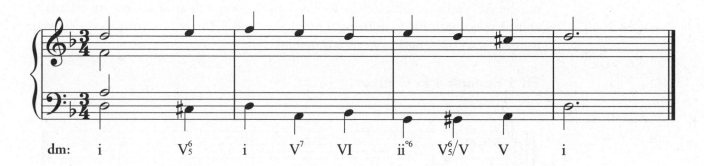

dm: i   V$_5^6$ i   V^7 VI   ii$^{\circ 6}$ V$_5^6$/V   V   i

STEP 3: Fill in the alto and tenor at the same time.

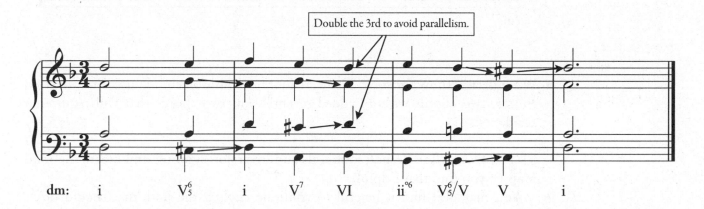

Double the 3rd to avoid parallelism.

dm: i   V$_5^6$ i   V^7 VI   ii$^{\circ 6}$ V$_5^6$/V   V   i

STEP 4: Check your work.
- ✔ Correct chord members
- ✔ Resolutions (including secondary dominant to the temporary tonic)
- ✔ No parallel fifths or eighths
- ✔ Spacing

Chord 3 has two roots, two thirds, and no fifth. This *is* acceptable as the triad is in *root position*. Moving the tenor up to the D puts him in position to move smoothly down to the C♯ and back to D. Leaving the tenor on A would also be acceptable.

ANSWERING FREE-RESPONSE PART-WRITING QUESTIONS

The last four examples in this chapter will be very similar to what you might see on the AP exam in difficulty as well as length. You will always have six chords to complete on both FR 5, realizing figured bass, and FR 6, part writing to the Roman numerals, so the length is never a variable.

FR 5 Example 1 in C minor

What do we know for sure? There are four root position chords and three inverted chords, two chords with an added seventh, and two chords that will require an accidental.

STEP 1: Determine Roman numerals and inversion symbols and create the road map (if you find that helpful).

You may also find it helpful to continue circling the note that should be in the bass according to the inversion symbols because it *confirms* the correct chord members and inversion—a system of checks and balances.

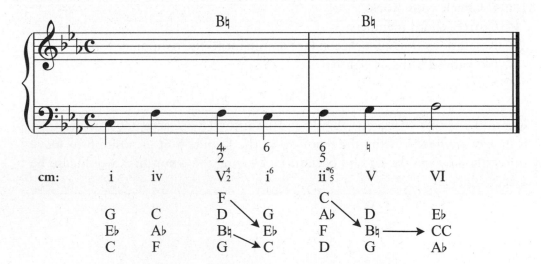

Connect the Dots: Note that the leading tone is **B♮**, the V$^4_2$ resolves to i^6, the supertonic seventh chord is half-diminished and resolves to the dominant chord. The cadence is *deceptive*. The dominant chord resolves to the major submediant; therefore, *Ti* must resolve to *Do*. The seventh of the ii$^{ø6}_5$ chord must resolve downward.

STEP 2: Write a melody that uses primarily contrary motion to the bass line.

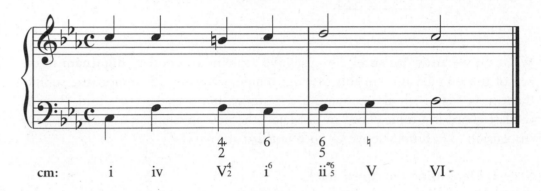

STEP 3: Fill in the alto and tenor at the same time.
Double-check accidentals to ensure correct chord quality.

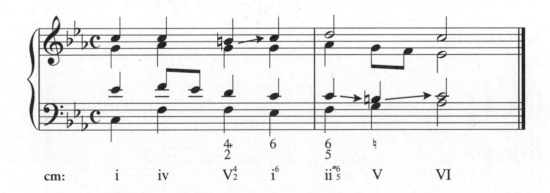

The added F in the alto in the penultimate (next to last) chord is not only a passing tone but also the seventh of that chord. If this was required by the figured bass, the figures below the staff would be 8–7.

FR 6 Example 1 in G Major

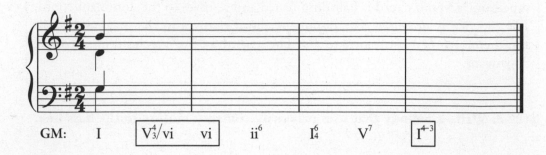

GM: I V^4_3/vi   vi   ii^6 I$^6_4$ V^7 I$^{4-3}$

What do we know for sure? This example contains a secondary **dominant** in the key of the submediant—in this case our temporary tonic is E minor (the submediant in G Major). It also contains a 4–3 suspension over the last chord. Because the last chord is a tonic chord in G Major, the note in the bass is G, making the suspension C (a **fourth** above G) to B (a **third** above G).

STEP 1: Determine the chord stack.
When determining secondary chords, identify the resolution chord *first* because this will be your temporary tonic, then identify the secondary function chord.

Create the road map.
Circle the notes that should be in the bass according to the inversion symbols.

Write the bass line.

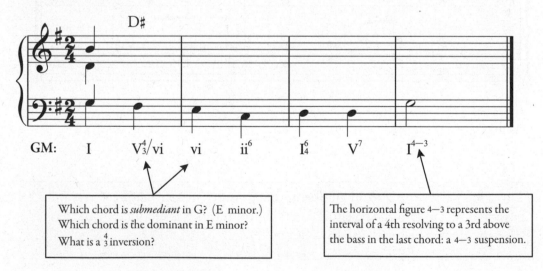

GM: I V^4_3/vi   vi   ii^6 I$^6_4$ V^7 I$^{4-3}$

Which chord is *submediant* in G? (E minor.)
Which chord is the dominant in E minor?
What is a $^4_3$ inversion?

The horizontal figure 4–3 represents the interval of a 4th resolving to a 3rd above the bass in the last chord: a 4–3 suspension.

STEP 2: Write a great melody.

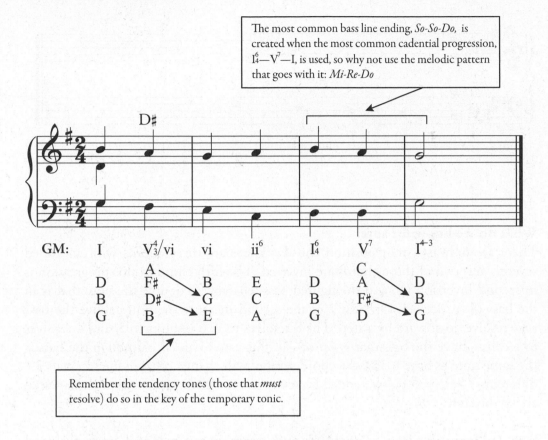

STEP 3: Fill in the alto and tenor at the same time.

FR 5 Example 2 in B minor

What do we know for sure?

There are only two root position chords. There are three chords with an added seventh and two of those chords are inverted. The fifth chord in this progression is in second inversion ($^6_4$), and the figured bass tells you to double the note that is in the bass (8 or octave). On beat 2 of the second measure the notes above the bass *each* resolve downward by a step. The $\hat{8}$ resolves to $\hat{7}$, $\hat{6}$ resolves to $\hat{5}$, and $\hat{4}$ resolves to a third above the bass that is *raised*—in this case to an A♯. Although the bass is the same note as beat 1 (F♯), the chord symbol will change because the intervals are different. There will be two added accidentals. As a reminder, write the accidental above the staff.

STEP 1: Determine Roman numerals and inversion symbols and create the road map (if you find that helpful).

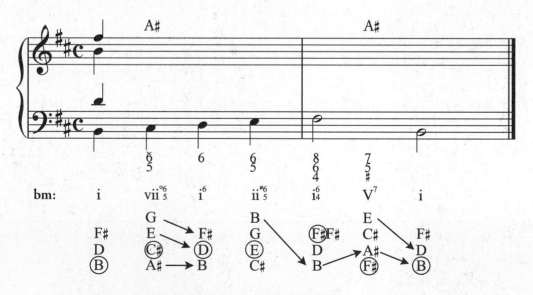

The leading-tone seventh chord is in first inversion and will have three resolutions. Because the half-diminished supertonic chord is not followed by the V chord, the seventh of the chord must **hold** on the B until it *can* resolve downward to the A♯.

STEP 2: Create a great melody in contrary motion where possible.

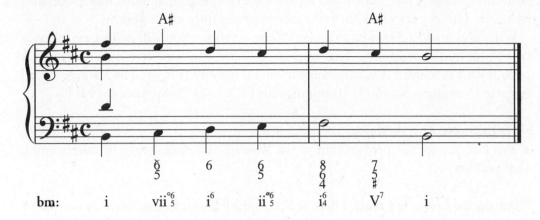

When the motion between the bass line and the melody is mostly contrary you will greatly reduce parallelism between those two voices, but don't forget to check inside voices when you have completed all four voices. Note that once again our bass line is **So-So-Do**, so we write what goes with that in the melody—**Me-Re-Do** (or **Do-Ti-Do** or **So-Fa-Me**).

STEP 3: Fill in the chords with the alto and tenor at the same time.
Be sure to add accidentals as needed and resolve all tendency tones.

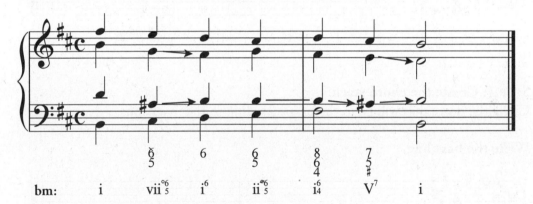

Let's look carefully at our realization. In the tenor voice in measure 1 we have written a diminished fourth between the D and A♯. That would be a two-point deduction in voice leading between chord 1 and chord 2 for writing a dissonant interval in the tenor voice. So how can we solve this without starting all over and changing the melody? The solution in this case is to create eighth notes on beat 2 in the tenor using C♯ and A♯ (both members of the chord) and eliminating the dim4.

Once again we see that when we have a complete seventh chord as we do in the penultimate chord, the chord that follows is *not complete*. It contains three roots and the third. This occurs when correctly following the rules of resolution.

What about adding non-chord tones? Keep it simple! You will *not* get extra credit for adding non-chord tones. This is a timed exam; you will have only 45 minutes to do both FR 5 and FR 6, *plus* harmonizing a melody (FR 7). The College Board suggests 15 minutes for FR 5, 10 minutes for FR 6, and 20 minutes for FR 7.

FR 6 Example 2 in A Major
In this last example of part writing to the Roman numerals, begin by determining what you know.

What do we know for sure? There is a secondary dominant seventh chord in first inversion followed by a second inversion tonic triad. Since this secondary dominant does *not* resolve to the **temporary tonic**, spell the temporary tonic to confirm your work, then spell the dominant in that key.

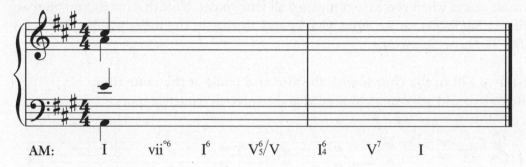

STEP 1: Create the chord stack.
Circle the notes that will be in the bass according to the inversions.

Write the bass line.

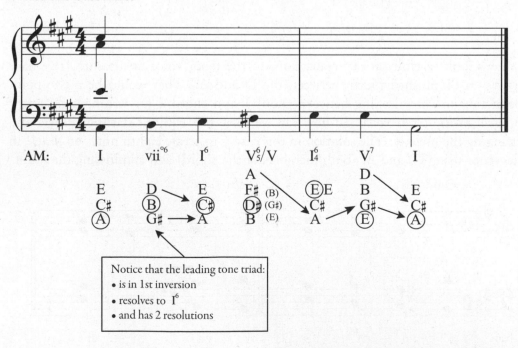

STEP 2: Create a melody.
Use contrary motion when possible.

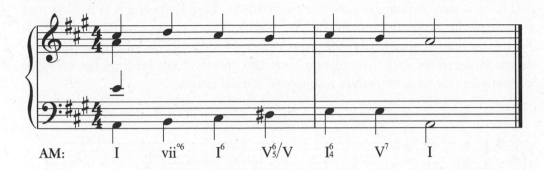

STEP 3: Fill in the alto and the bass at the same time.
Be aware of parallelism, and check and *recheck* your road map for resolutions and added accidentals.

Part writing requires knowledge of melody, interval, triads, inversions, seventh chords, cadences, non-chord tones, figured bass, chromatic harmony, resolution tendencies, and counterpoint as well as what is typical and/or prevalent for the Common Practice Period. Practicing this skill is an ideal way to reinforce all these concepts.

➡️ All of the examples from this chapter can be found in Appendix C for you to compose a new melody and complete for additional practice.

A Little About Scoring

Let's talk about the most common errors and how to avoid them. Free-Response 5 (FR 5) is part writing by realizing figured bass. Free-Response 6 (FR 6) is part writing to the Roman numerals. FR 5's possible high score is 25 and FR 6's is 18. Both are scored similarly with one point awarded for correct chord spelling and two points awarded for each "connection" between chords–voice leading. Let's look at a short example to demonstrate a couple of critical issues.

This example is in E minor; therefore, the V or V⁷ chord must have the raised 7th scale degree, in this case, D♯. Students lose more points for this error (omitting the accidental) than for any other, and it is a *critical* mistake. Without the sharp sign the chord is spelled incorrectly; that means a one-point deduction (or *zero* points added). Plus, because the chord is misspelled, there are *zero* voice leading points *into* chord 2, and *zero* points *out* of chord 2. That's what our graders call a "triangle affect."

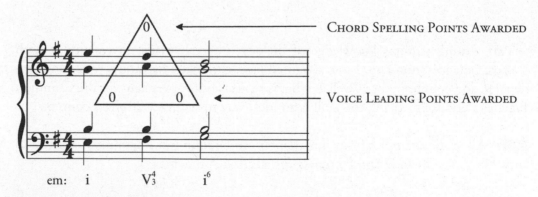

CHORD SPELLING POINTS AWARDED

VOICE LEADING POINTS AWARDED

By omitting just one accidental, five points are lost. Now let's look at another common mistake in chord 3. This chord has two thirds, two fifths, but no root. In a root position triad or seventh chord it is acceptable to omit the fifth, but not in an inverted chord, and *never* omit the root. This would be considered incorrect chord spelling, and once again zero points are awarded for chord spelling or voice leading. Chords 4 and 5 are both spelled correctly. The V⁷ chord has the accidental and both resolutions are correct; however, another major error has occurred. There are parallel fifths between the bass and tenor. This happened because the final tonic contains all three chord members. So many progressions end V⁷ to I or i, so here is the rule to remember:

When (root position)V^7 goes to (root position) I or i, **IF** the V^7 has all four members, **THEN** the tonic chord will have three roots, one third, and no fifth. **IF** the V^7 is *not* complete (leave out the fifth and *double the root*), **THEN** that will lead you to a complete (all three chord members) tonic triad. Here are the two ways this could have been corrected.

In this example the final tonic chord has three roots (E) and one third (G).

In this example the V^7 chord does *not* have the fifth. The root is doubled (B), and there is the third (D♯) and the seventh (A). The tonic chord is now complete with all three members (E–G–B).

So, how would these three critical errors affect our score on just chord spelling and voice leading?

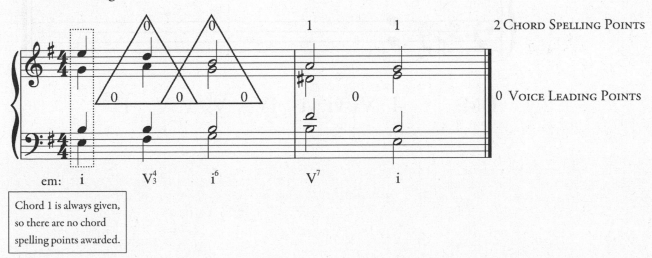

Chord 1 is always given, so there are no chord spelling points awarded.

Possible high score in this short example for chord spelling (4) and voice leading (8) = 12

Our score = 2

Additional Practice Examples

1.

$$\begin{matrix} & 6 & 4+ & 6 & 6 & \sharp \\ & 5 & 2 & & 5 & \end{matrix}$$

gm: i ___ ___ ___ ___ ___ ___

2.

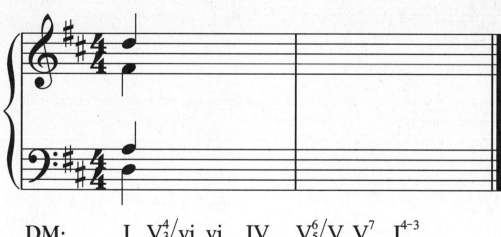

DM: I V_3^4/vi   vi   IV V_5^6/V V^7 I^{4-3}

3.

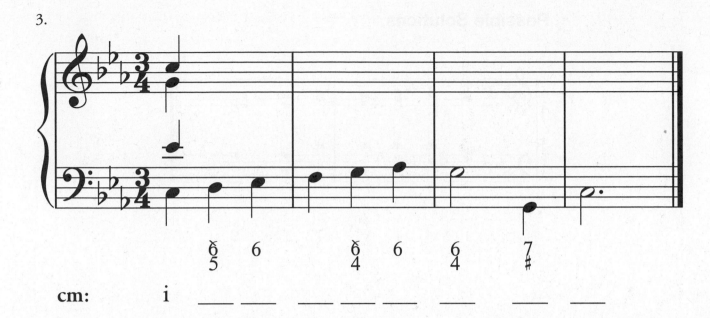

cm: i ___ ___ ___ ___ ___ ___ ___

4.

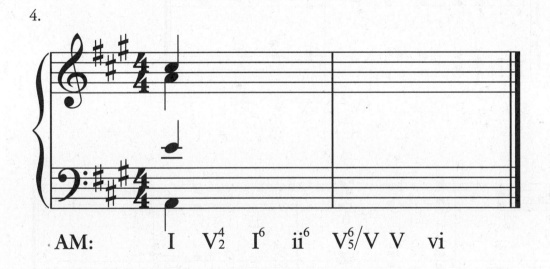

AM: I V_2^4 I^6 $ii^{\circ 6}$ V_5^6/V V vi

Possible Solutions

1.

gm: i   V$^6_5$ i   V$^4_2$ i^6 ii$^{ø6}_5$ V

2.

DM: I   V$^4_3$/vi   vi   IV   V$^6_5$/V   V^7 I$^{4-3}$

3.

cm: i   vii$^{ø6}_5$ i^6 iv   V$^6_4$/iv   iv^6 i$^6_{14}$ V^7 i

4.

AM: I   V$^4_2$ I^6 ii^6 V$^6_5$/V   V   vi

Chapter Summary

Review of Resolutions

1. When V goes to vi/VI or I/i, then *Ti* resolves to *Do*.
2. When V⁷, vii°, or vii°⁷ goes to I/i or vi/VI, then *Ti* resolves to *Do and Fa* resolves to *Mi*.
3. In *any* seventh chord, the seventh of the chord resolves downward by step or *holds* until it can.

Other Resolution Considerations

NOTE: V⁶ or V⁶₅ resolves to I or i; V⁴₂ resolves to I⁶ or i⁶.

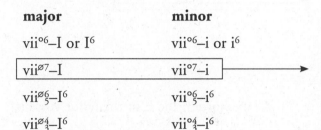

major	minor	
vii°⁶–I or I⁶	vii°⁶–i or i⁶	
vii⁰⁷–I	vii°⁷–i	Leading tone seventh chords are typically found in first inversion or second inversion. Root position and third inversion are *not* common.
vii⁰⁶₅–I⁶	vii°⁶₅–i⁶	
vii⁰⁴₃–I⁶	vii°⁴₃–i⁶	

- Do *not* add non-chord tones in part writing or figured bass realization.
- Do *not* double the leading tone (7̂).
- Double the fifth in ⁶₄ chords.
- V and vi are adjacent chords that will create parallelism if you double the root (because each chord member is a step away), so double the third in the submediant triad (vi) and use contrary motion.
- Sometimes the final chord in minor mode will feature the most common form of mode mixture—the **Picardy third**. The sharp or natural sign in the figured bass means to raise the third of the tonic triad, borrowing tonic from the parallel major. The Roman numeral must reflect this as well as the use of the accidental in the composition.
- Leading-tone chords will have three resolution tones. Note the only difference between the half-diminished and fully-diminished is that the seventh in the fully-diminished chord is a half-step lower than in the half-diminished chord.
- UNEQUAL fifths:

    – P5 to dim5 is acceptable
    – dim5 to P5 is not acceptable in common-practice style

- It is becoming increasingly common to see the use of secondary (chromatic) harmony particularly in part writing to the Roman numerals (FR 6), requiring the ability to:

    – Correctly identify the symbol *and* the resolution chord
    – Correctly determine the chord members
    – Correctly determine the appropriate resolutions in the temporary key

Practice Exercises

Questions 1–6 are based on the following example.

1. The cadence at the end of measure 2 is

   (A) an authentic cadence with a Picardy third
   (B) a deceptive cadence
   (C) an authentic cadence in the dominant key
   (D) a Phrygian half cadence

2. The error in voice leading between chords 2 and 3 would be identified as

   (A) inappropriate doubling
   (B) parallel octaves
   (C) parallel fifths
   (D) crossed voices

3. The error in voice leading in chords 4 and 5 would be identified as

   (A) a direct octave
   (B) an unresolved chordal seventh
   (C) an incomplete chord
   (D) a spacing error

4. In chord 3, the E in the tenor voice is

   (A) a retardation
   (B) an anticipation
   (C) an appoggiatura
   (D) an escape tone

5. The G♯ in the alto voice at 8 is all of the following **except**

   (A) the leading tone in A harmonic minor
   (B) the resolution of a 4–3 suspension
   (C) the third of the dominant triad
   (D) a chromatic incomplete neighbor

6. The harmonic analysis of the last three chords is

   (A) i^6–VI–I
   (B) i^6–IV^6–V♯
   (C) i^6–iv^6–V^{4-3}
   (D) I^6–IV^6–V

Questions 7–14 are based on the example below.

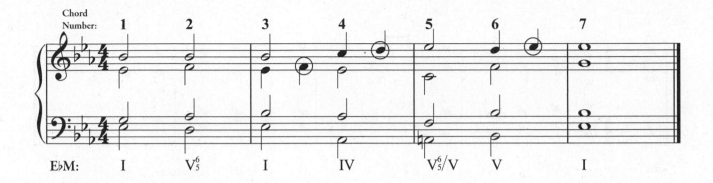

7. Chords 2 and 3 contain *two* voice-leading errors. They are

   (A) a spacing error and parallel fifths
   (B) unequal fifths and an improperly resolved chordal seventh
   (C) overlapping voices and an improperly doubled chord
   (D) a direct octave and crossed voices

8. Chords 4 and 5 contain what voice-leading error?

   (A) Parallel fifths
   (B) Parallel octaves
   (C) Direct octave
   (D) Overlapping voices

9. There are two errors in chords 5 and 6. They are

   (A) crossed voices and an unresolved chordal seventh
   (B) overlapping voices and parallel fifths
   (C) an incorrect chord member and an unresolved chordal seventh
   (D) a spacing error and parallel fifths

10. Chords 1, 2, and 3 represent what type of motion between the bass and the soprano?

    (A) Contrary
    (B) Oblique
    (C) Similar
    (D) Parallel

11. The error found in chord 3 is

    (A) crossed voices
    (B) the root is doubled
    (C) the third is missing
    (D) improper spacing

12. The circled non-chord tone in chord 3 is an

    (A) appoggiatura
    (B) upper neighbor
    (C) escape tone
    (D) accented neighbor tone

13. The circled non-chord tone in chord 4 is

    (A) an upper neighbor
    (B) an appoggiatura
    (C) a passing tone
    (D) a retardation

14. The circled non-chord tone in chord 6 is

    (A) an anticipation
    (B) a retardation
    (C) an appoggiatura
    (D) an accented neighbor

Questions 15–20 refer to the four-part harmonization below.

15. The error between chords numbered 1 and 2 is

    (A) the seventh of the chord resolves incorrectly
    (B) the inner voices are in a cross relationship
    (C) parallel octaves
    (D) the spacing is incorrect

16. The error in chord 2 is

    (A) a doubled leading tone
    (B) the root is missing
    (C) that it is not a viable cadential progression
    (D) a doubled root

17. The error between chords 3 and 4 is

    (A) parallel fifths
    (B) the seventh of the chord resolves incorrectly
    (C) total similar motion
    (D) improper spacing

18. The error between chords 5 and 6 is

    (A) improper harmonic progression
    (B) total contrary motion
    (C) improper resolution of the chordal seventh
    (D) improper resolution of the leading tone

19. The error with chord 6 is the

    (A) third is missing
    (B) fifth is doubled
    (C) fifth is in the bass
    (D) third is doubled

20. Both $^6_4$ chords found in measure 1 and measure 3 are

    (A) inverted seventh chords
    (B) pedal $^6_4$ chords
    (C) passing $^6_4$ chords
    (D) secondary dominants

ANSWER KEY

1. **D**	6. **C**	11. **C**	16. **A**
2. **B**	7. **B**	12. **B**	17. **B**
3. **C**	8. **A**	13. **C**	18. **D**
4. **A**	9. **D**	14. **A**	19. **A**
5. **D**	10. **B**	15. **C**	20. **C**

ANSWERS EXPLAINED

1. **(D)** The cadence at the end of this example is a Phrygian half cadence. This means it progresses from iv^6 to V, providing a half step from **Le** ($\hat{6}$) to **So** ($\hat{5}$). It is called Phrygian in reference to the mode (in E) ending $\hat{2}$ to $\hat{1}$.

2. **(B)** Parallel octaves occur between the soprano and the bass (C–D).

3. **(C)** This chord, the V$^4_2$ in A minor, is spelled E–**G♯**–B–D. The root of the chord (E) is doubled and the 5th of the chord (B) has been omitted. Use all members of a seventh chord or triad when the chord is inverted.

4. **(A)** The non-chord tone in chord 3 is a retardation. The note (E) is part of chord 2 and is held over into chord 3 and resolves *upward* to the note that *is* in the chord.

5. **(D)** The G♯ is the raised 7th scale degree (leading tone) in A minor, it is the third of the V chord (E–G♯–B) and is the *third* above the bass in the 4–**3** suspension. It is not a non-chord tone of any kind.

6. **(C)** The correct harmonic analysis is i^6–iv^6–V$^{4\text{-}3}$. Let's look at what makes the other answers incorrect. Answer (A) is just wrong—students often look at the note in the bass with no regard to the inversion, in this case thinking the F in the bass is the submediant chord. Answer (B) is wrong because the figured bass symbol (♯) does *not* belong with the Roman numeral V. Also, the subdominant chord is major and should be minor. Answer (D) uses all major chord symbols. In the correct answer, (C), the last chord is correctly identified as V$^{4\text{-}3}$.

7. **(B)** Between chords 2 and 3 there is an error of unequal fifths (d5 to P5) between the bass and tenor *and* an improperly resolved chordal seventh. The A♭ in the tenor should resolve downward to a G in the tenor.

8. **(A)** Chords 4 and 5 contain parallel fifths between the tenor and alto. Notice the similar motion in the top three voices.

9. **(D)** The errors between chords 5 and 6 are incorrect spacing (more than an octave between soprano and alto) and parallel fifths between tenor and alto.

10. **(B)** Oblique motion is used between the bass and soprano in chords 1–3. The soprano remains on the B♭ while the bass moves down by step then back to tonic.

11. **(C)** The third of the chord is missing. There is no G.

12. **(B)** The non-chord tone in chord 3 is an upper neighbor—a note above two of the same notes in the same voice. In this case, the added NCT also created parallel fifths between tenor and alto. Do *not* use non-chord tones on the exam.

13. **(C)** The NCT in chord 4 is a passing tone.

14. **(A)** The NCT in chord 6 is an anticipation. It leaves the chord and goes to the next chord early (anticipating the new harmony).

15. **(C)** The error is parallel octaves between the soprano and the tenor (one *great* reason to not use NCT in FR 5 or 6).

16. **(A)** The leading tone (which is also the third of the chord) is doubled in chord 2.

17. **(B)** The seventh of the chord in this example is C in the tenor and *should* resolve downward to a B♮. However, there is not a B♮ in the i⁶₄ chord, so *hold* the tenor on the C until it can resolve to the B♮ in the penultimate (V) chord.

18. **(D)** The 7th scale degree (*Ti*—in this case, B♮) should resolve upward to *Do*.

19. **(A)** The error with chord 6 is the third is missing. If you have to leave out a chord member for better voice leading you may leave out the fifth, but never leave out the third. It determines the quality of the triad.

20. **(C)** Both chords in the boxed areas are passing ⁶₄ chords occurring on weak beats connecting two notes in the bass that are a third apart.

Aural Skills Part III: Harmonic Dictation

15

HARMONIC DICTATION PREPARATION

In this Aural Skills chapter we break down the process of harmonic dictation into easily managed "chunks" of listening segments. Our goal is to prepare the brain **before** the ear hears, and to use all the tools at our disposal for successful harmonic dictation.

What Skills Are Required for Successful Harmonic Dictation?

- Understanding the relationship of chords to the tonal center
- Discriminating between chord qualities and recognizing inversions
- Recognizing familiar melodic patterns (*linear* movement) in the melody and bass and their placement within the example
- Recognizing and notating cadences
- Understanding the norms of the common-practice style

What Is the Actual Process of Harmonic Dictation?

There are two harmonic dictation questions in the Free-Response section of the exam—FR 3 and FR 4. The key is given to you; one will be in major and one will be in minor. Both examples contain nine chords with the first one complete (always tonic) and the remaining eight chords left blank. You are to fill in the soprano, the bass line, and the Roman numeral chord symbols, including inversions where appropriate. The meter is always simple. There are no rhythmic concerns. This is about hearing the progression of harmonies, how they logically relate to each other within the key, and correctly notating those chords on the grand staff. The progression will be played four times on a piano. There is a pause of thirty seconds after the first playing and a one-minute pause after each subsequent playing.

What Do We Know for Sure?

This information we must have stored and ready to use:

- The three harmonic areas or functions are tonic, subdominant (sometimes referred to as predominant), and dominant.
- The harmonies that represent these functions are

Tonic	Subdominant	Dominant
I and vi	IV and ii or ii^7	V or V^7 and vii° or vii°^{7}

- Other harmonic "truths" are

  - Root position chords are considered strong
  - The supertonic and leading-tone chords are commonly found in first inversion
  - The supertonic in first inversion (ii⁶, ii⁶₅) is a strong subdominant harmony (because it has *Fa* in the bass)

- Second inversion and sometimes first inversion harmonies are often used to **prolong** stronger harmonies. There are four basic ways of prolonging harmonies:

  - **Passing harmonies**   I $\boxed{\text{V}^6_4}$ I⁶   Bass line = *Do-* $\boxed{Re}$ *-Mi*

  - **Neighbor harmonies**   I $\boxed{\text{IV}^6_4}$ I   Creates neighbor in upper voice = *Mi-* $\boxed{Fa}$ *-Mi* and **pedal** in the bass = *Do-Do-Do*

  - **Arpeggiated harmonies**   I $\boxed{\text{I}^6 \quad \text{I}^6_4}$ Bass = *Do-Mi-So*

  - **Cadential harmonies** $\boxed{\text{I}^6_4}$ V I   Bass line = $\boxed{So}$ *-So-Do*

  This prolongs dominant function when it *precedes* V at the cadence.

- Harmonic progressions move in **T**onic to **S**ubdominant to **D**ominant to **T**onic (**T–S–D–T**)

$$\begin{array}{cccccc} \text{I} & \text{vi} & \text{IV} & \text{ii} & \text{V} & \text{V}^7 & \text{I} \\ \textbf{T} & & \textbf{S} & & \textbf{D} & & \textbf{T} \end{array}$$

- Dominant harmonies do not move to subdominant (retrogression)
- Chromatic chords (secondary dominants or secondary leading tones) are prolonging the harmony they lead to:

$$\begin{array}{ccc} \text{I} & \boxed{\text{V}^6_5/\text{V} \quad \text{V}} & \text{I} \\ \text{T} & \text{D} \longrightarrow \text{D} & \text{T} \end{array}$$

- Significant harmonic function changes usually occur on *strong* beats
- When the bass line is conjunct, harmonies are *generally* being prolonged
- When large skips or leaps occur in the bass it often signals a change of function

How Do We Connect the Dots Between Hearing and Notating?

- Understanding what commonly ends a phrase

  - Understand that *only* **I**, **V**, or **vi** can be the last chord
  - Understand cadential patterns—bass and soprano
  - Listen for basic patterns in the bass line
  - Be able to aurally identify cadences
  - ➤ **Understand what harmonies are implied from knowing the bass line**

- Understanding what commonly **begins** a phrase

  - Return to tonic
  - Listen for basic patterns in the bass line
  ➤ **Understand what harmonies are implied from knowing the bass line**

- Understanding what commonly occurs in the **middle** of a phrase

  - Common subdominant function
  - Possible use of chromatic harmony
  - Possible use of inverted chords for prolonging harmony
  - Listen for common basic patterns in the bass line
  ➤ **Understand what harmonies are implied from knowing the bass line**

IMPLIED HARMONIES

Let's start with what is common to each segment of a phrase—understanding what harmonies are implied from knowing the bass line.

Understanding Implied Harmonies		
When the bass is . . .	**The implied harmony is . . .**	**Or possibly . . .**
Do	I	IV_4^6
Ti	V^6 or V_5^6	$vii^{\o7}$ or vii^{o7}
La	vi	IV^6
So	V	I_4^6
Fa	IV	ii^6 or ii_5^6
Mi	I^6	
Re	ii	V_4^6, V_3^4, or vii^{o6}

Recognizing and Notating Cadences

We start with the way phrases *end*—the cadence. It is critical to understand how to aurally identify and correctly notate cadences. We have been practicing this all along, in part writing, harmonizing a melody, and singing—starting with the two most common bass line endings from our Top Ten. Those endings are *So-So-Do* and *Fa-So-Do*. Both imply an authentic cadence (V–I or V–i); however, they differ on the chord that comes *before* dominant.

		So So Do		So So Do
Major:	$I_4^6 - V^{(7)}$ I			
Minor:	$i_4^6 - V^{(7)} - i$			

FM: I_4^6 [V]   I   fm: i_4^6 [V]   i

           [V^7]   [V^7]

Fa-So-Do =

Major: $IV-V^{(7)}-I$ or ii^6 or $ii^6_5 - V^{(7)}-I$

Minor: $iv-V^{(7)}-i$ or $ii^{\circ 6}$ or $ii^{\circ 6}_5 - V^{(7)}-i$

IF we hear *So-So-Do* in the bass and recognize that as $I^6_4-V^7-I$, **THEN** what is commonly in the melody?

If we hear *Fa-So-Do* in the bass, we have two choices for implied harmony—IV or ii⁶; both would have *Fa* in the bass. How do we know which it is? One is major and the other is minor. **Our ear must confirm the correct answer.**

With *Fa-So-Do* in the bass these are the common melodic patterns:

- ii⁶–V⁷–I can harmonize with *Re-Re-Do*; IV–V–I *cannot*. Why? Because there is no *Re* in the IV chord.
- IV–V–I can be harmonized with *Do-Ti-Do* but not *Do-Re-Do* (parallel P5)
- ii⁶–V or V⁷–I can be harmonized with *Re-Re-Do* or *Re-Ti-Do*

*Remember that adjacent chords such as IV–V or V–vi will create parallelism unless contrary motion is used; listen for the **contrary motion** you anticipate.

Other Common Bass Lines	+	Implied Harmonies that End Phrases	=	Type of Cadence
Fa-So-La	+	IV–V–vi	=	Deceptive
Fa-So-Le	+	iv–V–VI		
So-So-La	+	I$^6_4$–V–vi	=	Deceptive
So-So-Le	+	i$^6_4$–V–VI		
Fa-Do	+	IV–I or iv–i	=	Plagal
Fa-So	+	IV–V or ii^6–V	=	Half
		iv–V or ii^{o6}–V		
Le-So	+	iv^6–V	=	Phrygian Half

Practice Exercises

Complete the Cadence—Major

Now we practice notating cadences. The first four exercises begin with the exact same progression, but the last three chords are left for you to complete. This exercise is an opportunity for you to **focus only on the cadence** chords. **Notate only the bass, soprano, and Roman numeral chord symbols, including inversions.**

Each question number will be announced, followed by the example played three times, with a short pause between each playing.

Access audio at *http://barronsbooks.com/ap/mtheory/*

1.

AM: I   V⁶   I   IV⁶   ___ ___ ___

2.

AM: I   V⁶   I   IV⁶   ___ ___ ___

3.

AM: I   V⁶   I   IV⁶   __ __ __

4.

AM: I   V⁶   I   IV⁶   __   __

Complete the Cadence—Minor

Now do the same type of exercise in minor. Prepare by considering what is necessary when notating cadences in the minor mode and what type of cadences might occur in this mode. **Notate only the bass, soprano, and Roman numeral chord symbols, including inversions.**

Each question number will be announced, followed by the example played three times, with a short pause between each playing.

5.

gm: i   V⁶   i   iv   __ __ __

6.

gm: i V⁶ i iv ___ ___ ___

7.

gm: i V⁶ i iv ___ ___ ___

8.

gm: i V⁶ i iv ___ ___ ___

Aural Identification of Cadences

Identify the cadence type, Roman numeral chord symbols including inversions, and the **soprano and bass only** of the requested chords, or fill in the notation as requested.

Each question number will be announced, followed by the example played three times, with a short pause between each playing.

9.

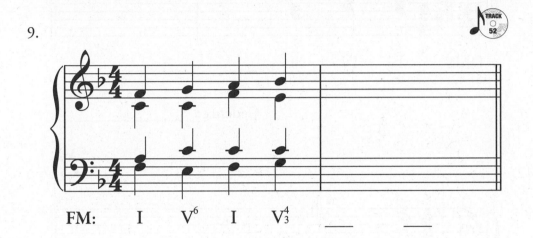

Cadence: _____

10.

Cadence: _____

11.

DM: I⁶   IV   vii°⁶   ___   ___

Cadence: _____

12.

gm: i⁶   iv   ___ ___ ___

Cadence: _____

13.

E♭M: I   V⁶   ___   ___   ___

Cadence: _____

14.

AM: I⁶   IV   ___ ___ ___

Cadence: _____

15.

dm: V⁶   i   V⁷   VI   — — — —

Cadence: _____

16.

Let chord *quality* help your ear discriminate.

B♭M: I⁶   IV   I⁶   ___ ___ ___ ___

Cadence: _____

17.

bm: i   V^6 i   i^6 ___ ___ ___

Cadence: _____

18.

FM: I   vi   ___   ___   ___

Cadence: _____

19.

GM: I   vi   IV^6 ___   ___

Cadence: _____

20.

fm: i V$_5^6$ i iv^6 ___ ___ ___

Cadence: _____

21.

E♭M: ii V ___ ___ ___

Cadence: _____

22.

DM: I V I ___ ___ ___

Cadence: _____

23.

am: i   ___   ___   ___   ___

Cadence: _____

Recognizing and Notating Phrase Beginnings

Now look at common bass lines that might *begin* a phrase.

Common Bass Lines	=	Implied Harmonies that Begin a Phrase:
1. *Do-Ti-Do*	=	I–V^6–I
2. *Do-Ti-Do*	=	I–V$^6_5$–I
3. *Do-Re-Mi*	=	I–V$^6_4$–I^6 or I–V$^4_3$–I^6
4. *Do-Re-Mi*	=	I–vii^{o6}–I^6
5. *Do-Do-Do*	=	I–IV$^6_4$–I
6. *Do-Fa-Mi*	=	I–V$^4_2$–I^6 (resolution in the bass)
7. *Do-Fa-Mi*	=	I–IV–I^6
8. *Do-Mi-So*	=	I–I^6–I$^6_4$

PHRASE BEGINNINGS IN MAJOR—
EXAMPLES

Notice how the progression and subsequent notation is altered when in a minor mode.

PHRASE BEGINNINGS IN MINOR—
EXAMPLES

The melodies used with these bass lines are examples of what commonly occurs when using these progressions, but they are not the only choices. Notice:

1. The use of familiar patterns (**sing** each bass line pattern; **sing** each melodic pattern)
2. The use of contrary motion
3. The **return** to tonic harmony

Anticipate the norm and let your ear confirm.

Practice Exercises

The next eight aural exercises (four in major and four in minor) contain the same cadence with **different phrase beginnings**. Each progression will contain seven chords of which the last three are ii°⁶–V⁷–i [in minor] or ii⁶–V⁷–I [in major], a PAC with predominant harmony. This exercise is an opportunity for you to focus on the beginning of the phrase (while continuing to hear standard cadence progressions).

Directions: Notate only the bass, soprano, and Roman numeral chord symbols, including inversions.

Each question number will be announced, followed by the example played three times, with a short pause between each playing.

Phrase Beginnings—Major

24.

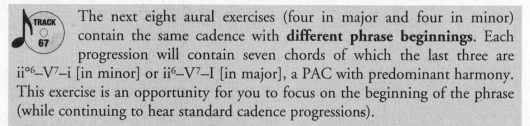

25.

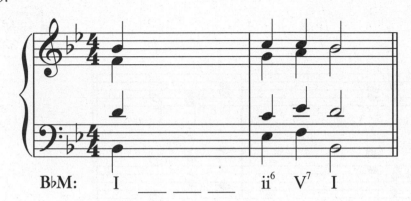

B♭M: I ___ ___ ___   ii⁶   V⁷   I

26.

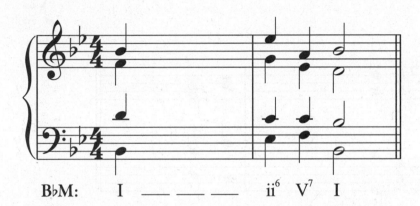

B♭M: I ___ ___ ___   ii⁶   V⁷   I

27.

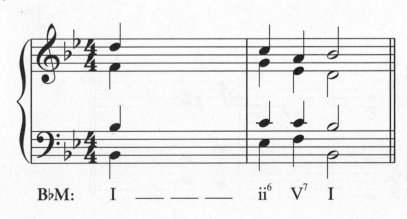

B♭M: I ___ ___ ___   ii⁶   V⁷   I

Phrase Beginnings—Minor

28.

gm: i —— —— —— ii°⁶ V⁷ i

29.

gm: i —— —— —— ii°⁶ V⁷ i

30.

gm: i —— —— —— ii°⁶ V⁷ i

31.

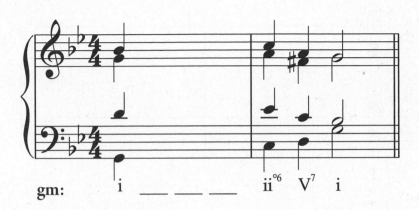

gm: i ___ ___ ___ ii°⁶ V⁷ i

Mix and Match—Major

Mix and match standard phrase beginnings *and* cadential endings with these two-measure exercises in D Major.

Each question number will be announced, followed by the example played three times, with a short pause between each playing.

32.

DM: I ___ ___ ___ ___ ___

33.

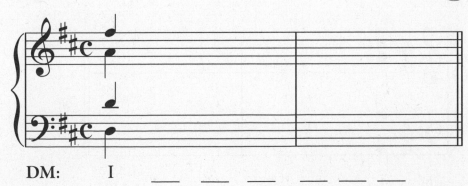

DM: I ___ ___ ___ ___ ___

34.

DM: I   __ __ __ __ __ __ __

35.

DM: I   __ __ __ __ __ __ __

Mix and Match—Minor

Mix and match standard phrase beginning and cadential endings in minor. This time the key is A minor.

Each question number will be announced, followed by the example played three times, with a short pause between each playing.

36.

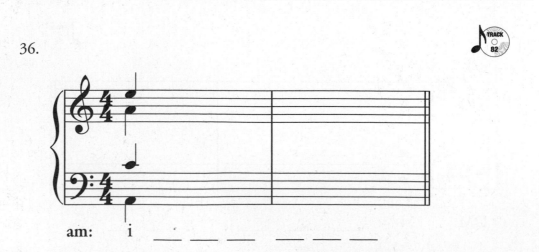

am: i   __ __ __ __ __ __ __

37.

am: i   _ _ _ _ _ _ _

38.

39.

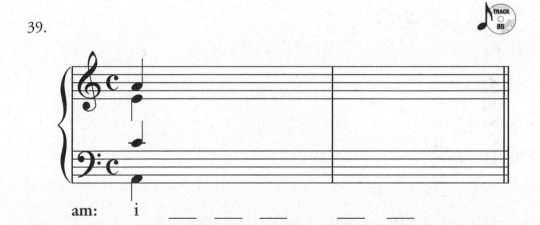

am: i   _ _ _ _ _ _ _

Recognizing and Notating the Mid-Phrase

Now we move on to the final portion of our harmonic dictation preparation—the middle. Something has to be sandwiched in between the beginning chords that focus on tonic, and the ending cadential progressions that generally feature dominant harmony before closing with the cadence. The middle three or four chords generally function as a transition between the beginning of the phrase and the cadence. Once past the beginning three or four chords, a phrase generally continues to *pro*gress in intensity and then culminates with the cadence. What harmonies function as transition? Subdominant or predominant harmonies (ii and IV) give us the full progression of **T–$\boxed{\text{S}}$–D–T**. Remember that ii is a strong subdominant function, especially if it is in first inversion and is stronger than subdominant when it has an added seventh (particularly in minor because the supertonic seventh chord is half-diminished). Let's look at a few common progressions, the implied harmony, *and* other elements that might be featured **in the middle**.

Common Bass Lines	=	Implied Mid-Phrase Harmonies
So-Fa-Mi	=	V–$\underline{\text{V}^4_2}$–I^6
Mi-Fa-So	=	I^6–ii$^6_5$–V
Do-La-Fa	=	I–vi–IV or I–vi–ii^6
La-Fa-Mi	=	vi–IV–I^6 or IV^6–IV–I^6
Fa-Mi	=	IV–I^6 or $\underline{\text{V}^4_2}$–I^6
Fa-Re	=	IV–ii
Fa-Fa	=	IV–ii^6 but not ii^6–IV
Fa-$\boxed{Fi}$-So	=	IV–$\boxed{\text{V}^6_5/\text{V}}$–V or ii^6–V$^6_5$/V–V
Fa-So-$\boxed{Si}$-La	=	IV–V–$\boxed{\text{V}^6_5/\text{vi}}$–vi
Me-$\boxed{Mi}$-Fa	=	i^6–$\boxed{\text{V}^6_5/\text{iv}}$–iv

The middle section uses inversions if the bass is moving stepwise; skips of a third are also frequently used. The **subdominant**, **supertonic**, and **submediant** are the most frequently used chords; therefore, this mid-section is generally considered "subdominant expansion." In the second harmonic dictation exercise on the AP Music Theory exam (FR 4), it is very common to have a secondary dominant occur somewhere from the middle "third" to the end of the example, usually with the accidental occurring in the bass or the soprano.

Here are some examples, but certainly not all possibilities, of mid-phrase progressions. We will start these mid-phrase progressions with tonic since the opening third often **returns to tonic**.

SOME MID-PHRASE PROGRESSIONS
THAT BEGIN WITH A RETURN TO TONIC

Practice Exercises

Mid-Phrase Dictation

 Following the pattern of focusing on a single area for dictation preparation, there are now eight excerpts that have the beginning and the end complete with three or sometimes four chords in the middle left for you to fill in the blanks. Once again, while you focus on the subdominant expansion, continue to recognize appropriate phrase beginnings and cadential progressions.

Each question number will be announced, followed by the example played three times, with a short pause between each playing.

40.

41.

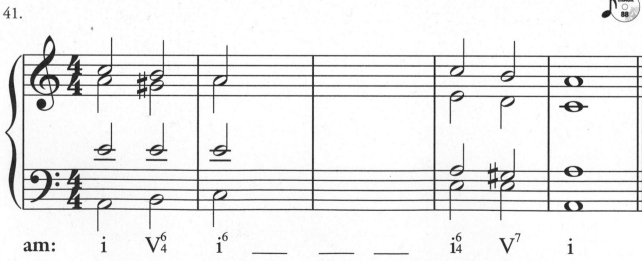

The Beginning, the Middle, and the Cadence

Now put it all together. The last five exercises are complete harmonic dictation examples with eight chords each. There are also **twelve more full harmonic dictation exercises** at the end of Chapter 20, Strategies for Harmonic Dictation.

Each question will be announced, followed by the excerpt played four times. There will be a 30-second pause after the first playing and a 1-minute pause after each subsequent playing.

48. Complete Harmonic Dictation in F Major

49. Complete Harmonic Dictation in C minor

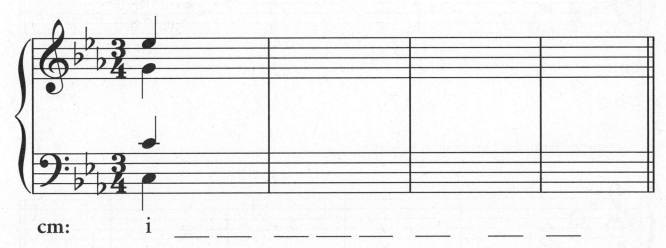

50. Complete Harmonic Dictation in D Major

DM: I ___ ___ ___ ___ ___ ___ ___

51. Complete Harmonic Dictation in E minor

em: i ___ ___ ___ ___ ___ ___ ___ ___ ___

52. Complete Harmonic Dictation in G Major

GM: I ___ ___ ___ ___ ___ ___ ___

ANSWERS EXPLAINED

Complete the Cadence—Major

1. Correct response.   What you heard.

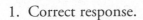

2. Correct response.   What you heard.

3. Correct response.   What you heard.

4. Correct response.   What you heard.

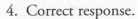

Complete the Cadence—minor

5. Correct response.

What you heard.

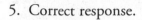

gm: i V⁶ i iv i⁶₁₄ V i

6. Correct response.

What you heard.

gm: i V⁶ i iv i⁶₁₄ iv⁶ V

7. Correct response.

What you heard.

gm: i V⁶ i iv i⁶₁₄ V⁷ VI

8. Correct response.

What you heard.

gm: i V⁶ i iv i⁶₁₄ V I

Aural Identification of Cadences

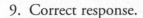

9. Correct response.

What you heard.

10. Correct response.

What you heard.

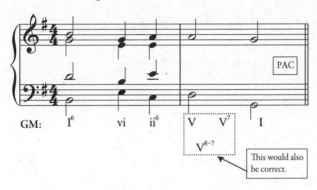

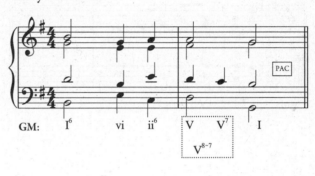

11. Correct response.

What you heard.

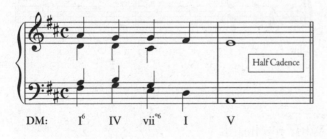

12. Correct response.

What you heard.

13. Correct response.

E♭M: I   V⁶   I   IV   I |Plagal|

What you heard.

E♭M: I   V⁶   I   IV   I |Plagal|

14. Correct response.

AM: I⁶   IV   ii⁶   V⁷   I |IAC|

What you heard.

AM: I⁶   IV   ii⁶   V⁷   I |IAC|

15. Correct response.

dm: V⁶   i   V⁷   VI   ii°⁶₅   V⁷   i |PAC|

What you heard.

dm: V⁶   i   V⁷   VI   ii°⁶₅   V⁷   i |PAC|

16. Correct response.

B♭M: I⁶   IV   I⁶   vi   ii°⁶₅   V   I |PAC|

What you heard.

B♭M: I⁶   IV   I⁶   vi   ii°⁶₅   V   I |PAC|

17. Correct response.　　　　　　　What you heard.

18. Correct response.　　　　　　　What you heard.

19. Correct response.　　　　　　　What you heard.

20. Correct response.　　　　　　　What you heard.

The V$^{8\text{-}7}$ refers to the B♭ passing tone in the soprano that is actually the added seventh of the chord (V^7). You might also see the Roman numerals of the last measure as ii^{6}V(V^7)VI.

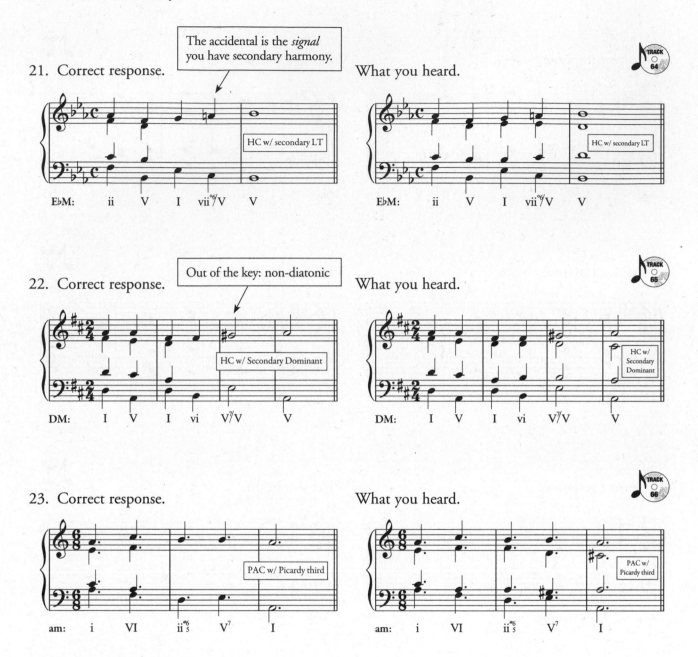

The accidental is the *signal* you have secondary harmony.

21. Correct response.

What you heard.

HC w/ secondary LT

EbM: ii   V   I   vii°⁷/V   V

Out of the key: non-diatonic

22. Correct response.

What you heard.

HC w/ Secondary Dominant

DM: I   V   I   vi   V⁷/V   V

23. Correct response.

What you heard.

PAC w/ Picardy third

am: i   VI   ii°⁶₅   V⁷   I

Phrase Beginnings—Major

Notice that even though these next four exercises all have the exact same cadence progression, the melody at the cadence is slightly different.

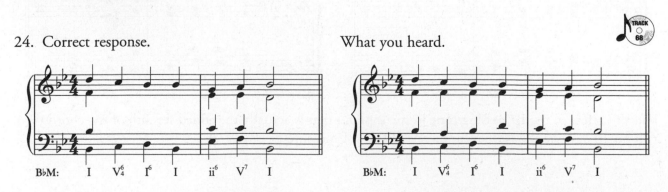

24. Correct response.

What you heard.

BbM: I   V⁶₄   I⁶   I   ii⁶   V⁷   I

25. Correct response.

What you heard.

26. Correct response.

What you heard.

27. Correct response.

What you heard.

Phrase Beginnings—Minor

28. Correct response.

What you heard.

29. Correct response.

What you heard.

gm: i   i⁶   i⁶₄   i⁶   ii°⁶   V⁷   i

gm: i   i⁶   i⁶₄   i⁶   ii°⁶   V⁷   i

30. Correct response.

What you heard.

gm: i   V⁴₂   i⁶   i   ii°⁶   V⁷   i

gm: i   V⁴₂   i⁶   i   ii°⁶   V⁷   i

31. Correct response.

What you heard.

gm: i   vii°⁶   i⁶   i   ii°⁶   V⁷   i

gm: i   vii°⁶   i⁶   i   ii°⁶   V⁷   i

Mix and Match—Major

32. Correct response.

What you heard.

DM: I   V⁶   I   vi   I⁶₄   V   I

DM: I   V⁶   I   vi   I⁶₄   V   I

33. Correct response.

What you heard.

This example contains a passing tone and an upper neighbor; however, non-chord tones are not usually part of the dictation on the exam.

34. Correct response.

What you heard.

35. Correct response.

What you heard.

Mix and Match—Minor

36. Correct response.

What you heard.

37. Correct response.

What you heard.

38. Correct response.

What you heard.

39. Correct response.

What you heard.

Listen for the difference between this pattern in #37 and #39, which have the same bass line.

Mid-Phrase Dictation

40. Correct response.

What you heard.

41. Correct response.

What you heard.

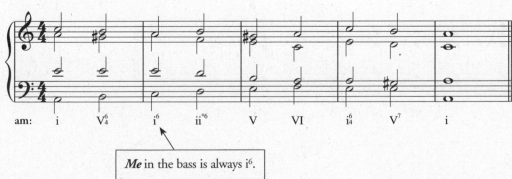

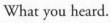 *Me* in the bass is always i⁶.

42. Correct response.

What you heard.

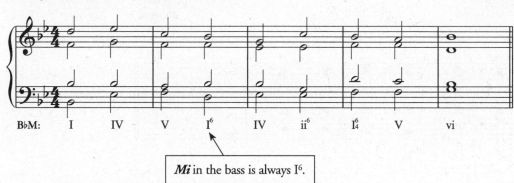

Mi in the bass is always I⁶.

43. Correct response.

What you heard.

44. Correct response.

What you heard.

45. Correct response.

What you heard.

46. Correct response.

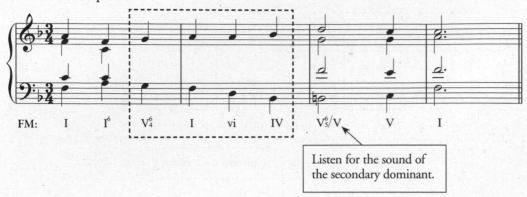

FM: I   I⁶   V⁴₆   I   vi   IV   V⁶₅/V   V   I

Listen for the sound of the secondary dominant.

What you heard.

FM: I   I⁶   V⁴₆   I   vi   IV   V⁶₅/V   V   I

Notice the chromaticism.

47. Correct response.

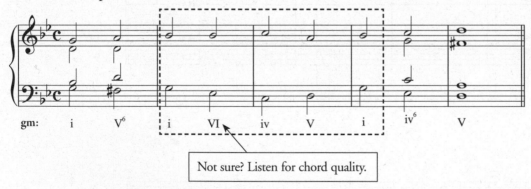

gm: i   V⁶   i   VI   iv   V   i   iv⁶   V

Not sure? Listen for chord quality.

What you heard.

gm: i   V⁶   i   VI   iv   V   i   iv⁶   V

The Beginning, the Middle, and the Cadence

48. Correct response.

FM: I   V$_5^6$ I   vi   IV   ii^6 I$_4^6$ V^7 I

What you heard.

FM: I   V$_5^6$ I   vi   IV   ii^6 I$_4^6$ V^7 I

49. Correct response.

cm: i   i^6 iv   V   V$_2^4$ i^6 iv   iv^6 V

What you heard.

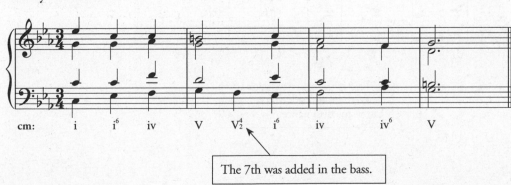

cm: i   i^6 iv   V   V$_2^4$ i^6 iv   iv^6 V

The 7th was added in the bass.

50. Correct response.

DM: I   V$_2^4$ I^6 V$_4^6$ I   vi   ii^6 V   I

What you heard.

DM: I   V$_2^4$ I^6 V$_4^6$ I   vi   ii^6 V   I

51. Correct response.

em: i   V^6 i   VI   iv   ii$^{ø6}_5$ $^{ø6}_{14}$ V^7 VI

What you heard.

em: i   V^6 i   VI   iv   ii$^{ø6}_5$ $^{ø6}_{14}$ V^7 VI

The 7th is an inside voice.
Listen for dissonance.

52. Correct response.

GM: I   V⁶   I   I⁶   IV   V⁶/V   V   V⁷   I

What you heard.

GM: I   V⁶   I   I⁶   IV   V⁶/V   V   V⁷   I

Visual Score Analysis Part I

- Alberti Bass
- Cadence
- Cadential Extension
- Canon, Canonic
- Chorus
- Coda
- Codetta
- Concert Pitch
- Contour
- Countermelody
- Fragment
- Instrumentation
    - Brass
    - Continuo
    - Percussion
    - Strings
    - Woodwinds
- Introduction
- Obbligato
- Ostinato
- Phrase
- Phrase Structure
    - Antecedent–Consequent
    - Contrasting
    - Double Period
    - Parallel Period
    - Period
- Rag, Ragtime
- Range
- Register
- Refrain

- Small Forms
    - Binary
    - Rondo
    - Sonata Allegro
    - Ternary
    - Theme and Variations
    - Through Composed
- Texture
    - Heterophony, Heterophonic
    - Homophony, Homophonic
        - Chordal Homophony,
            - Chordal Accompaniment,
            - Chordal Texture
        - Homorhythmic
        - Melody with Accompaniment
    - Monophony, Monophonic
        - Antiphonal
    - Polyphony, Polyphonic
        - Contrapuntal
        - Counterpoint
            - Imitative
            - Imitative Polyphony
            - Nonimitative Polyphony
            - Fugal Imitation
- Solo, Soli
- Song Form (aaba)
- Stanza
- Strophic
- Tessitura
- Theme
- Timbre
- Transposition
- Tutti
- Variation
- Verse
- Walking Bass

We have been looking at music from the very beginning of this guide. The next two chapters act as a culmination of visual score analysis, including providing tips and strategies for successful score analysis. Let's begin with the overall organization of a composition—the **form**.

PHRASE STRUCTURE AND SECTIONAL FORM

From Chapter 10 we learned that music, like language, consists of sentences or phrases punctuated by a cadence. Phrases often come in pairs to create a **period** and relate to each other like a question and answer does in language. The first phrase is called the **antecedent** and the second phrase is the **consequent**. The antecedent phrase ends with a less complete cadence while the consequent ends with a more complete or restful cadence. A **parallel period** occurs when the *beginning of the melody* is the same in both phrases (aa or aa¹). A **contrasting period** occurs when the beginning of the melody in each phrase is different (ab).

An analysis of phrase structure is called form. Phrases are labeled using small letters. One of the most common phrase structures is the **song form** or **aaba**. This tells us we probably (confirmed by cadences) have a parallel period with the first two phrases. You will generally see form structure labeled using arches. For example, "Home on the Range" is **aa¹ba¹** form beginning with a parallel period.

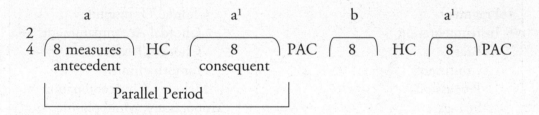

"Greensleeves" is **aa¹bb¹** and contains two parallel periods.

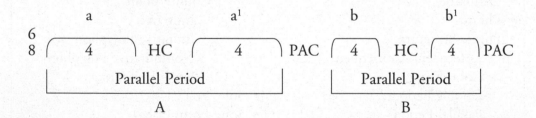

Phrases join together to make larger sections. Those sections are also labeled with letters, this time using capital letters to designate the larger sections over phrase structure. "Greensleeves" has two sections, A and B. This is called binary. When the first section ends with an authentic cadence in the original key it is called **sectional binary**. If any other cadence occurs at the end of the first section, or if the key modulates so that the first section ends in a different key, it is called **continuous binary**.

Strophic Form (AAAA)—In this form, the same music is used for each verse or stanza. Strophic form can be seen in art songs, ballads, hymns, and folksongs. Examples of strophic form are "Amazing Grace" and "Scarborough Fair" (also in Dorian mode).

Through-Composed Form is writing new music for each stanza, often written to reflect different moods or changing moods of each stanza. An example of this is *The Erl King* or *Der Erlkönig* by Franz Schubert. This also contains a rhythmic ostinato.

Binary Form (AB)—As the label says—*two* sections, often repeated (AABB). Binary might also be AA¹, two sections comprised of the same or similar melodic material. In common-practice style simple binary form was often used for dances, and the convention of the day was to maintain the same rhythmic feel but use different keys for each section. The music often moves to a new key in the B section, returning to tonic at the end of B. The beautiful piece for flute, *Badinerie* by Bach, is in binary form.

Ternary Form (ABA) has three sections generally with a **recapitulation** of the first (the return of A). Often the first section is repeated giving us AABA, very popular with eighteenth century operatic arias, and evolved into the thirty-two bar **song form** discussed earlier. "Anitra's Dance," from the *Peer Gynt Suite* by Edvard Grieg, is an example of ABA or ternary form.

Rounded Binary Form—Somewhere between binary form and ternary form lies the often mentioned, but frequently misunderstood rounded binary form. The name rounded binary is misleading. It's not really binary—it's ternary. But it's not "truly" ternary. Some theorists call rounded binary "incipient ternary"—incipient means "almost." Binary form is **AB**; ternary is **ABA**.

Rounded binary is also ABA but with one big difference—in rounded binary only a portion of the A material returns after the B section. It is usually *half* of the original A section's material (usually the latter half containing a PAC). Rounded binary is often written:

$$\|\!: \quad A \quad :\|\!\|\!: B \quad 1/2\,A \; :\|$$

or

$$\|\!: \quad A \quad :\|\!\|\!: B \quad \text{partial A} \; :\|$$

Just so we are clear, song form is *not* rounded binary because *all* of "a" is heard following the "b" phrase.

An example of rounded binary form is another piece by J. S. Bach, Minuet in G Major, no. 2.

Sonata–Allegro Form is a unique form that grew out of binary and ternary (with the **return** to the original material) and is found in the first movement of sonatas. It became the most important form of the classical period and was brought to its highest level of sophistication by Haydn, Mozart, and Beethoven. The three sections of sonata–allegro form are:

Exposition: The first theme is in the tonic key; the second theme is in the dominant key or the relative major key if the first theme is in minor.

Development: Previously presented themes are expanded and developed, often in new keys.

Recapitulation: A restating of the exposition with the first *and* second themes both in the tonic key, often concluding with a coda.

The relationship of the tonic and dominant keys is particularly important in sonata–allegro form. In the recapitulation, having both first and second themes in the tonic key provides a feeling of completion or of returning "home" after traveling through various keys during the development section. An example of sonata-allegro form is the first movement of *Eine Kleine Nachtmusik* by W. A. Mozart.

Rondo Form has a principal theme (sometimes called the motive) that alternates with one or more contrasting themes, generally called *episodes* or *digressions*. Most rondos fall into either a five-part (ABACA) or a seven-part (ABACABA) form. Arch form (ABCBA) resembles a symmetrical seven-part rondo without the intermediate repetition of the main theme. The last movement of *Eine Kleine Nachtmusik*, Serenade no. 13 for Strings in G Major (K 525), is an example of rondo form.

Theme and Variation Form has only one "section" and is repeated indefinitely (as in strophic form) but is varied each time ($AA^1A^2A^3A^4A^5A^6$). "American Salute," by Morton Gould, which is based on the song "When Johnny Comes Marching Home Again," is an example of theme and variation form.

A theme and variation may be an individual section of any shorter form such as binary or ternary. An important variation of this is the **passacaglia** and **chaconne** that feature a *repeating bass theme* (or **basso ostinato**) over which the rest of the musical structure is written.

Other terms related to form are:

Coda, Codetta—The closing few measures of a composition following the PAC, usually not a part of the main thematic material, but an ending added to give the composition closure.

The **coda sign** (⊕) is typically used in compositions that employ a **da capo** (D.C.) or **dal segno** (D.S.). Often the terms "D.S. al **coda**" or "D.C. al **coda**" are also used to indicate that the performer is to perform the **coda** portion of the composition after repeating to either the **sign** (𝄋) (D.S.) or to the beginning of the composition (D.C.).

Following is an example of D.C. al fine. "To the Color" is a military *bugle call* played to honor America in ceremonies when no band is available. The same courtesies are paid to "To the Color" as to our national anthem.

To the Color

TEXTURE

Texture is one of the basic elements of music. When you describe the **texture** of a piece of music, you are describing *how much is going on in the music* at any given moment. For example, the texture of the music might be thick or thin, or it may have many or few layers. It might be made up of rhythm only, or of a melody line with chordal accompaniment, or many independent melodies weaving together, sometimes referred to as counterpoint. In its most general sense, **counterpoint** involves the writing of musical lines that are distinct from each other, but sound harmonious when played together. **Chords** occur when three or more notes are grouped together *as a unit*; however, **counterpoint focuses primarily on linear interaction** and secondarily on the harmonies produced by the interaction of those lines. Good counterpoint requires two qualities: (1) some degree of independence or individuality within the lines themselves (a "horizontal" consideration—**melody**), and (2) a meaningful or harmonious relationship between the lines (a "vertical" consideration—**harmony**). You are trying to write good counterpoint when you harmonize a melody in FR 7.

There are many informal terms that can describe the texture of a piece of music (thick, thin, bass-heavy, rhythmically complex, and so on), but the formal terms that are used to describe texture all describe the **relationships of melodies and harmonies**. Here are definitions and examples of the four main types of texture.

1. **Monophonic** music has only one melodic line, with no harmony or counterpoint. There may be rhythmic accompaniment, but only one line that has specific pitches. Monophonic music can also be called **monophony**. Examples of monophony might be one person whistling a tune, a single bugle sounding "Taps," or a whole choir singing a melody in unison.

2. **Homophonic** music can also be called **homophony**. Homophony has one clearly melodic line; it's the line that naturally draws your attention. All other parts provide accompaniment or fill in the chords. In most well-written homophony, the parts that are not melody may still have a lot of melodic interest. They may follow many of the rules of well-written counterpoint, and they can sound quite different from the melody and be interesting to listen to by themselves. But when they are sung or played with the melody, it is clear that they are not independent melodic parts, either because they have the same rhythm as the melody (they are not independent) or because their main purpose is to fill in the chords or harmony (they are not really melodies). Examples of homophony are choral music in which the parts have mostly the same rhythms at the same time. Most traditional Protestant hymns and most "barbershop quartet" music is in this category.

   • **Chordal homophony** (may be referred to as chordal texture)—The beautiful melody on the next page ("Cranham," also known as "In the Bleak Midwinter" by Gustav Holst) is an example of chordal homophony—every line or voice moving together with exactly the same or nearly the same rhythm.

   • **Melody with accompaniment** is sometimes referred to as a form of homophony because it clearly has only one melodic line, but the harmony is not limited to chords moving together. A singer accompanied by a guitar player picking or strumming chords, or a small jazz combo with a bass, a piano, and a drum set providing the "rhythm" background for a saxophone improvising a solo, are examples of accompanimental texture. Some specific accompaniment types are ostinato, Alberti bass, and walking bass.

Cranham

Gustav Holst
(1874–1934)

– **Ostinato**—meaning obstinate or unceasing, an ostinato is a short **melodic**, **rhythmic**, or **harmonic** pattern that is repeated throughout an entire composition or some portion of a composition. Here is an example of an ostinato, played by the second violins, from the second movement of *St. Paul's Suite for String Orchestra*, by Gustav Holst.

St. Paul's Suite for String Orchestra

Ostinato - 2

Gustav Holst
(1874–1934)

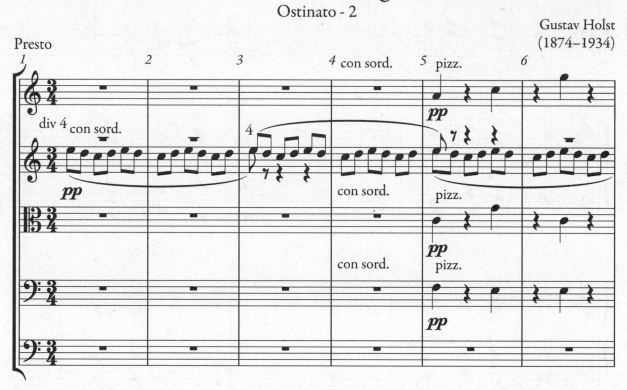

- **Alberti bass** is an **accompaniment** figure played on **a keyboard instrument with the left hand**. The chords of the Alberti bass are played as **arpeggios**, or **broken chords**, usually (1̂–5̂–3̂–5̂–3̂–5̂). Named for Domenico Alberti, Alberti bass is an example of homophony (melody with accompaniment) and is common to the works of Haydn, Beethoven, and in this example, Mozart, from *Sonata in C, K. 545, First Movement*.

- **Walking bass**—In popular music, a walking bass is a style of bass accompaniment or line that creates a feeling of regular quarter-note movement, similar to the regular alternation of feet while walking. Common to jazz, a walking bass line often uses a mixture of scale tones, arpeggios, and passing tones, including chromatic passing tones, to outline the chord progression of a song or tune. The melodic shape of a walking bass line alternately rises and falls in pitch over several bars, as you can see in the example below.*

*Courtesy of Aden Bubeck, professional bass player performing with Miranda Lambert.

– **Ragtime**, an American style of music popular at the turn of the twentieth century, features "ragged," or syncopated, rhythms. This example of a Scott Joplin **rag** shows monophonic texture in the first two measures with the right and left hand playing the identical melody in octaves, then the texture becomes melody with chordal accompaniment for the remainder of the excerpt. The first four measures are an **introduction** followed by two phrases with similar melodies; the first phrase ends with a plagal cadence (IV–I) in A♭ Major and the second with a PAC in E♭ Major.

The harmonies are actually quite complex, but at this point let's simply note the **sequence** of the melody (the repeated melodic pattern at a different interval) and the prominent use of the diminished fifth throughout the pattern. Observe that the diminished fifth (accented neighbors) resolves to a minor third in the melody over the bass line that remains diatonic until measure 10 moving into the cadence.

The Easy Winners
A Ragtime Two-Step

Scott Joplin
(1867 or 1868–1917)

3. **Polyphonic** music can also be called **polyphony**, **counterpoint**, or **contrapuntal** music. If more than one independent *melody* is occurring at the same time, the music is polyphonic. Examples of polyphony are rounds, canons, and fugues. Even if there is only one melody, if different people are singing or playing it at different times, the parts sound independent. Much Baroque music is contrapuntal, particularly the works of J.S. Bach, and most music for large instrumental groups such as bands or orchestras is contrapuntal at least some of the time.

Polyphony is usually divided into two main types: **imitative** and **nonimitative**. Either the various melodic lines in a polyphonic passage sound **similar** to one another, or they are **independent** in their rhythm and contour. If the individual lines are similar in their shapes and sounds, the polyphony is termed imitative; but if the voices show little or no resemblance to each other, it is nonimitative.

An accompanying, yet very important, part of the music is called a **countermelody**. It is a secondary melody or line written to be played simultaneously with a more prominent melody. "Air," from Suite No. 3 in D by Bach, is an example of polyphonic texture. The violin II is playing a countermelody with a very imitative quality that seems to be in response to the violin I part. Notice the octave leaps and the sequential pattern in the continuo part as well as the syncopation in the viola part.

Air, from Suite No. 3 in D

Johann Sebastian Bach
(1685–1750)
BWV 1068

A specific type of *imitative* polyphonic music is the **fugue**, a form of composition popular in the Baroque era, in which a theme or **subject** is introduced by one voice, and is imitated by other voices in succession. Generally the voices overlap and weave in and out of each other forming a continuous, tapestry-like texture. Imitative polyphony may feature **fugal imitation** and not be a fugue. This refers to a type of imitation of the antecedent or subject that *enters at a different pitch level,* usually the fourth or fifth, as in a fugue. Our next example is a Fugue, Opus 137, by Beethoven, for two violins, two violas, and a cello.

Fugue for String Quartet, Op. 137

Ludwig van Beethoven
(1770–1827)

4. In **heterophonic** music, there is only one melody, but different variations of it are being sung or played at the same time. **Heterophony** can be heard in American folk music such as Bluegrass, Cajun, and Zydeco traditions. Listen for the tune to be played by two instruments (say fiddle and banjo) *at the same time*, with each adding the embellishments, ornaments, and flourishes that are characteristic of the instrument. Some Middle Eastern, South Asian, central Eurasian, and Native American music traditions also include heterophony.

Other terms related to texture are:

- **Solo:** A single performer or a passage that is to be performed by a single performer
- **Soli:** A directive to perform an indicated passage of a composition with an entire **section** of an ensemble as opposed to a solo where only one member of the section performs or **tutti**, meaning "all" members play as opposed to a soli section or solo

INSTRUMENTATION AND IDENTIFICATION OF TIMBRE

Western instruments are often classified by their musical **range** in comparison with other instruments in the same family. These terms are named after **singing voice** classifications:

- Soprano instruments: flute, recorder, violin, clarinet, trumpet
- Alto instruments: alto saxophone, oboe, alto flute, viola, horn
- Tenor instruments: trombone, clarinet, tenor saxophone
- Baritone instruments: bassoon, English horn, baritone saxophone, baritone horn, bass clarinet, cello
- Bass instruments: contrabassoon, bass saxophone, double bass, tuba

Some instruments fall into more than one category: for example, the cello may be considered either tenor or bass, depending on how its music fits into the ensemble; the trombone may be alto, tenor, or bass; and the French horn may be bass, baritone, tenor, or alto, depending on which range it is played. The clarinet, having extended range, may be considered soprano, alto, or tenor range.

Many instruments have their range as part of their name: soprano saxophone, tenor saxophone, baritone saxophone, baritone horn, alto flute, bass flute, alto recorder, and bass guitar. Additional adjectives describe instruments above the soprano range or below the bass, for example: sopranino saxophone and contrabass clarinet. When used in the name of an instrument, these terms are relative, describing the instrument's range *in comparison to other instruments of its family* and not in comparison to the human voice range or instruments of other families.

Instruments are also classified in families pertaining to how the sound is produced, regardless of range. In the simplest of terms, families of instruments are **string** (plucked or bowed across strings), **woodwind** (blowing *into a tube* with or without a vibrating reed), **brass** (vibrating the lips against the tube to create sound), and **percussion** instruments (may be tuned or untuned) that are struck with a hand or a stick to produce sound. *How* the sound is produced, *what* the instrument is made of, and the range of an instrument all determine instrument **timbre**.

Other terms related to instrumentation and affecting timbre include:

Register refers to the division of the range of an instrument or singing voice. Usually registers are defined by a change in the quality of the sound between a lower range and a higher range as in the registers of a clarinet.

Tessitura is the general range of a performer (usually vocal) that is the most comfortable, and presents the best-sounding, most characteristic tone quality (timbre).

TRANSPOSITION

Transposition means to sound a pitch different from the one written. It also refers to rewriting music from one key to another. Music in a major key can be transposed to any other major key and music in a minor key can be transposed to any other minor key. A piece sounds higher or lower once it is transposed. Vocalists transpose music if the original key is too high or too low for their voice range, resulting in a much better performance. Instrumentalists may also find a piece easier to play if it is in a different key. Changing from major to minor or vice versa requires more than simple transposition because of the difference in major and minor scale patterns.

Instrumental Transposition

Let's briefly examine the concept of instrumental **transposition**. Many instruments read one note and sound another compared to what we call **concert pitch** (the actual notes as played by piano or sung by the voice). Instruments that are not in concert pitch require transposing and are often referred to as being in a certain "key." The instrument's key tells which pitch will sound when the performer plays a note written as "C," or another way to remember it is "Everybody reads C, but they **sound** the letter in their name." For example, when a B♭ clarinet reads a C on the staff, the note that sounds is a B♭—a full step lower than what is written. Transposing instruments need to have their music rewritten in a different key to sound the same pitches as non-transposing instruments (those in concert pitch are in the key of C). Most common transposing instruments fall into three groups. We transpose for them according to how they relate to C:

- **B♭** instruments sound a major second below the written concert pitch. Read a C, sound a **B♭**. These instruments are:

  - Bass clarinet (actually an octave *and* a M2)
  - B♭ clarinet
  - B♭ Cornet/B♭ trumpet
  - Flugelhorn
  - Soprano saxophone
  - Tenor saxophone (actually an octave *and* a M2)

- **F** instruments sound a perfect fifth below concert pitch. Read a C, sound an **F**. These instruments are:

  - English horn
  - French horn

- E♭ instruments sound a major sixth below (or a minor third above) concert. Read a C, sound an E♭. These instruments are:

  - Alto clarinet
  - Alto saxophone
  - Baritone saxophone (actually an octave *and* a major sixth)
  - E♭ clarinet (actually a minor third higher; the inversion of a major sixth)

With a few exceptions, other instruments are considered non-transposing C instruments—that is, what they play sounds exactly as written. Those exceptions are the orchestra bells and the piccolo, that sound an octave higher than written, and the double bass, which sounds an octave lower than written. Consider, too, the tenor voice, often written in treble clef and sung an octave lower.

Suppose you have four instruments that are in different keys: How do you create an arrangement so they can all play together in unison? The process of transposition can be accomplished in two ways. You *could* transpose each and every note individually by interval; or you can shift the key signature and recognize the relationship of the notes within the tonality. For example, if the concert pitch melody is **Do-Mi-Re-Fa-So-Ti-Do** in C Major, the notes are C–E–D–F–G–B–C. Transposed to D Major (the key signature is two sharps) for clarinet or trumpet, the pitches would be D–F♯–E–G–A–C♯–D. Transposed to G Major for horn, the key signature is 1 sharp and the pitches would be G–B–A–C–D–F♯–G.

The other side of transposition (and more often tested on the AP Music Theory exam) is reading what the instrument is playing and identifying what the concert pitch is. This is particularly important in score analysis. For example, if the French horn is reading an E♭, the clarinet is reading a D, and the alto saxophone is reading a D: What is the chord? What is the quality? Who is playing the third? The chord is F minor, and in concert pitch:

C: The clarinet is playing the fifth—concert C (and reading D).
A♭: The horn is playing the third—concert A♭ (reading E♭).
F: The saxophone is playing the root—concert F (reading a M6 above, which is D).

For the most common transposing instruments, the following process works:

IF you are looking at a transposed part and you need to identify the concert pitch, **THEN** go DOWN the appropriate interval to find concert pitch.

IF you are looking at concert pitch, **THEN** go UP the appropriate interval to correctly transpose.

> B♭ Clarinet is reading (*playing*) an A—go DOWN one whole step to find the concert pitch (G)
> Concert pitch is G—go UP one whole step to transpose for the clarinet to play

> Horn is reading (*playing*) an A♭—Go DOWN a perfect fifth to find the concert pitch (D♭)
> Concert pitch is D♭—Go UP a P5 to A♭ for the horn to play

> Alto saxophone is reading (*playing*) an F♯—go DOWN a M6 to find the concert pitch (A)
> Concert pitch is A—go UP a M6 to find the note that is the same pitch for alto sax (F♯)

An exception to this is the E♭ soprano clarinet that sounds higher than written. When the E♭ soprano clarinet plays an F♯, like the alto sax it also sounds an A—but the A that sounds is a minor third above (the inversion of a M6).

You can find more information about instruments, including names in various languages and instrument ranges, in Appendix A.

Chapter Summary

- Music, like language, consists of sentences or phrases punctuated by a cadence.
- Phrases often come in pairs to create a period and relate to each other like a question and answer does in language.

  - The first phrase is called the **antecedent** and the second phrase is the **consequent**. The antecedent phrase ends with a less complete cadence while the consequent ends with a more complete or restful cadence.
  - A **parallel period** occurs when the *beginning of the melody* is the same in both phrases.
  - A **contrasting period** occurs when the beginning of the melody in each phrase is different.

- Phrases and periods join together to make larger sections. Those sections are labeled using capital letters to designate the larger sections over phrase structure, which use small case.
- Sectional forms include:

  – Strophic form, through-composed form, binary form (AB or AA[1]), ternary form (ABA), sonata–allegro form, rounded binary form, theme and variations, and rondo

- **Texture** is one of the basic elements of music—described as how much is going on in the music at any given moment.

  – Formal terms that are used to describe texture all describe the relationships of melodies and harmonies. The basic types of textures are

    • Monophonic, homophonic, melody with accompaniment, heterophonic, polyphonic
    • Western instruments are classified by their musical range and how the sound is produced, regardless of range.

  – In the simplest of terms, families of instruments are string, woodwind, brass, and percussion.

- *How* the sound is produced, *what* the instrument is made of, and the range of an instrument all determine instrument timbre.
- **Transposition** is the changing of the key of a piece of music and/or sound a pitch different than written.

  – Many instruments read one note and sound another compared to what we call concert pitch (the actual notes as played by piano or sung by the voice). Instruments that are not in concert pitch require transposing and are often referred to as being in a certain "key."

- The instrument's key tells which pitch will sound when the performer plays a note written as "C."
- Most common transposing instruments fall into three groups: B♭, E♭, and F. We transpose for them according to how they relate to C.
- With a few exceptions, other instruments are considered non-transposing C instruments—that is, what they play sounds exactly as written, or as in the piccolo, an octave higher, or as in the double bass, an octave lower than written.
- The other side of transposition (and more often tested on the AP Music Theory exam) is reading what the instrument is playing and identifying what the concert pitch is. This is particularly important in score analysis. For most transposing instruments:

  – **IF** you are looking at a transposed part and you need to identify the concert pitch, **THEN** go *down* the appropriate interval to find the concert pitch.
  – **IF** you are looking at concert pitch, **THEN** go *up* the appropriate interval to correctly transpose.

Practice Exercises

Questions 1–6 are based on the opening eight measures of the *Fidelio Overture* by Beethoven.

Overture to Fidelio, Op. 72

1. What duration receives one full beat in this meter?

   (A) Half note
   (B) Quarter note
   (C) Dotted half note
   (D) Dotted quarter note

2. What is the texture of the first phrase to the dashed line?

   (A) Monophonic
   (B) Polyphonic
   (C) Homophonic
   (D) Melody with accompaniment

3. The transposition for the clarinet in A is

   (A) sounds a minor third lower than written
   (B) sounds a minor third higher than written
   (C) sounds a M2 lower than written
   (D) sounds a M2 higher than written

4. All of the following elements change in measure 5 **except**

   (A) tempo
   (B) texture
   (C) dynamic
   (D) meter

5. Since the fermata is on a rest, what else *could* have been used to indicate the same thing?

   (A) Caesura //
   (B) Dal segno
   (C) Da capo
   (D) ⁒

6. Identify the first cadence found in measures 3 and 4.

   (A) IAC in B Major
   (B) Half cadence in E Major
   (C) Half cadence in C# minor
   (D) Plagal cadence in B Major

Questions 7–10 are based on the excerpt of *Piano Trio, Opus 11*, by Beethoven.

Piano Trio, Op. 11
for Pianoforte, Clarinet or Violin and Violoncello

Ludwig van Beethoven
(1770-1827)

7. What is the texture of this excerpt?

   (A) Heterophonic
   (B) Melody with accompaniment
   (C) Polyphonic
   (D) Fugal imitation

8. The violoncello is playing

   (A) a pedal bass line
   (B) an arpeggio bass line
   (C) an Alberti bass line
   (D) a conjunct bass line

9. In measure 4 the clarinet is

   (A) sounding a whole step higher than written
   (B) playing the same melody played by the piano in measure 1 except up an octave
   (C) playing the exact melody played by the piano in measure 1
   (D) both A and C

10. The clarinet is sounding what chord member on the downbeat of measure 5?

    (A) The root of the chord
    (B) The third of the chord
    (C) The fifth of the chord
    (D) The seventh of the chord

Questions 11–14 are based on this excerpt from Bach's *Brandenburg Concerto No. 1*. This concerto features the use of a baroque instrument called the violino-piccolo, similar in size to a child-size violin and usually tuned a third higher.

Brandenburg Concerto No. 1 in F Major
First Movement

Johann Sebastian Bach
(1685-1750)

11. What is the texture of this excerpt?

    (A) Polyphony
    (B) Monophony
    (C) Homophony
    (D) Heterophony

12. The violin I and violino-piccolo are playing

    (A) in unison
    (B) in thirds
    (C) in fourths
    (D) an octave apart

13. What two instruments are sounding the same melody an octave apart?

    (A) Violoncello and violone grosso
    (B) Violin II and viola
    (C) Oboe I and oboe III
    (D) Fagotto (bassoon) and violoncello (cello)

14. The B♮ in this excerpt can be described as all of the following **except**

    (A) the leading tone in the key of the dominant
    (B) the raised 4th scale degree
    (C) a chromatic passing tone
    (D) the third of the V/V chord

Questions 15–17 are based on the excerpt below.

Ach Gott und Herr
Kirnberger Chorale Preludes

Johann Sebastian Bach
(1685–1750)
BWV 693

15. This piece would be performed by

    (A) a piano and a cello
    (B) two violins, a cello, and a bass
    (C) an organ
    (D) two pianos

16. The notes within the boxed areas can best be identified as

    (A) fragmented accompaniment
    (B) melodic motive
    (C) descending arpeggio
    (D) melodic sequence

17. What best describes the four descending half notes on the top staff measures 3–5?

    (A) It is the melody.
    (B) It is a countermelody.
    (C) It is a melodic ostinato.
    (D) It is a rhythmic augmentation of the motive.

Questions 18–20 pertain to this short excerpt from a *Sonatina* by Handel.

Sonatina in A minor

Georg Frederick Handel
(1685–1759)
HWV 584 (authentic?)

18. The texture associated with this excerpt is best described as

    (A) melody with accompaniment
    (B) polyphonic
    (C) homophonic
    (D) monophonic

19. The compositional device used in this excerpt is

    (A) variation
    (B) sequence
    (C) imitation
    (D) augmentation

20. Measure 5 clearly uses what scale pattern?

    (A) A Major
    (B) A harmonic minor
    (C) A melodic minor
    (D) B natural minor

ANSWER KEY

1. **A**	6. **B**	11. **A**	16. **B**
2. **A**	7. **B**	12. **A**	17. **D**
3. **A**	8. **C**	13. **A**	18. **D**
4. **D**	9. **C**	14. **C**	19. **C**
5. **A**	10. **C**	15. **C**	20. **C**

ANSWERS EXPLAINED

1. **(A)** The meter is alla breve or cut time. It is simple duple. The half note receives the beat.

2. **(A)** The texture is monophonic. Here is where you must be careful with identifying transpositions. At first glance it looks like it is homophonic; however, all instruments are playing unison octaves.

3. **(A)** The clarinet in A plays a C and sounds an A (such as a B♭ clarinet plays a C and sounds a B♭, or a French horn plays a C and sounds an F). The distance between A and C is a minor third. In the first measure, when the clarinet in A plays a G it is sounding a m3 lower, an E.

4. **(D)** The only thing that does not change is the meter.

5. **(A)** The caesura (∥), sometimes referred to as "railroad tracks," means there is a break of any length in the music at the discretion of the conductor.

6. **(B)** The first cadence (measure 4) is a half cadence in E Major.

7. **(B)** The texture is melody with accompaniment.

8. **(C)** The cello accompaniment figure is an Alberti bass.

9. **(C)** The clarinet imitates what the piano played in the introduction.

10. **(C)** The clarinet is playing a G and sounding an F on the downbeat of measure 5. F is the fifth of the tonic chord B♭–D–F.

11. **(A)** The texture features multiple independent lines performing at the same time—polyphony.

12. **(A)** The violin and the violino–piccolo are playing in unison. Notice that the key signatures are not the same. The violino–piccolo is in D Major while the violin is in F Major. Notice that both are playing ***Do-Mi-So-Do*** or $\hat{1}$–$\hat{3}$–$\hat{5}$–$\hat{8}$ in their respective keys.

13. **(A)** The violoncello (cello) and the violon grosso (double bass) are playing the same melody an octave apart. The double bass sounds an octave lower than written.

14. **(C)** The B natural is not a chromatic passing tone. It is the leading tone in C Major, and C Major is the dominant in the key of F. It is the raised fourth scale degree and the third of the G–B♮–D chord that functions as V/V in F Major.

15. **(C)** This piece by Bach was written for the organ. The lowest bass clef staff is played by the feet on the pedals.

16. **(B)** In the first thirteen measures of this excerpt, this four-note **motive** (C–B–A–G) is played seven times, most often in the pedal. This melodic pattern is easily recognizable throughout the excerpt.

17. **(D)** The passage in the top staff is an **augmentation** of the four-note motive (the four eighth-note pattern increased duration to four half notes).

18. **(D)** The texture is monophonic because only one line is playing at a time. This may also be called antiphonal (performing in alternation), as the left hand clearly imitates the right.

19. **(C)** The melody is based on one-measure imitative patterns.

20. **(C)** Measure 5, in the right hand, has the A melodic minor scale pattern starting from $\hat{5}$ to $\hat{5}$ (*So* to *So*).

Score Analysis Part II: Strategies for Multiple-Choice Part B 17

In this chapter, we reduce the elements found within a musical score to an outline form. The topics found on these two pages are all possible areas for exam questions—both visual and aural. The bulk of this chapter contains multiple-choice questions based on visual score analysis as the means to demonstrate types of questions and problem-solving strategies. If there are elements within this outline you are unsure of, consult the Table of Contents and review the necessary chapter(s) before continuing.

MUSICAL ELEMENTS

Scale Types

- Major, minor, modal, pentatonic, whole tone

Tonality

- Key signature, key center, modulation, accidentals, closely related keys
- Tonicization, chromaticism

Melody

- Melodic organization, recognizable patterns and identification of scale degrees, scale types, or scalar patterns
- Melodic patterns, sequences, motives and motivic development (variation, inversion, retrograde), melodic ornamentation

Phrase Structure

- Introduction, coda, antecedent–consequent, parallel or contrasting periods, double periods, phrase, verse, chorus, bridge, stanza, song form

Harmony

- Triads, seventh chords, inversion, secondary or chromatic harmony
- Cadences
- Harmonic function, harmonic progression
- Counterpoint, figured bass
- Roman numeral analysis
- Modulation

Meter

- Simple or compound, duple, triple, or quadruple
- Mixed meter, asymmetrical or symmetrical

Rhythm

- Aural and visual identification, correct notation including stemming and beaming, durational equivalents

Form

- Strophic, through-composed, binary, ternary, rounded binary, rondo, theme and variations

  - Road map elements—D.C. al Fine, D.S. al Fine, D.C. al Coda, D.S. al Coda, repeats, first and second endings
  - Harmonic elements of form—progression, cadences, harmonic rhythm, harmonic sequence, modulation, pivot chord, Picardy third
  - Melodic elements of form—motif, ostinato, theme, imitation, melodic sequence
  - Rhythmic elements of form—hemiola, augmentation, diminution, rhythmic ostinato

Textural Elements

- Monophonic, homophonic, melody with accompaniment, polyphonic, heterophonic

Instrumental Considerations

- Aural identification of instruments
- Pitch identification, register, tessitura, range, timbre, transposition

Performance Considerations
(see Appendix A for terms and definitions)

- Tempo, articulation, dynamics, style, ornamentation

Practice Exercises: Visual Analysis

Questions 1–4 are based on the excerpt from Robert Schumann's "Little Piece."

Little Piece
from Album für die Jugend, Op. 68

Robert Schumann
(1810–1856)

1. The texture features

   (A) Alberti bass
   (B) walking bass
   (C) arpeggiated bass
   (D) ostinato bass

2. This excerpt is an example of

   (A) contrasting period
   (B) parallel period
   (C) modulating period
   (D) repeated period

   You are comparing the *melody* of the phrases only.

3. The circled notes are:

   (A) escape tones
   (B) appoggiaturas
   (C) retardation
   (D) suspensions

   Look at what comes before and after the non-chord tone.

4. The cadence at measures 3 and 4 would best be analyzed as

   (A) V/iv–iv
   (B) V⁶₅/V–V
   (C) V/V–V
   (D) II–V

Questions 5–10 are based on the hymn tune below by Arthur Henry Mann. This excerpt contains four 4-measure phrases, each beginning with an anacrusis.

Angel's Story

Arthur H. Mann
(1850-1929)

5. Each phrase contains identical

   (A) rhythmic motive
   (B) harmonic progression
   (C) cadence
   (D) anacrusis pitch

   > Important word: identical

6. The phrase structure is

   (A) aba¹c
   (B) aa¹bb¹
   (C) abba
   (D) aaba

   > Remember you are looking at the melody only.

7. The second phrase implies the keys of

   (A) A minor and D Major
   (B) G Major and D Major
   (C) A Major and A minor
   (D) A Major only

   > I can't say it enough—look at the acciden-
   > tals and to what note they *lead*. Do they
   > occur more than once?

8. The cadence ending phrase 2 contains

   (A) a PAC in A Major
   (B) a half cadence in G Major
   (C) a suspension
   (D) an anticipation

   > Spell the cadence chords first and identify
   > the cadence. What belongs; what doesn't?

9. The cadence that concludes the second
   phrase (measures 7–8) contains what error in
   common-practice voice leading, doubling, or
   spacing?

   (A) Parallel octaves
   (B) The third of the chord is missing
   (C) The space between the tenor and the
        alto is too wide
   (D) Doubling the seventh of the chord
        and incorrect resolution of the
        chordal seventh

10. The A♯ in the melody that is the anacrusis
    to Phrase 3 can best be identified as

    (A) an accented upper neighbor
    (B) the third of a secondary dominant
    (C) the root of a secondary leading tone
    (D) a chromatic passing tone

Questions 11–17 are based on this excerpt from the introduction to *Panis Angelicus.*

Panis Angelicus
from Mass Solenelle, Op. 12

Cesar Franck
(1822–1890)

11. The **inversion** of the interval between the **bass** and the **solo voice** in the first chord Box 2 is

    (A) P5
    (B) dim6
    (C) m6
    (D) M3

    > This is what I call an "onion" question—you have to peel away more than one layer to get to the answer. The interval is compound; reduce it to a simple interval and invert.

12. The style markings would be defined as meaning

    (A) very soft, with vibrato
    (B) sing with great sadness
    (C) slow, with little energy
    (D) sweetly, in a very singing style

    > Know your performance terms. See Appendix A.

13. The circled note in the top staff on beat 1 in measure 3 is best identified as

    (A) a member of the chord
    (B) appoggiatura
    (C) upper neighbor
    (D) accented passing tone

    > **Clef:** Yes, it is very important to know tenor and alto clef. Simply put, you must know your non-chord tones. They *will* be on the exam in several questions.

14. The Roman numeral analysis of the chords in Box 1 would be identified as

    (A) $ii^6–V^6_5/V–V$
    (B) $ii^6–vii^{ø7}/V–I^6_4$
    (C) $ii–vii^{ø6}_5/V–I^6_4$
    (D) $IV–V^6_5/V–V$

    > **Step 1:** Identify the key. Note the clef for the solo instrument.
    > **Step 2:** LOOK AT THE BASS.
    > **Step 3:** It contains an accidental and implies secondary harmony.
    > **Step 4:** Is it major (secondary **dominant**) or is it diminished (secondary **leading tone**)?
    > **Step 5:** If you're not sure of the borrowed chord, look at the first chord and eliminate at least two of the answers.

15. The bass line in measures 4–8 is best described as

    (A) a pedal point
    (B) a suspension
    (C) an ostinato
    (D) monophonic

    > What can be eliminated by knowing you are looking at only the bass line?

16. Chords in Box 2 would be identified as

    (A) $vii°/vi–vi$
    (B) $III–V$
    (C) $v°–V$
    (D) $V^6_5/vi–vi$

17. The progression at the final cadence is

    (A) $V–V^7–I$
    (B) $I^6_4–V^7–I$
    (C) $ii^6–IV–V$
    (D) $ii^6–V–I$

    > What's your first clue? The bass line is *So-So-Do*.

Questions 18–24 are based on a more difficult excerpt from a courante by Bach.

French Suite 3 in B Minor

Johann Sebastian Bach
(1685–1750)
BWV 814

18. The durational value that is the equivalent of one beat in this meter is the

    (A) quarter note
    (B) half note
    (C) dotted half note
    (D) dotted quarter note

    > You must first determine the meter and the subdivision of the beat. The beaming of the eighth notes is a clue in this example.

19. Texture demonstrated in this excerpt is

    (A) fugal imitation
    (B) melody with accompaniment
    (C) homophonic
    (D) polyphonic

    > Is the melody imitated in various voices? If so, is the imitation **exact** or in a tonic–dominant relationship (fugal)?

20. The keys of this excerpt are best identified as

    (A) B minor only
    (B) D Major to A Major
    (C) B minor to E Major
    (D) B minor to A Major ending in F♯ minor

    > Keep your eyes on the accidentals—the occurrence of G♯ and E♯ are the biggest clues. Look for cadences to confirm tonality.

21. The cadence at measure 5 is

    (A) perfect authentic in B minor
    (B) imperfect authentic in B minor
    (C) Phrygian half cadence in B minor
    (D) half cadence in E Major

22. The accidental in measure 6 functions as

    (A) the leading tone to F♯
    (B) the third of a secondary dominant chord
    (C) the leading tone to A
    (D) an escape tone

23. In relationship to the key defined by the cadence at measure 7, the final phrase

    (A) remains in the same key
    (B) is in the key of the minor dominant
    (C) is in the key of the relative major
    (D) is in the key of the submediant

    > The question is giving you information. There is a cadence at measure 7, and it defines the key. The correct answer is **specific** to this information.

24. The final cadence is an example of

    (A) deceptive cadence in A Major
    (B) a PAC in B minor
    (C) Picardy third in F♯ minor
    (D) a Phrygian half cadence in B minor

ANSWER KEY

1. **A**	7. **A**	13. **D**	19. **D**
2. **B**	8. **C**	14. **B**	20. **D**
3. **B**	9. **D**	15. **A**	21. **B**
4. **C**	10. **D**	16. **D**	22. **C**
5. **A**	11. **D**	17. **B**	23. **D**
6. **A**	12. **D**	18. **C**	24. **C**

ANSWERS EXPLAINED

1. **(A)** The left hand accompaniment figure is an Alberti bass even though it is in treble clef and not bass.

2. **(B)** This excerpt has two phrases, each beginning with an anacrusis. You can eliminate answer (D) because a repeated period would have four phrases. There is a parallel relationship with the melody in m1–5 and m5–9. Phrase 1 is the antecedent and ends with a weak cadence (HC) followed by Phrase 2, the consequent ending with a strong cadence.

3. **(B)** The notes within the boxes are appoggiaturas.

4. **(C)** The cadence chords are D–F♯–A (the dominant) to G–B–D (the temporary tonic). The chords are V/V to V.

5. **(A)** Each of these four phrases contains the identical rhythm ♩. ♪ ♩ ♩.

6. **(A)** The phrase structure is a b a¹ c. The melody in Phrases 1 and 3 are **exactly** alike except for the anacrusis pitch. Answer (A) is the only choice that shows "a" for both Phrase 1 and Phrase 3. Some might argue that the second and fourth phrases are so similar that they are also the same melodic material. Although it was not an answer choice, that would be abab¹.

7. **(A)** The second phrase contains the keys of A minor and D Major. The addition of the accidental G♯ found in the E–G♯–B chord leading to A–C–E is a dominant-tonic relationship in the key of A minor. Beginning in measure 7 the G♯ is *not* present; however, F♯ (key signature) and C♯ are present and the phrase cadences with a D–F♯–A chord.

8. **(C)** The cadence in measure 8 contains a 4–3 suspension in the tenor voice. The G is the seventh of the V⁷ chord, which is held over to beat 3 when it resolves down to the F♯.

9. **(D)** We notice when answering Question 8 that there is no fifth in the penultimate chord of this phrase and the seventh of the chord is doubled. Having no fifth is acceptable; what is not acceptable in common-practice style is doubling a tendency tone (*Fa* or *Ti*) and incorrectly resolving the chordal seventh in an

outside voice especially. In this chord we have two Gs—one is resolved correctly with the suspension in the tenor, but the G in the soprano moves upward to *So* instead of resolving *Fa* to *Mi*.

10. **(D)** The A♯ in the soprano only occurs in this one place and serves as a chromatic passing tone to heighten the "pull" to B.

11. **(D)** Make sure you read *all* of the question. The interval between the bass and solo part (E♯–C♯) is a minor sixth; however, the question asks for the *inversion* of that interval. The answer is M3.

12. **(D)** Dolce, molto cantible means sweetly, in a very singing style. Know your performance terms; check out Appendix A.

13. **(D)** The E in the top line (tenor clef) is an accented (on the beat) passing tone. This solo part was written for cello.

14. **(B)** You can eliminate two answers by correctly identifying the first chord as ii⁶. The chord on beat 4 is spelled D♯–F♯–A–C♯. The D♯ makes the triad diminished and the chord half-diminished. It leads to an A Major chord in second inversion—ii⁶–vii°⁷/V–I⁶₄.

15. **(A)** The C in the bass begins in measure 4 and continues for four more measures creating a pedal. Notice that the C also occurs in the alto giving us a very strong sense of dominant.

16. **(D)** The chords in Box 2 are C♯–(E♯)–G♯–B to F♯–A–C♯. With the E♯ in the bass, the correct analysis is V⁶₅/vi–vi. The clue is the E♯ leading to F♯. The F♯ minor triad is the submediant (vi) in the key of A Major and the temporary tonic of the secondary dominant.

17. **(B)** The final progression is I⁶₄–V⁷–I. The *So-So-Do* in the bass is the big clue, but we must verify the chord members and also determine if the V has the added seventh, which it does, with the D in the alto line (correctly resolving downward to the C♯). Notice, too, the B in the cello moves *early* to the A, creating an anticipation.

18. **(C)** The meter is compound duple. The dotted half note gets one beat—dividing equally into three-quarter note subdivisions.

19. **(D)** The texture is clearly polyphonic. It does have a feel of imitation because of the rhythm, especially the eighth-note pattern following rests and/or ties, and the shape or contour of the lines; however, it is not a fugue.

20. **(D)** The tonalities functioning in this excerpt are B minor, shifting to A Major and ending in F♯ minor.

21. **(B)** The cadence at measure 5 is imperfect authentic in B minor.

22. **(C)** The G♯ in the tenor is the leading tone to A Major.

23. **(D)** The final phrase is in F♯ minor confirmed by the G♯ and the raised seventh scaled degree, E♯. It is the submediant in A Major and the relative minor.

24. **(C)** The final chord uses a Picardy third, raising the third of the chord (A♯) to create a major tonic on F♯.

Strategies for Multiple-Choice Part A 18

DEVELOPING YOUR LISTENING SKILLS

The Part A portion of the AP Music Theory exam is a daunting process at the very least. The prime objective for theory students is to combine theory fundamentals and aural skills training by listening to a piece of music and answering questions regarding the basic elements of the music they are hearing in "real time." To some students it seems an impossible task to "hear it all" when it goes by so fast with so few times to listen to the example. Contextual listening is a process of connecting all the dots and using all the tools you have available to match what the ear hears and the brain identifies. Contextual listening is a skill that musicians work on throughout their entire careers—mastery is not expected after one year of study. Don't get frustrated and stop listening. Listen smart and with a plan!

The basic elements of music such as pitch, duration, timbre, texture, form, melody, harmony, and cadences are found in every piece of music. The music in your band, choir, or orchestra class, the music on the radio or on your phone or tablet all have these elements, and therefore, provide you with many opportunities to develop your listening skills.

WHAT ELSE CAN YOU DO TO DEVELOP YOUR LISTENING SKILLS?

When you listen to music:

- Tap the beat, determine the meter, try conducting to confirm your answer (not during the exam), and consider what a particular rhythm might look like. Is there repetition of the rhythm?
- Listen for same and different. This is a *big* thing. All music is about same and different, and *if* it is different—*how* is it different? For example, what changes in the second phrase? What is the same?
- Name the instruments that are playing, and notice when instrumentation or tessitura changes.
- Identify performance elements such as tempo and dynamic, ritardando and crescendo, articulation, and ornaments such as grace notes and trills.
- Sing along! Sing the melody. Sing the bass line. Sing the root of the harmony. Use solfege. Does the melody have an anacrusis? Identify the scale degrees of the opening or closing few notes of a melody or bass line. If nothing else—sing **Do**!

- Listen for compositional elements like scale patterns, arpeggiated or broken chords, or Alberti bass.
- Determine the overall modality: Is it major or minor? Does it modulate?
- Identify lengths of phrases and the cadence type at the end of the phrase.

LISTEN TO MUSIC FOR THE PURPOSE OF IDENTIFYING ELEMENTS

Today we often have music playing all the time so it becomes background noise. Bring it to the front. Take notice. Focus your attention on the details. Don't be a passive listener.

EXPAND YOUR NORMAL LISTENING HABITS

Have you ever listened to a string quartet, a piano etude, an opera aria, or an oboe solo? To gain listening skills for the AP exam you must expand and vary your repertoire or playlist.

DEVELOP AN AURAL MEMORY

There is a certain amount of "must have" information that needs to be stored and easily (and confidently) retrieved. Many students find that they can listen in units or "chunks" of sound, rather than note by note, or one interval or chord at a time. By this, I mean have a working knowledge of these "chunks" of aural elements:

- **Major and minor scales:** scale patterns and arpeggios—ascending and descending
- **Melodic patterns:** Refer back to the "Top Ten Melodic Patterns," from Chapter 4.
- **Cadences:** By whatever means you have, whether it is to play them yourself on the piano, or practice with a software program or Internet website, learning to identify cadences by sound is a huge advantage in the aural and free-response portions of this exam. Chapter 15 will help with this.
- **Basic chord progressions:** such as I–ii⁶–V–I. (With this chord progression, what would the bass line be?) This is covered in more detail in Chapter 20, Strategies for Harmonic Dictation.

CONNECT THE EYES AND EARS

Throughout this guide we have discussed how all the processes overlap. See a melody and sing it. Hear a melody and notate it. See a bass line and create a melody. See the melody and create a bass line. It all works together. For example, when answering the first several multiple-choice identification questions in Part A, the most common approach is to first analyze the answers visually and identify what you **see**—*then* when the aural prompt is given, match what you hear to what is written. If you are unable to identify all four answers before the aural prompt is given, write in the margin what you hear, then go back when time allows and confirm the correct answer.

Prepare visually. Confirm aurally.

TIPS FOR CONTEXTUAL LISTENING

The contextual listening examples vary in length from a short excerpt of 4–16 measures to an entire piece. *Read the information* about the example and note how many times the excerpt will be repeated. Read the questions thoroughly in the silent times between questions.

Here are some additional tips for contextual listening.

TIP 1

Be sure to look at the terms and directions within the questions very carefully.

These include:

- **Best describes** . . .
- Includes all of the following **except** . . .
- **Ends** with or **Begins** with . . .
- **Lengthened** by . . .
- **Outside** voices (a very specific direction)
- **ONLY** (as in "listen for the rhythm <u>only</u>")
- **Characterized** by the use of . . .
- The **bass line** *of the accompaniment* begins with . . . (a very specific direction)
- **Embellished** with
- **Compared** to

TIP 2

Circle the important words that are relevant to answering correctly.

- Be proactive in answering. The questions many times will direct your ear to a **specific place** in the music (phrase 2, last 3 notes, beginning progression). Prepare your brain and your ear for those specific places. Questions, and also answers, will direct you to **listen *for*** something specific (rhythm only, bass line, melody, timbre, texture, etc.). This is critical information. These terms are clues. Use them to your advantage and stay focused on the *requested task*.

TIP 3

Read each question twice.

TIP 4

Know how to answer the error-detection questions.

Within Part A there are four questions having to do with error detection. The example will be a two-part piano piece. The score is written correctly; however, the performance you hear will have four errors in either pitch or rhythm. You will hear the example four times. There are several ways you can strategize to work these questions. The directions will tell you what measures contain the errors. Circle the measures that contain the errors and *prepare first* before listening to the

> **TIP**
>
> FOCUS on what is asked for. Don't try to see the whole forest if what you need to see is only the color of the leaves.

example. What does the example tell you visually? Identify patterns you will expect to hear, such as tonic arpeggios, rhythm patterns (e.g., dotted notes), ascending and descending motifs, or use and placement of rests. Many students find it effective to focus on the right hand one time and the left hand the second time. If the errors are in measures 1, 3, 5, and 7, another strategy is to focus on measures 1 and 5 on the first listening and on measures 3 and 7 on the second listening. Your goal is to have three out of four identified at the end of the second listening. Use the third listening to identify the remaining answer and confirm the other three. Use the fourth listening to check your answers.

TIP 5 — **What do I know just by looking at the question? How much can I logically deduce before even hearing the music?**

- There is often information revealed in the one or two sentences printed before each section of questions. This is another opportunity to *prepare* your ear. For example, if the excerpt is an orchestral piece, would it most likely have a walking bass line? No, probably not. If the excerpt is from a jazz ensemble, then a walking bass is *very* likely, as is syncopation, or change of timbre.

- If a question asks about the motion of the **outer voices**—what is the *expected* motion? Contrary, of course. Once again, let your ear confirm—but at least you are thinking of what is the "norm," are *actively listening*, and have your brain engaged.

- A very common question will ask you to identify the notes using scale degrees at the beginning or the end of a phrase or section. If it is melody, what pitches commonly end a phrase? Here is where using solfege helps identify pitch. **You must be able to sing the tonic in order to be able to determine whether the last note is tonic or not, and/or how it relates to tonic.** Keep *Do* in your ear.

- Meter questions are common in the multiple-choice section. Here are four typical answers: (A) $\frac{2}{4}$, (B) $\frac{4}{4}$, (C) $\frac{6}{8}$, and (D) $\frac{3}{8}$. What do we know by just looking at the answers? There are two duple meters, one triple meter, and one quadruple meter. Since there is only one triple meter answer, the question is significantly easier if that is the answer. It is highly unlikely that it would be $\frac{2}{4}$ or $\frac{4}{4}$ because they are so similar. But $\frac{2}{4}$ and $\frac{6}{8}$ would require knowing not only the grouping of the beats but also the division of the beat. *Now* you are prepared to listen.

- In many of the multiple-choice questions, one answer is correct, two answers are close to the correct answer, and one answer is far from the correct answer. Sometimes an answer is not even possible. For example, when asked to identify the structure that Phrases 1 and 2 form, the answer cannot be a parallel double period. A **double period** requires four phrases. Remember, the more you can eliminate, the closer you are to answering or even guessing correctly.

- How are the answers the same or different? Particularly with questions about progression, there are usually two answers that are similar to each other. *Listen to the bass.* Chord progressions tell you what note is in the bass. Figure out the solfege for the bass line of each multiple-choice answer. On the first listening you should be able to eliminate two of the answers. Two may start with I–V–I and two start with I–IV–V. Sometimes it's the ending that can help you discriminate between the progression answers because endings imply cadence.

- Look for something that *you* can identify aurally . . . perhaps the last two notes are ***Ti-Do***, the first two notes are m3 apart, the beginning is chromatic, or the ending is a melodic minor pattern . . . **prepare visually**, **listen *for* something, and confirm aurally**.

6 Fill in the answers for the multiple-choice questions as you go along—not at the end.

Many states have standardized testing that students prepare for diligently in public school. The questions are multiple choice, and a bubble sheet is used for the answers. For most states these standardized tests are not timed and many teachers practice a strategy of answering all the questions first, *then* filling in the answer sheet at the end. *Do not do this on the AP exam.* There is a time limit on each portion of the exam, and a clock should be visible to all students during the exam. It's better to run out of time with three more questions to answer then run out of time with all the questions answered but only half transferred to the answer sheet.

7 To guess or not to guess? That's a good question!

Total scores on the multiple-choice sections are based on the number of questions answered correctly. Points are not deducted for incorrect answers and no points are awarded for blank answers. Therefore, if you are not sure, guess!

- It's not always about knowing the correct answer. Sometimes we can arrive at the correct answer by eliminating the answers we know are wrong—leaving us with fewer choices.

The next part of this chapter features multiple-choice questions based on aural prompts. You have been doing these types of questions all along in the aural units, but here we have added **tips and strategies** to maximize your success with Part A multiple-choice, including contextual listening. We begin with several examples of aural identification similar to what would be on the AP exam.

Practice Exercises

Questions 1–8 ask you to identify the pitch patterns that are played. In each case, the question number will be announced. You will have **10 seconds** to read the choices; then you will hear the musical example played twice, with a brief pause between playings. Remember to read the choices for each question after the number is announced. Now listen to the music for **Questions 1–8** and identify the pitches that are played.

Access audio at *http://barronsbooks.com/ap/mtheory/*

1. Which of the following pitches is played?

(A)

(B)

(C)

(D)

2. Which of the following pitches is played?

(A)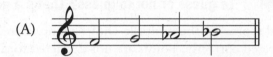

(B)

(C)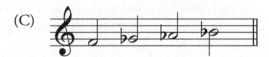

(D)

Answers A and B both have a whole step between the first two notes while C and D have a half step. Eliminate two of the answers after the first playing. If you hear a whole step between the first two notes, then determine that A is W–W and B is W–H.

Another strategy is to look for recognizable scale patterns; for example, (A) is part of the F minor scale and (B) is the F Major scale.

Pitch pattern, played twice.

Pitch pattern, played twice.

3. Which of the following pitches is played?

(A)

(B)

(C)

(D)

Identify the interval between the first two pitches:
(A) = M3, (B) = M2, (C) = M3, and (D) = P4. After
the first playing, if it is M3, you have narrowed it down
to (A) or (C).

Pitch pattern, played twice. 𝄞

These are recognizable scale patterns. Make sure you
observe the **clef**!

4. Which of the following is played?

(A)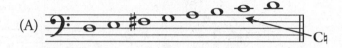

(B)

(C)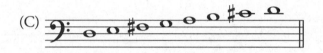

(D)

There is no key signature, so recognizing notes that are
natural (without an accidental) may imply a specific
scale pattern.

Pitch pattern, played twice. 𝄞

5. Which of the following pitches is played?

(A)

(B)

(C)

(D)

6. Which of the following is played?

(A)

(B)

(C)

(D)

Once again, look for what you know. Prepare *before* you listen. Does solfege work for you? Try that. Identify by interval or by pattern.

Identify the interval and mark it to the side. Let your ear confirm.

Pitch pattern, played twice.

Pitch pattern, played twice.

7. Which of the following is played?

(A)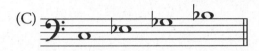

(B)

(C)

(D)

8. Which of the following is played?

(A)

(B)

(C)

(D)

> Recognizable seventh chords.

> Notice not only the quality of the triad but also the inversion.

Pitch pattern, played twice.

Pitch pattern, played twice.

Go on to the next group of questions.

TRACK
102
Questions 9–10 ask you to identify the rhythms. After a question is announced, you will have **10 seconds** to read the choices carefully before the example is played. Each example is played twice, with a brief pause between playings. Now listen to the music for **Questions 9–10** and identify the rhythm that matches the example played.

9. Which of the following represents the rhythm played?

RHYTHM ONLY

Rhythm pattern, played twice.

10. Which of the following represents the rhythm played?

(A)

(B)

(C)

(D)

RHYTHM ONLY

Rhythm pattern, played twice.

Go on to the next group of questions.

The next section contains several questions based on contextual listening examples. For this chapter on strategies, the most important aspects of the questions are in bold lettering.
Tips and clues are also provided below the questions.

♪ TRACK 103 **Questions 11–18** are based on a traditional Irish Air containing four phrases with repeated sections. The first section contains two phrases and is repeated. You will hear it played twice, followed by the full excerpt also played twice. Before listening to the first section for the first time, read **Questions 11–15**.

First of all, the information above reveals you are about to hear FOUR PHRASES—this **suggests** periodic structure. You know to listen for the same and different melodic content. READ ALL THE QUESTIONS and **prioritize** what can be heard in the first hearing—meter (11), beginning of phrase scale degree identification (13), and possibly a pretty good idea of Questions 12 and 14. You may not be ready to answer—but put a check by the answer you think it is and use the second playing to confirm.

11. The **meter** of this example is

  (A) simple duple
  (B) simple triple
  (C) compound duple
  (D) compound triple

Tap your foot or tap the beat on your leg or hand (it CANNOT be out loud), but most important, listen for the subdivision of the beat. Sing eighth notes to yourself under the beat or sing "triplets" to confirm simple or compound.

12. The **melody** contains **all** of the following elements **except**

  (A) anacrusis
  (B) dotted rhythms
  (C) hemiola
  (D) conjunct and disjunct movement

The word "**except**" is the most important. Which one of these answers is LEAST likely to occur?

13. The flute melody of the first phrase **begins with** what three-note scale degree pattern?

  (A) $\hat{3}$–$\hat{2}$–$\hat{1}$
  (B) $\hat{5}$–$\hat{3}$–$\hat{1}$
  (C) $\hat{1}$–$\hat{2}$–$\hat{3}$
  (D) $\hat{1}$–$\hat{7}$–$\hat{1}$

START HERE. It may be Question 3 in this set, but the answer to this question is the very first thing you will hear from the melody.

14. The **phrase structure** would correctly be described as a

  (A) parallel period
  (B) contrasting period
  (C) double parallel period
  (D) repeated parallel period

The opening information tells you, "the first section contains two phrases and is repeated," which eliminates two of the answers.

15. The repeat is **different** from the first two phrases in

  (A) timbre
  (B) range
  (C) rhythmic accompaniment
  (D) texture

What is different in the last two phrases? Timbre suggests a different voice or instrument, range suggests the last two phrases are higher or lower. Answer (C) or (D) suggests something changes in the accompaniment.

The first section will now be played the first time. 𝄞

The first section will now be played a second time. 𝄞

Before listening to the entire excerpt, read **Questions 16–18**.

16. The second section begins with an **anacrusis**. What are the pitches of the anacrusis and the downbeat performed in B♭ Major?

   (A) D–C   B♭
   (B) B♭–C   D
   (C) F–F   B♭
   (D) F–G–A   B♭

> You are going to listen specifically to where the new material comes in. Every answer has **scale degree 1** (*Do*) as the downbeat except one. Three answers have a two-note pickup and one has a three-note pickup. What is the most common anacrusis? In B♭ Major, what are those pitches?

17. The final phrase ends with what scale degrees?

   (A) $\hat{3}$–$\hat{2}$–$\hat{1}$
   (B) $\hat{1}$–$\hat{7}$–$\hat{1}$
   (C) $\hat{4}$–$\hat{3}$–$\hat{2}$–$\hat{1}$
   (D) $\hat{2}$–$\hat{7}$–$\hat{1}$

> Final phrase ENDING (17) and cadence information (18)—these two questions can be "heard" and answered at the same time.

18. The final cadence features

   (A) 4–3 suspension
   (B) rhythmic augmentation
   (C) Picardy third
   (D) an appoggiatura

> The excerpt would have to be in minor to have a Picardy third. Is it? By now you know whether this answer is even an option. The other three answers are very specific in what they suggest.

The entire excerpt will now be played. 𝄞

The entire excerpt will now be played a second time. 𝄞

Go on to the next group of questions.

Questions 19–22 are based on an excerpt that will be played four times. The score is printed correctly, but in the version you will hear there are errors in either pitch or rhythm in several measures. The questions ask you to identify those errors. Before listening to the music for the first time, please read **Questions 19–22** and look at the score.

19. Measure **1** contains an error in the

    (A) rhythm in the melody staff
    (B) rhythm in the bass staff
    (C) pitch in the melody staff
    (D) pitch in the bass staff

Circle the measures where there are errors. LOOK carefully at the score for recognizable melodic patterns and rhythms. During the first playing, look at the melody staff. When you hear a mistake, write **P** for pitch or **R** for rhythm by that measure.

20. Measure **3** contains an error in the

    (A) rhythm in the melody staff
    (B) rhythm in the bass staff
    (C) pitch and rhythm in the melody staff
    (D) pitch and rhythm in the bass staff

During the second playing, look at only the bass staff. When you hear a mistake, write **P** for pitch or **R** for rhythm by that measure.

21. Measure **5** contains an error in the

    (A) rhythm in the melody staff
    (B) rhythm in the bass staff
    (C) pitch in the melody staff
    (D) pitch in the bass staff

During the third playing, concentrate on the question and measure(s) unanswered.

22. Measure **7** contains an error in the

    (A) rhythm in the melody staff
    (B) rhythm in the bass staff
    (C) pitch in the melody staff
    (D) pitch in the bass staff

During the fourth playing, check your answers.

The excerpt will now be played for the first time.

The excerpt will now be played a second time.

The excerpt will now be played a third time.

The excerpt will now be played a final time.

Go on to the next group of questions.

Questions 23–27 are based on an excerpt from a suite. The excerpt will be played three times. Before listening to the excerpt for the first time, please read **Questions 23–27**.

23. The **first two phrases** have *melodies* that are

(A) played by the same instrument
(B) harmonized differently
(C) inverted and played by different instruments
(D) repeated but played by different instruments

24. The **second phrase** features which of the following performance techniques in the *accompaniment?*

(A) Glissando
(B) Legato
(C) Slur
(D) Staccato

25. The **first two phrases** both *end with*

(A) a half cadence
(B) an imperfect authentic cadence
(C) a perfect authentic cadence
(D) a deceptive cadence

> Notice that the first three questions pertain to ONLY the first two phrases. Each question gives specific directions regarding **where** to listen and **what** to listen for.

26. All of the following elements are heard except

(A) anacrusis
(B) imitation and sequence
(C) trills
(D) irregular phrase length

27. Which of the following best describes the **phrase structure** of the entire excerpt?

(A) a b a
(B) a a¹ b a
(C) a a b b¹
(D) a b a b

> With questions about phrase structure, you are listening to only the melody.

The excerpt will now be played for the first time. 🎼

The excerpt will now be played a second time. 🎼

The excerpt will now be played a third time. 🎼

Go on to the next group of questions.

♪ TRACK
○
106

Questions 28–33 are based on an excerpt from a Mozart symphony. The excerpt, in *Presto* tempo, has two segments. The first segment will be played twice, followed by the full excerpt, including the second segment, played twice. Before listening to the first segment for the first time, please read **Questions 28–31**.

28. The opening two measures contain a unison melodic statement in D Major. What are the *scale degree numbers* of the first two measures?

(A) $\hat{8}$–$\hat{7}$–$\hat{6}$–$\hat{5}$–$\hat{3}$
(B) $\hat{8}$–$\hat{5}$–$\hat{5}$–$\hat{5}$–$\hat{3}$
(C) $\hat{5}$–$\hat{3}$–$\hat{3}$–$\hat{3}$–$\hat{1}$
(D) $\hat{8}$–$\hat{5}$–$\hat{3}$–$\hat{3}$–$\hat{1}$

Be ready for the tempo.

29. The second two measures (measures 3 and 4) of the unison melodic statement are different from the first two measures because they contain what accidental?

(A) ♭5
(B) ♭3
(C) ♯5
(D) ♯4

♭5 and ♯4 are enharmonic and sound alike. The raised 4th scale degree implies "leading" to 5.

30. The opening statement (first eight measures) ends with what type of cadence?

(A) Half cadence
(B) Authentic cadence
(C) Plagal cadence
(D) Deceptive cadence

31. After the first cadence, the second phrase begins in measure 9 with the strings playing scale patterns accompanied by three accented chords. What is the Roman numeral progression of the three accompaniment chords?

(A) I–ii⁶–V
(B) I–IV–I
(C) I–V–I
(D) I–V–vi

Listen to the bass.

Now listen to the first segment for the first time and answer **Questions 28–31**. 𝄞

The first segment will now be played a second time. 𝄞

Before listening to the full excerpt, including the second segment, please read **Questions 32–33**.

32. The second segment employs which of the following compositional techniques?

(A) Direct modulation
(B) Literal repetition
(C) Melodic sequence
(D) Circle of fifths progression

33. Which statement best describes the second segment?

   (A) It modulates to the dominant and ends with a PAC in major.
   (B) It modulates to the dominant and ends with a HC in the parallel minor.
   (C) It modulates to the relative minor and ends with a PAC.
   (D) It modulates to the dominant but returns to the original key and ends with a HC.

Now listen to the full excerpt containing both segments for the first time and answer **Questions 32–33.** 𝄞

The full excerpt will now be played a second time. 𝄞

ANSWER KEY

1. **B**		8. **A**		15. **B**		22. **C**		29. **D**
2. **A**		9. **B**		16. **C**		23. **D**		30. **A**
3. **D**		10. **A**		17. **D**		24. **D**		31. **C**
4. **A**		11. **B**		18. **B**		25. **A**		32. **C**
5. **A**		12. **C**		19. **D**		26. **A**		33. **B**
6. **B**		13. **B**		20. **D**		27. **C**		
7. **C**		14. **D**		21. **B**		28. **B**		

ANSWERS EXPLAINED

1. **(B)** The pitches played were a whole step followed by a half step.

2. **(A)** The pitches were the first four notes of the F minor scale.

3. **(D)** The first two pitches are a P4 apart.

4. **(A)** This is the Mixolydian scale (lowered seventh of the major (Ionian) scale). If you are unable to confirm what the scale pattern *is*—can you tell what it is *not*? It is not (B), the D natural minor scale, or (C), the D major scale, or (D), the D harmonic minor scale.

5. **(A)** The solfege is *Do-Mi-Fa-Re-Ti-Do*.

6. **(B)** The interval played is a minor sixth.

7. **(C)** The chord played was a *half*-diminished seventh chord. If you listen for the quality of the triad—Answers (A) and (D) both had a major triad, while (B) was minor and (C) was diminished.

8. **(A)** The triad played was a D minor triad in first inversion. Answer (A) is the only answer that is minor (regardless of inversion).

9. **(B)** Beat 2 of measure 1 is identical in Answers (A) and (D). Answer (B) is the only choice with the dotted note in the middle of beat 1.

10. **(A)** Answer (A) is the only choice that starts with two equal eighth notes.

11. **(B)** The meter is simple triple.

12. **(C)** The melody *does* begin with an anacrusis, has dotted rhythms, as well as triplet rhythms. It does not have hemiola.

13. **(B)** The flute melody begins with *So-Mi-Do*, the descending tonic triad. *So* and *Mi* are the anacrusis, and *Do* is the downbeat.

14. **(D)** The first two phrases are a parallel period because the melody begins exactly the same. Those two phrases are repeated.

15. **(B)** On the repeat, the flute plays the same notes an octave higher.

16. **(C)** The beginning of the second section (Phrase 5) begins *So-So-Do*. In B♭ Major those notes are F–F–B♭.

17. **(D)** The final phrase ends with **Re-Ti-Do** (as do Phrases 2 and 4—all exactly the same). The phrase structure is aa¹ aa¹ ba¹.

18. **(B)** The durations in the final cadence are twice as long as the cadence we hear in Phrases 2 and 4, creating the feeling of closure or coming to the end.

Questions 19–22: This was played.

19. **(D)** The error is pitch in the bass staff. What is played is **Do-(So-Ti)**, written as **Do-(Ti-Re)**.

20. **(D)** What is played is a dotted quarter and eighth note rhythm in the bass, which also changes the pitch.

21. **(B)** The rhythm in the bass clef, beat 1, is played dotted-eighth sixteenth but written as two equal eighth notes.

22. **(C)** What is written in the last two measures of the RH melody is **Fa-Mi-Re-Ti-Do**; what is played is **Fa-Re-Do-Ti-Do**.

23. **(D)** The melodies are the same but the timbre is different between Phrases 1 and 2 because different instruments are used.

24. **(D)** In the second phrase the strings are playing staccato.

25. **(A)** Both Phrases 1 and 2 end with a half cadence (V).

26. **(A)** This excerpt uses imitation and sequence to achieve the polyphonic texture. Trills are also used extensively, as are the irregular phrase lengths. The irregular phrase length in the third and fourth phrase is due to an elided cadence on the downbeat of measure 12, which ends the third phrase and also begins the fourth phrase. The phrases all begin on the first beat of the measure without anacrusis.

27. **(C)** The phrase structure is a a b b[1].

28. **(B)** When answering aural questions such as these, pay close attention to information given in the directions or the questions themselves regarding **where** and **what** to listen for. The first three questions pertain to the opening eight measures "in Presto tempo." This is your clue that it is going to be *very fast*. Be prepared before the music starts. The opening statement is ***Do-So-So-So-Mi*** ($\hat{8}$–$\hat{5}$–$\hat{5}$–$\hat{5}$–$\hat{3}$) in D Major.

29. **(D)** The second two measures of the unison melodic statement contain the raised $\hat{4}$ scale degree (***Fi***). In D Major that pitch is G♯.

30. **(A)** The cadence at the end of eight measures is a half cadence ending on the dominant (V).

31. **(C)** The scale patterns are accompanied by the progression I-V-I.

32. **(C)** The second segment moves to the key of A Major (the dominant) through a melodic sequence pattern that moves up by step to A.

33. **(B)** After modulating to A Major, this segment ends with a cadence in the key of the parallel minor, A minor.

Strategies for Melodic Dictation: FR 1 and FR 2

19

Melodies—they're everywhere. We sing them in sight-singing exercises, we write them in part-writing exercises, we analyze them in phrase structure examples, and we have been performing them in bands, choirs, and orchestras for years. So why is melodic dictation so hard for students?

It is for one of two reasons:

1. **Melody memory.** You can't write down what you can't remember. That's where using a system of solfeggio or numbers helps. It identifies the pitch with a label or name the brain can remember.

2. **Notation breakdown.** If you can retain the melody and are able to sing it back but cannot correctly put the melody down on paper, the problem is notation; that is, a lack of understanding how the melody looks on paper. This skill also has two sides—pitch and rhythm. Some students understand what the pitches are but can't correctly write the rhythm *in the correct place* within the measure. Some students get the rhythms correct but miss the pitches by a step or a third.

For most students it is a combination of both. For some the anxiety is so great they fail to get much of anything written on the paper. We are going to look at this process, break it down step by step, and come up with a plan to maximize your potential for success with melodic dictation.

TIPS FOR SUCCESSFUL MELODIC DICTATION

TIP 1   **If you can't get it all, get all that you can.**

Students lose points on the melodic dictation portion of the exam simply by struggling to get it *all*. They become frustrated and end up with nearly nothing. We, the teachers, evaluators, and readers, want you to demonstrate how much you know . . . it is *not* about knowing everything. Once again, start with a plan and work smart!

TIP

2   Use logic and plan ahead.

The music will tell you so much to help you prepare. I call it the **IF–THEN** method. What is given? The clef, the key signature, the time signature, the number of measures, and the first pitch are given. From that we can deduce the key, the probable last note, and a possible half cadence (V = *So* or *Ti* or *Re*) in the middle.

- CLEF–CLEF–CLEF! If you make the mistake of overlooking the clef, your entire melody could possibly be wrong (as in sight-singing). Write down the KEY in big letters somewhere on the paper. Just the physical act of connecting pencil to paper helps you to focus.
- What pitches are connected to what solfege or numbers? Once again, write it down somewhere in the margin of the paper. Use your time to *prepare your brain* for what might occur—ANTICIPATE.

$\hat{5}$	$\hat{1}$	$\hat{2}$	$\hat{3}$	$\hat{4}$	$\hat{5}$	$\hat{6}$	$\hat{7}$	$\hat{8}$
B♭	E♭	F	G	A♭	B♭	C	D	E♭
So	*Do*	*Re*	*Mi*	*Fa*	*So*	*La*	*Ti*	*Do*

- The last note is always *Do* ($\hat{1}$). *Pencil in that pitch* at the end of the last measure (could be high or low). *Anticipate* what is likely to happen and let your ear confirm it.
- Knowing the time signature will give you a clue to the **duration** of the last note. If the time signature is $\frac{4}{4}$, the last note is probably a half note. If the time signature is $\frac{6}{8}$, the probable last note is a dotted quarter note.
- Is there an **anacrusis**? If so, that usually tells you two things. Since an anacrusis is commonly *So* most often going to *Do*, the first note on the *downbeat* most likely will be *Do* ($\hat{1}$). You must also consider the change in the durations in the last measure. If the time signature is $\frac{4}{4}$ with a quarter-note anacrusis, the last measure will most probably have a dotted-half note. Make sure the anacrusis and the last measure equal a full measure.
- Are you in minor? An accidental must be used to create the **leading tone**. A melodic dictation example in minor will always have at least one leading tone that requires writing an accidental. Evaluators—whether that's your classroom teacher, the readers grading your exam, or the college professor assessing your skills for acceptance into a music school—will all want to know that you can:

  – recognize the various forms of minor when you *hear* them,
  – anticipate the use of the raised 7th scale degree, and
  – recognize the possible use of the melodic form of minor in an ascending pattern (almost always in the scale pattern *So-La-Ti-Do* instead of harmonic minor *So-Le-Ti-Do*). The use of *Te* from natural minor is also a common alteration particularly as a complementing descending pattern following melodic minor, as in the following example.

HARMONIC   MELODIC   NATURAL

 Write the name of the leading tone in BIG letters underneath the key signature to jog your memory when you begin to write in harmonic minor.

- Are you in compound meter? One of the examples will be in ⁶⁄₈ time. If rhythm is problematic—use a *rhythm menu* (see Chapter 11). Plan ahead by thinking about and writing down what possible rhythms are going to be used. You can't write down every possible combination, but you can certainly *anticipate* the most often-used rhythms. Recognize, but don't write as part of the menu, other rhythms that are primarily variations of sixteenth-note subdivisions and dotted rhythms.

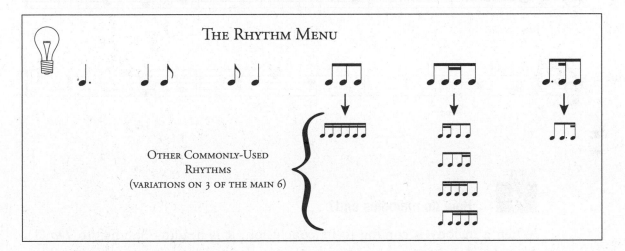

THE RHYTHM MENU

OTHER COMMONLY-USED
RHYTHMS
(VARIATIONS ON 3 OF THE MAIN 6)

With the rhythm menu in place, much of the guesswork is gone; you have narrowed down the choices to these six 1-beat rhythms. Just the process of writing the rhythm menu prepares your **brain** and your **ear** for what is possible *and* you know how to notate it. Are these six the only compound rhythms used? No, of course not, but you are anticipating and preparing. Using a rhythm menu is a great tool, especially when you are practicing and building your skills for melodic dictation. When taking the AP Music Theory exam, remember your time limit, write only the part of the rhythm menu that helps you focus on the meter.

- What about the possibility of a chromatic note in a **major** key? It could occur—just like it could occur in harmonic dictation (FR 4), harmonizing the melody (FR 7), and sight–singing (SS 2)—**because the skills overlap**.

From our study of chromatic harmony we have learned that the most common chromatic notes are #4̂ (*Fi*), #5̂ (*Si*), and sometimes #1̂ (*Di*). By far the most common pattern is *Fa-Fi-So* or *So-Fi-So*.

| Do | Re | Mi | Fa | So | **Fi** | So | La | **Si** | La | Ti | So | Do |

TIP 3   How do melodies begin?

Many melodies have similar beginnings. We use this approach in harmonic dictation as well. The two most common beginnings of melodies are **Do-Re-Mi** and **Do-Mi-So** in both major and minor. A very common beginning in a minor key is **Do-Ti-Do** because that pattern requires the writing of an accidental.

TIP 4   How do melodies end?

When a melody is coming to its conclusion, it is heading "home" to **Do** (1̂). Here are the commonly used endings in melodic dictation:

- *Mi-Re-Do* or *So-Fa-Mi-Re-Do*
- *Do-Ti-Do* or *Do-Re-Do*
- *Re-Ti-Do* or *Ti-Re-Do*
- *Fa-Ti-Do* (the tritone is created between *Fa* and *Ti* in both major and harmonic minor); also *So-Ti-Do* and *Mi-Ti-Do*.

SOUNDS DIFFERENT IN MAJOR AND MINOR | **SOUNDS IDENTICAL IN MAJOR AND HARMONIC MINOR**

GM:

Mi Re Do   So Fa **Mi** Re Do   Do Re Do   Re Ti Do   Fa Ti Do

gm:

Me Re Do   So Fa **Me** Re Do

Go back and review the Top Ten Melodic Patterns (Chapter 4).

TIP 5   What's in the middle?

Now the middle is not so easy. What can you expect?

Anticipate mostly stepwise motion with one or two skips or leaps. If there is a leap (more than a third) it is most often *going to **Do*** or ***So*** or *coming from **Do*** or ***So***. Another common occurrence is a half cadence in the middle of the example. Because this is melody only, there is no harmony; but, melody implies harmony, particularly in specific places within the phrase. If a four-measure example ends on ***Do*** (Î), that would *imply* a perfect authentic cadence. Most of the melodic dictation exercises are symmetrical, meaning balanced into two equal halves. Anticipate a weaker cadence (HC) somewhere near the end of the second measure to create an antecedent–consequent relationship within the melody. This cadence is generally *not* marked by significantly longer durations, but more by shape and contour of the line as well as pitches from the dominant triad (***So-Ti-Re***). Remember that half cadences don't always occur at the very end of the measure. Often the antecedent phrase will end with the HC and the next phrase will begin with an anacrusis. Think about the shape or contour of a melody. If the shape is flowing downward at the end of the first phrase, an anacrusis beginning the next phrase will normally start with an ascending movement.

> In the last ten years, eighteen out of twenty melodic dictation exercises have implied an HC or IAC near the middle of the example and seventeen out of twenty followed the implied HC with an anacrusis leading into the next phrase; twenty out of twenty have ended on ***Do*** (Î) !

To prepare for this, near the halfway point, write the names of the pitches above the measure that are *So-Ti-Re* ($\hat{5}$–$\hat{7}$–$\hat{2}$), as a reminder of what you are anticipating. **Prepare** your brain for what might occur and let your ear confirm it.

TIP 6 Don't write until you have heard the entire example.

I teach with this method because I find that if you start writing immediately upon hearing the first measure, your brain is no longer focused on the melody but on one measure or pattern. Use 100 percent of your attention to hear the melody through to the end, assigning solfege or numbers to the melodic patterns you are able to identify on the first hearing. **Try and sing the melody to yourself internally**, then write. Other teachers may suggest that students should begin to write while the music is playing. Try both methods and identify your own strengths to determine which process to use. After the first hearing your goal should be to be able to write the first and last measures, and to have an idea of the shape or contour of the melody and the exact location of an implied HC. Other things to listen for are where *Do* or *So* occurs, or if rhythm is an easier element for you, "sketch" out rhythms and where they are located within the measure. The melody *will* come back to *Do*, usually more than once.

TIP 7 Don't be afraid to use the back door.

You may be able to get the first two measures, draw a blank in the middle, but come back in toward the end. Perhaps you hear a *Ti-Do* ending but are not sure what comes before that. Does the melody approach the pattern *Ti-Do* from above *Ti* or below *Ti*? Think about the shape or line of the melody and what pitches that implies, and once again—listen for patterns. **Work backward** from what you know to find what you don't know.

This is two familiar patterns *So-La-Ti-Do* and *Re-Ti-Do* but rhythm may confuse.

So recurring from an earlier pattern helps identify the interval *So-Ti* at the end OR if you can identify *So-Ti* at the end—knowing that may help identify the earlier pattern.

TIP

8   **When you are done knowing—GUESS.**

If you have written notes in the spaces around the staff suggesting solfege or pitch numbers, and/or contour, and/or rhythm—GUESS. What looks like a viable melody? Does it match the shape and rhythm? You can even go back to the melodic dictation pages when you have finished other portions of the Free-Response section and fill in the blanks with educated guesses. When a reader sees a melodic dictation example with the first two notes written and then a completely blank staff—that's a signal that the student did not have a plan.

Hopefully you have been practicing your aural skills fundamentals with Chapter 11, Aural Skills Part II, which provides progressive exercises (fifteen two-measure examples in compound meter and eight three-measure examples in simple meter) in preparation for these sample exercises, which are similar in difficulty to what you may find on the AP Music Theory exam. After you have completed the progressive exercises, you are ready to practice for the exam with these sample questions.

Practice Exercises

Directions: Here are twenty melodies for you to practice taking melodic dictation: ten examples in simple meter and ten in compound meter. Half the examples are in bass clef and half are in treble clef, as well as half in major and half in minor.

The first ten examples (1–10) are equivalent to **Free-Response Question 1** on the exam. These ten examples will be **played three times** each. There will be a pause of **30 seconds** after the first playing and a **1-minute pause** after each subsequent playing. There are no rests in the melody. Each question number will be announced, followed by one measure of tempo clicks. The pitch of the first note has been provided. Be sure to complete the note with stems and flags as needed.

Access audio at *http://barronsbooks.com/ap/mtheory/*

1. The melody will be be performed by a bassoon.

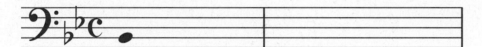

2. The melody will be performed by a violin.

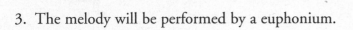

3. The melody will be performed by a euphonium.

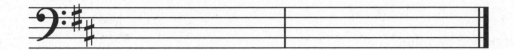

4. The melody will be performed by an oboe.

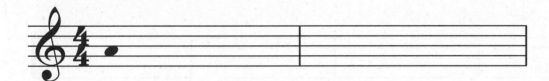

5. The melody will be performed by a cello.

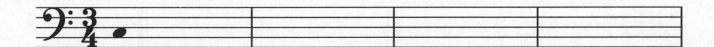

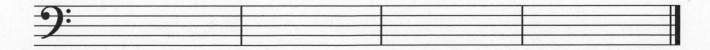

6. The melody will be performed by a violin.

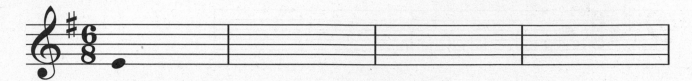

7. The melody will be performed by a flute.

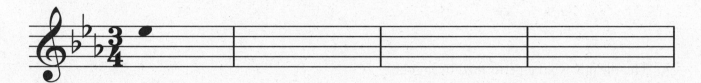

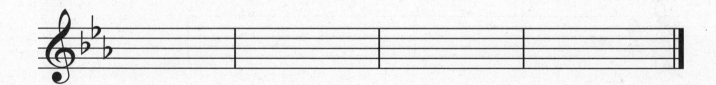

8. The melody will be performed by a euphonium.

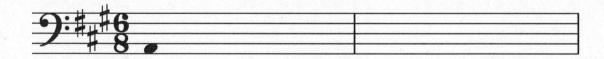

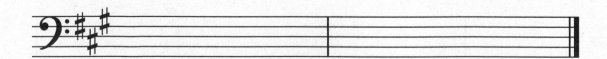

9. The melody will be performed by a cello.

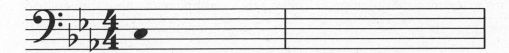

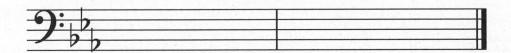

10. The melody will be performed by an oboe.

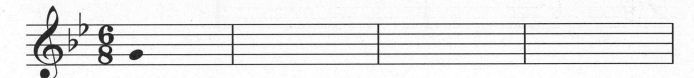

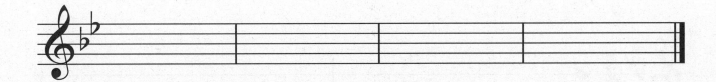

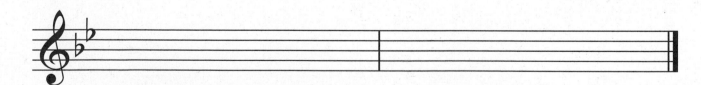

Directions: The next ten examples (11–20) are equivalent to **Free-Response Question 2** on the exam. These ten examples will be **played four times** each. There will be a pause of **30 seconds** after the first playing and a **1-minute pause** after the next three playings. There are no rests in the melody. Each question number will be announced, followed by one measure of tempo clicks. The pitch of the first note has been provided. Be sure to complete the note with appropriate stems and flags.

11. The melody will be performed by a cello.

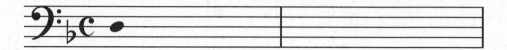

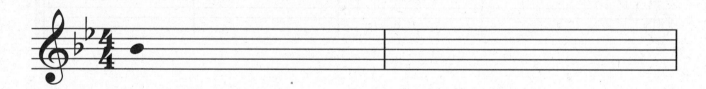

12. The melody will be performed by a violin.

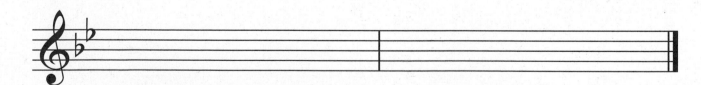

13. The melody will be performed by a euphonium.

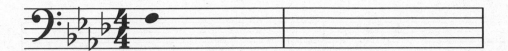

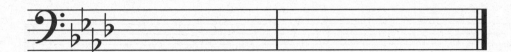

14. The melody will be performed by a violin.

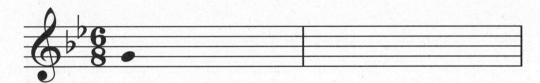

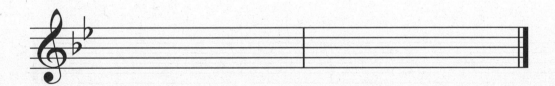

15. The melody will be performed by a flute.

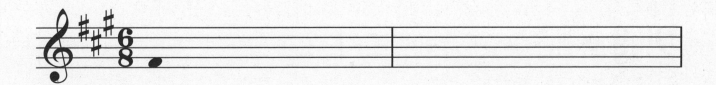

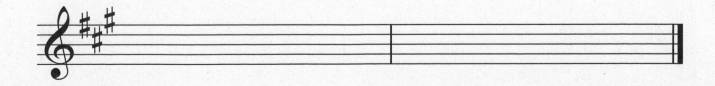

16. The melody will be performed by a cello.

17. The melody will be performed by a flute.

18. The melody will be performed by a bassoon.

19. The melody will be performed by an oboe.

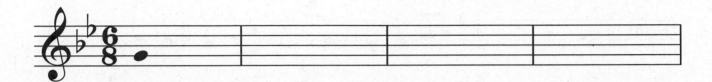

20. The melody will be performed by a cello.

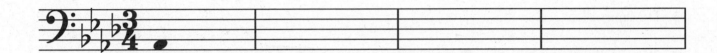

ANSWERS EXPLAINED

1. B♭ Major

2. F Major

3. D Major

4. A minor

5. C Major

6. E minor

7. E♭ Major

8. A Major

9. C minor

10. G minor

11. D minor

12. B♭ Major

13. F minor

14. G minor

15. F♯ minor

16. G Major

The FR 2 examples, exercises 11–20, contain chromatic harmony. The accidental must be written correctly because there is implied harmony. Enharmonic spellings are not accepted. In exercise 16, the D♯ in measure 2 cannot be written as E♭.

17. B♭ Major

18. D minor

19. G minor

20. A♭ Major

Strategies for Harmonic Dictation: FR 3 and FR 4

20

PREPARING FOR HARMONIC DICTATION

Students often lack confidence when doing harmonic dictation. It does require an advanced level of understanding and the ability to associate and connect several overlapping skills. Harmonic dictation requires knowledge of the function of chords within the tonality and their relationship to each other, as well as skills to aurally identify quality and inversion.

If you have completed the progressive studies in harmonic dictation found in Chapter 15, you are well on your way to successful dictation of four-part harmony.

Let's answer a few remaining questions and then practice with twelve more examples.

HOW CAN I PREPARE BEFORE THE FIRST PLAYING STARTS?

The key is given—write the chord menu so you don't have to think of what notes go with which chord while trying to hear, identify, and notate. If nothing else, write the name of the pitch that is the leading tone—*especially* if the key is minor. Notice the similarities between C Major and C minor:

		(C)		(C)	(F)		(A)
	G	A	C	A	D	E	F
	E	F	A	F♯	B	C	D
	C	D	F	D	G	A	B
CM:	I	ii⁽⁷⁾	IV	V⁷/V	V	vi	vii⁰⁷⁾

		(C)		(C)	(F)		(A♭)
	G	A♭	C	A	D	E♭	F
	E♭	F	A♭	F♯	B♮	C	D
	C	D	F	D	G	A♭	B♮
cm:	i	ii⁰⁽⁷⁾	iv	V⁷/V	V	VI	vii°⁽⁷⁾

465

WHAT STEPS SHOULD I FOLLOW <u>DURING</u> THE AURAL PROMPTS TO ACHIEVE THE MOST SUCCESS?

There are several ways to "listen" . . . there is not just one way to hear harmonic dictation. The best thing to do is determine what works best for *you* and develop your own strategy. Here are two methods that work well.

- **Method 1** is hearing vertically—identifying the function and quality of chords first and then confirming with the bass and soprano line.

  PLAYING 1: **Listen for "chunks" of the phrase for familiar patterns top to bottom.** In other words, listen to the full chord to recognize the sound of tonic moving to dominant and back to tonic, not just linear listening as outlined in Method 2. Fill in the blank with correct Roman numeral chord symbols. You will confirm the inversion when you listen specifically to the bass line. **Identify and notate the cadence.** The cadence will usually be in root position and will have recognizable melodic patterns in both bass and soprano.

  PLAYING 2: **Listen to the bass line to confirm chord quality and inversion.** Notate the bass line.

  PLAYING 3: **Listen to the soprano—expect contrary motion to the bass line.** Listen for recognizable and familiar patterns. Notate as much of the soprano and bass line as possible. Listen for dissonance that may indicate a seventh chord, and in FR 4 anticipate and prepare your ear for the possibility of chromatic harmony with the accidental often occurring in the soprano or bass.

  PLAYING 4: **Listen specifically for what you have left blank.** Review and check your work.

Most students tend to be linear listeners since, unless they are pianists, students who sing soprano, or play the clarinet or cello look at music one line at a time and therefore generally hear music one line at a time.

- **Method 2** is the linear method—listening for the bass line first and then the soprano as separate lines and logically determining the chord symbols (implied harmony) based on the counterpoint. Some students find it easier to hear the soprano or melody line first and then add the bass line and chord quality. Do what works for you.

  PLAYING 1: **Listen to the bass line.** While you are listening the first time try to pick out the bass line and sing the bass notes in your head right after you hear it. As you sing the bass, assign solfege to the pitches. The solfege tells you the placement of the notes within the scale and also implies harmony. **Identify and notate the cadence.** The cadence will usually be in root position and will have recognizable melodic patterns in both bass and soprano.

PLAYING 2: **Listen to the soprano.** Notice the shape or contour of the soprano compared to the bass. Remember that the bass and soprano most often move in contrary motion. The melody will be mostly steps and skips while the bass tends to be more disjunct. Notate as much of the melody as you can and fill in Roman numeral chord symbols that you have already identified.

PLAYING 3: **Listen vertically for the chord quality.** Determine the chord symbols as you review both bass line and soprano. Listen for identifiable patterns in both melody and bass line. By now, many two-chord progressions such as V to I should be easily recognizable. Remember the progression usually returns to tonic on the third or fourth chord and that you may hear V–I in places other than the cadence. Listen for dissonance that may indicate a seventh chord, and in FR 4 anticipate and prepare your ear for the possibility of chromatic harmony.

PLAYING 4: **Listen specifically for what you have left blank.** Review and check your work.

REVIEW

Understand what harmonies are implied from knowing the bass line.

When the bass is:	The implied harmony is:	Or possibly:
Do	I	IV^6_4
Ti	V^6 or V^6_5	$vii^{ø7}$ or vii^{o7}
La	vi	IV^6
So	V	I^6_4
Fa	IV	ii^6 or ii^6_5 or V^4_2
Mi	I^6	
Re	ii	V^6_4 or vii^{o6}

Common Bass Lines	=	Implied Harmonies that *Begin* a Phrase:
1. *Do-Ti-Do*	=	$I–V^6–I$
2. *Do-Ti-Do*	=	$I–V^6_5–I$
3. *Do-Re-Mi*	=	$I–V^6_4–I^6$
4. *Do-Re-Mi*	=	$I–vii^{o6}–I^6$
5. *Do-Do-Do*	=	$I–IV^6_4–I$
6. *Do-Fa-Mi*	=	$I–V^4_2–I^6$ (resolution in the bass)
7. *Do-Fa-Mi*	=	$I–IV–I^6$
8. *Do-Mi-So*	=	$I–I^6–I^6_4$

Common Bass Lines	+	Implied Harmonies that *End* Phrases	=	Type of Cadence
So-So-Do	+	I_4^6–V–I or i_4^6–V–i	=	Authentic
So-So-Do	+	V–V–I or V–V–i	=	Authentic
Fa-So-Do	+	IV–V–I or iv–V–i	=	Authentic
Fa-So-Do	+	$ii^6(ii_5^6)$–V–I or $ii^{o6}(ii^{ø6}_5)$–V–i	=	Authentic
Fa-So-La	+	IV–V–vi	=	Deceptive
Fa-So-Le	+	iv–V–VI	=	Deceptive
So-So-La	+	I_4^6–V–vi	=	Deceptive
So-So-Le	+	i_4^6–V–VI	=	
Fa-Do	+	IV–I or iv–i	=	Plagal
Fa-So	+	IV–V or ii^6–V iv–V or ii^{o6}–V	=	Half
Le-So	+	iv^6–V	=	Phrygian half

Common Bass Lines	=	Implied Mid-Phrase Harmonies
So-Fa-Mi	=	V–V_2^4–I^6
Mi–Fa-So	=	I^6–ii_5^6–V
Do-La-Fa	=	I–vi–IV or I–vi–ii^6
La-Fa-Mi	=	vi–IV–I^6 or IV^6–IV–I^6
Fa-Mi	=	IV–I^6 or V_2^4–I^6
Fa-Re	=	IV–ii
Fa-Fa	=	IV–ii^6 but not ii^6–IV
Fa-Fi-So	=	IV–V_5^6/V–V or ii^6–V_5^6/V–V
Fa-So-Si-La	=	IV–V–V_5^6/vi–vi
Me-Mi-Fa	=	i^6–V_5^6/iv–iv (in minor)

OTHER TIPS TO MAXIMIZE SUCCESS

- If you have left several blanks on the exam, start to make note of what you can positively identify, and write a reminder in the margin or near the answer blank and when in doubt make an educated guess. **Do not leave any blanks.**
- Does your progression move in **T–S–D–T** fashion? It should. Check for retrogression.
- Have you written parallel fifths or octaves between the soprano and bass? If so, one or possibly both are wrong. If you change your bass you've changed your chord symbol too.
- Is the last note the correct value?
- Have you used stems and filled in note heads where necessary?
- The perfect authentic cadence is used most often *and* the most common PAC is I$^6_4$–V^7–I.
- In the perfect authentic cadence **V^7** is used more often than **V**.

> To avoid running out of time, use the facing page of staff paper for writing the chord menus and for scratch paper only. **Do all your work on the question page.** If you do use the staff paper, remember to allow yourself enough time to transfer information to the question page.

You are now ready for more practice of four-part harmonic dictation. The following twelve exercises are the same length and approximate difficulty as on the AP Music Theory exam.

Practice Exercises

Directions: For each of these questions, you will hear a four-part harmonic progression. The progression will be played **four** times for each example. There will be a pause of 30 seconds after the first playing and a **1-minute pause** after each subsequent playing.

You are to notate only the soprano and bass voices. Do not notate the alto and tenor. On the lines provided under each staff, write the Roman and Arabic numerals that indicate the chords and possible inversions. Each progression has nine chords; the Roman numeral and notes of the first chord are given.

Access audio at *http://barronsbooks.com/ap/mtheory/*

1. Harmonic Dictation in A Major

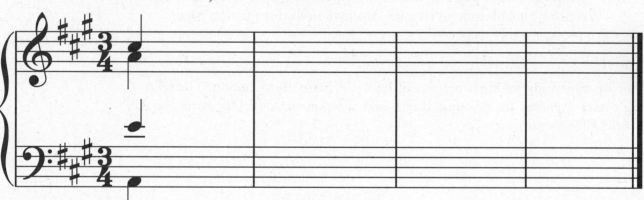

AM: I ___ ___ ___ ___ ___ ___ ___ ___

2. Harmonic Dictation in G minor

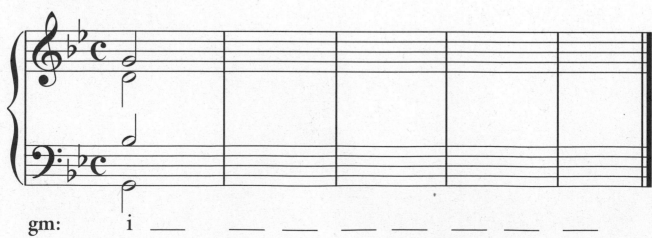

gm: i ___ ___ ___ ___ ___ ___ ___ ___

3. Harmonic Dictation in B♭ Major

B♭M: I   _ _ _ _ _ _ _ _ _ _

4. Harmonic Dictation in D minor

dm: i   _ _ _ _ _ _ _ _ _ _ _

5. Harmonic Dictation in E minor

em: i   _ _ _ _ _ _ _ _ _

6. Harmonic Dictation in C Major

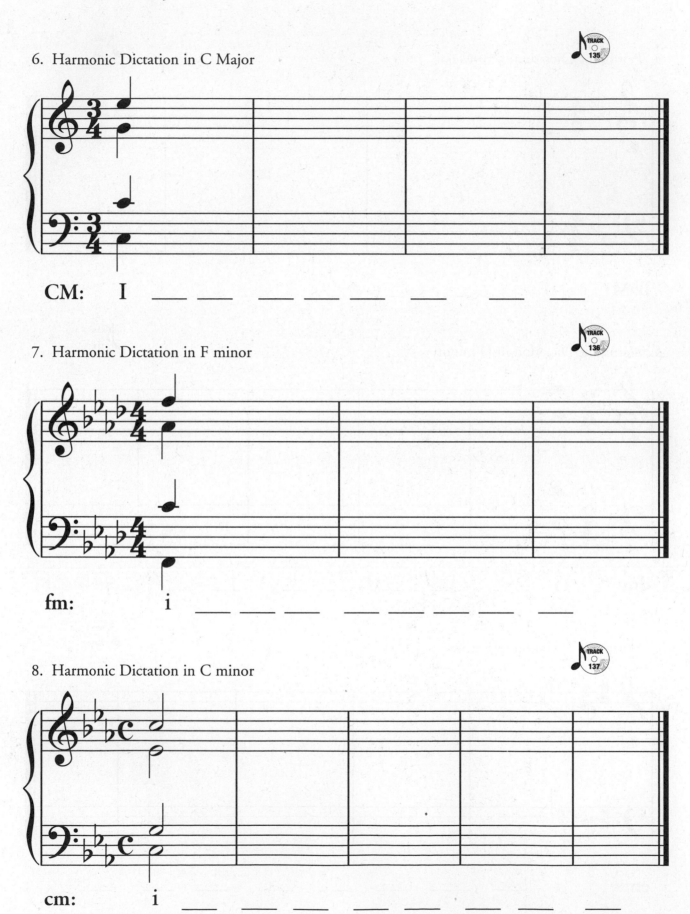

CM: I __ __ __ __ __ __ __

7. Harmonic Dictation in F minor

fm: i __ __ __ __ __ __ __

8. Harmonic Dictation in C minor

cm: i __ __ __ __ __

9. Harmonic Dictation in A♭ Major

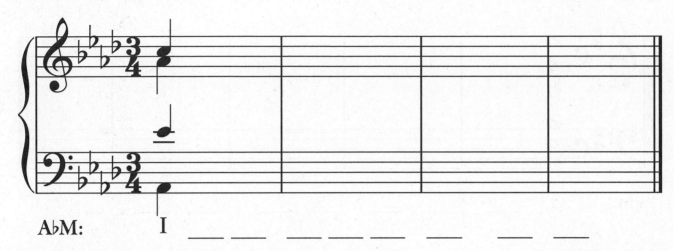

A♭M: I   _   _   _   _   _   _   _   _

10. Harmonic Dictation in D minor

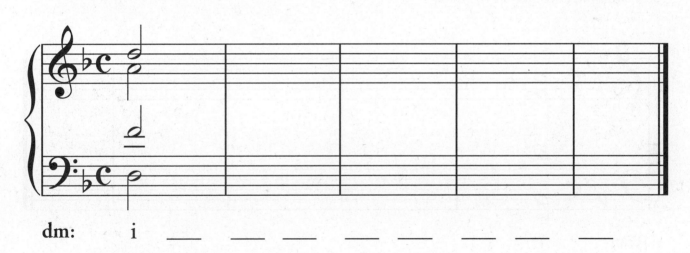

dm: i   _   _   _   _   _   _   _   _   _

11. Harmonic Dictation in E minor

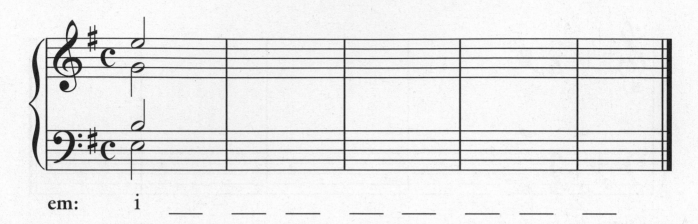

em: i _ _ _ _ _ _ _ _ _ _ _ _ _ _

12. Harmonic Dictation in B♭ Major

B♭M: I _ _ _ _ _ _ _ _ _ _ _ _ _

ANSWERS EXPLAINED

1. Harmonic Dictation in A Major

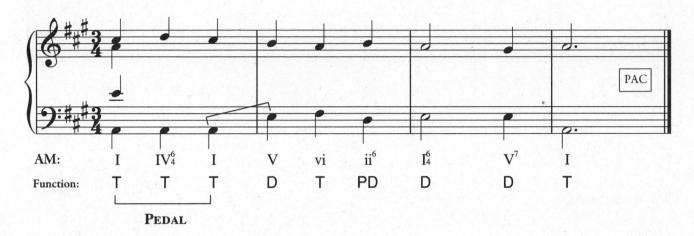

What you heard.

Same note in the bass = pedal $^6_4$ and, as we learned, the upper neighbor in the soprano. The melodic ending is ***Do-Ti-Do*** ($\hat{1}$–$\hat{7}$–$\hat{1}$) and ***So-So-Do*** in the bass—the most common bass ending. If we back up one chord we have ***Fa*** in the bass with the ii⁶—very common *pre*dominant harmony.

Notice that there is a leap in the bass between measures 1 and 2. Remember that leaps often occur between ***Do*** and ***So*** (as it is here) and a leap in the bass often indicates function change. The first measure is all about tonic, but the second measure leaps into dominant function with the root position V.

2. Harmonic Dictation in G minor

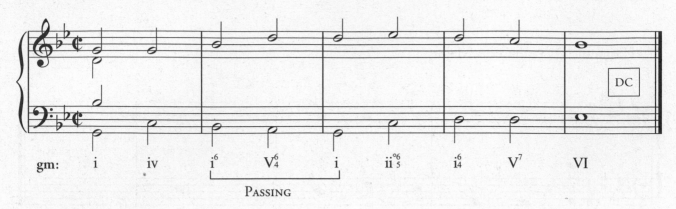

What you heard.

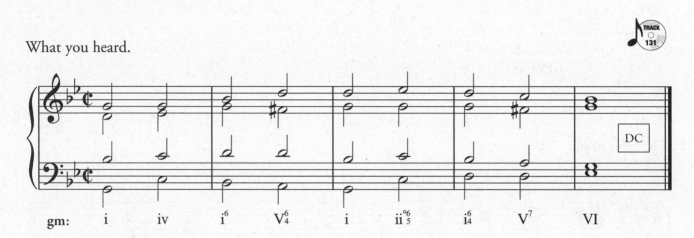

This exercise begins with *Do-Fa* in the bass and then descends by step. Note the use of the passing $^6_4$ chord (we have often used this progression to create the ascending *Do-Re-Mi*—here it is descending *Mi-Re-Do*). A classic deceptive cadence occurs as the bass line concludes with *Do-Fa-So-So-Le*; your ear anticipates the tonic but there is a cadence on VI instead.

3. Harmonic Dictation in B♭ Major

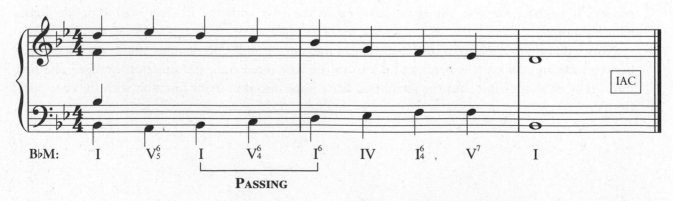

What you heard.

BbM: I   V⁶₅   I   V⁶₄   I⁶   IV   I⁶₄   V⁷   I

In this example, we have a very common beginning paired with a very common ending; however, you must hear that the last note in the soprano is *not **Do*** in order to get the cadence correct. Connecting these two is a stepwise passage using the passing V⁶₄ chord. As you listen to the aural prompt, notice the shape (contour) of the outside voices; or if you are not able to hear both at the same time, note the shape of just the melody. This is a clue as it continues to descend *past* the tonic. If you hear the tonic chord but not ***Do*** in the melody, it can only be ***Mi*** or ***So*** . . . . Work backward from what you know to help you determine what you don't know. When in doubt, GUESS!

4. Harmonic Dictation in D minor

dm: i   V⁶₄   i⁶   V⁴₂   i⁶   V   VI   iv⁶   V

What you heard.

dm: i   V⁶₄   i⁶   V⁴₂   i⁶   V   VI   iv⁶   V

When you know you are in minor, it is wise to anticipate what *might* be played and think about what that implies. Always consider the leading tone and realize it is often in the soprano or the bass because it requires writing the accidental, *and* realize that where there is $\hat{7}$ there should be a $\hat{1}$ right after it. The Phrygian half cadence occurs only in minor. Although it is not frequently used, it has appeared in harmonic dictation examples. Listen for the half-step **Le-So** in the bass at the cadence.

5. Harmonic Dictation in E minor

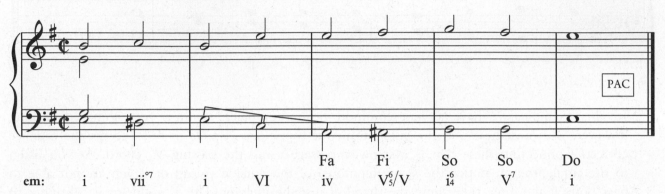

What you heard.

In this example, we have **Do-Ti-Do** at the beginning, with the leading tone in the bass (accidental required) and the seventh of the chord in the soprano—both imperative resolutions. Notice that the mid-phrase progression descends in thirds, leading to the secondary dominant—**Fa-Fi-So**. What's the ending pattern in the melody? Take what you have learned from part writing, and apply it to harmonic dictation.

6. Harmonic Dictation in C Major

What you heard.

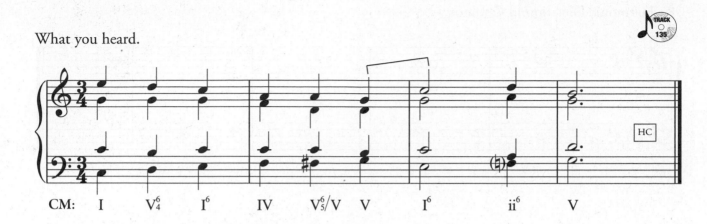

CM: I   V$^6_4$ I^6 IV   V$^6_5$/V   V   I^6 ii^6 V

Here we have an ascending stepwise pattern similar to Question 4, this time in major, utilizing a secondary dominant chord and ending with a half cadence. Once again a leap, this time in the melody, is *So* to *Do*. Hearing the leading tone in the melody on the last note is automatically a half cadence. The dominant chord is the only chord that includes $\hat{7}$ that is used at the end of a cadence.

7. Harmonic Dictation in F minor

fm: i   V$^4_2$ i^6 V$^6_5$/iv   iv   ii$^{\circ6}$ i$^6_4$ V^7 i

What you heard.

fm: i   V$^4_2$ i^6 V$^6_5$/iv   iv   ii$^{\circ6}$ i$^6_4$ V^7 i

This example begins *Do-Fa-Me* in the bass, which is the seventh of the V^7 resolving downward in the bass, leading to a chromatic chord that intensifies the subdominant (iv). The chromatic pattern is *Me-(Mi)-Fa*. The melody is a pattern we have often seen in minor using the leading tone on beat 2 (*Do-Ti*) followed by the natural minor descending pattern—*Do-Te-Le*.

8. Harmonic Dictation in C minor

cm: i   vii°$^{6}_{5}$ i^{6} ii°$^{6}_{5}$ V   i^{6} ii°^{6} V^{7}/V   V

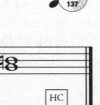

What you heard.

cm: i   vii°$^{6}_{5}$ i^{6} ii°$^{6}_{5}$ V   i^{6} ii°^{6} V^{7}/V   V

This example begins with an ascending pattern using the fully-diminished leading-tone seventh chord in first inversion. The leading-tone seventh chord is often in first inversion and, as it does here, it moves frequently to the i^{6}. The progression ends with a half cadence preceded by the V^{7} of V in root position.

9. Harmonic Dictation in A♭ Major

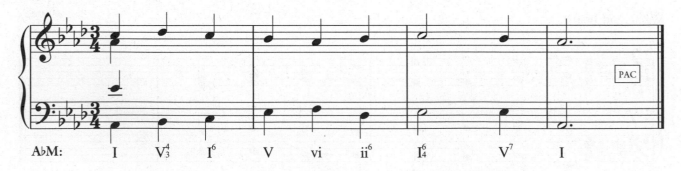

A♭M: I   V$^{4}_{3}$ I^{6} V   vi   ii^{6} I$^{6}_{4}$ V^{7} I

What you heard.

$A\flat M$:   I V^4_3 I^6 V   vi $ii^{\circ 6}$ I^6_4 V^7 I

This example has a passing chord between the I and I^6, in this case a V^4_3, a deceptive progression in measure two, and by now a familiar PAC cadence.

10. Harmonic Dictation in D minor

dm: i V^4_2 i^6 VI $ii^{\circ 6}$ V^6_5/V i^6_4 V^7 VI

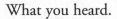

What you heard.

dm: i V^4_2 i^6 VI $ii^{\circ 6}$ V^6_5/V i^6_4 V^7 VI

This exercise requires the use of three accidentals, all in the outside voices and all leading tones. The V^6_5/V does not resolve to the dominant as you expect (so the D in the melody holds) but does resolve to the substitute (I^6_4), which also has *So* in the bass. It ends with a deceptive cadence.

11. Harmonic Dictation in E minor

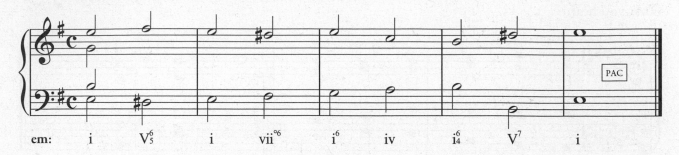

em: i   V$_5^6$ i   vii^{o6} i^6 iv   i$_4^6$ V^7 i

What you heard.

em: i   V$_5^6$ i   vii^{o6} i^6 iv   i$_4^6$ V^7 i

The example in E minor has one tricky chord in the second measure – the vii^{o6} triad. It is acting as a passing chord between the i and i^6.

12. Harmonic Dictation in B♭ Major

B♭M: I   V$_4^6$ I^6 V^7/IV   IV   ii   V   V^7 I

What you heard.

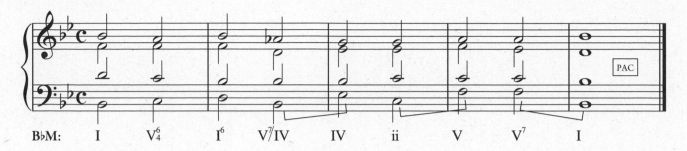

This last example in B♭ Major has a circle progression from the fourth chord to the end. This particular example is easier to hear since all the chords are in root position. You must recognize that this **So-So-Do** ending is not the I$_4^6$, but the V followed by the V^7.

Strategies for Harmonizing a Melody: FR 7

21

REVIEW THE PROCESS

In Chapter 9 we learned the fundamentals of how to harmonize a melody. This portion of the AP Music Theory exam is challenging because it requires the student to understand melodies and their implied harmonies, harmonic progression, cadences, and counterpoint. It can be overwhelming because of the fact that there are many possible correct solutions—not just one right answer—to harmonizing a melody. Let's review the process and identify strategies for success. This is a timed exam, so:

1. The key is given. Identify notes in the melody using solfege or scale degree numbers. If you need to, write out the I ii$^{(7)}$ IV V$^{(7)}$ vi in a chord stack, then immediately . . .
2. Identify cadences and work them first.
3. Identify possible chord choices and **start phrases with tonic**, if possible.
4. Determine what harmonic rhythm you are going to use. This is when you choose which notes you are going to harmonize and which notes will not be part of the harmony (non-chord tones).
5. Make your selection of the chord and inversion, keeping in mind standard progressions, T-S-D-T (function), the desired contrary motion of the bass against the melody, and **creating a bass line that is a *consonant* counterpoint to the melody**.
6. Check your work to look for parallelism, retrogression, and correct resolution of tendency tones if they are in the bass (such as V$^4_2$–I^6).

THE MENU

These are the choices that are easiest to work with and will create the necessary progressions that are the *norm* of common-practice style. *Prepare* for the possibility of chromatic harmony. KISS—Keep It Simple for Success—it is not necessary to use iii, vii°, or vii°^{7} chords in FR 7.

			(F)		(B♭)
C	D	F	D	G	A
A	B♭	D	B♮	E	F
F	G	B♭	G	C	D
F: I	**ii**(7)	**IV**	**V⁷/V**	**V**(7)	**vi**

Most common
(but not only) choice

> Is there a chromatic (non-diatonic) note in the melody? Look for the accidental and the note it **leads to**. The accidental is *usually* a leading tone in a new key and the note the accidental leads *to* is the new tonic.

TIPS FOR WRITING CADENCES

- Use *only* I/i, vi/VI, or V as the last chord of a cadence
- Do *not* invert at the cadence
- Write a PAC for the last (final) cadence

> These are the *most common* melodic endings. Harmonize with the *norm* for all cadences.

Authentic Cadences (V–I)

- **IF** the final cadence melody ends with *Mi-Re-Do* ($\hat{3}$–$\hat{2}$–$\hat{1}$) or *Do-Ti-Do* ($\hat{1}$–$\hat{7}$–$\hat{1}$) or *Do-Re-Do* ($\hat{1}$–$\hat{2}$–$\hat{1}$), **THEN** harmonize with *So-So-Do*—meaning chord progression I$^6_4$–V$^{(7)}$–I.
- Use I$^6_4$ on a **strong beat** followed by the V or V⁷ on a weak beat:

> *So-So-Do* is the most common bass ending!

- **IF** the melody ends with (final cadence) *Re-Ti-Do* ($\hat{2}$–$\hat{7}$–$\hat{1}$) or possibly *Fa-Ti-Do* ($\hat{4}$–$\hat{7}$–$\hat{1}$) or even *Do-Ti-Do* ($\hat{1}$–$\hat{7}$–$\hat{1}$) **THEN** harmonize with *Fa-So-Do* in the bass and the chord progression: ii⁶–V–I or IV–V–I.

> *Fa-So-Do* is the second most common bass ending!

Half Cadences (V)

- In FR 7 at least one cadence will usually end the phrase with a *So*, *Ti*, or *Re*.

  - If the melody ends with *Ti* ($\hat{7}$) or *Re* ($\hat{2}$) your *only* choice is a half cadence.
  - *So* ($\hat{5}$) could be half cadence or an IAC.

- **IF** you harmonize as a half cadence, **THEN** write a **root position V**.
- What comes *before* V? The same three chords that came before V in the PAC: I^6_4, ii^6, or IV.

  - Harmonize *Re*, *Fa*, or *La* in the melody with *Fa* in the bass and IV or ii^6.
  - Harmonize *Do*, *Mi*, or *So* in the melody with *So* in bass and I^6_4.
  - The **Phrygian half** cadence (iv^6–V) occurs only in minor. The bass line *must be* *Le-So* and the melody is commonly *Fa-So*.

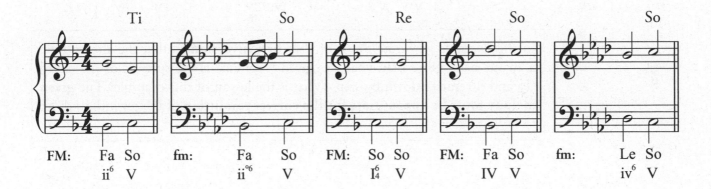

One of these examples is *not* correct. Which one?

> Here's where you must be careful not to write parallel octaves between the bass and soprano. If the melody is *Fa-So*, it does indeed imply ii^6 to V or IV to V; however, do *not* write the same thing in the bass that is in the soprano. The second example creates parallel octaves B♭ to C even though the passing tone moves the B♭ to beat 2. It is still parallel octaves and is considered an egregious error.

- **IF** two cadences both end with *So* ($\hat{5}$), both could be a half cadence or one could be a half cadence and one an IAC.
- **IF** the melody (in this case at a cadence) ends with *So* and is preceded by *Fi* (the raised 4th scale degree), **THEN** harmonize *Fi* with root position V/V or V⁷/V and *So* with root position V.

In this example we wrote the V of V in **first inversion** so that the altered note is in the bass. Note that what was given (soprano) is the seventh of the chord (F) and it resolves down by step. What is the lesson of this example? The **given melody must be appropriate for the correct resolution** of the seventh in order to harmonize it this way.

Deceptive Cadences (V–vi or V–VI)

- What pitches in the melody would imply a deceptive cadence? *Do* or *Mi* ($\hat{1}$–$\hat{3}$). Why not *La*? Because with *La* in the soprano and *La* in the bass you would have parallel octaves! If the phrase end is *Mi* or *So*, you have choices: PAC or DC.
- **IF** you harmonize with a deceptive cadence, **THEN** the two-chord progression should be root position V–vi (V–VI in minor).
- What comes *before* V? Haven't we already answered that question? *Predominant* harmony ii⁶ or IV; or I⁶₄ **IF** it is on a strong beat.

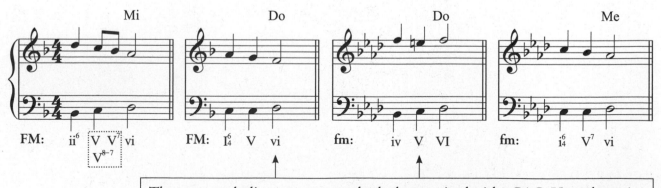

These two melodic patterns may also be harmonized with a PAC. Use a deceptive cadence if this melodic pattern is phrase 2 or 3. Use a PAC if this pattern ends the final phrase.

Plagal Cadence (IV–I or iv–i)

- What pitches in the melody might imply a plagal cadence? *Fa*, *La*, or *Do* (the IV chord—$\hat{4}$–$\hat{6}$–$\hat{1}$) going to *Do*, *Mi*, *So* (the I chord—$\hat{1}$–$\hat{3}$–$\hat{5}$).
- What melodic endings *usually* produce a plagal cadence? *Fa-Mi* (*Fa-Me* in minor) or *La-So* (*Le-So*) are the two most common. For either of these phrase endings harmonize with root position IV–I (or iv–i in minor).

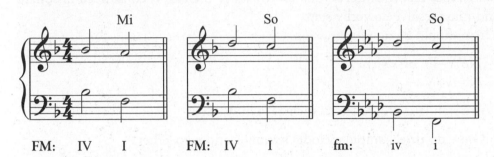

TIPS FOR WRITING PHRASE BEGINNINGS

Once all the cadences have been written you have completed half the exercise! Here are a few tips for beginning each phrase:

- Observe the melody of the first phrase that has been harmonized for you. Are any of the other phrases similar? Sometimes you can gain insight and even clues by studying what has been done for you in the first cadence. Look at the melodic patterns and see if you can use the same progression.
- What is the last chord written? Does it contain an imperative resolution? The last chord is often written as V^6 or V^6_5, *requiring* the next chord to be I, or a V^4_2, *requiring* the next chord to be I^6.
- Remember that a new phrase is just like starting over—you do *not* have to resolve tendency tones. For example, if the cadence ends with V and the next chord you write is I, *Ti* does not have to resolve to *Do* because the tonic chord starts the new phrase.
- As we have seen in our study of progression and harmonic dictation, the beginning of phrases generally starts with tonic and very often returns to tonic on the third or fourth chord. Most common bass lines that begin phrases are:

  - I–V^6–I   same bass if it is I–V^6_5–I = ***Do-Ti-Do***
  - I–IV^6_4–I   creating a pedal in the bass = ***Do-Do-Do***
  - I–V^6_4–I^6 creating a passing tone bass with V^4_3 = ***Do-Re-Mi***

TIPS FOR WRITING EVERYTHING ELSE

- You do *not* have to harmonize every single beat.
- Do not use non-chord tones in the bass (**KISS**).
- Do not invert carelessly. Second inversion $^6_4$ chords, in particular, must have a function—cadential (strong beat), passing, or pedal (weak beat).
- Do *not* use seventh chords except at cadences.
- Remember that the interval of a fourth above the bass is considered dissonant and must resolve down by step.
- There should be no retrogression.

  - No V–IV or V–ii⁶
  - No ii–IV

- Write standard progressions, such as vi–ii–V–I.

We will now do three sample melodic harmonizations together.

EXAMPLE 1 IN F MAJOR

What do we know for sure?

After identifying the scale degree numbers or solfege of the melody we can determine that the use of **Fi** in measure 4 requires a chord outside of F Major and the B♭ at the end of the measure is simply the return to the diatonic 4th scale degree. Phrase 2 (the "Start here" phrase) cadence will have a secondary dominant resolving to the dominant to create a half cadence. Phrase 3 ends on **Re**; therefore, the cadence must also be a half cadence. Why? Because the chords ending a cadence are *only* I, V, or vi. The only chord that includes $\hat{2}$ or **Re** is the V; therefore, it is a half cadence. The fourth phrase ends with **Mi-Re-Do**; that's our signal to write I$_4^6$–V^7–I in the bass for a PAC.

STEP 1: Complete the cadences.

The Phrase 2 cadence chords function as V–I in the key of C Major, signaled by the B♮ (the leading tone in C Major). It is in root position, as are the two cadence chords in Phrase 3, to keep it simple.

STEP 2: Start the phrases with I (tonic), if possible, then decide on the harmonic rhythm.

This establishes what notes are to be harmonized and what notes are to be considered non-chord tones. It is not necessary to harmonize every beat and do *not* harmonize every NOTE when eighth notes are added to the melody. Do not use non-chord tones in the bass line. When in doubt, list the choices for possible harmonization.

STEP 3: Fill in the beats between the cadences.

Notice the anacrusis to Phrase 3 is *Fa* leading to *Mi*. We harmonized it with a root position V^7 resolving to I. Measure 6 has *Fa-Mi* in the melody as well, which we also harmonized with a V^7.

The numbers between the staves represent the intervals between the soprano and bass. Remember you are creating a consonant counterpoint. This system of checking also quickly shows if you have parallel fifths or octaves.

EXAMPLE 2 IN G MAJOR

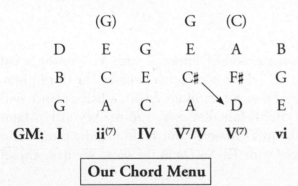

Our Chord Menu

What do we know for sure?

The harmonization of beat 3 in measure 3 with a V tells us the B is functioning as an accented passing tone and is an NCT. The use of the *Fi* in measure 6 requires a chord outside of G Major and the C♮ in measure 7 is simply the return to the diatonic 4th scale degree.

STEP 1: Complete the cadences.

We have harmonized the cadence at the end of Phrase 2 with V, creating a half cadence. The note in the melody is *Ti*—there is no other choice. The third phrase ends with $\hat{5}$ (*So*) but is preceded by *Fi*, so we harmonize with a half cadence with a secondary dominant. Those two chords function as V–I in the key of D Major, signaled by the C♯ (the leading tone in D Major). Our final melodic phrase ends with *Re-Ti-Do*, which we know goes with *Fa-So-Do* in the bass. We have chosen ii⁶–V–I. Aim for contrary motion.

STEP 2: Start with I (tonic) if possible, then decide on the harmonic rhythm.
This establishes what notes are to be harmonized and what notes are to be considered non-chord tones. Remember you only need two chords per measure. It is not necessary to harmonize every beat and do *not* harmonize every note when eighth notes are added to the melody.

Do not use non-chord tones in the bass line. When in doubt, list the three (sometimes four) choices for possible harmonization.

STEP 3: Fill in the beats between the cadences.

Remember that each phrase is like starting at the beginning. In Phrase 2 we used tonic and dominant harmony and chose to use the tonic triad in root position in both places and the dominant triad in first inversion. Why? First, it provides contrary motion. Second, if we had used all root-position triads we would have P8–P5–P8–M3 in the counterpoint between bass and soprano. By inverting the dominant triad we have P8–m3–P8–M3 and eliminated the direct fifth and direct octave (similar motion into a perfect interval in bass–soprano voice pair). The last phrase works nicely harmonizing the C♮ with the supertonic and identifying the B as a passing tone, and using the suggested progression of vi–ii–V–I to end the phrase. It works well by using the supertonic in the common first-inversion position for the *Fa-So-Do* bass line.

The third phrase ends with a half cadence preceded by the V of V in root position. In measure 5 we have chosen to harmonize beats 1 *and* 2 with tonic to keep it simple. The B is a passing tone. The IV⁶ leads us "gracefully" to V⁶ where *Ti* must go to *Do*.

Step 4: Check your work!
   ✔ Is there contrary motion between the bass and soprano? Check for parallelism.
   ✔ Does the progression follow the T–PD–D–T progression?
   ✔ If you have written V–I or V–vi OR used a seventh chord in any inversion, do the tendency tones resolve?
   ✔ Have you written viable cadences with only I, V, or vi at the fermatas? Are cadence chords (two chords per cadence) in root position?

EXAMPLE 3 IN A♭ MAJOR

A♭M: I   vii°⁶   I⁶   I   IV   V   I

STEP 1: Complete the cadences first.
Create the chord stack in the key. Label the melody using solfege or numbers if this technique is helpful. Watch your time!

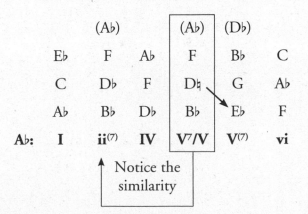

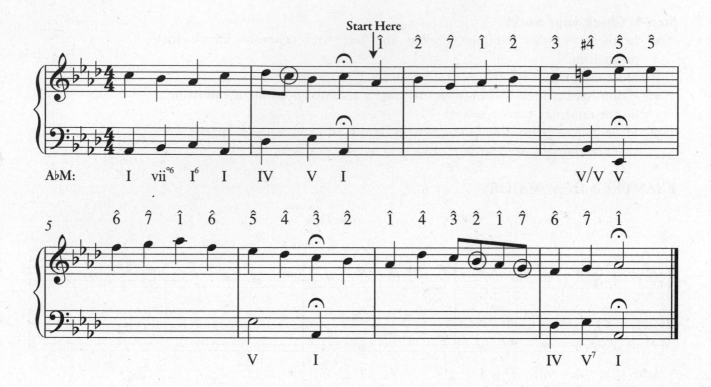

We notice in Phrase 1 the use of the leading-tone triad in first inversion leading to I⁶ (the NORM) forming an ascending pattern in the bass and ending with an IAC. Phrase 2 features *Fi* passing between *Mi* and *So* at the cadence, and the third and fourth phrase both look like they imply dominant–tonic harmony.

STEP 2: Decide on the harmonic rhythm. Determine available choices starting with I if possible.

To avoid a direct fifth we started the second phrase with I^6 and harmonized both $\hat{2}$ and $\hat{7}$ in measure 3 with root position V. Once again we choose a I^6 because an A♭ here would have created parallel octaves. The V^6_4 on beat 4 is a passing $^6_4$. Notice the segment in the box is essentially in the temporary key of E♭ Major so the progression vi^6–V/V–V is the same as ii^6–V–I in the key of the dominant. We begin Phrase 3 with root position tonic and once again employ ii^6–V–I leaving only one more chord before completing Phrase 3. We decided to see what it would look like if we opt to use two quarter notes for V and V^7 in the next measure. Looks good! Now we fill in the remaining blanks.

STEP 3: Fill in the beats between the cadences.

Phrases 3 and 4 both lend themselves to the use of dominant seventh chords. In Phrase 3 the $\hat{4}$–$\hat{3}$ melodic pattern provides the correct resolution of the seventh and again in Phrase 4 where this time we started the phrase with the familiar I–V$^6_5$–I and ***Do-Ti-Do*** in the bass.

STEP 4: Check your work!

Remember, there's more than one way to harmonize a melody, just as there are many possible solutions to the part-writing examples.

✔ Is there contrary motion most often between the bass and soprano? Check for parallelism.

✔ Does the progression follow the T–S–D–T progression?

✔ If you have written V–I or V–vi OR used a seventh chord in any inversion, do the tendency tones resolve?

✔ Have you written viable cadences with only I, V, or vi at the fermatas? Are cadence chords in root position?

A FEW MORE COMMENTS ABOUT EXAM STRATEGY

Since time is limited to 45 minutes to accomplish both part-writing examples (FR 5 and 6) *and* harmonizing the melody (FR7), I suggest you *begin* with FR7. Identify the melody with solfege or numbers and complete all three cadences. Then go directly to the part-writing exercises and complete both. Finish harmonizing the melody with your remaining time. In this way you will be sure to earn 3 points (out of 8) for correctly completing the cadences should you run out of time. Make sure you practice timing yourself on these three free-response questions.

Additional Practice Examples

1.

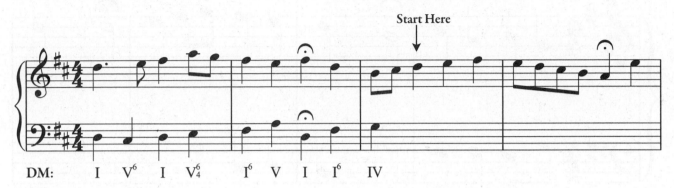

- Complete the cadences first. You are looking for standard patterns so you can write standard progression. Remember you are writing in common-practice style.
- Look for familiar patterns in the melody, such as *Fa* to *Mi*, that imply harmonization (V^7–I).
- Remember to use contrary motion more than similar motion.
- Observe T–S–D–T.
- Keep it simple. Use root position primary chords (I, ii, IV, V).

2.

Start Here

GM: I   vi   V⁶   V⁶₅   I   I⁶   IV   V⁴₂

5

3.

E♭M: I V$_4^6$ I^6 V$_5^6$ I ii V I IV IV^6 V

5

POSSIBLE SOLUTIONS

1.

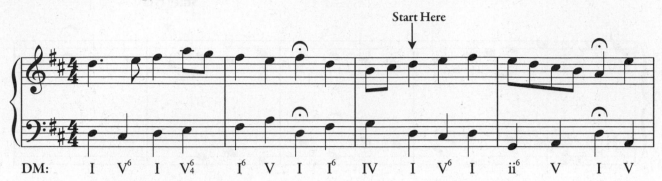

Comments

Phrase 2 ends with an IAC. Phrase 3 ends with an HC with secondary dominant (G♯ is *Fi*), and the final cadence is PAC. Although the ending melody is *Mi-Re-Do*, we did not harmonize with *So-So-Do* and the I$^6_4$. Why? The I$^6_4$ chord should occur on a *strong* beat and not on beat 4 of the measure. The V$^6_4$ in measure 7 is a passing $^6_4$ chord, and the eighth note in measure 5 is not part of the implied harmony. It is a passing tone.

2.

Comments

The Start Here phrase must begin with a I^6 as it follows the V^4_2. The second fermata is ***So***; therefore, it can be harmonized with a I or a V. The third phrase has ***Fi-So*** implying secondary harmony and the final phrase ***Mi-Re-Do***.

3.

Comments

The third fermata has ***Do*** in the melody and can be harmonized with an authentic cadence or a deceptive cadence. Notice I harmonized the last phrase with the same three chords as the opening phrase, gathering inspiration from what was already written and using the $^6_4$ chord.

Strategies for Sight-Singing

22

For many students the prospect of having to sing two melodies on the AP exam can be a frightening and traumatic experience. It doesn't have to be. In order to be truly confident, or at least reasonably comfortable, you have to do one thing—practice singing. The students who do not do well on the exam are those who gave up in the beginning. Remember, it is not about being perfect, although many will sing the examples flawlessly. It is about demonstrating what you *can* do to the best of your ability. That means staying calm and focused and singing as much of the exercise as correctly you can, recovering if you falter. Many students feel a certain amount of anxiety because it is as close to "performing" as there is on the exam. If that is the case, take steps to eliminate anxiety just like you would if you were about to sing a solo on stage: Take deep breaths, have centered and focused thought, and *prepare* ahead of time.

FIVE TIPS FOR SUCCESSFUL SIGHT-SINGING

TIP
1   **Sing!**

Sing every day. Sing for five minutes a day while you're fixing your hair or driving to school. Establish a routine. Sing the scale degree finder in major and then repeat it in minor. Sing a major scale and intervals, plus the scale in thirds. Sing it in the parallel minor. Sing the tendency tone patterns:

Do-Mi-So-Mi-Do//Fa-Mi//La-So//Ti-Do//Re-Do//So-Do

Combine the Top Ten Melodic Patterns into these three exercises. Sing in major and minor.

1. *Do-Re-Mi-Fi-So-Fa-Mi-Re-Do-Mi-So-Mi-Do-↓So-La-Ti-Do*
2. *↓So-Do-Mi-Re-Fa-Mi-So-Fa-La-So-Mi-Fa-Re-Mi-Do-Re-Ti-Do*
   (*↓So* to *Do* is an anacrusis)
3. *Do-Ti-Do-Mi-So-So-Do   Do-Re-Mi-Do-Fa-So-Do*
   I V⁶ I I⁶ I⁶₄ V I   I V⁶₄ I⁶ I ii⁶ V I
   Now you're connecting the dots!

(This is a bass line.
What chords are implied?)

507

TIP 2

Have a strategy.

Plan to sing with syllables, numbers, or just on *La*. Don't sing nonsense, don't sing "tut" (too much "T" sound), but do sing with the same system each and every time a new melody is sung. Do not whistle and do not hum. Practice a "Plan B"—attempt the solfege and if you get flustered, then drop the syllables and go with *Dah* or *Lah* or even *Noo* (New). Solfege can be a valuable tool to help determine interval and pitch; however, some students feel that if they are not completely comfortable, it almost seems like singing in a foreign language where using the right "words" outweigh the desired goal—correct pitch and rhythm.

TIP 3

Perform with a *steady* tempo and a slower tempo.

Do not start and stop when you sing. You get one point for *not hesitating*. It is called the "flow point." The flow of the melody is an important part of the evaluation, so your performance needs to be consistent and steady. You don't get points for singing fast, or with vibrato or great tone quality. If you sing very slowly, make sure you are prepared for holding out long notes the appropriate length.

TIP 4

Be rhythmically accurate.

Make sure you give full durational value to the rhythms you sing, particularly with the last note of the melody. Students often sing a perfect melody and then lose one full point because the last note is not held to full duration. This is most common in compound meter when the last note is usually a dotted quarter note.

TIP 5

Know your own range and the range of the example.

This is so important. The exam will present the first note of the example that is to be sung (usually *Do*). You do *not* have to sing it in that key. However, you must maintain the key (and tempo) you establish with your first two notes. One of the examples will be in bass clef. Women are not expected to sing the example in bass clef, but in their own range. If you have a comfortable range of one octave look at the example and see how far below and above *Do* it is written. Rarely will both examples start on low *Do* (1̂) and extend to high *Do* (8̂). What is common is for the example to start on 1̂, move below *Do* to *So*, and then move above *Do* also to *So* or to *La*, usually ending on the original *Do*. You may indeed have to sing an octave, but the octave may be between low *So* and high *So* and not from *Do* to *Do*. Therefore, if you begin the example singing on the lowest note of your range you have nowhere to go. **Determine what note is the center of the example and make that note the center of your range.**

OTHER HINTS

Here are some more helpful tips:

1. Practice the melody *out loud*. Start singing from the second your time begins. Sing while you circle or write, or simply start singing at the beginning and work through to the end. Sing strong and confidently. Don't be afraid of your own voice.

2. Check the clef. One example will be in bass and one will be in treble.

3. Check the key signature and determine the key you are to sing in. This information is *not* given. You must make that identification and begin practicing immediately. One example will be in major and one will be in minor.

4. Determine the meter, establish your beat and tempo, look for tricky rhythms, and tap out the rhythm. One will be in simple meter and one will be in compound.

5. Sing the scale associated with the example (major or minor) and the tonic triad including low *So*: Î–Ŝ–Ŝ–Ŝ–Î–↓Ŝ–Î.

6. **Look for the patterns.** There will be many familiar patterns and very often ***Do-Mi-So*** or ***Do-Re-Mi*** at the beginning.

7. With a pencil, (yes, pencils are allowed in sight-singing) circle all the ***Dos*** and also mark any "tricky" solfege. You do *not* need to pencil in every single solfege syllable—it takes way too long and you have only 75 seconds. Remember, while you are marking you should be singing.

8. Look for the tricky melodic patterns, perhaps a ***Fa-Fi-So***, an awkward leap, or a tricky rhythm. Isolate that tricky place and practice that. Sometimes you can "find" a pitch by working up the scale or down the scale or by using the Scale Degree Finder.

9. Work out any places that fell apart or that were incorrect.

10. Perform the melody again correctly before the practice time is over.

Understand about scoring.

Scoring the sight-singing portion of the exam is done in half-measure segments. In $\frac{4}{4}$ time that is the equivalent of two quarter notes and in $\frac{6}{8}$ time it is the equivalent of three eighth notes. For every half-measure segment that is correct in pitch and rhythm, one point is awarded; plus one point is awarded for *not hesitating*—the "flow point." The high score is 9 points. Alternate scoring is also possible through grading of pitch only (high score is 4 points) or rhythm only (high score is 2 points).

As you are preparing for the sight-singing portion of the exam:

• Practice the way you will do it on the exam.
• Limit your practice time to 75 seconds.
• After 75 seconds, sing the example straight through **once** with no stops.
• Record your performance if possible.
• After performing, review your mistakes and determine whether it was the correct melody by playing it on the piano or another instrument.
• Ask your teacher to help with the scoring for a more accurate assessment of your skill.

Melodies for Sight-Singing Practice

These examples are comparable to sight-singing Questions 1 and 2.

8.

9. Now try the same melody in the relative minor with a "twist." Note that A♭ Major in bass clef and F minor in treble clef look exactly the same on the staff.

10. Notice the three-note melodic sequence in the first three beats: each time the motif is up a m3 and the note below is a half step. The second phrase includes a natural minor descending pattern.

11. This example contains **Di**—raised scale degree $\hat{1}$. Harmonically it would be V/ii. The E natural is the leading tone of F (Major or minor).

12.

13.

14.

15.

La-Si-La is V/vi; F♯ is the leading tone in the relative key of G minor.

16.

17.

18.

19. Be careful.

20.

21.

22.

23.

24.

PRACTICE TESTS

In this section, you will have the opportunity to test your knowledge. The following tests were modeled after the actual AP Music Theory exam. Each exam is approximately 2 hours and 40 minutes long, with a total of 84 questions, including 2 sight-singing questions. Section I is worth 45 percent of the total grade; Section II is worth 55 percent.

Answer all of the multiple-choice questions on the answer sheet provided. Note that five spaces are provided on the answer sheet but only four answer choices are given on the exam. Do not fill in answer choice E. This is similar to the format you will see on the actual exam. Remember that you are only filling in answer choices A–D.

Write your answers to the Section II free-response questions on the staves provided for each question. If you need scratch paper you may use a separate sheet of blank paper or staff paper. Have a recording device handy for the sight-singing section (Section II, Part B). You may wish to review your sight-singing with your teacher to see how you might have been graded.

NOTE: The AP Music Theory exam has only four answer choices, A–D. Do not mark choice E.

SECTION I: PART A

1. Ⓐ Ⓑ Ⓒ Ⓓ Ⓔ	12. Ⓐ Ⓑ Ⓒ Ⓓ Ⓔ	23. Ⓐ Ⓑ Ⓒ Ⓓ Ⓔ	34. Ⓐ Ⓑ Ⓒ Ⓓ Ⓔ
2. Ⓐ Ⓑ Ⓒ Ⓓ Ⓔ	13. Ⓐ Ⓑ Ⓒ Ⓓ Ⓔ	24. Ⓐ Ⓑ Ⓒ Ⓓ Ⓔ	35. Ⓐ Ⓑ Ⓒ Ⓓ Ⓔ
3. Ⓐ Ⓑ Ⓒ Ⓓ Ⓔ	14. Ⓐ Ⓑ Ⓒ Ⓓ Ⓔ	25. Ⓐ Ⓑ Ⓒ Ⓓ Ⓔ	36. Ⓐ Ⓑ Ⓒ Ⓓ Ⓔ
4. Ⓐ Ⓑ Ⓒ Ⓓ Ⓔ	15. Ⓐ Ⓑ Ⓒ Ⓓ Ⓔ	26. Ⓐ Ⓑ Ⓒ Ⓓ Ⓔ	37. Ⓐ Ⓑ Ⓒ Ⓓ Ⓔ
5. Ⓐ Ⓑ Ⓒ Ⓓ Ⓔ	16. Ⓐ Ⓑ Ⓒ Ⓓ Ⓔ	27. Ⓐ Ⓑ Ⓒ Ⓓ Ⓔ	38. Ⓐ Ⓑ Ⓒ Ⓓ Ⓔ
6. Ⓐ Ⓑ Ⓒ Ⓓ Ⓔ	17. Ⓐ Ⓑ Ⓒ Ⓓ Ⓔ	28. Ⓐ Ⓑ Ⓒ Ⓓ Ⓔ	39. Ⓐ Ⓑ Ⓒ Ⓓ Ⓔ
7. Ⓐ Ⓑ Ⓒ Ⓓ Ⓔ	18. Ⓐ Ⓑ Ⓒ Ⓓ Ⓔ	29. Ⓐ Ⓑ Ⓒ Ⓓ Ⓔ	40. Ⓐ Ⓑ Ⓒ Ⓓ Ⓔ
8. Ⓐ Ⓑ Ⓒ Ⓓ Ⓔ	19. Ⓐ Ⓑ Ⓒ Ⓓ Ⓔ	30. Ⓐ Ⓑ Ⓒ Ⓓ Ⓔ	41. Ⓐ Ⓑ Ⓒ Ⓓ Ⓔ
9. Ⓐ Ⓑ Ⓒ Ⓓ Ⓔ	20. Ⓐ Ⓑ Ⓒ Ⓓ Ⓔ	31. Ⓐ Ⓑ Ⓒ Ⓓ Ⓔ	42. Ⓐ Ⓑ Ⓒ Ⓓ Ⓔ
10. Ⓐ Ⓑ Ⓒ Ⓓ Ⓔ	21. Ⓐ Ⓑ Ⓒ Ⓓ Ⓔ	32. Ⓐ Ⓑ Ⓒ Ⓓ Ⓔ	43. Ⓐ Ⓑ Ⓒ Ⓓ Ⓔ
11. Ⓐ Ⓑ Ⓒ Ⓓ Ⓔ	22. Ⓐ Ⓑ Ⓒ Ⓓ Ⓔ	33. Ⓐ Ⓑ Ⓒ Ⓓ Ⓔ	

SECTION I: PART B

44. Ⓐ Ⓑ Ⓒ Ⓓ Ⓔ	52. Ⓐ Ⓑ Ⓒ Ⓓ Ⓔ	60. Ⓐ Ⓑ Ⓒ Ⓓ Ⓔ	68. Ⓐ Ⓑ Ⓒ Ⓓ Ⓔ
45. Ⓐ Ⓑ Ⓒ Ⓓ Ⓔ	53. Ⓐ Ⓑ Ⓒ Ⓓ Ⓔ	61. Ⓐ Ⓑ Ⓒ Ⓓ Ⓔ	69. Ⓐ Ⓑ Ⓒ Ⓓ Ⓔ
46. Ⓐ Ⓑ Ⓒ Ⓓ Ⓔ	54. Ⓐ Ⓑ Ⓒ Ⓓ Ⓔ	62. Ⓐ Ⓑ Ⓒ Ⓓ Ⓔ	70. Ⓐ Ⓑ Ⓒ Ⓓ Ⓔ
47. Ⓐ Ⓑ Ⓒ Ⓓ Ⓔ	55. Ⓐ Ⓑ Ⓒ Ⓓ Ⓔ	63. Ⓐ Ⓑ Ⓒ Ⓓ Ⓔ	71. Ⓐ Ⓑ Ⓒ Ⓓ Ⓔ
48. Ⓐ Ⓑ Ⓒ Ⓓ Ⓔ	56. Ⓐ Ⓑ Ⓒ Ⓓ Ⓔ	64. Ⓐ Ⓑ Ⓒ Ⓓ Ⓔ	72. Ⓐ Ⓑ Ⓒ Ⓓ Ⓔ
49. Ⓐ Ⓑ Ⓒ Ⓓ Ⓔ	57. Ⓐ Ⓑ Ⓒ Ⓓ Ⓔ	65. Ⓐ Ⓑ Ⓒ Ⓓ Ⓔ	73. Ⓐ Ⓑ Ⓒ Ⓓ Ⓔ
50. Ⓐ Ⓑ Ⓒ Ⓓ Ⓔ	58. Ⓐ Ⓑ Ⓒ Ⓓ Ⓔ	66. Ⓐ Ⓑ Ⓒ Ⓓ Ⓔ	74. Ⓐ Ⓑ Ⓒ Ⓓ Ⓔ
51. Ⓐ Ⓑ Ⓒ Ⓓ Ⓔ	59. Ⓐ Ⓑ Ⓒ Ⓓ Ⓔ	67. Ⓐ Ⓑ Ⓒ Ⓓ Ⓔ	75. Ⓐ Ⓑ Ⓒ Ⓓ Ⓔ

Practice Test 1

SECTION I

TOTAL TIME: APPROXIMATELY 80 MINUTES
NUMBER OF QUESTIONS: 75
45% OF TOTAL SCORE

TRACK 142 **Directions:** Each of the questions or incomplete statements below is followed by four suggested answers. Select the best answer in each case and fill in the corresponding circle on the multiple-choice answer sheet. Throughout the exam you will see the treble clef icon, 𝄞, which will let you know when music will be played.

Part A

TIME: APPROXIMATELY 48 MINUTES

Questions 1–6 ask you to identify pitch, interval, melodic patterns, or triads that are played. In each case the question number will be announced. You will have 10 seconds to read the choices; then you will hear the musical example played twice, with a brief pause between playings. Remember to read the choices for each question after the number is announced. Now listen to the music for **Questions 1–6** and identify the patterns that are played.

1. Which of the following pitch patterns is played?

(A)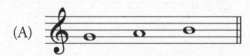

(B)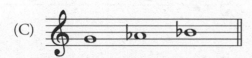

(C)

(D)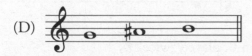

2. Which of the following pitch patterns is played?

(A)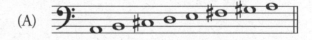

(B)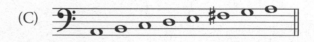

(C)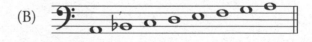

(D)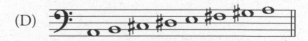

Question 1, played twice. 𝄞

Question 2, played twice. 𝄞

3. Which of the following pitch patterns is played?

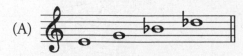

(A)

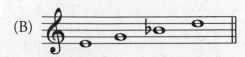

(B)

(C)

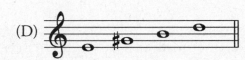

(D)

Question 3, played twice.

4. Which of the following intervals is played?

(A)

(B)

(C)

(D)

Question 4, played twice.

5. Which of the following triads is played?

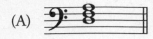

(A)

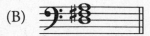

(B)

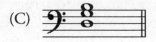

(C)

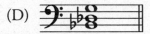

(D)

Question 5, played twice.

6. Which of the following pitch patterns is played?

(A)

(B)

(C)

(D)

Question 6, played twice.

Go on to the next group of questions.

Questions 7–8 ask you to identify rhythm as it is performed within a melody. After the question is announced you will have 10 seconds to read the question. It is important that you read the question and choices carefully before the aural example is given. Each example will be played twice with a brief pause between playings. Now listen to the music for **Questions 7–8**. Identify the rhythm that correctly matches the example that is played.

7. Which of the following rhythms is played?

Question 7, played twice.

8. Which of the following rhythms is played?

Question 8, played twice.

Go on to the next group of questions.

PRACTICE TEST 1

Questions 9–13 are based on an excerpt from a Mozart piano sonata arranged for solo instrument. It contains four phrases. You will hear the excerpt played two times. Before listening to the excerpt for the first time, read **Questions 9–13**.

9. The accompaniment in this excerpt can best be described as:

   (A) a countermelody
   (B) Alberti bass
   (C) contrary motion to the melody
   (D) all tonic harmony

10. The ornamentation used by the melody (soloist) is

    (A) suspension
    (B) trill
    (C) turn
    (D) tremolo

11. At the end of the second phrase the rhythm in the melody demonstrates

    (A) syncopation
    (B) hemiola
    (C) diminution
    (D) augmentation

12. The third phrase begins

    (A) with new material
    (B) as a literal repetition of the first phrase
    (C) with the same melody as the first phrase in the relative minor
    (D) with the same melody as the first phrase in the parallel minor

13. This excerpt ends with a

    (A) Phrygian half cadence
    (B) plagal cadence
    (C) Picardy third
    (D) deceptive cadence in minor

Now listen to the excerpt for the first time and answer **Questions 9–13**.

The excerpt will now be played a second time.

Go on to the next group of questions.

Questions 14–19 are based on an excerpt that has two segments from a work representing the Romantic period. The first segment will be played two times; the second segment will be played once, followed by the entire excerpt played once. Before listening to the first segment for the first time, please read **Questions 14–17**.

14. What is the meter?

    (A) Simple quadruple
    (B) Compound triple
    (C) Simple triple
    (D) Simple duple

15. How would you describe the texture of the first segment?

    (A) Chordal homophony
    (B) Primarily melody with accompaniment
    (C) Heterophonic
    (D) Polyphonic

16. Which of the following performance considerations is featured in this segment?

    (A) Moderato tempo
    (B) Terraced dynamics
    (C) Poco stringendo
    (D) Arco and pizzicato

17. Relative to the opening tonic, the first segment ends in what key?

    (A) Tonic
    (B) Subdominant
    (C) Mediant
    (D) Dominant

Now listen to the first segment for the first time and answer **Questions 14–17**.

The first segment will now be played a second time.

Before listening to the second segment, please read **Questions 18–19**.

18. In the second segment, the melodic material features what compositional device(s)?

    (A) Melodic sequence and imitation
    (B) Melodic inversion and imitation
    (C) Melodic variation
    (D) Melodic augmentation and imitation

19. When the original melody returns, it is the same in all the following ways EXCEPT

    (A) texture
    (B) mode
    (C) articulation
    (D) tempo

Now listen to the second segment and answer **Questions 18–19**.

The entire excerpt will now be played one time.

TRACK
146

Questions 20–25 are based on a piece for piano by Johann Strauss, Jr. After a short introduction, all other phrases contain eight measures. You will hear the first segment played once, the second segment played twice, and then the entire excerpt played once. Before listening to the first segment, read **Questions 20–21**.

20. The meter of this excerpt is

(A) simple duple
(B) simple triple
(C) compound duple
(D) compound triple

21. Segment 1 contains two phrases that create a

(A) parallel period
(B) contrasting period
(C) modulating parallel period
(D) repeated parallel period

Now listen to the first segment for the first time and answer **Questions 20–21**. &

Segment 2 contains **four phrases**. Before listening, read **Questions 22–24**. &

22. The first two phrases begin with the same melody. The cadences at the end of each of these two phrases are

	Phrase 1	Phrase 2
(A)	Imperfect Authentic	Deceptive
(B)	Half	Perfect Authentic
(C)	Imperfect Authentic	Half
(D)	Half	Plagal

23. The third phrase in segment two contains all of the following **except**

(A) descending chromatic scale patterns in the melody
(B) melody with accompaniment texture
(C) broken chord accompaniment
(D) ascending stepwise motion in the bass

24. The last phrase in segment two can be described as all of the following **except**

(A) containing an ascending chromatic scale
(B) acting as a transition into the next segment
(C) a literal repetition
(D) containing oblique motion between the melody and the bass

Now listen to segment two and answer **Questions 22–24**. &

Segment two will now be played a second time. &

Before hearing the full excerpt, read **Question 25**. &

25. The form of this excerpt is

(A) binary
(B) ternary
(C) through-composed
(D) strophic

The full excerpt will be played one time. Answer **Question 25** and review all your answers. &

Go on to the next group of questions.

Questions 26–29 are based on a musical example that will be played four times. The score is printed correctly below; however, what you will hear has several errors in either pitch or rhythm. The questions ask you to identify those errors. Before listening to the example for the first time, read **Questions 26–29** carefully and look at the score.

26. In measure 1, there is an error in the

    (A) rhythm in the treble staff
    (B) pitch in the bass staff
    (C) rhythm in both the treble and bass staff
    (D) pitch in both the treble and bass staff

27. In measure 3, there is an error in

    (A) rhythm in the treble staff
    (B) pitch in the bass staff
    (C) both rhythm and pitch in the treble staff
    (D) both rhythm and pitch in the bass staff

28. In measure 4, there is an error in the

    (A) rhythm in the treble staff
    (B) rhythm in the bass staff
    (C) pitch in the treble staff
    (D) pitch in the bass staff

29. In measure 7, there is an error in

    (A) rhythm in both treble and bass staff
    (B) pitch in both treble and bass staff
    (C) both pitch and rhythm in the treble staff
    (D) both pitch and rhythm in the bass staff

Listen as the entire example will now be played for the first time, and answer **Questions 26–29.**

The example will now be played a second time.

The example will now be played a third time.

The example will now be played a final time. Review your answers for **Questions 26–29.**

Go on to the next group of questions.

Questions 30–32 are based on a short excerpt from a contemporary piano solo. You will hear the excerpt two times. Before listening to the excerpt, please read **Questions 30–32**.

30. Following the introduction, the opening melodic pattern contains which four scale degrees?

(A) $\hat{6}$–$\hat{5}$–$\hat{2}$–$\hat{1}$
(B) $\hat{8}$–$\hat{5}$–$\hat{3}$–$\hat{1}$
(C) $\hat{8}$–$\hat{7}$–$\hat{6}$–$\hat{5}$
(D) $\hat{5}$–$\hat{4}$–$\hat{2}$–$\hat{1}$

31. Taking into consideration that all the phrases are two measures long, what is the time signature?

(A) $\frac{3}{4}$

(B) $\frac{4}{4}$

(C) $\frac{6}{8}$

(D) $\frac{12}{8}$

32. What compositional technique is used in this excerpt?

(A) Change of meter
(B) Retrograde
(C) Fragmentation
(D) Diminution

The excerpt will now be played for the first time.

The excerpt will now be played a final time.

Go on to the next group of questions.

Questions 33–38 are based on an excerpt in two segments of a Celtic reel. The first segment includes four phrases that will be played twice. The second segment also has four phrases and will be played once, followed by the playing of the entire excerpt. Before listening to the first segment for the first time, please read **Questions 33–35**.

33. In the opening melody, what is the prominent rhythmic motive?

(A)

(B)

(C)

(D)

34. On what interval above the first instrument does the second instrument enter?

(A) 4th
(B) 6th
(C) 5th
(D) 3rd

35. Which of the following best describes the texture after the entrance of the third instrument?

(A) Imitative polyphony
(B) Melody with accompaniment
(C) Homophonic
(D) Monophonic

Now listen to the first segment played for the first time and answer **Questions 33–35**.

The first segment will now be played a second time.

Before listening to the second segment, please read **Questions 36–37**.

36. Compared to the first phrase, the second phrase of this section features

(A) an exact repetition
(B) a change of tessitura
(C) a harmonization of the original melody
(D) a shift of modality

37. The third and fourth phrases feature

(A) imitative polyphony
(B) a melodic inversion
(C) a sequential repetition
(D) an added rhythmic accompaniment

The second segment will now be played once.

Before listening to the **entire excerpt**, please read **Question 38** and review all your answers for **Questions 33–38**.

38. The form of this excerpt can best be identified as

(A) ABBA
(B) AABA
(C) AABC
(D) ABCB

The entire excerpt will now be played.

Go on to the next group of questions.

PRACTICE TEST 1

Questions 39–43 are based on an excerpt from an aria in an opera by Handel. You will hear one segment containing two phrases. The excerpt will be played three times. Before listening to the first playing, read **Questions 39–43.**

39. In this meter the half note gets the beat. What is the time signature?

(A) Alla breve
(B) $\frac{2}{2}$
(C) $\frac{9}{4}$
(D) $\frac{3}{2}$

40. The melody begins on what scale degree?

(A) 1
(B) 2
(C) 3
(D) 4

41. The tempo marking that applies to this excerpt is

(A) Largo
(B) Andante
(C) Allegro
(D) Maestoso

42. The harmonic progression for the excerpt (both phrases) is

(A) I – – | ii^7 – – | V$^{4-3}$ – – | I – – | IV – – | V$^4_2$ I^6 – | ii$^6_5$ I$^6_4$ V | I

(B) I – – | IV – – | V – – | V – – | I – – | IV I^6 – | ii I$^6_4$ V | I

(C) I – – | IV – – | V^6 – – | I – – | IV – – | V$^4_2$ I^6 – | ii$^6_5$ V V^7 | vi

(D) I – – | ii^7 – – | V^6 – – | I – – | V – – | V$^4_2$ I^6 – | I I V | I

43. The non-chord tone at the final cadence is

(A) Upper neighbor
(B) Escape tone
(C) Suspension
(D) Anticipation

Now listen to the excerpt for the first time and answer **Questions 39–43.**

The excerpt will now be played a second time.

The excerpt will now be played a final time.

THIS IS THE END OF PART A

Part B

TIME: 35 MINUTES

44. What pitch is subdominant in the relative major of F♯ minor?

    (A) B
    (B) C♯
    (C) D
    (D) D♯

45. All of the following are diminished fifths except

    (A)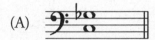

    (B)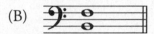

    (C)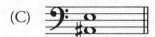

    (D)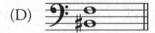

46. Which of the following is ii°7 in C♯ minor?

    (A)

    (B)

    (C)

    (D)

47. Which of the following scales represents the Phrygian mode?

    (A)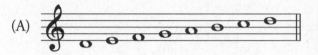

    (B)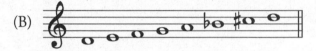

    (C)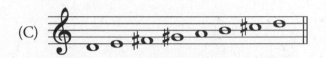

    (D)

48. The durational value that represents the beat in the time signature $\frac{6}{4}$ is a

    (A) quarter note
    (B) dotted quarter note
    (C) dotted half note
    (D) half note

49. In what key would this chord function as the V^6_5/ii ?

    (A) B♭ Major
    (B) F minor
    (C) E♭ Major
    (D) F Major

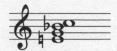

50. If the raised submediant pitch is C♯, the key signature is

    (A)

    (B)

    (C)

    (D)

Questions 51–53 are based on the melody printed below.

51. Which of the following meter signatures best fits this melody?

    (A) $\frac{6}{8}$
    (B) $\frac{9}{8}$
    (C) $\frac{6}{4}$
    (D) $\frac{2}{4}$

52. The melody contains all of the following EXCEPT a

    (A) secondary dominant
    (B) melodic minor pattern
    (C) natural minor pattern
    (D) rhythmic augmentation

53. What cadence would harmonize the half note in measure 2?

    (A) Imperfect authentic
    (B) Plagal
    (C) Half
    (D) Deceptive

Questions 54–57 are based on the following four-part harmonic example. There are four errors in this example that do not adhere to strict eighteenth-century guidelines for doubling, spacing, and voice-leading. Choose the answer that best describes the errors in the indicated chords.

54. The error at chord 4 is

    (A) overlapping voices
    (B) an incorrect chord spelling
    (C) an unresolved chordal seventh
    (D) an error in spacing

55. The error between chords 6 and 7 is

    (A) unequal fifths
    (B) an unresolved chordal seventh
    (C) crossed voices
    (D) an improperly resolved leading tone

56. The error between chords 7 and 8 is

    (A) an error in spacing that is the result of parallel fifths
    (B) parallel octaves
    (C) oblique motion
    (D) an incorrect chord member

57. The error between chords 11 and 12 is

    (A) crossed voices
    (B) parallel fifths
    (C) unresolved chordal seventh
    (D) an improperly resolved leading tone

58. Which term indicates the general range of a melody or voice part that presents the most characteristic timbre?

   (A) Obbligato
   (B) Tremelo
   (C) Tessitura
   (D) Melisma

59. The non-chord tone in this example is

   (A) a retardation
   (B) an appoggiatura
   (C) a 4–3 suspension
   (D) an escape tone

Questions 60–63 accompany the following excerpt of a string quartet.

String Quartet No. 17 in Bb Major
Excerpt

Wolfgang Amadeus Mozart
(1756–1791)
K. 458

60. The key of the excerpt is best identified as

    (A) C Major
    (B) B♭ Major
    (C) G minor
    (D) F Major

61. What chord occurs on the downbeat of measure 101?

    (A) V^7
    (B) V
    (C) ii^7
    (D) $vii°^7$

62. Which of the following figures prominently throughout the excerpt?

    (A) Arpeggiation
    (B) Use of suspensions
    (C) Secondary dominant chords
    (D) Syncopation

63. The cadence in measures 105–106 signals a shift to the key of the

    (A) dominant
    (B) relative minor
    (C) parallel minor
    (D) subdominant

Questions 64–68 accompany Schubert's 36 *Original Dances, #33*

36 Original Dances (First Waltzes), Op 9, No. 33

Franz Schubert
(1797–1828)
D. 365

64. Which of the following best represents the harmonic rhythm of measures 5–8?

(A)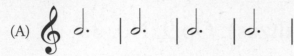

(B)

(C)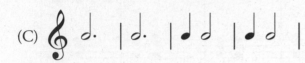

(D)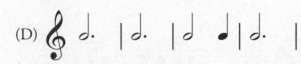

65. Measures 14–24 show a temporary shift into what key?

(A) A♭ Major
(B) E♭ Major
(C) F minor
(D) D♭ Major

66. The cadence in measures 15–16 can best be described as

(A) half cadence
(B) plagal cadence
(C) perfect authentic cadence
(D) imperfect authentic cadence

67. The D in the upper voice on beat 3 of both measures 1 and 2 is best described as

(A) an accented passing tone
(B) an unaccented passing tone
(C) an accented upper neighbor tone
(D) a chord tone

68. The first two phrases of this excerpt (measures 1–8) are identified as a

(A) repeated period
(B) contrasting period
(C) parallel period
(D) modulating period

Questions 69–71 are based on this short excerpt of *Salve Regina* by Couperin.

Salve Regina

F. Couperin
(1668–1733)

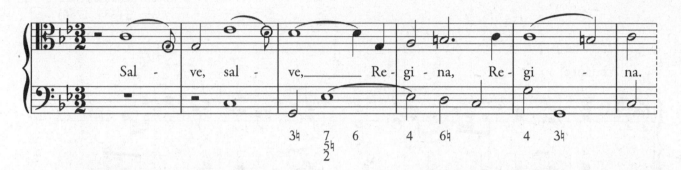

69. The meter and key of this excerpt is

   (A) simple triple in B♭ Major
   (B) compound triple in G minor
   (C) simple triple in C minor
   (D) compound triple in C minor

70. The accidental represented by the altered figures within the figured bass is

   (A) F♯
   (B) A♭
   (C) A natural
   (D) B natural

71. The circled notes in the first two measures would be considered

   (A) suspension
   (B) retardation
   (C) anticipation
   (D) lower neighbor tones

PRACTICE TEST 1

Questions 72–75 are based on this excerpt of *Nun komm, der Heiden Heiland* by J. S. Bach.

Nun komm, der Heiden Heiland

Johann Sebastian Bach
(1685–1750)
BWV 36

72. The chord marked 1 can best be identified as

    (A) supertonic
    (B) dominant
    (C) dominant seventh
    (D) leading tone seventh

73. The two chords in box 2 can best be identified as

    (A) a plagal cadence in D Major
    (B) an authentic cadence in G Major
    (C) a deceptive cadence in B minor
    (D) V^7/V–VI in B minor

74. The Roman numeral analysis of the three chords in box 3 would be

    (A) VI–V–i
    (B) iv–V^7–i
    (C) ii–V^7–i
    (D) ii°⁶–V–i

75. The final chord of this excerpt can be described as all of the following **except** as

    (A) borrowed from the relative minor
    (B) an example of mode mixture
    (C) containing a Picardy third
    (D) a major tonic

THIS IS THE END OF SECTION I, PART B.

Please continue to Section II and restart the audio.

SECTION II

TOTAL TIME: APPROXIMATELY 1 HOUR AND 20 MINUTES
NUMBER OF QUESTIONS: 9
55% OF TOTAL SCORE

Access audio at
http://barronsbooks.com/ap/mtheory/

Part A

TIME: APPROXIMATELY 68 MINUTES

TRACK 151

Directions: Answer **Questions 1–7** in the space provided. You may want to have blank staff paper available, or use your own blank scratch paper. On the exam, the questions are written on one side of the test booklet and the facing page is blank staff paper. During the actual exam, if you write your answer on the blank staff paper, make sure you allow yourself time to write your final answer in the answer space or clearly indicate on the question page that your answer is on the facing page.

Questions 1–2
On the staff provided for each question, notate to the best of your ability the correct pitch and rhythm of a short melody you will hear. Make sure that any accidentals are appropriate to the key signature that has been provided. In each case, the pulse will be provided before the melody is first played.

Question 1: The melody will be played **three times**. There will be a pause of 30 seconds after the first playing and a pause of 1 minute after each subsequent playing. There are no rests in this melody, which is played on a bassoon.

The pitch of the first note has been provided. Be sure to complete the note with stems and flags as appropriate. Now listen to the melody for the first time and begin to notate.

1.

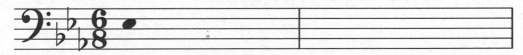

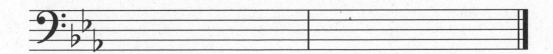

The melody for **Question 1** will now be played a second time.

The melody for **Question 1** will now be played a third and final time.

Question 2: The melody will be played **four times**. There will be a pause of 30 seconds after the first playing and a pause of 1 minute after each subsequent playing. There are no rests in this melody, which is played on a trumpet.

The pitch of the first note has been provided. Be sure to complete the note with stems and flags as appropriate. Now listen to the melody for the first time and begin to notate.

2.

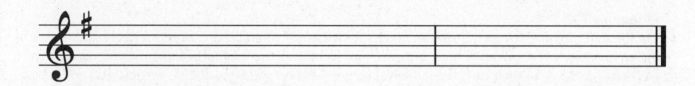

The melody for **Question 2** will now be played a second time.

The melody for **Question 2** will now be played a third time.

The melody for **Question 2** will now be played a final time.

Go on to the next group of questions.

Questions 3–4

For the next two questions you will hear a four-part harmonic progression. In both examples the progression will be played **four times**. There will be a pause of 30 seconds after the first playing and a pause of 1 minute after each subsequent playing.

1. For each question you are to notate *only* the bass and the soprano on the staff provided. Do *not* write the alto and the tenor.
2. On the lines underneath the staff you are to write the Roman numeral chord symbols, including the Arabic numbers for any appropriate inversion.

Question 3: Before listening to the progression for the first time, look at the staff below and notice that there are nine chords in the progression, with the first one provided for you.

Now listen to the harmonic progression for the first time and begin notating. 𝄞

3.

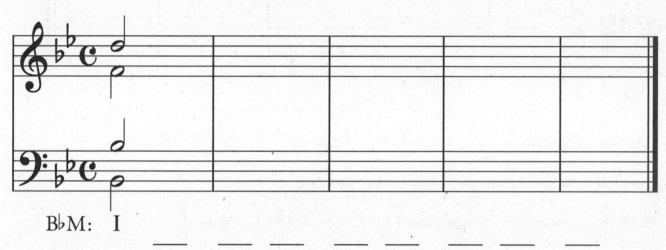

B♭M: I   ___ ___ ___ ___ ___ ___ ___ ___

Question 3 harmonic progression played a second time. 𝄞

Question 3 harmonic progression played a third time. 𝄞

The harmonic progression for **Question 3** will now be played a fourth and final time. 𝄞

Question 4: Before listening to the progression for the first time, look at the staff below and notice that there are once again nine chords in the progression. The first one has been done for you. You are to fill in *only* the soprano, bass, and chord symbols, including appropriate inversions, for the remaining eight chords.

Now listen to the harmonic progression for the first time and begin notating.

4.

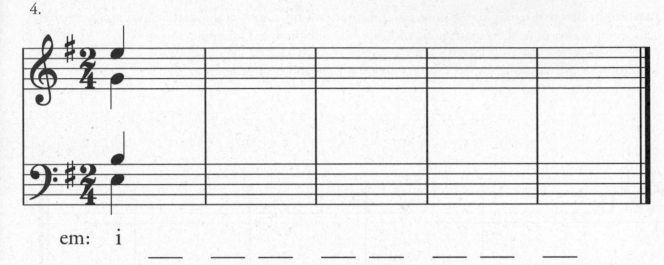

em: i   ___ ___ ___ ___ ___ ___ ___ ___

Question 4 harmonic progression played a second time.

Question 4 harmonic progression played a third time.

The harmonic progression for **Question 4** will now be played a final time.

The remaining three Free-Response questions do not require aural prompts. You may answer them in the order you choose, but your time is limited to 45 minutes to complete all three questions. A suggested time for each question is printed in your Practice Exam next to each question number. Read the questions carefully and use your time efficiently. Now, pause the audio, turn the page, and begin working.

Question 5 (Suggested time: 15 minutes)
You are to realize the figured bass below in four voices following traditional eighteenth-century voice-leading procedures. Continue in the same fashion from the spacing of the first chord, which is given to you. In the space below each chord, fill in the appropriate Roman numeral chord symbol and inversion.

5.

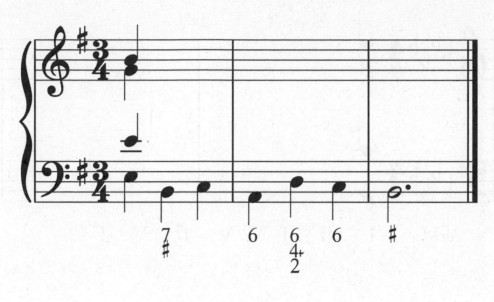

em: _____ _____ _____   _____ _____ _____ · _____

Question 6 (Suggested time: 10 minutes)
You are to write the following progression in four voices following eighteenth-century voice-leading procedures. Continue in the same fashion from the spacing of the first chord, which is given to you. Use only quarter and half notes.

6.

A♭M: I   vii°⁶   I⁶   V⁶₅/V   I⁶₄   V⁷   I⁴⁻³

Question 7 (Suggested time: 20 minutes)

Complete the bass line for the melody below. Place the Roman numerals with inversion symbols below the bass line to indicate the harmony implied by the soprano and bass. Follow these guidelines:

1. Your bass line should make melodic sense in relation to the soprano.

   - Give melodic interest to the bass line and vary the motion of the bass in relation to the soprano.
   - Use note values ranging from half notes to eighth notes.

2. Your bass line and choice of chord symbols should make harmonic sense with the melody.

   - Use appropriate cadences at each phrase ending.
   - Use at least two chords per measure or two positions of the same chord.

3. Do not notate the alto and tenor lines.

7.

STOP

THIS IS THE END OF THE WRITTEN EXAM.

SECTION II: PART B—SIGHT-SINGING

TOTAL TIME: APPROXIMATELY 10 MINUTES

Directions: For each of the melodies, sing the pitches in accurate pitch and rhythm using a steady, consistent tempo. For each melody you will hear the starting pitch at the beginning of the practice period. You will have 75 seconds to practice singing the melody. At the end of the practice time you will have 30 seconds to perform the melody. A recorded announcement will tell you when it is time to stop practicing and start performing. On the actual exam you will be recording your performance digitally, and the file will be saved in an MP3 format.

During your performance:

- You may sing solfege syllables (***Do-Re-Mi***), scale degree numbers ($\hat{1}$–$\hat{2}$–$\hat{3}$), a neutral syllable (for example ***Ta*** or ***Da***) or note names (C–D–E). You may whistle if you prefer.
- Even though you will hear the starting pitch you do *not* have to sing it in that key. You may transpose the melody to a register that is comfortable for you.
- You should use all of the practice time to sing out loud. You may write on the music if you want to.
- You may not use any device such as a metronome or any musical instrument to help you in your practice or performance.
- You will be evaluated on pitch accuracy relative to the opening tonic you choose, rhythm, and continuity—maintaining a steady tempo without hesitating or breaking the flow of the melody. You may start over if you need to, but there *will* be a deduction from your score. You are not evaluated on the quality of your singing voice.

Access audio at
http://barronsbooks.com/ap/mtheory

Question 1: Look over the melody and begin practicing. You have 75 seconds to practice the melody. You will now hear the starting pitch of the printed melody.

1.

Question 2: Look over the melody and begin practicing. You have 75 seconds to practice the melody. You will now hear the starting pitch of the printed melody.

2.

ANSWER KEY
Practice Test 1

SECTION I: PART A

1. **D**	12. **D**	23. **D**	34. **D**
2. **B**	13. **C**	24. **C**	35. **B**
3. **C**	14. **C**	25. **B**	36. **C**
4. **C**	15. **B**	26. **C**	37. **D**
5. **D**	16. **D**	27. **C**	38. **D**
6. **B**	17. **D**	28. **D**	39. **D**
7. **D**	18. **A**	29. **D**	40. **C**
8. **C**	19. **B**	30. **A**	41. **A**
9. **B**	20. **A**	31. **D**	42. **A**
10. **C**	21. **C**	32. **B**	43. **D**
11. **A**	22. **C**	33. **A**	

SECTION I: PART B

44. **C**	52. **D**	60. **D**	68. **C**
45. **D**	53. **D**	61. **A**	69. **C**
46. **C**	54. **B**	62. **A**	70. **D**
47. **D**	55. **D**	63. **C**	71. **C**
48. **C**	56. **B**	64. **D**	72. **C**
49. **C**	57. **B**	65. **A**	73. **B**
50. **D**	58. **C**	66. **C**	74. **D**
51. **C**	59. **B**	67. **C**	75. **A**

ANSWERS EXPLAINED

Section I: Part A

1. **(D)** This pattern would be the *last* three pitches in the B harmonic minor scale with the interval of an A2 between G and A♯. When possible, look at patterns holistically instead of note-to-note.

2. **(B)** These are all scale patterns. Answer (A) is Major, (B) is Phrygian, (C) is Dorian, and (D) is Lydian. The A Phrygian scale with lowered scale degree 2 from minor was played.

3. **(C)** Holistically this pattern is a minor triad with a minor seventh.

4. **(C)** The interval played (A–F) is a minor sixth.

5. **(D)** Remember to use your time wisely; determine *during the silence* between questions the quality of each triad. Answer (A) is a minor triad, (B) is Major, (C) is also Major but in second inversion, and (D) is diminished in first inversion. If after the first listening you can determine that the example is *not* a major triad, you have eliminated two answers.

6. **(B)** When looking at each pattern it should be discernible that every answer could be in the tonality of G. While answers (B) and (D) are in G minor, answer (C) is in Major and (A) could really be both. Answers (A), (C), and (D) begin with a ***So-Do*** relationship (P4) while Answer (B) begins with ***So-Re*** (P5). What was played (B) is ***So-Re-Fa-Me-Do***.

7. **(D)** When answering rhythm questions, look at beginnings and endings and *compare*. By recognizing that the opening rhythm is *not* two equal eighth notes, you immediately eliminate two answers. Remember to always listen *for* something.

8. **(C)** In this set of answers, what is similar is the endings. Answers (C) and (D) had the same ending; however, the ♩. ♪♪ beginning pattern (C) is correct.

9. **(B)** The piano accompaniment is playing an Alberti bass figure, which means it is an arpeggiated chord usually using (in scale degrees) 1-5-3-5 repeatedly.

10. **(C)** The ornamentation is a turn, in this instance notated as .

    It consists of four slurred notes after the main tone: the note above the main tone, the main tone, the note below the main tone, and finally back to the main tone again. It is performed as

11. **(A)** The second phrase ends with syncopation on both beats 1 and 2. In simple quadruple meter the rhythm is ♩ ♩ ♫ ♩ ♫ ♩

12. **(D)** This is the same melody but it is not a literal repetition because the mode changes from Bb Major to Bb minor—the parallel minor.

13. **(C)** The excerpt ends with a Picardy third, meaning the final harmony is a MAJOR tonic (raising the third of the chord). This is an example of mode mixture.

14. **(C)** The meter has three beats per measure (triple); each beat is divided into two parts (simple).

15. **(B)** The texture is primarily melody with accompaniment with some areas of monophony.

16. **(D)** This segment features the strings playing *arco* (with the bow) and *pizzicato* (plucked).

17. **(D)** The key shifts to the dominant. The pizzicato melody ends $\hat{5}$–$\hat{1}$, a 5th above the original tonic. Try to sing the last 2 notes and retain the "new *Do*" in your head when the original melody repeats. Note that the original tonic is lower by a P5.

18. **(A)** The second segment features **melodic sequence** and **imitation** as one section plays pizzicato in a descending line, followed by legato imitation of the same melody, and then the same pattern slightly lower (sequence) played pizzicato and imitated legato.

19. **(B)** The melody returns in major. This is a change of mode.

20. **(A)** The meter is $\frac{2}{4}$, simple duple.

21. **(C)** Because the segment contains only 2 phrases, answer D can be eliminated because a repeated parallel period has 4 phrases. In this excerpt, the two phrases begin with the same melody but the end of the second phrase modulates.

22. **(C)** In segment two, the first phrase is an imperfect authentic cadence and the second phrase is a half cadence.

23. **(D)** The third phrase begins with two measures of descending chromatic patterns followed by descending major scale patterns, two measures of contrary motion (a two-voice counterpoint between the left and right hands), and ends with an ascending chromatic scale pattern with a PAC. The bass line is not in an ascending step-wise motion.

24. **(C)** The last phrase is definitely a transition into the next segment. It contains an ascending chromatic scale pattern in the right hand against a resounding tonic pedal in the bass. It is not a literal repetition.

25. **(B)** The form of this excerpt is ternary: A B A.

Questions 26–29: This is what was seen.

Questions 26–29 This is what was played.

26. **(C)** There is a rhythm mistake in *both* the treble staff and the bass staff. What was played was three even quarter notes in the bass staff and the dotted-quarter and eighth-note rhythm was played in the treble staff.

27. **(C)** The eighth-note rhythm was on beat 1 instead of beat 2 and pitch was also slightly different.

28. **(D)** Pitch is different in the bass line. An ascending pattern beginning with a m3 was played instead of a descending M3 followed by an ascending P4.

29. **(D)** What was written was an ascending major scale pattern leading up to B♭, which includes parallel perfect octaves created going into measure 8. What was played was oblique motion in the bass staying on F and avoiding the parallelism.

30. **(A)** The opening melodic pattern is 6̂–5̂–2̂–1̂.

31. **(D)** If each phrase has 2 measures, then there are four beats per measure. This is compound meter; therefore, the time signature is $\frac{12}{8}$.

32. **(B)** This composition uses retrograde. This means it is the reverse of the previous line.

33. **(A)** The prominent rhythmic motive is

34. **(D)** When the second violin enters he plays a 3rd above the first violin.

35. **(B)** When the piano enters the texture is melody with accompaniment.

36. **(C)** The second phrase of the second section harmonizes the original melody with the melody heard in the first phrase.

37. **(D)** The third and fourth phrases are different because the drum enters and plays a rhythmic accompaniment. The rhythm that is played is

38. **(D)** The form of this piece is ABCB. The B sections are the same, except the final B section is performed an octave higher and with rhythm accompaniment. Remember that timbre, texture, range, or the addition of the drum rhythm does not change the melodic content.

39. **(D)** This excerpt is in simple triple meter. The time signature is $\frac{3}{2}$. Alla breve and $\frac{2}{2}$ are the same, two beats per measure and the half note gets the beat. The signature $\frac{9}{4}$ represents compound triple meter.

40. **(C)** The melody begins on scale degree 3 (*Mi*).

41. **(A)** The tempo marking that applies to this excerpt is Largo meaning very slow; broadly, dignified.

42. **(A)** Listen *for* the bass line in a harmonic progression question. The bass line implies the Roman numeral. Listen *for* the cadence(s). Both cadences are authentic; that eliminates answers (B) and (C). The bassline ending the last two measures is *Fa-So-So-Do*. That eliminates answer (D).

43. **(D)** The non-chord tone at the ending cadence is an anticipation. There is also a non-chord tone at the first phrase cadence. It is a suspension. Here is the soprano and bass line from this aria.

Section I: Part B

44. **(C)** First you have to know what key is the relative major of F♯ minor: it is A Major. The subdominant is the 4th scale degree or D (natural).

45. **(D)** This interval of B♯–F is doubly diminished. The interval B–F is diminished, so by adding a sharp to the lower pitch, you are making the interval even smaller.

46. **(C)** The key of C♯ minor has four sharps (F♯, C♯, G♯, D♯). The ii⌀7 (half-diminished) chord is spelled D♯–F♯–A–C♯. It is a diminished triad and a minor seventh.

47. **(D)** Phrygian mode lowers the second scale degree from the natural minor, or in this case adds one flat to the key signature.

48. **(C)** The time signature $\frac{6}{4}$ is a compound duple meter. Any time signature with 6 as the top number has two beats per measure; therefore, the dotted half note gets the beat. The time signature $\frac{6}{4}$ represents the *subdivision* of the beat or the equivalent of six quarter notes per measure.

49. **(C)** What do we know for sure? The chord is C–E♮–G–B♭ and functions as a secondary dominant of a *temporary tonic* key. If C is dominant, the tonic is F; therefore, the temporary tonic is F minor. The chord symbol V/ii tells us that F minor is ii in our original key. If F is ii, then tonic (I) is E♭ Major.

50. **(D)** Raised submediant only occurs in the melodic form of minor. If C♯ is scale degree 6, then 7 (also raised) is D♯ and tonic is E. The key signature of E minor is one sharp.

51. **(C)** The meter is compound duple and the meter signature is $\frac{6}{4}$.

52. **(D)** Augmentation is not used in this excerpt. Melodic minor is identified in the last measure. A secondary dominant is implied with the A♯ (_**Fi**_) leading to B (_**So**_).

53. **(D)** The E natural could be harmonized with a tonic (i) or a submediant (VI)—that would mean PERFECT authentic cadence (because the root of the chord _**Do**_ is doubled in the soprano) or deceptive cadence. Since perfect authentic is not a choice, the answer is deceptive.

54. **(B)** The chord symbol at #4 is the ii$^{\varnothing7}$ chord in first inversion. In the key of E minor that would be F♯–A–C–E with the A in the bass. There is no seventh (E).

55. **(D)** The leading tone in E minor is D♯. Especially if it is in an outside voice, the leading tone should always resolve to the tonic.

56. **(B)** There are parallel octaves between the soprano and the bass.

57. **(B)** There are parallel fifths between the bass and tenor in the last two chords. To avoid this, remember that at a cadence when V^7 goes to I in root position, the V^7 should have all four members and, if you correctly observe the resolutions, the tonic chord will contain three roots and one third (no fifth).

58. **(C)** Tessitura is the most acceptable and comfortable vocal range (less frequently, instrumental range), which provides the performer with the best-sounding or characteristic timbre.

59. **(B)** An appoggiatura occurs when you leap upward from the preparation chord to the note that is not part of the chord, and resolve downward by step to the chord tone. An appoggiatura is always on the beat. The B natural in the melody is the appoggiatura.

60. **(D)** The tonality of this excerpt is F Major. Here is a perfect example to reinforce that you must look at the music and not just the key signature or the title. Key is always confirmed by cadence. E natural is present throughout and there is a PAC on the downbeat of measure 98.

61. **(A)** The chord at measure 101 is V^7. The cello plays C, viola G, violin II has B♭ (the seventh of the chord), and violin I has the third (C–E–G–B♭).

62. **(A)** Notes of a triad or seventh chord played one after the other (arpeggio) are present in nearly every measure, in at least one voice.

63. **(C)** The cadence in measure 105–106 is V^7–i, shifting the tonality to the parallel minor where the tonic triad is F–A♭–C.

64. **(D)** The harmonic rhythm is one chord per measure in 5 and 6, two chords in measure 7 with the harmony changing on beat 3, and back to one harmony per measure in 8.

65. **(A)** The key temporarily shifts to A♭ Major.

66. **(C)** The cadence at 16 is a perfect authentic cadence in the key of A♭ Major.

67. **(C)** The D in the upper voice occurs several times in this motive (measures 1, 5, 9) and is an upper neighbor. It is accented because it is *on the beat*, not because it has an accent articulation.

68. **(C)** The first two phrases (measures 1–8) create a **parallel period**. The second two phrases (measures 9–16) create a modulating parallel period—the first phrase is in FM and the second phrase is in A♭ M.

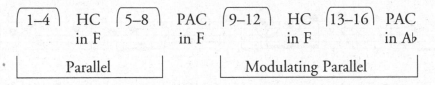

FYI: The last four phrases (measures 17–32) create a double parallel period. **Parallel** because the melodic content is essentially the same, and **double** because the first three cadences are weak with only one strong cadence at the end of the fourth phrase.

69. **(C)** The meter is simple triple. The key of this excerpt is C minor. The key signature may suggest B♭ Major or G minor, but the analysis is clearly C minor because the figured bass indicates B natural, and the cadence *confirms* the tonality of C.

70. **(D)** The altered figures in this excerpt are B natural. Make sure you are correctly identifying the pitches in alto clef.

71. **(C)** The small notes (grace notes) are anticipations, arriving early at the new harmony.

72. **(C)** This chord (F♯–A♯–C♯–E) is the dominant seventh chord in B minor.

73. **(B)** This is an authentic cadence in G Major. The final chord in this phrase is G Major (G–B–D) preceded by D–F♯–A–C♮, the V⁷ chord in G. The "red flag" is the C natural, diatonic to G but not to B minor.

74. **(D)** This progression is ii°⁶–V–i in B minor. (C♯–Ⓔ–G to Ⓕ♯–A♯–C♯ to Ⓑ–D–F♯)

75. **(A)** The final chord is a major tonic borrowed from the *parallel* major, not the relative. It is considered mode mixture and the raised third is called Picardy.

Section II: Part A

There is only one correct answer to Questions 3 and 4; however, for Questions 1 and 2, grading is such that you can achieve points for correctly notating a section of the melody even if it is misplaced in the measure. That's one of the reasons you are always listening for patterns. Make sure you understand the components of these four exercises.

1. E♭ Major

Measure 1: The very first interval is **Do-Mi**, then descending **Fa-Mi-Re**.

Measure 2: The leap is up to **So** in the second measure with a **So-La-So** (**La** is the upper neighbor). Leading into measure three there is a chromatic pitch leading to **So**. It is the raised 4th scale degree—**Fi**.

Measure 3: The pattern descends scale-wise from **So** down to **Do**. The A♭ is back to the key signature (**Fa**). The flat sign is *not* necessary because you are in a new measure.

Measure 4: The ending pattern is **Re-↓So-Do**.

2. E minor

Trumpet in B♭

What you *heard* and what was *seen* by the trumpet player is different because the trumpet is a transposing instrument. The trumpet *plays* in F♯ minor to *sound* in E minor (up a M2).

Measure 1: Measure 1 begins the way many minor melodies begin, by going down a half step to the leading tone. Remember that when notating in minor the leading tone requires an accidental, in this case D♯.

Measure 2: The difficulty level increases with both the sixteenth notes on beat one *and* the dotted-quarter-note pattern on beat three.

Measures 2 and 3: The area between the brackets is the melodic minor form of the scale from low **So** to **Me**. This example ends with **Re-↑So-Do**.

Before going any further, please notice that the completed harmonic progression for Questions 3 and 4, and for that matter *any* harmonic progression in this guide, looks like what you should write for Question 7. Are you connecting the processes? What harmonies are used? What inversions? Observe the motion between the two lines, and notice that the counterpoint (line against line) is made up of consonant intervals. If the interval is dissonant (second, fourth, or seventh), it *must* resolve to a consonant. Let's continue

3. B♭ Major

This example begins with a pedal in the bass (I–IV$^6_4$–I), then continues with an ascending bass line, and concludes with a deceptive cadence. This is a very conjunct bass line that features oblique and contrary motion between the bass and soprano.

Full harmonization

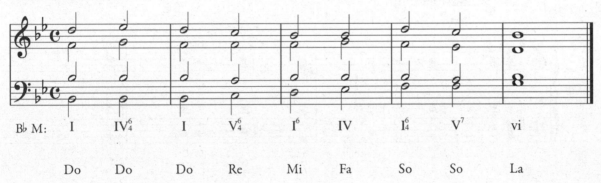

4. E minor

Full harmonization

em: i V^4_2 i^6 V^6_4 i V^4_2/iv iv^6 iv   i

Did you remember to write the leading tone (D♯) in big letters as a reminder before you started? Notice that it is used in the melody and requires the accidental. This progression is a little more challenging and requires hearing the P4 (***Do-Fa***) in the bass between the first two chords. Also remember that whenever you hear the leading tone, *two things must register in your brain:* (1) The leading tone is only in V and vii, and (2) the leading tone in an outside voice must always resolve upward to ***Do***. The bass line descends in stepwise motion using ***Te*** and not ***Ti*** as it moves past ***Do***. At the same time there is a chromatic pattern in the melody ***Me-Mi-Fa*** that signals a raised 3rd scale degree leading to ***Fa***. This example ends with a plagal cadence.

5. Possible solution

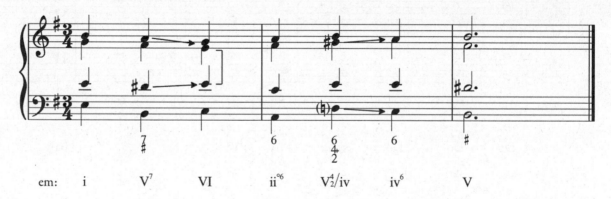

em: i V^7 VI $ii^{\circ 6}$ V^4_2/iv iv^6 V

There are possible variables in the solution of this figured bass exercise. What is *not* a variable is the correct chord analysis, which leads you to the correct chord members. Start with that correct information, and you are well on your way to success. A deceptive progression in measure one should lead you to double the third in the VI chord to avoid parallelism. The secondary dominant is V^4_2 of iv^6. The temporary tonic is A minor (iv) and its dominant is E–G♯–B–D. The figured bass shows a #4 above the bass (D) which is the G♯. There is a half cadence at the end and the sharp sign under the final chord indicates to *raise* the note a third above the bass to (D♯), the leading tone. This is an example of a Phrygian half cadence. Be careful between the last two chords not to double the third (C) and resolve it to the D♯ (that would create an A2 interval in voice leading), nor to double the third (C) and resolve it to B (that would create parallel octaves between the soprano and bass).

A secondary function seventh chord *always* includes an accidental. Remember that the chord underneath the slash is the temporary tonic. Practice writing these chords until you are comfortable with the process. These are the errors most often committed in Questions 5 and 6.

- Wrong chord members
- Failure to add accidentals
- Failure to resolve the leading tone and/or the seventh of a chord

> A chord spelled incorrectly either by misspelling a chord member or by leaving out an accidental is a costly error, losing up to 5 points.

6. Possible Solution

This example uses the vii°⁶ triad, which requires two resolutions *Ti* to *Do* (G–A♭) and *Fa* to *Mi* (D♭ to C). The V⁶₅ of V (B♭–D♮–F–A♭) does not resolve to V but to a strong substitute for dominant, the I⁶₄. The I⁶₄ does not contain the pitch that A♭ *should* resolve to (G); therefore, you must hold the A♭ until it *can* resolve in the V⁷ chord. This concludes with an authentic cadence with a 4–3 suspension over the tonic chord.

7. Possible Solution

Composition of a bass line with Roman numerals is the most creative of all the free-response questions. It is fairly easy to earn a high score, and it is the question that students make more careless errors on than all the rest. Keep it simple.

- *Don't add NCT to the bass.*
- Use root position chords as much as you can, especially at the cadence (two chords).
- Use contrary motion.
- Write consonant counterpoint: Notice that the numbers between the voices in the solution equal the interval between the bass and the soprano.
- Don't write retrogression (V–ii⁶, or V–IV).
- Write appropriate cadences.

This is a fairly simple harmonization of this melody reusing a fragment of the progression from the first two given measures: the I–V⁶–I progression. The second fermata has a melodic pattern of *Fa-Fi-Sol*, so use the root position V/V or V⁷/V. This is a timed exam, so remember you are not required to harmonize in quarter notes. Look for pitch patterns that can utilize the same harmony. The third fermata is harmonized with a half cadence. Recognize the relationship of the melody notes (A–G♯) as a half-step relationship (*Fa-Mi*) in the key of the dominant, and note that the melody can be also harmonized with V⁷/V, this time in first inversion putting the chromatic pattern in the bass. The final cadence harmonizes the familiar *Re-Ti-Do* with ii⁶–V⁷–I.

Section 2: Part B

1.

This example is in simple quadruple meter in C minor. It has elements of harmonic minor at the end of measure two, and a melodic minor passage at measure three. The last measure begins with an interval of a descending minor third (*Le-Fa*) and ends with *Fa-Me-Re-Do*.

2.

The range of this example is from high *So* (D) to low *Mi* (B natural), so the key to successful singing is to find a tonal center (*Do*) that allows you to go up a fifth to *So*, but also down a sixth to *Mi* while staying in a comfortable singing range for you. You do *not* have to sing in the given key. Another helpful pointer is to recognize how many times you return to *Do*. *Use this* to retain your pitch.

Measure 2 contains an ascending scalewise melody with the chromatic pattern *So-Fi-So* into measure three. You can expect to see chromatic pitches in SS2. Measure 3 descends diatonically from high *So* to *Do*, and then the pattern is the familiar *Do-So-Mi.* In the last measure the leap from *Fa* up to *Re* is an M6; however, instead of thinking about going from interval to interval, think about the patterns. The example ends with the familiar *Re-Ti-Do* ending, so it goes from *Do-So-Mi* to *Re-Ti-Do* with *Fa* as the connector. Choose a tempo that will not rush you in compound meter. Take your time, but make sure you hold the last pitch full value.

Self-Scoring Guide

Section I: Parts A and B—Multiple-Choice

75 questions—**aural** and **non-aural**—for **45%** of total score

Section II: Part A—Free-Response

7 questions graded uniquely for **45%** of total score

Questions 1, 2: Melodic Dictation
Scoring: **9** points each = **18** total points

1 point for each correct half-measure segment in *both* pitch and rhythm (8) plus 1 point added when at least one segment (any one half-measure) is correct. *Note:* No enharmonic equivalents are permitted, plus notation must correctly place accidentals and dots, and use stems, flags, or beams.

Questions 3, 4: Harmonic Dictation
Scoring: **24** points each = **48** total points

Correct pitches = 16 points
Correct chord symbols with both Roman and Arabic numerals = 8 points
Note: Enharmonic equivalents are not permitted. Rhythmic duration is not considered.

Question 5: Realizing Figured Bass
Scoring: **25** points

Correct Roman and Arabic numeral chord symbols = 7 points (1 point each)
Chord spelling = 6 points (1 point each)
Voice leading = 12 points (2 points per connection between chords)

Question 6: Part Writing to Roman Numeral
Scoring: **18** points

Chord spelling = 6 points (1 point each)
Voice leading = 12 points (2 points per connection between chords)

Question 7: Melodic Harmonization
Scoring: **9** points

Bass line (Counterpoint) and Harmonies (Roman numerals) are awarded points by phrase. Phrase 2 = 2 points. Phrases 3 and 4 = 3 points each plus 1 point for being consistently accurate, or aesthetically musical.

Section II: Part B—Sight-Singing

2 questions performed individually for **10%** of total score

> **Questions 1, 2: Sight-Singing**
> Scoring: **9** points each = **18** total points
>
> 1 point is awarded for every half-measure that is correct in pitch and rhythm, including consistent tempo, and 1 point is added for no hesitation or stopping (the flow point).

HOW TO CALCULATE YOUR SCORE

It is important to note that on the actual AP Music Theory Exam not all questions are weighted the same. Calculating the composite score of the exam remains fairly standardized from year to year and questions are weighted according to difficulty. You can calculate your percentage score to show **relative emphasis**, and use the table below to get an idea of your AP score.

Composite Score of: _____%

No Recommendation	**1** = 0–20% accuracy on all parts of the exam
Possibly Qualified	**2** = 21–39% accuracy on all parts of the exam
Qualified	**3** = 40–52% accuracy on all parts of the exam
Well Qualified	**4** = 53–65% accuracy on all parts of the exam
Extremely Well Qualified	**5** = **above 65%** accuracy on all parts of the exam

Most students do not achieve consistently on all sections of the exam. Some may score 35 percent accuracy on the aural multiple-choice but 68 percent on the non-aural, or score 55 percent accuracy on melodic dictation but only 15 percent accuracy on sight-singing. Remember that the subscores calculate aural and non-aural to create the composite score. **If your goal is a passing composite score of 3, then you are looking for approximately 45 percent accuracy on all parts of the exam**.

AURAL	NON-AURAL
Multiple-Choice Part A	Multiple-Choice Part B
FR 1, 2—Melodic Dictation	FR 5—Realization of Figured Bass
FR 3, 4—Harmonic Dictation	FR 6—Part Writing to Roman Numerals
SS 1, 2—Sight-Singing	FR 7—Melodic Harmonization

Test Analysis

Section I: Multiple-Choice, Part A

Number correct (out of 43): _____ × 1.0465 = _____
Aural Subtotal

Section I: Multiple-Choice, Part B

Number correct (out of 32): _____ × 1.4063 = _____
Non-aural Subtotal

Aural Subtotal + Non-aural Subtotal = _____
Weighted Section 1 Score
(If less than 0, enter 0;
do not round.)

Note: Do not round any subtotals.

Section II: Free-Response

Melodic Dictation Question 1 = _____ × 1.0185 = _____
(out of 9) *(Do not round)*

Melodic Dictation Question 2 = _____ × 1.0185 = _____
(out of 9) *(Do not round)*

Harmonic Dictation Question 3 = _____ × 0.3819 = _____
(out of 24) *(Do not round)*

Harmonic Dictation Question 4 = _____ × 0.3819 = _____
(out of 24) *(Do not round)*

Sight-Singing Question 1 = _____ × 1.0185 = _____
(out of 9) *(Do not round)*

Sight-Singing Question 2 = _____ × 1.0185 = _____
(out of 9) *(Do not round)*

Aural Subtotal = _____

Part Writing from Figured Bass
Question 5

= _____ × 0.7333 = _____
  (out of 25)   (*Do not round*)

Part Writing from Roman
Numerals Question 6

= _____ × 0.7639 = _____
  (out of 18)   (*Do not round*)

Composition of a Base Line
Question 7

= _____ × 2.5463 = _____
  (out of 9)   (*Do not round*)

Non-aural Subtotal = _____

Aural Subtotal + Non-aural Subtotal = _____
                                       Weighted Section 1 Score
                                       (If less than 0, enter 0;
                                       do not round.)

Composite Score

_____ + _____ = _____
Weighted Score, Section I   *Weighted Score, Section II*   ***Composite Score***
                                                          (rounded to the nearest
                                                          whole number)

_____ + _____ = _____
Multiple-Choice   *Free-Response*   ***Aural Subscore***
Aural Subtotal   *Aural Subtotal*   *(rounded to the nearest*
                                                          whole number)

_____ + _____ = _____
Multiple-Choice   *Free-Response*   ***Non-aural Subscore***
Non-aural Subtotal   *Non-aural Subtotal*   *(rounded to the nearest*
                                                          whole number)

Final Score Range	AP Score*
132–200	5
105–131	4
78–104	3
47–77	2
0–46	1

*The score range corresponding to each grade varies from exam to exam and is approximate.

ANSWER SHEET
Practice Test 2

NOTE: The AP Music Theory exam has only four answer choices, A–D. Do not mark choice E.

SECTION I: PART A

1. Ⓐ Ⓑ Ⓒ Ⓓ Ⓔ
2. Ⓐ Ⓑ Ⓒ Ⓓ Ⓔ
3. Ⓐ Ⓑ Ⓒ Ⓓ Ⓔ
4. Ⓐ Ⓑ Ⓒ Ⓓ Ⓔ
5. Ⓐ Ⓑ Ⓒ Ⓓ Ⓔ
6. Ⓐ Ⓑ Ⓒ Ⓓ Ⓔ
7. Ⓐ Ⓑ Ⓒ Ⓓ Ⓔ
8. Ⓐ Ⓑ Ⓒ Ⓓ Ⓔ
9. Ⓐ Ⓑ Ⓒ Ⓓ Ⓔ
10. Ⓐ Ⓑ Ⓒ Ⓓ Ⓔ
11. Ⓐ Ⓑ Ⓒ Ⓓ Ⓔ

12. Ⓐ Ⓑ Ⓒ Ⓓ Ⓔ
13. Ⓐ Ⓑ Ⓒ Ⓓ Ⓔ
14. Ⓐ Ⓑ Ⓒ Ⓓ Ⓔ
15. Ⓐ Ⓑ Ⓒ Ⓓ Ⓔ
16. Ⓐ Ⓑ Ⓒ Ⓓ Ⓔ
17. Ⓐ Ⓑ Ⓒ Ⓓ Ⓔ
18. Ⓐ Ⓑ Ⓒ Ⓓ Ⓔ
19. Ⓐ Ⓑ Ⓒ Ⓓ Ⓔ
20. Ⓐ Ⓑ Ⓒ Ⓓ Ⓔ
21. Ⓐ Ⓑ Ⓒ Ⓓ Ⓔ
22. Ⓐ Ⓑ Ⓒ Ⓓ Ⓔ

23. Ⓐ Ⓑ Ⓒ Ⓓ Ⓔ
24. Ⓐ Ⓑ Ⓒ Ⓓ Ⓔ
25. Ⓐ Ⓑ Ⓒ Ⓓ Ⓔ
26. Ⓐ Ⓑ Ⓒ Ⓓ Ⓔ
27. Ⓐ Ⓑ Ⓒ Ⓓ Ⓔ
28. Ⓐ Ⓑ Ⓒ Ⓓ Ⓔ
29. Ⓐ Ⓑ Ⓒ Ⓓ Ⓔ
30. Ⓐ Ⓑ Ⓒ Ⓓ Ⓔ
31. Ⓐ Ⓑ Ⓒ Ⓓ Ⓔ
32. Ⓐ Ⓑ Ⓒ Ⓓ Ⓔ
33. Ⓐ Ⓑ Ⓒ Ⓓ Ⓔ

34. Ⓐ Ⓑ Ⓒ Ⓓ Ⓔ
35. Ⓐ Ⓑ Ⓒ Ⓓ Ⓔ
36. Ⓐ Ⓑ Ⓒ Ⓓ Ⓔ
37. Ⓐ Ⓑ Ⓒ Ⓓ Ⓔ
38. Ⓐ Ⓑ Ⓒ Ⓓ Ⓔ
39. Ⓐ Ⓑ Ⓒ Ⓓ Ⓔ
40. Ⓐ Ⓑ Ⓒ Ⓓ Ⓔ
41. Ⓐ Ⓑ Ⓒ Ⓓ Ⓔ
42. Ⓐ Ⓑ Ⓒ Ⓓ Ⓔ
43. Ⓐ Ⓑ Ⓒ Ⓓ Ⓔ

SECTION I: PART B

44. Ⓐ Ⓑ Ⓒ Ⓓ Ⓔ
45. Ⓐ Ⓑ Ⓒ Ⓓ Ⓔ
46. Ⓐ Ⓑ Ⓒ Ⓓ Ⓔ
47. Ⓐ Ⓑ Ⓒ Ⓓ Ⓔ
48. Ⓐ Ⓑ Ⓒ Ⓓ Ⓔ
49. Ⓐ Ⓑ Ⓒ Ⓓ Ⓔ
50. Ⓐ Ⓑ Ⓒ Ⓓ Ⓔ
51. Ⓐ Ⓑ Ⓒ Ⓓ Ⓔ

52. Ⓐ Ⓑ Ⓒ Ⓓ Ⓔ
53. Ⓐ Ⓑ Ⓒ Ⓓ Ⓔ
54. Ⓐ Ⓑ Ⓒ Ⓓ Ⓔ
55. Ⓐ Ⓑ Ⓒ Ⓓ Ⓔ
56. Ⓐ Ⓑ Ⓒ Ⓓ Ⓔ
57. Ⓐ Ⓑ Ⓒ Ⓓ Ⓔ
58. Ⓐ Ⓑ Ⓒ Ⓓ Ⓔ
59. Ⓐ Ⓑ Ⓒ Ⓓ Ⓔ

60. Ⓐ Ⓑ Ⓒ Ⓓ Ⓔ
61. Ⓐ Ⓑ Ⓒ Ⓓ Ⓔ
62. Ⓐ Ⓑ Ⓒ Ⓓ Ⓔ
63. Ⓐ Ⓑ Ⓒ Ⓓ Ⓔ
64. Ⓐ Ⓑ Ⓒ Ⓓ Ⓔ
65. Ⓐ Ⓑ Ⓒ Ⓓ Ⓔ
66. Ⓐ Ⓑ Ⓒ Ⓓ Ⓔ
67. Ⓐ Ⓑ Ⓒ Ⓓ Ⓔ

68. Ⓐ Ⓑ Ⓒ Ⓓ Ⓔ
69. Ⓐ Ⓑ Ⓒ Ⓓ Ⓔ
70. Ⓐ Ⓑ Ⓒ Ⓓ Ⓔ
71. Ⓐ Ⓑ Ⓒ Ⓓ Ⓔ
72. Ⓐ Ⓑ Ⓒ Ⓓ Ⓔ
73. Ⓐ Ⓑ Ⓒ Ⓓ Ⓔ
74. Ⓐ Ⓑ Ⓒ Ⓓ Ⓔ
75. Ⓐ Ⓑ Ⓒ Ⓓ Ⓔ

Practice Test 2

SECTION I

TOTAL TIME: APPROXIMATELY 80 MINUTES

NUMBER OF QUESTIONS: 75

45% OF TOTAL SCORE

 Directions: Each of the questions or incomplete statements below is followed by four suggested answers. Select the best answer in each case and fill in the corresponding circle on the multiple-choice answer sheet. Throughout the exam you will see the treble clef icon, 𝄞, which will let you know when music will be played.

Part A

TIME: APPROXIMATELY 48 MINUTES

Questions 1–6 ask you to identify pitch, interval, melodic patterns, or triads that are played. In each case the question number will be announced. You will have 10 seconds to read the choices; then you will hear the musical example played twice, with a brief pause between playings. Remember to read the choices for each question after the number is announced. Now listen to the music for **Questions 1–6** and identify the patterns that are played.

1. Which of the following pitch patterns is played?

(A)

(B)

(C)

(D)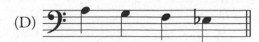

Question 1, played twice. 𝄞

2. This melody reflects what mode?

(A) Aeolian
(B) Phrygian
(C) Dorian
(D) Lydian

Question 2, played twice.

3. Which of the following intervals is played?

(A)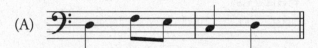

(B)

(C)

(D)

Question 3, played twice.

4. Which of the following pitch patterns is played?

(A)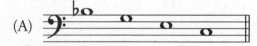

(B)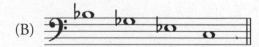

(C)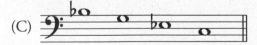

(D)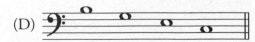

Question 4, played twice.

5. Which of the following pitch patterns is played?

(A)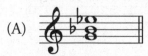

(B)

(C)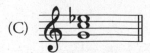

(D)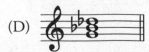

Question 5, played twice.

6. Which of the following triads is played?

(A)

(B)

(C)

(D)

Question 6, played twice.

Go on to the next group of questions.

Questions 7–8 ask you to identify rhythm as it is performed within a melody. After the question is announced, you will have 10 seconds to read the question. It is important that you read the question and choices carefully before the aural example is given. Each example will be played twice with a brief pause between playings. Now listen to the music for **Questions 7–8**. Identify the rhythm that correctly matches the example that is played.

7. Which of the following rhythms is played?

Question 7, played twice.

8. Which of the following rhythms is played?

Question 8, played twice.

Go on to the next group of questions.

Questions 9–12 are based on an excerpt that will be played four times. The score is printed correctly below; however, what you will hear has several differences in either pitch or rhythm. The questions ask you to identify those errors. Before listening to the excerpt for the first time, please read **Questions 9–12** carefully and look at the score.

TRACK
157

9. In measure 2, the error occurs in

   (A) pitch in the treble staff
   (B) rhythm in the treble staff
   (C) pitch in the bass staff
   (D) rhythm in the bass staff

10. The error in measure 3 occurs in

   (A) pitch in the treble staff
   (B) rhythm in both the treble and bass staff
   (C) pitch in both the treble and bass staff
   (D) pitch only in the bass staff

11. The error that occurs in measure 5 is

   (A) pitch and rhythm in the bass staff
   (B) rhythm in the bass staff
   (C) rhythm in the treble staff
   (D) pitch and rhythm in the treble staff

12. In measure 6, the error that occurs is

   (A) rhythm only in the treble staff
   (B) pitch and rhythm in the treble staff
   (C) pitch and rhythm in the bass staff
   (D) rhythm only in the bass staff

The excerpt will now be played for the first time.

The excerpt will now be played a second time.

The excerpt will now be played a third time.

The excerpt will now be played a final time.

Go on to the next group of questions.

Questions 13–17 are based on music for the ballet. The first section will be played twice, followed by the entire excerpt played twice. Before listening to Section 1 for the first time, please read **Questions 13–15**.

13. The time signature of this excerpt is most likely

(A) $\frac{6}{8}$

(B) $\frac{2}{4}$

(C) $\frac{9}{8}$

(D) $\frac{3}{4}$

14. The second phrase contains a modulation to the

(A) parallel minor
(B) mediant
(C) dominant
(D) subdominant

15. The prominent element in the repeat of the first two phrases is

(A) the dynamic and the addition of percussion to the rhythmic accompaniment
(B) a countermelody in the woodwinds
(C) an arpeggiated figure in the inside voices
(D) a scalewise accompaniment in low strings and low brass

Section 1 will now be played for the first time. 𝄞

Section 1 will now be played a second time. 𝄞

Before listening to the entire excerpt, please read **Questions 16–17**.

16. The second section is different from the first section in all of the following elements EXCEPT

(A) dynamic
(B) articulation
(C) timbre
(D) tempo

17. The form of the entire excerpt would best be described as

(A) A B A
(B) ‖:A:‖ B coda
(C) A B C
(D) A A^1 A^2 coda

The entire excerpt will now be played for the first time. 𝄞

The entire excerpt will now be played a final time. 𝄞

PRACTICE TEST 2

Go on to the next group of questions.

Questions 18–21 are based on an excerpt from a Baroque suite by Bach. You will hear the excerpt twice. Before listening to the excerpt for the first time, read **Questions 18–21**.

18. The rhythm of the opening melodic statement is

19. The overall texture of this excerpt is

(A) monophonic
(B) homophonic
(C) heterophonic
(D) unison

20. What compositional technique is **not** used in this excerpt?

(A) Imitation (call and response)
(B) Sequence
(C) Rhythmic augmentation
(D) Modulation

21. The excerpt ends with what type of cadence?

(A) Imperfect authentic
(B) Perfect authentic
(C) Plagal
(D) Half

Now listen to the excerpt for the first time and answer **Questions 18–21**.

The excerpt will now be played a second time.

Go on to the next group of questions.

22. The rhythm of the prominent melodic theme is correctly notated as

23. The first two phrases are two measures each. The second phrase can be described as

    (A) the consequent phrase
    (B) a sequence
    (C) ending with a deceptive cadence
    (D) modulating to the dominant

24. What compositional device is used during this introductory segment?

    (A) voice exchange
    (B) rhythmic
    (C) melodic inversion
    (D) cadenza

25. The introduction can best be described as

    (A) in simple triple meter
    (B) based on the pentatonic scale
    (C) containing arpeggiated material
    (D) containing several suspensions

The introduction will now be played one time. 𝄞

Before listening to both the introduction and the verse, read **Questions 26–27**. 𝄞

26. Both the introduction and verse use

    (A) monophony
    (B) the same timbre
    (C) countermelody fragments
    (D) an inconclusive final cadence

27. What are the melodic intervals of the last three pitches sung in the verse?

    (A) Minor 2nd, Minor 2nd
    (B) Major 2nd, Perfect unison
    (C) Minor 3rd, Perfect unison
    (D) Major 3rd, Minor 2nd

Listen to the entire excerpt and answer **Questions 26–27**. 𝄞

The entire excerpt will now be played a final time.

Review all your answers to **Questions 22–27**. 𝄞

PRACTICE TEST 2

Go on to the next group of questions.

Questions 28–32 are based on an excerpt from a dance suite. The excerpt contains two sections. Section I will be played once, followed by the entire excerpt, including the second section, played twice. Before listening to Section 1, please read **Questions 28–29**.

28. The opening melody begins with which three scale degrees?

   (A) $\hat{1}$–$\hat{3}$–$\hat{5}$
   (B) $\hat{6}$–$\hat{1}$–$\hat{3}$
   (C) $\hat{5}$–$\hat{1}$–$\hat{3}$
   (D) $\hat{3}$–$\hat{5}$–$\hat{1}$

29. The accompaniment of the opening melody includes all of the following EXCEPT

   (A) the low strings playing on the beat
   (B) brass playing on the upbeats
   (C) accents and syncopation
   (D) the woodwinds playing a countermelody

Section 1 will now be played. 𝄞

Before listening to the entire excerpt for the first time, please read **Questions 30–32**.

30. In the second section, all of the following musical elements are present EXCEPT

   (A) dynamic change
   (B) tempo fluctuation
   (C) meter change
   (D) rhythmic syncopation

31. What is the cadence at the end of the second section?

   (A) Phrygian half
   (B) Perfect authentic
   (C) Deceptive
   (D) Plagal

32. Which of the following best describes the harmonic content of the second section?

   (A) 12-bar blues
   (B) Modulation
   (C) Circle of fifths progression
   (D) Moving down by thirds

The entire excerpt will now be played for the first time. 𝄞

The entire excerpt will now be played a final time. Review your answers to **Questions 28–32**. 𝄞

Go on to the next group of questions.

Questions 33–38 are based on an excerpt that features an introduction (two measures) and one segment containing four phrases. You will hear the entire excerpt played three times. Before listening to the first playing, read **Questions 33–38**.

33. The duration that gets the beat in this meter is the

    (A) quarter note
    (B) eighth note
    (C) half note
    (D) dotted-quarter note

34. The harmony represented throughout the introduction and first two phrases is

    (A) IV–V
    (B) I–IV
    (C) I–IV–V–I
    (D) I–V

35. After the introduction, the first two phrases of this excerpt are an example of a

    (A) parallel period
    (B) contrasting period
    (C) literal repetition
    (D) double period

36. The third phrase features a

    (A) change in modality
    (B) change in meter
    (C) change in timbre
    (D) change in articulation

37. All of the following statements are true of the fourth phrase **except** that

    (A) it is longer than the other three phrases
    (B) it contains a ritardando
    (C) it contains an expansion of the thematic material
    (D) it contains a circle of fifths progression

38. The end of this excerpt contains

    (A) a perfect authentic cadence in the original key
    (B) a perfect authentic cadence in the key of the dominant
    (C) a melodic ending of scale degrees 4-3-2-1
    (D) both B and C

The excerpt will now be played for the first time.

The excerpt will now be played for a second time.

The excerpt will now be played a final time. Review your answers to **Questions 33–38**.

Go on to the next group of questions.

TRACK
163

Questions 39–43 are based on a section from a movement of a mass from the classical era. The excerpt will be played two times. Before listening to the excerpt for the first time, please read **Questions 39–43**.

39. The opening three chords include which of the following?

(A) A passing $^6_4$ chord
(B) A secondary dominant
(C) A pedal $^6_4$ chord
(D) All root position chords

40. Which of the following best describes the texture?

(A) Homophonic only
(B) Polyphonic only
(C) Polyphonic with occasional homophonic sections
(D) Homophonic with occasional polyphonic sections

41. This excerpt relies heavily on what compositional device?

(A) Inversion
(B) Imitation
(C) Ostinato
(D) Variation

42. Which of the following is demonstrated throughout this section?

(A) Scalar variance
(B) Tremolo
(C) Rubato
(D) Melisma

43. At the end of the excerpt, what is the repeated harmony as the choir sings "in excelsis"?

(A) I–IV–I
(B) I–V^7–I
(C) IV–V–I
(D) ii^6–V–I

Now listen to the excerpt for the first time and answer **Questions 39–43**.

The excerpt will now be played a final time. Review your answers for **Questions 39–43**.

THIS IS THE END OF PART A.

Part B

TIME: 35 MINUTES

44. If E is subtonic, what pitch is supertonic?

    (A) G
    (B) G#
    (C) D#
    (D) A#

45. The pitch that is in the bass of the V$^6_5$/vi chord in D Major is

    (A) F#
    (B) G#
    (C) D#
    (D) A#

46. The interval shown is

    (A) an augmented fifth
    (B) a minor sixth
    (C) a major sixth
    (D) a diminished sixth

47. This scale pattern represents what mode?

    (A) Ionian
    (B) Aeolian
    (C) Phrygian
    (D) Mixolydian

48. The correct beaming of the following rhythm into two measures in simple triple meter would be

49. The chord below will function diatonically in what two keys?

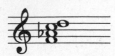

(A) F minor and E♭ Major
(B) F minor and A♭ Major
(C) C minor and F minor
(D) C minor and E♭ Major

50. What single note fills an entire measure in $\frac{3}{2}$ time signature ?

(A)

(B)

(C)

(D)

Questions 51–56 are based on the following example.

51. The musical example above contains an example of

    (A) augmentation
    (B) secondary dominant
    (C) cross relation
    (D) hemiola

52. The chord marked 1 has an error that does not reflect common eighteenth-century voice-leading practice. That error is

    (A) a direct fifth
    (B) an unresolved chordal seventh
    (C) parallel octaves
    (D) crossed voices

53. The chord marked 2 would correctly be identified as

    (A) V^7
    (B) V$^6_5$/vi
    (C) V$^4_3$
    (D) vii$^{ø6}_5$

54. The chord marked 3 has an error that does not reflect common eighteenth-century voice-leading practice. That error is

    (A) crossed voices
    (B) overlapping voices
    (C) spacing
    (D) doubled leading tone

55. The musical example above contains all of the following non-chord tones except

    (A) 4–3 suspension
    (B) anticipation
    (C) passing tone
    (D) 9–8 suspension

56. The cadence is an example of

    (A) Phrygian half cadence
    (B) octave displacement
    (C) cadential $^6_4$ chord
    (D) mode mixture

Questions 57–61 are based on the excerpt below.

Fleur Melodiques, Op. 100
Quatrième Suite, No. 10

Johann Friedrich Franz Burgmüller
(1806–1874)

57. Measures 9–14 indicate a shift of tonality

   (A) from the original tonic to the relative minor

   (B) from the original tonic to the key of the dominant

   (C) to the key of the mediant

   (D) from F♯ minor to the relative major

58. All of the following would be considered a correct description of measures 15–16 **except**

   (A) cadential extension

   (B) transition material

   (C) modulation sequence

   (D) recapitulation

59. This composition is an example of

   (A) fugal counterpoint

   (B) Alberti Bass

   (C) melodic ostinato

   (D) imitative polyphony

60. The form of this piece is

   (A) binary

   (B) rounded binary

   (C) ternary

   (D) rondo form

61. The marking *dim. e poco rall.* means to

   (A) slow down a little and get louder

   (B) get softer and gently fade away

   (C) gradually get softer and get much slower

   (D) gradually get softer and slow down a little

PRACTICE TEST 2

Questions 62–65 are based on "Air" from the *Aylesford Pieces* by Georg Friedrich Handel.

Air
from the Aylesford Pieces

Georg Friedrich Handel
(1685–1759)

62. The meter is

    (A) simple duple
    (B) simple triple
    (C) compound duple
    (D) compound triple

63. What is the harmonic progression in measures 18–20?

    (A) i^6–vii^{o6}–i–V–i in G minor
    (B) I–vii^{o6}/vi–vi–V/vi–vi in B♭ Major
    (C) i–V^7–i–V-i in G minor
    (D) i^6–vii^o–i^6–V^7–i in G minor

64. The final cadence contains what non-chord tone?

    (A) Anticipation
    (B) Retardation
    (C) Suspension
    (D) Appoggiatura

65. The ornamentation used in this excerpt is

    (A) mordent
    (B) turn
    (C) tremolo
    (D) grace note

Questions 66–70 are based on the following excerpt by J. S. Bach.

B Minor Mass - Aria
Quoniam tu solus sanctus

Johann Sebastian Bach
(1685–1750)
BWV 232, Part I, No. 11

66. The figured bass symbols at Box 1 indicate

    (A) a first inversion tonic triad followed by a root position dominant triad
    (B) a second inversion dominant triad preceded by passing tones
    (C) a second inversion tonic triad followed by a root position dominant triad
    (D) a first inversion tonic triad followed by a second inversion tonic triad resolving to a root position dominant triad

67. The horn in D at Box 1 sounds what chord member (beat 2 of the measure)?

    (A) the root
    (B) the third
    (C) the fifth
    (D) the seventh

68. The harmonic analysis of Box 2 is

    (A) ii^7–V in D Major
    (B) V^7/V–V in D Major
    (C) V^7–V in A Major
    (D) V^7/V–V in G Major

69. The progression at Box 3 implies a

    (A) brief shift to G Major
    (B) plagal cadence
    (C) modulation to the key of the dominant
    (D) circle of fifths progression

70. What is the root of the chord at Box 4?

    (A) G
    (B) E
    (C) B
    (D) A

Questions 71–72 are based on the excerpt below, by Beethoven.

Piano Trio in B♭ Major
excerpt from First Movement

71. The texture of this excerpt is

   (A) monophonic changing to homophonic
   (B) homophonic changing to polyphonic
   (C) monophonic changing to polyphonic
   (D) chordal homophony

72. Considering transposition and range, this piano trio is for piano, cello, and most likely what other instrument playing the top staff?

   (A) Violin
   (B) Oboe
   (C) Clarinet
   (D) Horn

Questions 73–75 are based on this excerpt by Grieg.

Aase's Death
from Peer Gynt Suite No. 1, Op. 46

Edvard Grieg
(1843–1907)

73. What is the cadence at measure 4?

    (A) Authentic cadence in D Major
    (B) Authentic cadence in B minor
    (C) Half cadence in B minor
    (D) Authentic cadence in F♯ minor

74. The chord within the box in measure 5 contains what interval between the double bass and violin II?

    (A) Major third
    (B) Augmented sixth
    (C) Major sixth
    (D) Diminished fifth

75. The last four measures of this excerpt reflect a shift in tonality to the key of

    (A) A Major
    (B) the parallel major
    (C) the mediant
    (D) the dominant

THIS IS THE END OF SECTION I, PART B.

Please continue to Section II and restart the audio.

SECTION II

TOTAL TIME: APPROXIMATELY 1 HOUR AND 20 MINUTES
NUMBER OF QUESTIONS: 9
55% OF TOTAL SCORE

Part A

TIME: APPROXIMATELY 68 MINUTES

Directions: Answer **Questions 1–7** in the space provided. You may want to have blank staff paper available, or use your own blank scratch paper. On the exam, the questions are written on one side of the test booklet and the facing page is blank staff paper. During the actual exam, if you write your answer on the blank staff paper, make sure you allow yourself time to write your final answer in the answer space or clearly indicate on the question page that your answer is on the facing page.

Questions 1–2
On the staff provided for each question, notate to the best of your ability the correct pitch and rhythm of a short melody you will hear. Make sure that any accidentals are appropriate to the key signature that has been provided. In each case, the pulse will be provided before the melody is first played.

Question 1: The melody will be played **three times**. There will be a pause of 30 seconds after the first playing and a pause of 1 minute after each subsequent playing. There are no rests in this melody, which is played on a bassoon.

The pitch of the first note has been provided. Be sure to complete the note with stems and flags as appropriate. Now listen to the melody for the first time and begin to notate.

1.

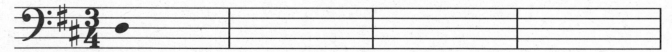

The melody for **Question 1** will now be played a second time.

The melody for **Question 1** will now be played a third and final time.

Question 2: The melody will be played **four times**. There will be a pause of 30 seconds after the first playing and a pause of 1 minute after each subsequent playing. There are no rests in this melody, which is played on a flute.

The pitch of the first note has been provided. Be sure to complete the note with stems and flags as appropriate. Now listen to the melody for the first time and begin to notate.

2.

The melody for **Question 2** will now be played a second time.

The melody for **Question 2** will now be played a third time.

The melody for **Question 2** will now be played a final time.

Go on to the next group of questions.

Questions 3–4

For the next two questions you will hear a four-part harmonic progression. In both examples the progression will be played four times. There will be a pause of 30 seconds after the first playing and a pause of 1 minute after each subsequent playing.

1. For each question you are to notate *only* the bass and the soprano on the staff provided. Do *not* write the alto and the tenor.
2. On the lines underneath the staff, you are to write in the Roman numeral chord symbols, including the Arabic numbers for any appropriate inversion.

Question 3: Before listening to the progression for the first time, look at the staff below and notice that there are nine chords in the progression, with the first one provided for you.

Now listen to the harmonic progression for the first time and begin notating.

3.

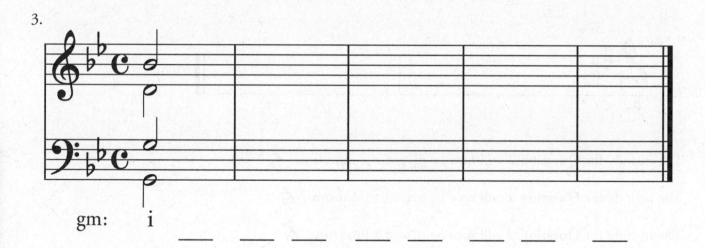

Question 3 harmonic progression played a second time.

Question 3 harmonic progression played a third time.

The harmonic progression for **Question 3** will now be played a fourth and final time.

Question 4: Before listening to the progression for the first time, look at the staff below and notice that there are once again nine chords in the progression. The first one has been done for you. You are to fill in *only* the soprano, bass, and chord symbols, including appropriate inversions, for the remaining eight chords.

Now listen to the harmonic progression for the first time and begin notating.

4.

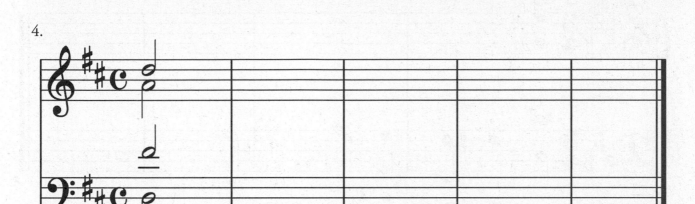

DM   I

_____   _____   _____   _____   _____   _____   _____   _____

Question 4 harmonic progression played a second time.

Question 4 harmonic progression played a third time.

The harmonic progression for **Question 4** will now be played a final time.

The remaining three Free-Response questions do not require aural prompts. You may answer them in the order you choose, but your time is limited to 45 minutes to complete all three questions. A suggested time for each question is printed in your Practice Exam next to each question number. Read the questions carefully and use your time efficiently. Now, pause the audio, turn the page, and begin working.

PRACTICE TEST 2

Question 5 (Suggested time: 15 minutes)
You are to realize the figured bass below in four voices following traditional eighteenth-century voice-leading procedures. Continue in the same fashion from the spacing of the first chord, which is given to you. In the space below each chord, fill in the appropriate Roman numeral chord symbol and inversion.

5.

Question 6 (Suggested time: 10 minutes)
You are to write the following progression in four voices following eighteenth-century voice-leading procedures. Continue in the same fashion from the spacing of the first chord, which is given to you. Use only quarter notes and half notes.

6.

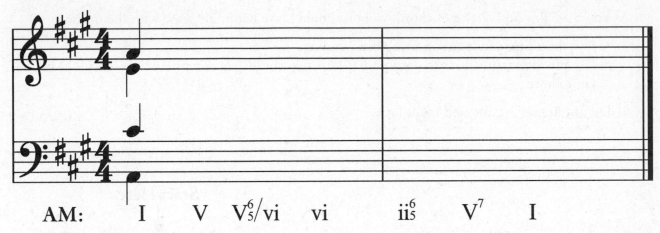

AM: I   V   V$^6_5$/vi   vi   ii$^{\circ 6}_5$ V^7 I

Question 7 (Suggested time: 20 minutes)
Complete the bass line for the melody below. Place the Roman numerals with inversion symbols below the bass line to indicate the harmony implied by the soprano and bass. Follow these guidelines:

1. Your bass line should make melodic sense in relation to the soprano.

   • Give melodic interest to the bass line and vary the motion of the bass in relation to the soprano.
   • Use note values ranging from half notes to eighth notes.

2. Your bass line and choice of chord symbols should make harmonic sense with the melody.

   • Use appropriate cadences at each phrase ending.
   • Use predominantly quarter notes and at least two chords per measure or two positions of the same chord.

3. Do not notate the alto and tenor lines.

7.

SECTION II: PART B—SIGHT-SINGING

TOTAL TIME: APPROXIMATELY 10 MINUTES

Directions: For each of the melodies, sing the pitches in accurate pitch and rhythm using a steady, consistent tempo. For each melody you will hear the starting pitch at the beginning of the practice period. You will have 75 seconds to practice singing the melody. At the end of the practice time you will have 30 seconds to perform the melody. A recorded announcement will tell you when it is time to stop practicing and start performing. On the actual exam you will be recording your performance digitally, and the file will be saved in an MP3 format.

During your performance:

- You may sing solfege syllables (***Do-Re-Mi***), scale degree numbers ($\hat{1}$–$\hat{2}$–$\hat{3}$), a neutral syllable (for example ***Ta*** or ***Da***), or note names (C–D–E). You may whistle if you prefer.
- Even though you will hear the starting pitch you do *not* have to sing it in that key. You may transpose the melody to a register that is comfortable for you.
- You should use all of the practice time to sing out loud. You may write on the music if you want to.
- You may not use any device such as a metronome or any musical instrument to help you in your practice or performance.
- You will be evaluated on pitch accuracy relative to the opening tonic you choose, rhythm, and continuity—maintaining a steady tempo without hesitating or breaking the flow of the melody. You may start over if you need to, but there *will* be a deduction from your score. You are not evaluated on the quality of your singing voice.

Access audio at
http://barronsbooks.com/ap/mtheory/

Question 1: Look over the melody and begin practicing. You have 75 seconds to practice the melody. You will now hear the starting pitch of the printed melody.

1.

Question 2: Look over the melody and begin practicing. You have 75 seconds to practice the melody. You will now hear the starting pitch of the printed melody.

2.

ANSWER KEY
Practice Test 2

SECTION I: PART A

1. **B**	12. **B**	23. **B**	34. **D**
2. **C**	13. **D**	24. **D**	35. **C**
3. **C**	14. **C**	25. **B**	36. **A**
4. **B**	15. **A**	26. **C**	37. **D**
5. **A**	16. **D**	27. **B**	38. **D**
6. **A**	17. **B**	28. **C**	39. **C**
7. **B**	18. **B**	29. **D**	40. **C**
8. **C**	19. **B**	30. **C**	41. **B**
9. **B**	20. **C**	31. **B**	42. **D**
10. **C**	21. **B**	32. **C**	43. **A**
11. **A**	22. **D**	33. **D**	

SECTION I: PART B

44. **B**	52. **B**	60. **C**	68. **B**
45. **D**	53. **C**	61. **D**	69. **A**
46. **B**	54. **D**	62. **B**	70. **D**
47. **D**	55. **C**	63. **A**	71. **A**
48. **C**	56. **D**	64. **A**	72. **C**
49. **D**	57. **B**	65. **A**	73. **C**
50. **B**	58. **D**	66. **D**	74. **B**
51. **D**	59. **D**	67. **C**	75. **D**

ANSWERS EXPLAINED

Section I: Part A

1. **(B)** Looking at the patterns from the highest note *or* the lowest note, they all correspond to a particular scale pattern. (A) is descending A minor, (B) is descending to tonic in E minor, (C) is descending A Major, and (D) is E♭ Lydian.

2. **(C)** This is based on the E Dorian scale. The tonal center is E, but has two sharps with the added raised 6th scale degree.

3. **(C)** This is a P4 from D to G. Always check the clef.

4. **(B)** When you listen to the pattern holistically (as a descending arpeggiated seventh chord) it is a half-diminished seventh chord: a diminished triad (C–E♭–G♭) with a minor seventh (B♭).

5. **(A)** All four patterns look like they are centered around D. (A) is minor with no leading tone, (B) is minor *with* the leading tone, (C) is definitely major, and (D) could be either. Answers (A) and (B) begin with a m3, (C) with a P4, and (D) with a M2. Find something you know for sure and listen *for* something.

6. **(A)** This is major in first inversion. (A) is the only answer that is major.

7. **(B)** Answers (A), (B), and (C) all begin exactly alike, and (A) and (D) end very similarly. The only difference is the last beat of the second measure.

8. **(C)** This pattern begins with the dotted quarter and eighth note.

Questions 9–12
This was SEEN.

This was PLAYED.

9. **(B)** The error is in rhythm in the treble staff. The dotted eighth sixteenth rhythm is on beat 2 and not on beat 1.

10. **(C)** The error is pitch in both the treble and bass staff. The melody stays on D instead of leaping down to B, while the bass skips down by thirds instead of by step.

11. **(A)** The error is *both* in pitch and rhythm in the bass staff. What is played is an upper neighbor and back to G.

12. **(B)** The error is in *both* pitch and rhythm in the treble staff. What is played is a leap down of a P5 to A and then two equal eight notes.

13. **(D)** The time signature is most likely $\frac{3}{4}$.

14. **(C)** The second phrase features a modulation to the key of the dominant.

15. **(A)** The dynamic is louder and the brass rhythmic pattern is heard prominently on the repeat of the first two phrases.

16. **(D)** What remains the same is the tempo, the texture, and the mode (we remain in the same key). The dynamic, the timbre, and the articulation are all different in this section.

17. **(B)** The first section is a repeated parallel period: ‖: a a :‖. The second section has a "b" phrase, then back to the "a" melody played once and then ends with a coda. The form is binary (two parts) with coda, or ‖ : A : ‖ B coda.

18. **(B)** To be able to correctly answer this question you must first know the meter, which is compound duple.

19. **(B)** The overall texture is homophonic, where one melody predominates over the accompanying lines that support it.

20. **(C)** This excerpt uses chromatic sequence, imitation, and modulation. It does not include any rhythm augmentation.

21. **(B)** The end of this excerpt modulates to the key of the dominant and ends with a perfect authentic cadence.

22. **(D)** In order to correctly answer this question, you must first identify the meter (simple quadruple) and that there is an anacrusis.

23. **(B)** The melody begins with an anacrusis *So-Do*. The second time the pattern begins on *Do* and goes up to *Fa*, the interval of a P4. It is a melodic sequence.

24. **(D)** During the introduction the solo instrument, the flute, plays a short cadenza during which all other accompaniment ceases.

25. **(B)** The introduction is based on the pentatonic scale, a scale containing only five pitches within the octave.

26. **(C)** Both introduction and verse contain fragments of a countermelody. A countermelody is briefly stated in the introduction while the accompaniment texture of the countermelody is expanded in the verse.

27. **(B)** The solfege of the last three pitches is *Te-Do-Do*, a major second and a perfect unison.

28. **(C)** The opening three notes in the melody are $\hat{5}$–$\hat{1}$–$\hat{3}$.

29. **(D)** There is no woodwind countermelody.

30. **(C)** The meter does not change. There is a change in dynamic and tempo fluctuation as well as rhythmic syncopation.

31. **(B)** The cadence is perfect authentic (PAC). Listen for the bass line and for common melodic patterns.

32. **(C)** The second section moves in a circle of fifths progression.

33. **(D)** Before you can determine the answer to this question, you must be able to tell if it is simple or compound. In this case, it is compound; therefore, there is only one viable answer because in compound meter the beat is always dotted.

34. **(D)** The harmonic progression is tonic (I) to dominant (V) in every measure.

35. **(C)** The first two phrases are a literal repetition. Yes, the second phrase does have the same melody, but that does not make it a parallel period. There must be an antecedent-consequent (weak-strong) relationship in the cadences. These two phrases are identical, both ending with half cadences.

36. **(A)** The third phrase changes mode from major to the relative minor.

37. **(D)** The fourth phrase is longer than the first three *because* it contains an expansion of the thematic material. There is a ritardando but *not* a circle of fifths progression.

38. **(D)** The end of this excerpt is a PAC in the key of the dominant. The melodic ending is ***Fa-Mi-Re-Do*** or scale degrees 4-3-2-1.

39. **(C)** The opening three chords are an example of the pedal $^6_4$ chord. The bass note stays the same and the upper voices move to the upper neighbor and then back down.

40. **(C)** The texture is almost always polyphonic; however, music rarely stays in one texture for very long. We like to hear variety. This excerpt goes to chordal homophony at the very end of Section 1 on the words "**in excelsis.**"

41. **(B)** This excerpt features imitation.

42. **(D)** Melisma (multiple pitches on one syllable) is used extensively throughout the first section.

43. **(A)** The repeated harmony is I–IV–I (***Do-Fa-Do***).

Section I: Part B

44. **(B)** If E is subtonic, then you are in F♯ minor. The supertonic ($\hat{2}$) is G♯.

45. **(D)** In order to determine the answer find the temporary tonic in V$^6_5$/vi in DM, which is bm (vi). The V$^6_5$ in bm is F♯–A♯–C♯–E with A♯ in the bass.

46. **(B)** The interval G♯ to E in alto clef is a minor sixth.

47. **(D)** The scale pattern is Mixolydian in A. Mixolydian lowers the seventh scale degree in major, or adds a flat to the key signature. In the case of sharp scales like this, it decreases the key signature by one sharp.

48. **(C)** Correct beaming requires understanding that the purpose is to clearly define the beat.

49. **(D)** The chord is D–F–A♭–C, a half-diminished seventh chord. This chord functions as the vii° in a major key and the supertonic (ii°) in the relative minor. If D is leading tone, then tonic is E♭ and the relative minor is C minor.

50. **(B)** The dotted whole note fills the entire measure in $\frac{3}{2}$ time.

51. **(D)** This example contains hemiola in the last three measures. Hemiola occurs when the triple meter is altered by rhythm or ties to reflect duple meter.

52. **(B)** Chord #1 is B–D♯–F♯–A. The seventh of the chord (A) does not resolve downward.

53. **(C)** Chord #2 is B–D♯–F♯–A with F♯ in the bass (second inversion). In the key of E minor that is V$_3^4$.

54. **(D)** Chord #3 doubles the leading tone (D♯).

55. **(C)** This excerpt does not include a passing tone.

56. **(D)** The cadence includes a Picardy third, or mode mixture, borrowing the major tonic from the parallel major by raising the third of the chord.

57. **(B)** The original key is D Major. The excerpt modulates directly to AM (the dominant) at measure 9.

58. **(D)** Measures 15 and 16 are a melodic sequence that transitions the melody back to the original key of D Major. It is a non-accompanied passage that extends the cadence. It is not a recapitulation. The recapitulation (restating of earlier melodic material) begins in measure 17.

59. **(D)** This composition is imitative polyphony. There are two separate independent voices that imitate rhythm and contour but not literally or exactly.

60. **(C)** The form of this piece is ternary (ABA). Measure 1–8 = A, 9–14 = B, 15–16 = extension; 17–24 = A.

61. **(D)** The marking *dim e poco rall* means to gradually get softer (*dim.*) and (*e*) slow down a little (*poco rall.*).

62. **(B)** The meter is simple triple: three beats in a measure and the eighth note gets the beat.

63. **(A)** The progression begins i^6–vii^{o6}–i in G minor. Compare the answers and be selective with what you identify. There is usually no reason to do a complete analysis of the whole phrase. You can determine the answer by identifying the first two chords.

64. **(A)** The final cadence contains an anticipation, as does the cadence at measures 11 and 12 and 19 and 20.

65. **(A)** The mordent is an ornament indicating that the note is to be played with a *single* rapid alternation with the note above or below.

66. **(D)** The figured bass symbols represent a first inversion tonic triad, second inversion tonic triad, and root position dominant triad. (I^6–I$_4^6$–V).

67. **(C)** The horn is *reading* a G and *sounding* an A on beat 2 of the measure. It is the fifth of the tonic triad (D–F♯–A). Remember that with any instrumental transpositions, when they read C they sound their name. This score indicates the horn is in D. Therefore:

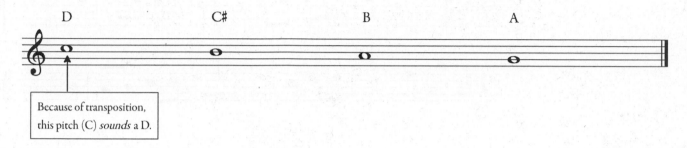

68. **(B)** The progression is V⁷/V–V in D Major. The horn is sounding a G♯, the third of the E–G♯–B–D chord resolving to V (A–C♯–E). This is easily determined by looking at the figured bass.

69. **(A)** The progression implies a shift to the subdominant (G Major). The progression is ii₃⁴–V⁷–I in G Major.

70. **(D)** This is a V⁷ chord in third inversion A–C♯–E–Ⓖ with the G in the bass.

71. **(A)** This example begins with monophonic texture. All voices are playing the same pitch in octaves. At measure 5 it shifts to homophonic texture, where the piano plays the harmonized motive from measures 1 and 2. You must recognize that the top staff is for a transposing instrument.

72. **(C)** The top voice is the clarinet. When the cello and piano have a key signature of two flats, the transposition for clarinet (a B♭ instrument) would be no sharps or flats. The violin and oboe are non-transposing instruments. They would have the same key signature as the cello and piano. The horn in F would have a key signature of one flat.

73. **(C)** This is a half cadence in B minor.

74. **(B)** The interval is an augmented sixth. This is an augmented sixth chord, specifically the French Augmented Sixth (Fr+6). It is usually found between the sixth degree of the minor scale (G) and the raised fourth scale degree (E♯).

75. **(D)** The last four measures of this excerpt shift to the key of F♯ minor (the dominant of B minor). Notice the addition of the G♯ as well as the E♯ that occurs in the viola. The only key containing both E♯ and G♯ is F♯ minor or F♯ Major. F♯ Major would also have A♯ and D♯, which this excerpt does not.

Section II: Part A

1. D Major

Phrase 1: Begins with the tonic triad, going up to *La* and descending scale-wise to *Re*. Again scale-wise, beginning with the dotted quarter note and ending on *So-La-So* at the HC.

Phrase 2: Begins with an anacrusis *Ti* leading to high *Do* followed by the descending tonic arpeggio *Do-So-Mi*. In measure 6, there is a skip of a third from *Re* to *Fa*. It concludes with a scale-wise descending pattern and ends *Ti-Do*.

2. B minor

This example has the same key signature as FR 1, so observe your clef and accidentals carefully. This is in B minor, and it reflects harmonic minor in measures 1 and 2 with the raised seventh scale degree (A♯), descending natural minor in measure 3, and melodic minor in the last measure. Although there is no chromatic harmony in this example, there are all three forms of minor.

3. G minor

This example begins with an ascending bass line ***Do-Re-Me-Fa***, using a passing $\frac{6}{4}$ chord. The mid-phrase bass is ***Le-Fa*** and the cadence is ***So-So-Do***. Remember that in minor, whenever you hear the leading tone you must write the accidental.

Let's look at the completed progression.

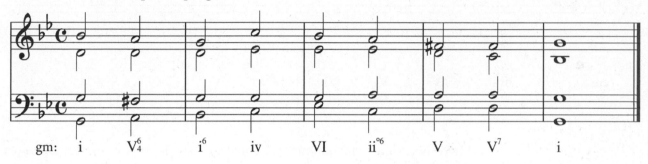

4. D Major

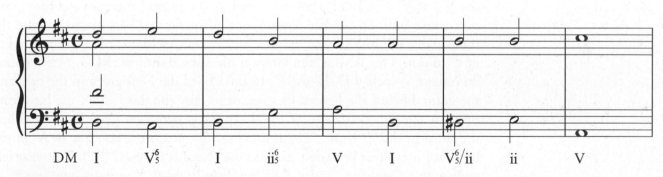

Full harmonization

The FR4 example in D Major ends with a half cadence preceeded by a secondary dominant V_5^6/ii going to ii. The opening progression ***Do-Ti-Do*** uses the V_5^6 chord. The mid-phrase, ***Fa-So-Do***, could easily be an ending phrase with a ii$_5^6$–V–I progression. Remember that progressions very often return to ***Do*** (I) and the harmonies that come before tonic are often the same as they are at the end of the phrase. Make sure you can hear and write V and V^7–I.

5. Possible solution

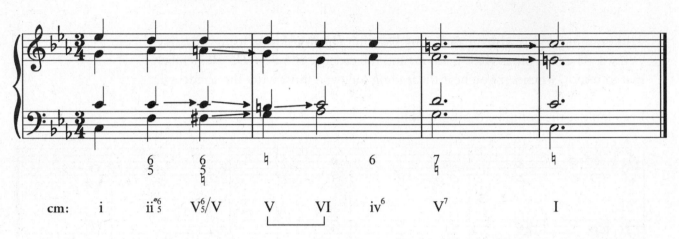

There is a significant amount of chromaticism in this example. The second chord is a half-diminished supertonic in first inversion (the seventh of the chord, C, *cannot* resolve, so hold it in the same voice until it can) followed by the V_5^6 of V. Not sure? The first chord in the second measure is a root position chord built on G. The natural sign in the figured bass means to raise the third above the bass (Bb) to natural, making it a G Major triad (V) in the key of C minor. This is your temporary tonic. The dominant of G, or secondary dominant, is spelled D–F#–A♮–C. In this chord the F# is given in the bass and the natural below the figured bass means to raise the third above the bass from Ab to A natural. Be careful of the deceptive progression (V–VI) by doubling the third in the VI chord. The third chord in measure 2 also has an Ab in the bass, but it is a first inversion triad, so the chord is F–Ab–C (iv^6). This example ends with an authentic cadence with a Picardy third. You must raise the Eb to E natural and also write the Roman numeral as major I.

6. Possible solution

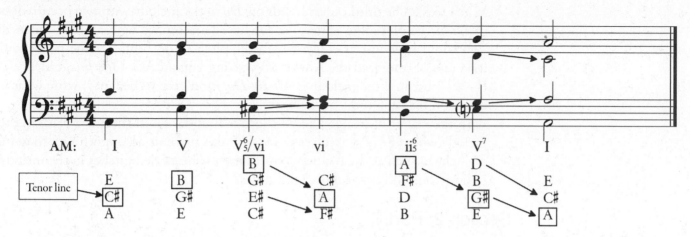

This progression has three seventh chords, including one secondary dominant. All three require correct resolution of the chordal seventh. When writing with secondary harmony you must first correctly identify the temporary tonic chord (in this case, vi in the key of A Major is F#–A–C#), then spell the dominant in the key of the temporary tonic (C#–E#–G#–B). Remember that all imperative resolutions in secondary harmony resolve in the key of the temporary tonic. Observe that since the tenor voice starting pitch was given a C#, the remaining line for the tenor almost writes itself based on required resolutions.

7. If we employ the **KISS** method, we want to use root position chords as much as possible, write appropriate standard cadences, and start phrases with tonic when possible. We don't want to use unnecessary seventh chords or second inversion triads. Write contrary motion between the melody and the base line.

The "Start Here" cadence has ***Mi-Fi-So*** in the melody, so we write V/V (or V⁷/V) to V. The third cadence ends on ***Do*** in the melody with two occurrences of ***La*** in the preceding pattern, so we have harmonized with a plagal cadence. You could have just as easily chosen the pitch G on beat 2 as the non-chord tone and harmonized the A with a V, giving you an AC. Our *final* cadence is I$^6_4$–V⁷–I because the melody is ***Mi-Re-Do***. Don't try to be fancy; write what is common for "common-practice" style.

In the key of B♭ Major, the V⁷ chord is F–A–C–E♭. If there is a place in the melody where E♭ (***Fa***) resolves to D (***Mi***) this presents an opportunity to write a V⁷ chord such as the pick up to measure 5. The circled pitches in the melody indicate our choice for non-chord tones.

Section 2: Part B

1.

This melody is in F♯ minor; the leading tone is E♯. The range of this example is just over an octave, from low ***Ti*** to high ***Do***. The melody begins with a scalewise pattern and ends with the arpeggiated tonic triad. Measure 3 will be the most difficult because the pattern between beats 1 and 2 and beats 3 and 4, although rhythmically the same, are not intervallically the same. Note that ***Do*** occurs five times in this exercise.

2.

This melody is in E♭ Major and begins with the ***Do-Mi-Do*** pattern. It then proceeds up to high ***So*** and down stepwise. Measure two leaps down to low ***So*** from ***Re***. The next rhythm is not difficult, but you must count carefully. Don't lose points with an easy pitch pattern by singing the rhythm incorrectly. Measure 2 ends with a chromatic pattern of ***Do-Di-Re***. The E natural is raised ***Do*** and leads to ***Re***. Measure 3 uses the dotted-eighth sixteenth pattern and descending tonic triad. (Don't let the accidental fool you.) The example ends with ***Ti-Mi-Re-Do***. The interval from ***Ti*** to ***Mi*** is a perfect fourth, but it is a little more difficult to sing from ***Ti***. Sing scalewise from ***Ti*** up to ***Mi*** until you find your interval. Go back and forth several times to secure the sound in your head before inserting the interval into the pattern.

Self-Scoring Guide

Section I: Parts A and B—Multiple-Choice

75 questions—**aural** and **non-aural**—for **45%** of total score

Section II: Part A—Free-Response

7 questions graded uniquely for **45%** of total score

Questions 1, 2: Melodic Dictation
Scoring: **9** points each' = **18** total points

1 point for each correct half-measure segment in *both* pitch and rhythm (8)
plus 1 point added when at least one segment (any one half-measure) is correct.
Note: No enharmonic equivalents are permitted, plus notation must
correctly place accidentals and dots, and use stems, flags, or beams.

Questions 3, 4: Harmonic Dictation
Scoring: **24** points each = **48** total points

Correct pitches = 16 points
Correct chord symbols with both Roman and Arabic numerals = 8 points
Note: Enharmonic equivalents are not permitted. Rhythmic duration is not
considered.

Question 5: Realizing Figured Bass
Scoring: **25** points

Correct Roman and Arabic numeral chord symbols = 7 points (1 point each)
Chord spelling = 6 points (1 point each)
Voice leading = 12 points (2 points per connection between chords)

Question 6: Part Writing to Roman Numeral
Scoring: **18** points

Chord spelling = 6 points (1 point each)
Voice leading = 12 points (2 points per connection between chords)

Question 7: Melodic Harmonization
Scoring: **9** points

Bass line (Counterpoint) and Harmonies (Roman numerals) are awarded
points by phrase. Phrase 2 = 2 points. Phrases 3 and 4 = 3 points each
plus 1 point for being consistently accurate, or aesthetically musical.

Section II: Part B—Sight-Singing

2 questions performed individually for **10%** of total score

> **Questions 1, 2: Sight-Singing**
> Scoring: **9** points each = **18** total points
>
> 1 point is awarded for every half-measure that is correct in pitch and rhythm, including consistent tempo, and 1 point is added for no hesitation or stopping (the flow point).

HOW TO CALCULATE YOUR SCORE

It is important to note that on the actual AP Music Theory Exam not all questions are weighted the same. Calculating the composite score of the exam remains fairly standardized from year to year and questions are weighted according to difficulty. You can calculate your percentage score to show **relative emphasis**, and use the table below to get an idea of your AP score.

Composite Score of: _____%

No Recommendation	**1** = 0–20% accuracy on all parts of the exam
Possibly Qualified	**2** = 21–39% accuracy on all parts of the exam
Qualified	**3** = 40–52% accuracy on all parts of the exam
Well Qualified	**4** = 53–65% accuracy on all parts of the exam
Extremely Well Qualified	**5** = **above 65%** accuracy on all parts of the exam

Most students do not achieve consistently on all sections of the exam. Some may score 35 percent accuracy on the aural multiple-choice but 68 percent on the non-aural, or score 55 percent accuracy on melodic dictation but only 15 percent accuracy on sight-singing. Remember that the subscores calculate aural and non-aural to create the composite score. **If your goal is a passing composite score of 3, then you are looking for approximately 45 percent accuracy on all parts of the exam.**

AURAL	NON-AURAL
Multiple-Choice Part A	Multiple-Choice Part B
FR 1, 2—Melodic Dictation	FR 5—Realization of Figured Bass
FR 3, 4—Harmonic Dictation	FR 6—Part Writing to Roman Numerals
SS 1, 2—Sight-Singing	FR 7—Melodic Harmonization

Test Analysis

Section I: Multiple-Choice, Part A

Number correct (out of 43): _____ × 1.0465 = _____

Aural Subtotal

Section I: Multiple-Choice, Part B

Number correct (out of 32): _____ × 1.4063 = _____

Non-aural Subtotal

Aural Subtotal + Non-aural Subtotal = _____

Weighted Section 1 Score
(If less than 0, enter 0;
do not round.)

Note: Do not round any subtotals.

Section II: Free-Response

Melodic Dictation Question 1 = _____ × 1.0185 = _____
                               (out of 9)   *(Do not round)*

Melodic Dictation Question 2 = _____ × 1.0185 = _____
                               (out of 9)   *(Do not round)*

Harmonic Dictation Question 3 = _____ × 0.3819 = _____
                                (out of 24)   *(Do not round)*

Harmonic Dictation Question 4 = _____ × 0.3819 = _____
                                (out of 24)   *(Do not round)*

Sight-Singing Question 1 = _____ × 1.0185 = _____
                           (out of 9)   *(Do not round)*

Sight-Singing Question 2 = _____ × 1.0185 = _____
                           (out of 9)   *(Do not round)*

Aural Subtotal = _____

Part Writing from Figured Bass
Question 5

= _____ × 0.7333 = _____
   (out of 25)   (*Do not round*)

Part Writing from Roman
Numerals Question 6

= _____ × 0.7639 = _____
   (out of 18)   (*Do not round*)

Composition of a Base Line
Question 7

= _____ × 2.5463 = _____
   (out of 9)   (*Do not round*)

Non-aural Subtotal = _____

Aural Subtotal + Non-aural Subtotal = _____
                                       Weighted Section 1 Score
                                       (If less than 0, enter 0;
                                       do not round.)

Composite Score

_____ + _____ = _____
Weighted Score, Section I   *Weighted Score, Section II*   ***Composite Score***
                                                        (rounded to the nearest
                                                        whole number)

_____ + _____ = _____
Multiple-Choice   *Free-Response*   ***Aural Subscore***
Aural Subtotal   *Aural Subtotal*   *(rounded to the nearest*
                                                        whole number)

_____ + _____ = _____
Multiple-Choice   *Free-Response*   ***Non-aural Subscore***
Non-aural Subtotal   *Non-aural Subtotal*   *(rounded to the nearest*
                                                        whole number)

Final Score Range	AP Score*
132–200	5
105–131	4
78–104	3
47–77	2
0–46	1

*The score range corresponding to each grade varies from exam to exam and is approximate.

Appendix A

Additional Information

THE CIRCLE OF FIFTHS

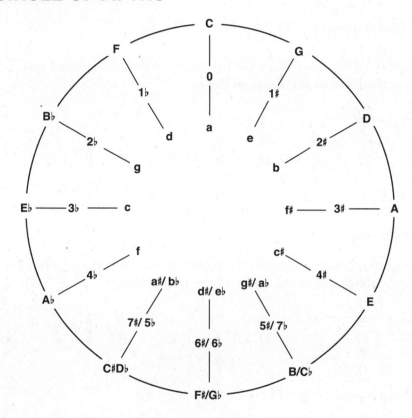

Here's another way to show the same thing in chart form:

C

minor	Major		Major	minor
Flats			**Sharps**	
d	F	1	G	e
g	B♭	2	D	b
c	E♭	3	A	f♯
f	A♭	4	E	c♯
b♭	D♭	5	B	g♯
e♭	G♭	6	F♯	d♯
a♭	C♭	7	C♯	a♯
minor	**Major**		**Major**	**minor**

Memorization of all major and minor key signatures is a necessary tool for success on the AP exam.

THE KEY SIGNATURE TOOL*

"When you cross the line—Add the sign . . ."

For Major Keys

Starting with C, go to the right for the names of the sharp keys—when you *cross the line*, **add sharp to the name of the key**.

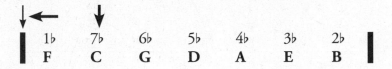

6♯	7♯	1♯	2♯	3♯	4♯	5♯	
F	C	G	D	A	E	B	

MAJOR Sharps Keys: G   D   A   E   B   F♯   C♯

Starting with C, go to the left for the names of the flat keys—when you *cross the line*, **add flat to the name of the key**.

1♭	7♭	6♭	5♭	4♭	3♭	2♭	
F	C	G	D	A	E	B	

MAJOR Flat Keys: F   B♭   E♭   A♭   D♭   G♭   C♭

For Minor Keys

Starting with A, go to the right for the names of the sharp keys—when you *cross the line*, **add sharp to the name of the minor key**.

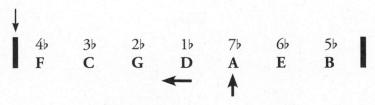

3♯	4♯	5♯	6♯	7♯	1♯	2♯	
F	C	G	D	A	E	B	

Minor Sharp Keys: E   B   F♯   C♯   G♯   D♯   A♯

Starting with A, go to the left for the names of the flat keys—when you *cross the line*, **add flat to the name of the key**.

4♭	3♭	2♭	1♭	7♭	6♭	5♭	
F	C	G	D	A	E	B	

Minor Flat Keys: D   G   C   F   B♭   E♭   A♭

---

*Courtesy of Brandon Pedigo's AP Music Theory class, Plano East Senior High, Plano, Texas.

THE CIRCLE OF MAJOR TRIADS*

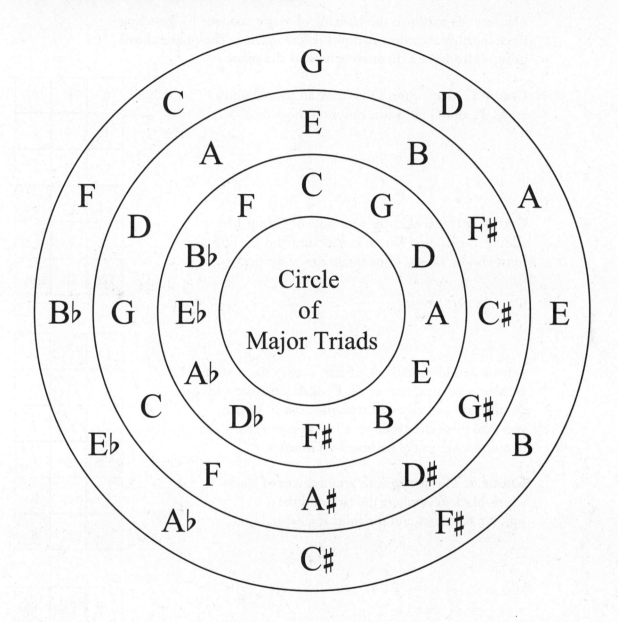

Start from the center circle and read outward to spell major triads. Each circle is a "Circle of Fifths." Every pitch to the right (clockwise) is P5 **above**. Every pitch to the left (counter clockwise) is a P4 **above**.

*Courtesy of Mary Elizabeth.

HOW TO VISUALLY IDENTIFY MAJOR TRIADS

One way to reinforce the learning of major triads is by grouping them together according to how they are notated. **The major chord groups also have a distinctive look at the piano.**

GROUP 1: Major chords that have all natural notes are **C**, **F**, and **G** (all white notes on the piano).

1.	C	E	G
	F	A	C
	G	B	D

GROUP 2: If you alter the root note of Group 1 by adding a sharp or a flat, then the third and the fifth must also be altered to maintain major quality.

2.	C#	E#	G#
	F#	A#	C#
	G#	B#	D#

GROUP 3: This group has a black note in the middle creating a major chord on **D**, **E**, or **A**. The root and the fifth are natural and the third is sharp. When you take these chords down a half step you create the opposite look on the keyboard—**Group 4**.

3.	D	F#	A
	E	G#	B
	A	C#	E

GROUP 4: This group is an arrangement of black–white–black keys where the root and the fifth are flat notes and the third is a natural note.

4.	Db	F	Ab
	Eb	G	Bb
	Ab	C	Eb

GROUPS 5 and 6: The B and B♭ group are opposites of each other. The **B Major chord** is white–black–black, while the **B♭ Major** chord is black–white–white.

5.	B	D#	F#
6.	Bb	D	F

MODAL KEY SIGNATURES

Modal music can be written using standard key signatures or may use altered notes or accidentals to create the modality. If you use the method of altering major and minor scale patterns to identify modes, **start with what you know for sure**.

- **Lydian (major + #4):** While C Major has no sharps or flats, C Lydian corresponds with a key signature of one sharp (adding F#—the raised 4th scale degree).

> **In relation to *major* key signatures, Lydian mode adds one sharp.**
> G Major has one sharp; therefore, G Lydian has two sharps. If you use this method of identifying the key signatures of major modes you must remember that adding a sharp to a flat key signature simply means to take away one flat; therefore, because B♭ Major has two flats, B♭ Lydian has one flat.

- **Mixolydian (major + ♭7):** Compared to the C Major scale, the C-Mixolydian mode would add a B♭, so its key signature has one flat.

> **In relation to *major* key signatures, Mixolydian mode adds one flat.**
> B♭ Major has two flats so B♭ Mixolydian has three flats. And likewise, adding a flat to a sharp key signature takes away one sharp; therefore, because G Major has one sharp, G Mixolydian has no sharps or flats.

- **Dorian (natural minor + #6):** In comparing the minor modes we'll use A natural minor, which has no sharps or flats; therefore, the A Dorian scale would have an F# and correspond with a key signature of one sharp.

> **In relation to *minor* key signatures, Dorian mode adds one sharp.**
> E minor has one sharp; therefore, E Dorian has two sharps. If you use this method of identifying the key signatures of minor modes you must remember that adding a sharp to a flat key signature simply means to take away one flat; therefore, because D minor has one flat, D Dorian has no sharps or flats.

- **Phrygian (natural minor + ♭2):** In comparing A minor with A Phrygian, the Phrygian scale has B♭, so the corresponding key signature would be one flat.

> **In relation to *minor* key signatures, Phrygian mode adds one flat.**
> D minor has 1 flat, so D Phrygian has two flats. Likewise, adding a flat to a sharp key signature takes away one sharp. B minor has two sharps; therefore, B Phrygian has one sharp.

Remembering Modal Key Signatures*

Rearrange the modes into

pad MIL = **P**hrygian <u>**A**eolian</u> **D**orian **M**ixolydian <u>**I**onian</u> **L**ydian

Aeolian (natural minor) in the center of the group; lowercase to remind you that the tonic chord is minor

	p	**a**	**d**	
ADD:	1♭		1♯	to **minor** key signature

Ionian (Major) in the center of the major tonic group; uppercase to remind you that the tonic chord is major

	M	**I**	**L**	
ADD:	1♭		1♯	to **Major** key signature

(beginning with the rarely used Locrian)

This provides you with all seven modal key signatures in order:

	l	**p**	**a**	**d**	**M**	**I**	**L**
When tonic is D:	3♭	2♭	1♭	0	1♯	2♯	3♯
When tonic is C:	5♭	4♭	3♭	2♭	1♭	0	1♯
When tonic is B♭:	7♭	6♭	5♭	4♭	3♭	2♭	1♭
When tonic is A:	2♭	1♭	0	1♯	2♯	3♯	4♯

ALL SEVEN KEY SIGNATURES WITH THE TONIC OF A

A Locrian	A Phrygian	A Aeolian	A Dorian	A Mixolydian	A Ionian	A Lydian
l	p	a	d	M	I	L

---

*Courtesy of Dr. JoAnn Groom, Coordinator of Music Theory, University of North Texas, Denton, Texas.

SIDE-BY-SIDE COMPARISON OF DIATONIC TRIADS AND SEVENTH CHORDS BETWEEN ANY MAJOR TONALITY AND THE PARALLEL HARMONIC MINOR

Fill in the blanks on this chart using *any* major and *parallel* minor key such as F Major and F minor.

TONALITY	M	m	M	m	M	m	M	m	M	m	M	m	M	m
Seventh														
Fifth														
Third														
Root														
Triad Chord Symbol	I	i	ii	ii°	iii	III (natural minor)	IV	iv	V	V	vi	VI	vii°	vii°
Seventh Chord Symbol	I⁷	i⁷	ii⁷	iiø⁷	iii⁷	III⁷ (natural minor)	IV⁷	iv⁷	V⁷	V⁷	vi⁷	VI⁷	viiø⁷	vii°⁷
Quality Triad/Seventh	M/M	m/M	m/m	dim/m	m/m	M/M	M/M	m/m	M/m	M/m	m/m	M/M	dim/m	dim/dim

HALF Diminished

FULLY Diminished

THE STRING FAMILY

PRACTICAL WRITTEN RANGES OF THE STRING FAMILY OF INSTRUMENTS

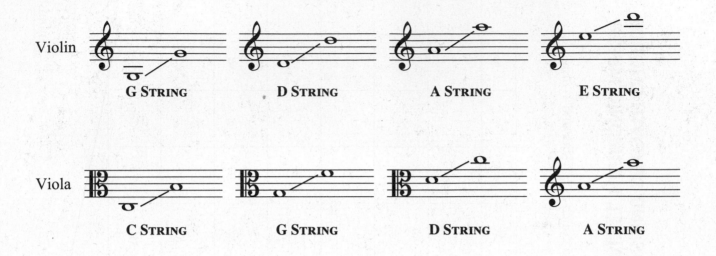

Violin — G STRING, D STRING, A STRING, E STRING

Viola — C STRING, G STRING, D STRING, A STRING

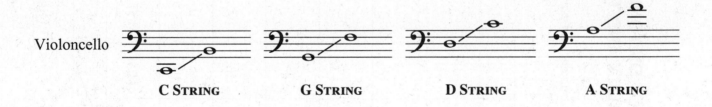

Violoncello — C STRING, G STRING, D STRING, A STRING

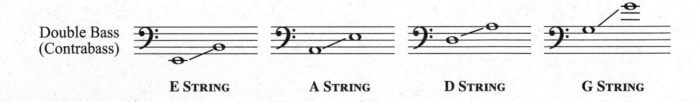

Double Bass (Contrabass) — E STRING, A STRING, D STRING, G STRING

THE WOODWIND FAMILY

PRACTICAL WRITTEN RANGES OF THE WOODWIND FAMILY OF INSTRUMENTS

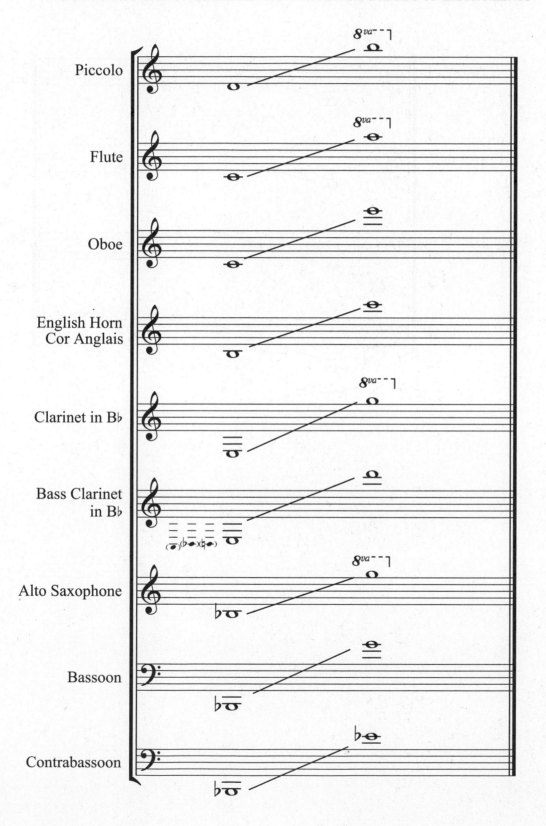

THE BRASS FAMILY

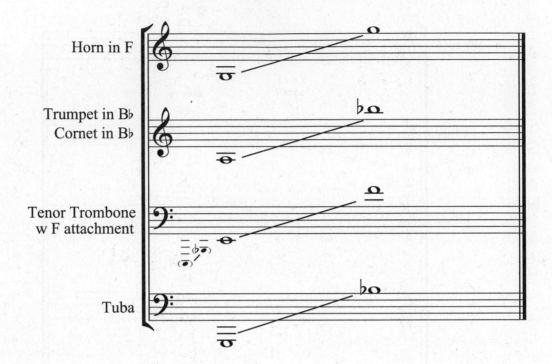

PRACTICAL WRITTEN RANGES OF THE BRASS FAMILY OF INSTRUMENTS

INSTRUMENT NAMES

English	Italian	German	French
Woodwinds	**Legni** *or* **Fiati**	**Holzbläser**	**Bois**
Piccolo	Ottavino *or* Flauto Piccolo	Kleine Flöte *or* Pickelflöte	Petite flûte
Flute	Flauto	Flöte	Flûte
Oboe	Oboe	Oboe *or* Hoboe	Hautbois
English horn *or* Cor anglais	Corno inglese	Englisch horn	Cor anglais
Clarinet	Clarinetto	Klarinette	Clarinette
Bassoon	Fagotto	Fagott	Basson
Saxophone	Sassofono	Saxophon	Saxophone
Brass	**Ottoni**	**Blechinstrumente**	**Cuivres**
Horn	Corno	Horn	Cor
Trumpet	Tromba	Trompete	Trompette
Trombone	Trombone	Posaune	Trombone
Tuba	Tuba	Tuba	Tuba
Percussion	**Percussione**	**Schlagzeug**	**Batterie**
Timpani	Timpani	Pauken	Timbales
Xylophone	Xilofono *or* Silofono	Xylophon *or* Holzharmonika	Xylophone *or* Claquebois
Marimba	Marimba	Marimbaphon	Marimba
Glockenspiel *or* Orchestral Bells	Campanelli *or* Campanette	Glockenspiel *or* Stahlspiel	Jeu de timbres *or* Carillon
Vibraphone	Vibrafono	Vibraphon	Vibraphone
Snare Drum	Tamburo piccolo *or* Tamburo militare	Kleine Trommel	Tambour *or* Caisse claire
Triangle	Triangolo *or* Acciarino	Triangel	Triangle
Tambourine	Tamburino *or* Tamburo basco	Schellentrommel *or* Tamburin	Tambour de basque
Strings	**Archi**	**Streichinstrumente**	**Cordes**
Harp	Arpa	Harfe	Harpe
Violin	Violino	Violine *or* Geige	Violon
Viola	Viola	Bratsche	Alto
Violoncello *or* Cello	Violoncello	Violoncell	Violoncelle
Double Bass *or* Contrabass	Contrabasso	Kontrabass	Contrebasse

PERFORMANCE CONSIDERATIONS

Clarifying Terms

These terms help clarify performance. For example, *L'istesso tempo* and *Simile* refer to terms or directions that appeared earlier in the piece. The other terms in the list are combined with specific dynamics, tempo, style, and articulation terms in order to make them more precise or otherwise clarify what is meant.

STAYING THE SAME

L'istesso tempo	At the same tempo
Sempre	Always
Simile	In the same manner

CHANGING SLOWLY

Poco a poco	Little by little

CHANGING QUICKLY

Subito	Suddenly

A SMALL AMOUNT

Non troppo	Not too much
Poco	Little
Un poco	A little

A LARGE AMOUNT

Assai	Very
Molto	Very

LESS

Meno	Less
Mezzo	Half

MORE

Più	More

WITH

Con	With

Dynamics

Dynamic indicators not only tell performers how loud or soft to play but also inform musicians about the character or mood of a piece and greatly contribute to creating a musical and sensitive performance.

ppp	***pp***	***p***	***mp***	***mf***	***f***	***ff***	***fff***
pianississimo	pianissimo	piano	mezzo piano	mezzo forte	forte	fortissimo	fortississimo

SOFTEST VOLUME ⟶ MEDIUM VOLUME ⟶ LOUDEST VOLUME

These terms and symbols also have to do with dynamics:

cresc. ⟍⟋ From *crescendo*, meaning "increasing in loudness."

dim. ⟋⟍ From *diminuendo*, which means "decreasing in loudness."

decresc. ⟋⟍ From *decrescendo*, which means "decreasing in loudness."

fp From *fortepiano*, meaning "*forte* immediately followed by *piano*."

rf rfz From *rinforzando*, meaning "a sudden increase in loudness."

Tempo

The speed of the beat is known as *tempo*. Performers use tempo indicators to convey the character of the work. Tempos are customarily indicated with markings in Italian and may be accompanied by a metronome marking such as **M.M.** = 120, referring to "**M**aelzel **M**etronome." In 1814, Johann Maelzel invented the **metronome**, a device for sounding adjustable *beats per minute* and therefore fixing the tempo of a composition.

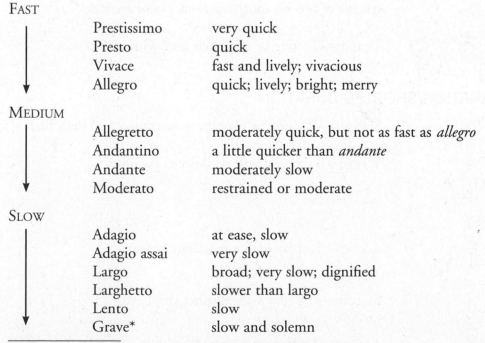

FAST
Prestissimo	very quick
Presto	quick
Vivace	fast and lively; vivacious
Allegro	quick; lively; bright; merry

MEDIUM
Allegretto	moderately quick, but not as fast as *allegro*
Andantino	a little quicker than *andante*
Andante	moderately slow
Moderato	restrained or moderate

SLOW
Adagio	at ease, slow
Adagio assai	very slow
Largo	broad; very slow; dignified
Larghetto	slower than largo
Lento	slow
Grave*	slow and solemn

*Note that *Grave* is pronounced with two syllables: GRAH vay.

These terms and symbols also have to do with tempo. Any of these terms can be combined with *poco* or *molto*.

SPEEDING UP

accel.   From *accelerando*—to gradually increase the tempo.

string.   From *stringendo*—to press forward.

SLOWING DOWN

rall.   From *rallentando*—to gradually slow down.

rit.   From *ritardando*—to gradually slow down, or *ritenuto*—
               to suddenly slow down.

riten.   From *ritenuto*—to suddenly slow down.

OTHER TEMPO CHANGES

Rubato   To take out of the stated tempo.

Articulations

Articulation marks indicate *how* a note, phrase, or melody should be performed. Remember that this is an *aspect of sound* called *envelope*—how a note is begun (attack), how it is sustained, and how it is ended (release).

CONNECTION

Slur—to smoothly connect two or more notes with different pitches. This is called legato singing or playing. For singers, the slur is an indication to sing more than a single syllable of text on more than one pitch: *melisma.*

Tenuto—To sing or play each note with its full value.

SEPARATION/SHORTED DURATION

Staccato—To sing or play the note shorter and detached.

Wedge—To play a note as short as possible.

STRESS

Accent—To play with a moderate accent.

Marcato—To play with distinct emphasis.

Tenuto—To lean on a note.

fz	From *forzando*, meaning "forced" or "played with a sudden accent."
sfz	From *sforzato*, meaning "played with sudden emphasis."
sf	From *sforzato*, meaning "played with sudden emphasis."

STRESS COMBINED WITH DYNAMIC

| *fzp* | From *forzando piano*, meaning "played with a sudden accent and immediately becoming *piano.*" |

Style Markings

Amoroso tender and affectionate

Animato animated, lively

Calando gradually softer and slower

Cantabile in a singing style

Con anima with life and animation

Con brio with vigor and spirit

Con dolore with sadness

Con forza with force

Con fuoco with fire, in a fiery manner

Con moto with motion

Deciso decisively

Détaché detached

Dolce sweetly

Doloroso sorrowfully

Espressivo expressively

Furioso furious

Giocoso humorous

Grandioso with grandeur

Grazioso gracefully

Legato smooth and connected

Leggiero lightly

Maestoso majestically

Marcato marked and stressed

Marzial in the style of a march

Morendo dying away

Pesante heavy

Religioso solemn, religious

Semplice simple

Sostenuto sustained

Soto voce in an undertone

Staccato short and detached

Tranquillo tranquil

Additional Playing Indications

arco	Play with a bow, as opposed to plucking (*pizzicato*)—used for string instruments. If there is no marking, arco playing is assumed.
	Arpeggio—the notes of a chord played in sequence, rather than simultaneously. An arpeggio may be written as individual notes or indicated by an arpeggio line placed to the left of the chord.
//	**Caesura** or **cesura**—a complete break in sound: a pause, sometimes called *railroad tracks*.
Con sord./ Senza sord.	From **Con sordino** (pl. *Con sordini*)/**Senza sordino** (pl. *Senza Sordini*)—Play with a mute/remove the mute.
D.C. al Coda	From **Da capo al Coda**—Go back to the start of the piece and play until you reach the marking *To Coda*, and then jump to the coda.
D.S. al Coda	From **Dal segno al Coda**—Go back to the 𝄋 sign and play until you reach the marking *To Coda*, and then jump to the coda.
D.C. al Fine	From **Da capo al Fine**—Go back to the start of the piece and play until you reach the marking *Fine*, and then stop.
D.S. al Fine	From **Dal segno al Fine**—Go back to the 𝄋 sign and play until you reach the marking *Fine*, and then stop.
	Grace note—A miniature note, with or without a slash. It is not counted in the rhythm of the measure, but is played quickly, almost together with the next note.
	Octave sign—a line and symbol placed above notes as a signal to play the material an octave higher than written. A similar line with a *b* instead of an *a* and placed beneath notes is a signal to play the material an octave lower than written: 8vb---⌐
	Mordent—an ornament to the notes that are written. The notes indicated are the first three notes of a downward trill, beginning with the note that is written, with the second occurrence of the main note held for the remaining duration.
	Pedal line—a symbol to guide a pianist in the use of the sustain pedal.
pizz.	From **pizzicato**—play by plucking: used for string instruments that are usually played with a bow.

♪   **Tremolo**—a rapid repetition of the same note, indicated by one or more strong diagonal lines across the stem of a note or between the stems of two notes.

tr〜〜〜   **Trill**—an ornament in which two tones a major or minor second apart are alternated rapidly.

      Turn—an ornament consisting of four slurred notes: the note *above* the main tone, the main tone, the note *below* the main tone, and finally back to the main tone. A turn may start *with* the main tone and then move to the note above (1) or start directly on the note above the main tone (2), depending on the placement of the sign.

Additional Terms

Alberti bass—An accompaniment pattern using a three-note chord. The notes of the chord are played (usually in eighth notes) root-fifth-third-fifth.

Cadenza—A solo section usually in a concerto or similar work that is used to display the performer's technique, sometimes at a considerable length.

Opus (Op.)—Work. The term is usually used with a number to indicate the chronological order of music written by that composer.

Tre corde—Release the soft (left) pedal on the piano.

Una corda—Depress the soft (left) pedal.

Vibrato—The pulsating or vibrating element of some sounds that is produced by a full, resonant quality of tone. Vibrato is a very slight fluctuation of the pitch of a note. Since the nineteenth century, vibrato has been used almost constantly because of its enhancement of tone.

Appendix B

Music for Further Study

Aberystwyth

Joseph Parry
(1841–1903)

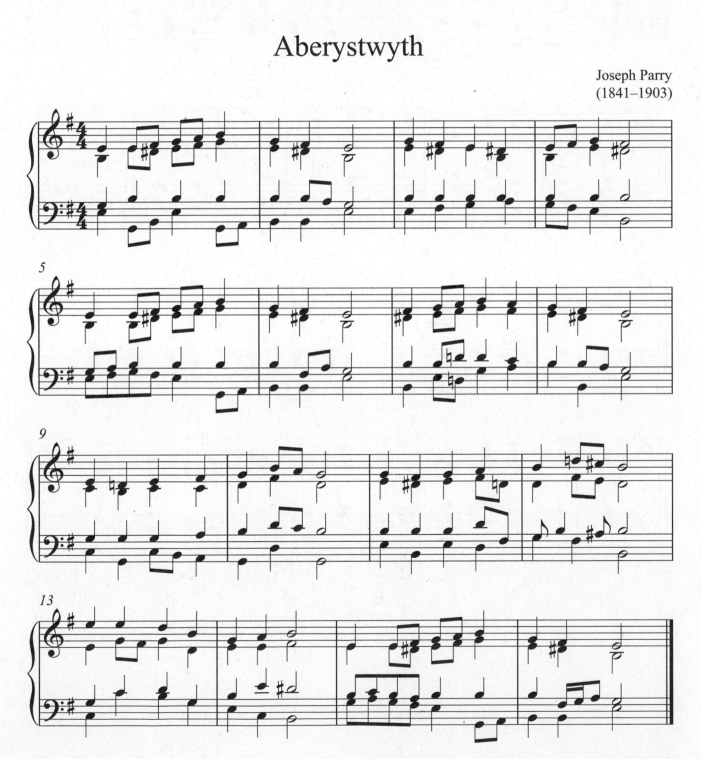

Angel's Story

Arthur H. Mann
(1850–1929)

Aurelia

Samuel Wesley
(1810–1876)

Austria

Adapted from
Franz Joseph Haydn
(1732–1809)

Crusader

A. H. Hoffman von Fallersleben,
Schlesiche Volkslieder
arr. Richart Storrs Wills
(1819–1900)

Ein feste Burg ist unser Gott

Martin Luther
Harm. Johann Sebastian Bach (1685–1750)
BWV Anh. 49 (doubtful)

Ellacombe

Gesangbuch der Herzogl W. k.
Hofkapelle, Wurttemberg, 1784.
Harm. William H. Monk
(1823–1889)

Eventide

William H. Monk
(1823–1889)

Olivet

Lowell Mason
(1792–1872)

Rustington

C. Hubert H. Parry
(1848–1918)

Salzburg

From a melody by Jakob Hintze
Harm. by Johann Sebastian Bach
(1685–1750)

Was Gott tut

Severus Gastorius, 1681
Harm. *Common Service Book,* 1917

Appendix C

Part-Writing and Melodic Harmonization Examples

PART-WRITING EXAMPLES

1. C minor

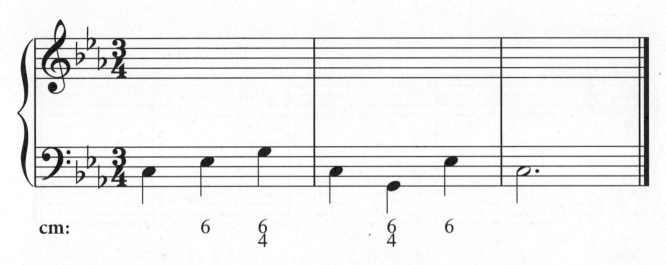

2. D Major

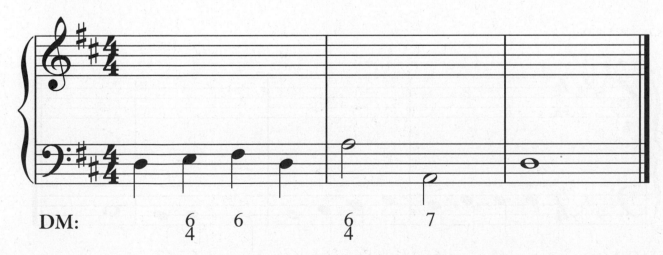

3. F Major

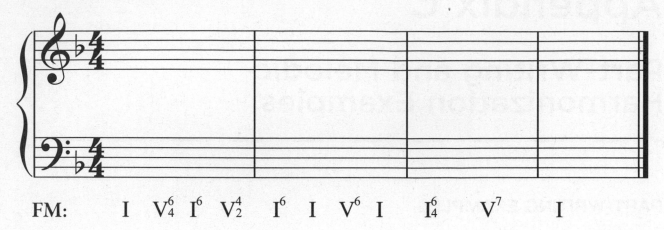

FM: I V$^6_4$ I^6 V$^4_2$ I^6 I V^6 I I$^6_4$ V^7 I

4. A minor

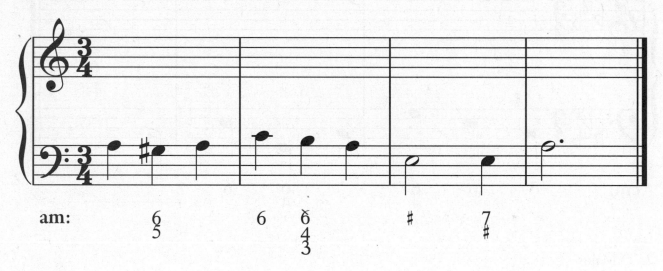

am: $^6_5$ 6 $^6_{4\ 3}$ # $^7_\#$

5. E♭ Major

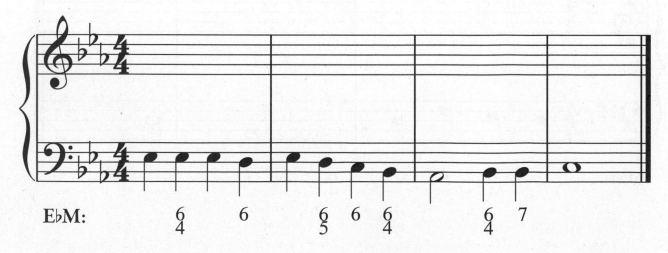

E♭M: $^6_4$ 6 $^6_5$ 6 $^6_4$ $^6_4$ 7

6. F minor

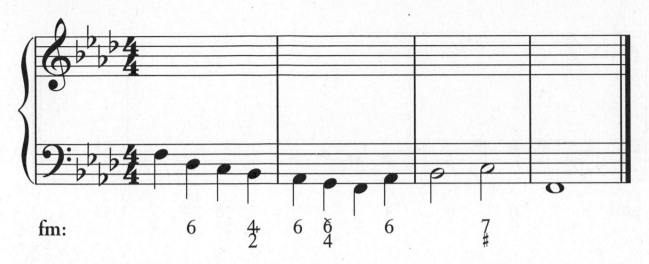

fm: 6 $\begin{smallmatrix}4\\2\end{smallmatrix}$ 6 $\begin{smallmatrix}6\\4\end{smallmatrix}$ 6 $\begin{smallmatrix}7\\\sharp\end{smallmatrix}$

7. F Major

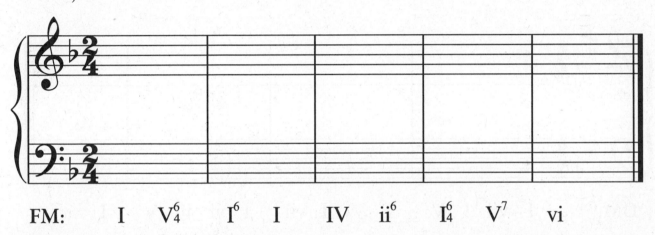

FM: I V^6_4 I^6 I   IV ii^6 I^6_4 V^7 vi

8. A minor

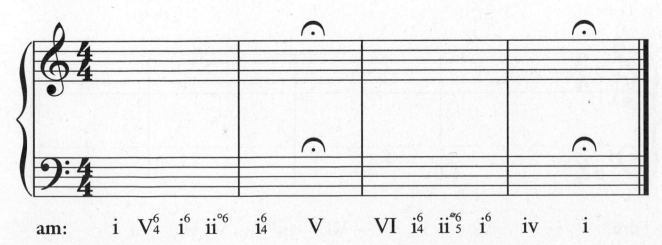

am: i V^6_4 i^6 $ii^{\circ 6}$ i^6_4 V   VI i^6_4 $ii^{\circ 6}_5$ i^6 iv   i

9. G minor

10. D Major

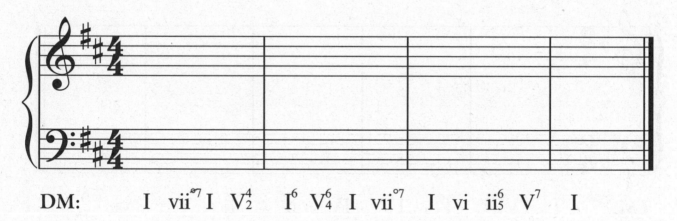

DM: I vii°⁷ I V₂⁴ I⁶ V₄⁶ I vii°⁷ I vi ii₅⁶ V⁷ I

11. D minor

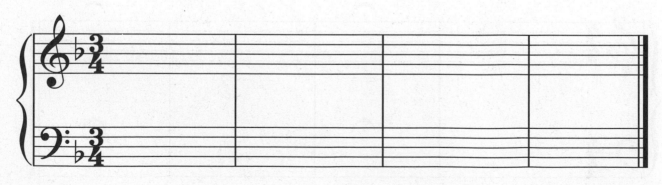

dm: i V₅⁶ i V⁷ VI ii°⁶ V₅⁶/V V i

12. C minor

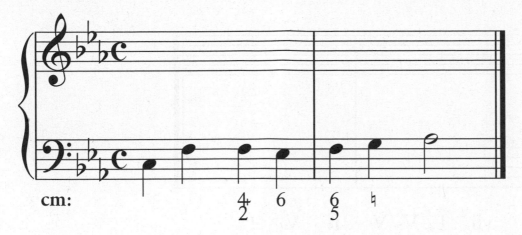

cm:

$\begin{smallmatrix}4\\2\end{smallmatrix}$ 6 $\begin{smallmatrix}6\\5\end{smallmatrix}$ ♮

13. G Major

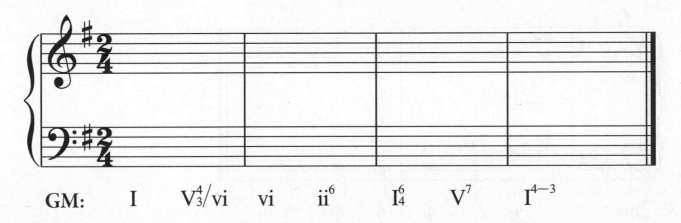

GM: I   V$_3^4$/vi   vi   ii^6 I$_4^6$ V^7 I$^{4-3}$

14. B minor

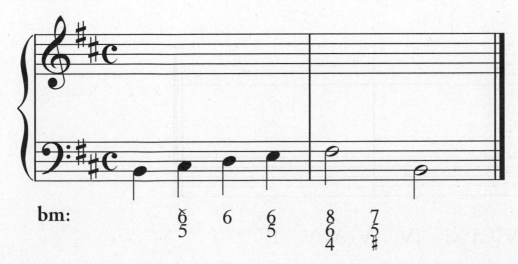

bm: $\begin{smallmatrix}6\\5\end{smallmatrix}$ 6 $\begin{smallmatrix}6\\5\end{smallmatrix}$ $\begin{smallmatrix}8\\6\\4\end{smallmatrix}$ $\begin{smallmatrix}7\\5\\\#\end{smallmatrix}$

15. A Major

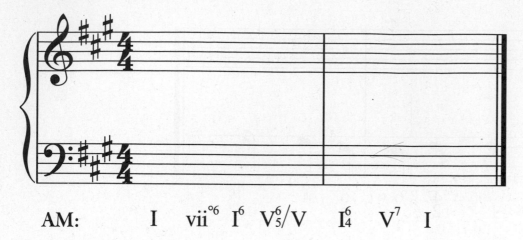

AM: I vii°⁶ I⁶ V⁶₅/V I⁶₄ V⁷ I

16. G minor

gm: ⁶₅ ⁴₂ 6 ⁶₅ ♯

17. D Major

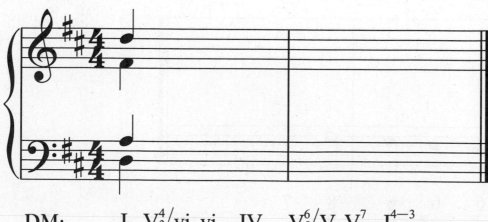

DM: I V⁴₃/vi vi IV V⁶₅/V V⁷ I⁴⁻³

18. C minor

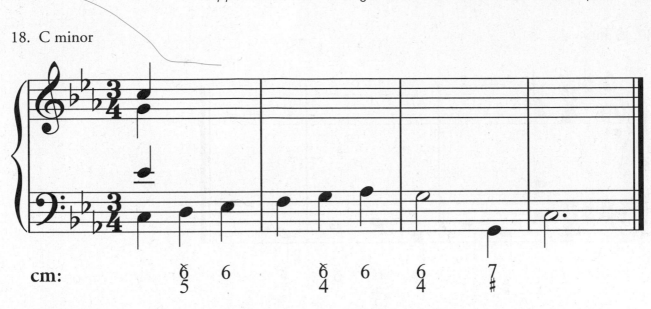

cm: $\overset{6}{\underset{5}{}}$ 6 $\overset{6}{\underset{4}{}}$ 6 $\overset{6}{\underset{4}{}}$ $\overset{7}{\underset{\sharp}{}}$

19. A Major

AM: I V$_2^4$ I^6 ii^6 V$_5^6$/V V vi

20. E minor

em: i __ __ __ __ __ __ __

21. A♭ Major

A♭M: I   vii°⁶   I⁶   V⁶₅/V   I⁶₄   V⁷   I⁴⁻³

22. C minor

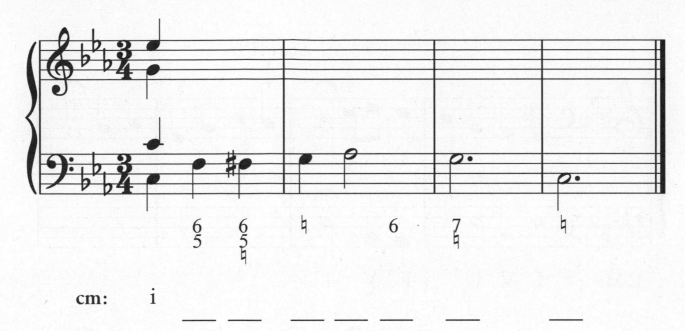

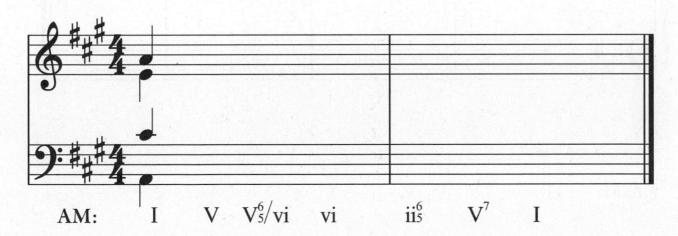

cm: i

23. A Major

AM: I   V   V$^6_5$/vi vi   ii$^6_5$ V^7 I

MELODIC HARMONIZATION EXAMPLES

1. Key E♭

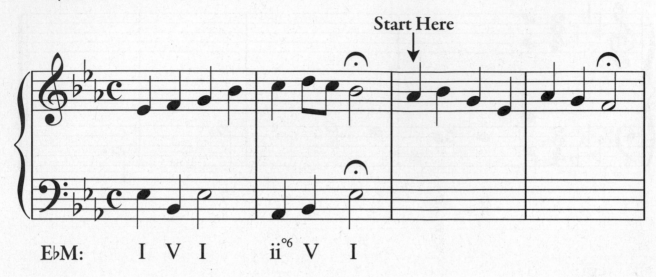

E♭M: I V I   ii°⁶ V I

2. F Major

FM: I   V⁶ I I⁶   ii   V⁷ I   ii⁶ V

5

3. G Major

GM: I   I⁶ ii⁶ V   vi V I   I IV V

4. A♭ Major

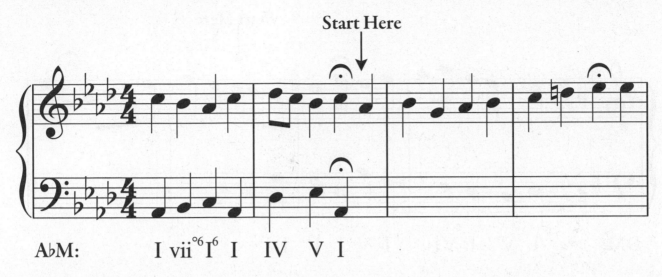

A♭M: I vii°⁶I⁶ I   IV   V   I

5. D Major

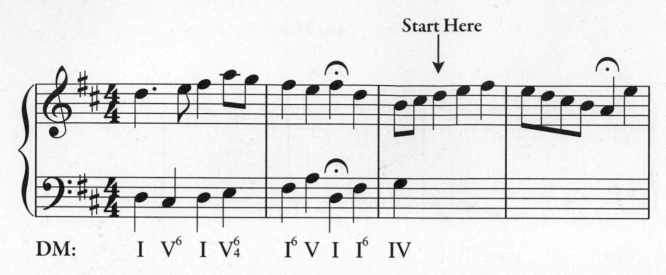

DM: I V⁶ I V⁴₆   I⁶ V I I⁶ IV

6. B♭ Major

Start Here

B♭M: I   IV   V   V$_5^6$/V V I^6

5

7. G Major

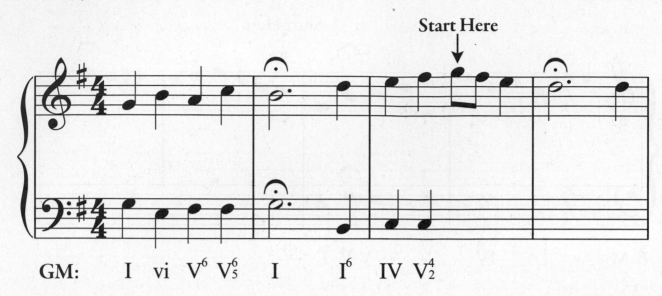

GM: I   vi   V^6 V$^6_5$ I   I^6 IV   V$^4_2$

5

8. E♭ Major

E♭M: I   V$^6_4$ I^6 V$^6_5$ I   ii   V   I   IV   IV^6 V

9. A Major

AM: I V⁶ I I⁶ ii⁶   V   I V⁶ I

10. B♭ Major

B♭M: I   V$^6_4$ I^6 ii   V^6 I   V   I^6 I   ii

5

Appendix D

Index of Contextual Listening Aural Examples

Aural Unit I: Multiple-Choice Questions for Chapters 1–3

Questions 13–20:   Wolfgang Amadeus Mozart: Piano Sonata in A Major, op. K 331

Aural Unit II: Multiple-Choice Questions for Chapters 5–7

Questions 17–22:   *Fearful Clan Warfare*

Questions 23–27:   Karl (Carl) Stamitz: "Rondo," from Konzert D Dur

Aural Unit III: Multiple-Choice Questions for Chapters 10, 12, 13

Questions 10–16:   Georges Bizet: "La Garde Montante" from *Carmen,* Suite no. 2

Questions 17–20:   Jean-Philippe Rameau: Miniature in E Minor

Questions 21–25:   Ludwig van Beethoven: The second movement (Allegretto Scherzando), from Symphony no. 8, op. 93

Chapter 18: Strategies for Multiple-Choice: Part A

Questions 11–18:   "Lark in the Clear Air" (Traditional Irish Folk Song)

Questions 23–27:   Georg Philipp Telemann: Vivace, from Suite no. 6 in D Minor

Questions 28–35:   Ludwig van Beethoven: Finale Presto, from Symphony no. 35 in D Major

Practice Test 1

Questions 9–13:   Wolfgang Amadeus Mozart: Piano Sonata no. 12 (arranged for clarinet)

Questions 14–19:   Edvard Grieg: "Anitra's Dance," from *Peer Gynt Suite*

Questions 20–25:   Johan Strauss: *Tritsch-Trasch Polka*

Questions 30–32:   Steve Peisch: *Palindrome*

Questions 33–38:   World Music: *C'est Reels*

Questions 39–43:   George Frideric Handel: *Laschia ch 'io piango*

Practice Test 2

Questions 13–17:	Friedrich Burgmuller: Peasant Pas de Deux, from the ballet, *Giselle*
Questions 18–21:	Johann Sebastian Bach: Gigue, from Suite no. 3 in D Major, BWV 1068
Questions 22–27:	Guowajiamaoji: "The Goddess of Snow Mountains"
Questions 28–32:	Johannes Brahms: Hungarian Dance no. 5
Questions 33–38:	Gabriel Faure: Berceuse, op. 16
Questions 39–43:	Wolfgang Amadeus Mozart: "Gloria in Excelsis Deo," from Great Mass in C Minor, K 427

Index

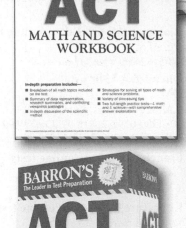
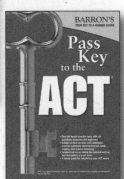

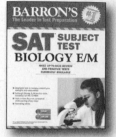